THE MAKING OF THE MEXICAN BORDER

JUAN MORA-TORRES

The Making of

the Mexican Border

UNIVERSITY OF TEXAS PRESS  AUSTIN

Requests for permission to reproduce material from this work should be sent to Permissions, University of Texas Press, P.O. Box 7819, Austin, TX 78713-7819.

⊗ The paper used in this book meets the minimum requirements of ANSI/NISO Z39.48-1992 (R1997) (Permanence of Paper).

LIBRARY OF CONGRESS CATALOGING-IN-PUBLICATION DATA

Mora-Torres, Juan, 1956–

The making of the Mexican border : the state, capitalism, and society in Nuevo León, 1848–1910 / Juan Mora-Torres.— 1st ed.

   p.   cm.

Includes bibliographical references and index.

ISBN 0-292-75252-0 (cloth : alk. paper) —

ISBN 0-292-75255-5 (pbk. : alk. paper)

   1. Nuevo León (Mexico : State)—Economic conditions.   2. Nuevo León (Mexico : State)—Social conditions.   3. Nuevo León (Mexico : State)—History.   4. Industrialization—Mexico—Nuevo León (State) 5. Social classes—Mexico—Nuevo León (State)—History. 6. Mexican-American Border Region—History.   I. Title.

HC137.N8 M665   2001

972'.1304—dc21

2001027537

En memoria de mi hermanita, Magdalena,
mujer combatiente que dedicó su juventud
a crear un mundo sin fronteras.

Dedico este libro a mis padres,
Magdaleno y Esther,
por sus esfuerzos y sacrificios.

Para Lorraine, mi esposa,
e hijos, Juan Ignacio y Magdalena Irene.

Para Tlalpuhajua, Michoacán,
mi pueblo natal,
que tiene sus hijos y hijas regados en
México, Estados Unidos, y Canadá.

Contents

Acknowledgments

I have been fortunate in meeting many people in universities, neighborhoods, and community organizations with whom I established strong and lasting friendships. I learned much from Professors John Coatsworth, Adolfo Gilly, James Grossman, Friedrich Katz, Ricardo Romo, Ramón Ruiz, and Carlos Vásquez. They have provided me with guidance, counsel, and encouragement and have always placed rigorous scholarly demands on me. I hope this book does not disappoint them.

Félix Almaraz, Bernadette Andrea, Marianne Bueno, Antonio Calabria, Kolleen Guy, Michael Harrington, José Angel Hernández, Gilberto Hinojosa, Patrick Kelly, Yolanda Leyva, Raquel Márquez, Louis Mendoza, Ben Olguín, Kamala Platt, Rodolfo Rosales, Irma Sánchez, Lee and Lucy Valadez, Ronald Zeller, and Arturo Vega provided me with a warm and intellectually engaging environment in San Antonio. I will always treasure their friendship, support, and hospitality. My bonds with Louis, Art, Antonio, Raquel, José Angel, Ben, and Rudy, all from the University of Texas at San Antonio, provided a *carnalismo* that went beyond camaraderie. I owe a debt of gratitude to the Rosales family (Rudy, Rosa, Rudy Jr., Miguel, and Gabriel), who made San Antonio a second home for my family.

In Chicago I had the pleasure of discussing history and politics with Oswaldo Alfaro, Nick Ceh, Ernesto Chairez, Irene Chávez Pimsler, Rosie Contreras, Jesus García, the Hinojosa family (Raúl, Bertha, Raúl Jr., and María), Lupe Lozano, Martin Pimsler, Francisco Piña, Rogelio Reyes, Sergio Rodríguez, and William Taylor. I would also like to thank the staff of the Center for Latin American Studies at the University of Chicago, where I was a Visiting Scholar from 1998 to 1999. Professor José Cuello and the staff of the Center for Chicano-Boricua Studies at Wayne State University made every effort to make my stay in Detroit as enjoyable as possible. Moreover, I would like to thank them for inviting me to be the Chávez/King/Parks Visiting Professor for the 1991–1992 academic year.

Mario Cerutti, Celso Garza Guajardo, Rocio González Maíz, Abraham Nuncio, Javier Rojas, Meynardo Vásquez, Oscar Flores Torres, and the members of the Oficina de Información y Difusión del Movimiento Obrero (OIDMO) welcomed me to Monterrey and taught me much about the city and the Mexican northeast. In Mexico City I have enjoyed the collegiality of Primitivo Rodríguez, Jesús Martínez, Beatriz Nava, Juan Manuel Sandoval, and the members of the Seminario Permanente de Estudios Chicanos y de Fronteras. Juan Manuel Sandoval, one of Mexico's foremost experts on Chicanos, deserves special mention for his generosity and hospitality.

I would like to thank the staffs of the following archives and libraries for their professionalism: Archivo General de la Nación, Archivo de Relaciones Exteriores, Biblioteca Nacional, Archivo General del Estado de Nuevo León, Capilla Alfonisa de la Universidad Autónoma de Nuevo León, and Archivo Municipal de Monterrey.

I would also like to thank Professor John Hart and the second outside reviewer of this manuscript for their comments and helpful suggestions. I owe special thanks to Theresa May of the University of Texas Press for her encouragement, enthusiasm, and timely help. Many thanks also to Kathy Lewis for her editing.

My parents, Esther and Magdaleno, are largely responsible for this book. Their love, warmth, encouragement, guidance, patience, and wise advice have always kept me on track. They have been the main source of my inspiration: my *jefito* has been an ardent Cardenista since his youth, when he labored as a *campesino,* miner, and factory worker in Mexico. He first came to the United States as a *bracero* and retired as a railroad worker; my *jefita,* a retired cannery worker, inculcated in her children the importance of education as a tool for advancing the interest of the poor. My brothers— Ignacio, Carmelo, Gregorio, and Hugo—have always been there for me. *Gracias, carnales.*

I have enjoyed a second childhood with my children, Juanito and Maggie, who constantly raised provocative questions (Why are the women always working? Why don't the waiters make more money than restaurant owners? — they do all the work). Finally, Lorraine, my *compañera,* has been my best friend and most profound critic on this journey. Her love, political idealism, and *cariño* kept us going.

THE MAKING OF THE MEXICAN BORDER

Introduction

This is how one pictures the angel of history. His face is
turned toward the past. Where we perceive a chain of events,
he sees one single catastrophe which keeps piling wreckage
and hurls it in front of his feet. The angel would like to stay,
awaken the dead, and make whole what has been smashed.
But a storm is blowing in from Paradise; it has got caught in
his wings with such a violence that the angel can no longer
close them. The storm irresistibly propels him into the future
to which his back is turned, while the pile of debris before
him grows skyward. That storm is what we call progress.

WALTER BENJAMIN, *ILLUMINATIONS*

Boundaries are points of contact between nations. This does not mean that
all neighboring nations are equal in military and economic terms. In one
of his most famous quotes, Porfirio Díaz summarized the power that the
United States had manifested over Mexico: "Poor Mexico, so far from God
and so near to the United States." Díaz, the ruler of Mexico from 1876 to
1910, meant that whether Mexicans wanted to or not, and for better or
worse, Mexico could not escape from the shadow of its northern neighbor.
At least since 1848 (and more precisely since the independence of Texas in
1836), the United States has been a major force shaping Mexico's economy,
politics, culture, and society, and its greatest influence has been manifested
in the border states.

What makes the U.S.-Mexican boundary so unique is that it has historically functioned as both a link and a barrier between two nations that
have different economic systems, political systems, and cultural values.
From its creation in 1848 to the present, this boundary has separated the
United States, the land of plenty, from Mexico and Latin America, the land
of want. In spite of heavy policing, the U.S.-Mexican border is not exactly
the Iron Curtain, a line that divided a society into two different and an-
tagonistic entities from its post–World War II inception to 1989. Border

areas are also zones of permanent contact, and in the U.S.-Mexican border-lands national differences have engaged each other since 1848, binding the world's most powerful nation to its "developing" southern neighbor. These national differences, especially in the economic and cultural spheres, have undergone processes of mutation, creating a border society that is profoundly different from the interiors of both countries.

This study explores Mexico's "frontier to border" phase of this historical development by focusing on the northeastern state of Nuevo León, in particular the city of Monterrey, the industrial capital of the nation and the birthplace of the most powerful business groups in twentieth-century Mexico. The northeast was the first region in Mexico to come into permanent contact with the westward-expanding U.S. territorial state and economy. The starting point for this study is 1848, when the international boundary was created, and it ends in 1910, on the eve of the Mexican Revolution, the watershed event that established the foundations of modern Mexico. During this time the Mexican border region emerged as a geographical zone with distinctive economic, political, social, and cultural features. This period constitutes a well-defined historical era for northern Mexico, characterized by the transition from the "closing of the frontier," a phrase first used by Frederick Jackson Turner in his famous 1893 frontier essay, to the emergence of the border as the next stage of territorial development.

This study begins with the premise that the frontier populations of pre-1848 northern Mexico shared a common experience that had evolved over a period of two hundred years. That experience was primarily conditioned by the long and deep-seated history of conflict between native people and colonists and by the frontier's geographic isolation from larger economies and the centers of political authority. The imposition of the 1848 international boundary prompted a series of profound changes that eventually brought an end to this isolation. Over the next sixty years two parallel processes ended the period of the northern frontier as the border emerged as the new stage of territorial development: first, the incorporation of the frontier into a centralized political system, a project that was completed during the dictatorship of Porfirio Díaz; second, the integration of the frontier into the capitalist economy, a process that foreign investors accelerated with massive infusions of capital into northern Mexico.

The strengthening of the Mexican state and the rapid spread of capitalism transformed the north from the "frontier" to the "border," especially during the Porfiriato (1876–1910). The northern states emerged as the showcase of the Porfirian economic "miracle" with its impressive railroad network linking cities, mining and industrial sites, and agricultural complexes to the United States and central Mexico. One of the far-reaching consequences of this "frontier to border" transition was that the center of economic gravity in Mexico tilted toward the north. As the zone binding Mexico and the United States, the border states leaped from their "peripheral" status vis-à-vis emergent capitalist development in Mexico to a "core" position.

During these years the Mexican border states acquired the peculiarities that would distinguish them from other regions in the country. In addition to fostering a political culture that revolved around federalism, liberalism, and anticlericalism, the border states produced a capitalist economy more complex than that in the rest of Mexico, including a regional economy that was largely an appendage to the U.S. economy; the ascent of fairly new native capitalist groups that in all probability would have merged into larger and more powerful groupings if it had not been for the Mexican Revolution, which eliminated most of them as the dominant classes in their regions;[1] and, finally, a regional labor market based on free labor and dependent on large inflows of migrants who were lured by higher wages in the north. Indeed, the new north of 1910 was but a shadow of its former self. Ironically, the Mexican Revolution originated in the border states, the region where capitalist development had been most intense, suggesting a strong correlation between the rapid spread of capitalism and rebellion.

This book traces the development of the border as a continuously changing territory, but not by following a strictly diplomatic, evolutionary, and chronological format as other histories have done. It approaches the border as a location in which broad processes of state-building, emergent capitalism, and growing linkages to the United States transform localities and identities and shape class formations and struggles. The following chapters examine the key "frontier to border" transformations in Nuevo León, including the metamorphic evolution of classes from frontier merchants to industrialists; the creation of new classes; class conflict; the transformation of identities; the recasting of relations between periphery and center; and, finally, as the countryside declined economically, demographically, and politically, the ascent of Monterrey, the capital of Nuevo León, from a small and insignificant frontier town to Mexico's most important industrial center and the largest city in the north.

THE CONCEPTUAL BACKGROUND

In 1893 Frederick J. Turner lamented the closing of the frontier in his famous and controversial essay "The Significance of the Frontier in American History." He argued that the western frontier experience shaped both the American national character and its institutions, particularly its democratic tradition. His frontier thesis defined the historical canon until the 1960s, when a new generation of historians questioned his arguments and turned most of his assertions upside down. In spite of the new scholarship that has successfully challenged the Turner thesis, no new thesis has come close to replacing it entirely; as a result, it continues to be one of the most provocative ideas in U.S. history.

Mexico has produced neither a Mexican Turner nor such an alluring thesis to follow, challenge, or reinterpret for two reasons. First, no Mexican intellectual of Turner's generation lamented the closing of Mexico's frontier. Most intellectuals viewed Mexican history and society through the lens of Mexico City, the center of authority, and assessed the history of the north as one that went against the grain of nation-building. Second, a frontier thesis like Turner's cannot directly apply to Mexico, a country whose history has been dictated not by one large and overarching experience but rather by the multiple experiences of the "many Mexicos."

As a proponent of the "many Mexicos" approach to understanding national history, I strongly believe that one of the implicit weaknesses of Mexican regional history is the near-absence of interpretive studies on the relationship between and meaning of regions in the making of a national history. For the most part, historians have examined regional and local histories in isolation from the broader processes of state-building and capitalist development. Consequently, historians of the Mexican borderlands have the task of exploring and explaining what makes the north so different from the rest of Mexico. Why, for instance, did the north play a leading role not only in the unmaking of Mexico during the Mexican Revolution but also in its remaking when the victorious *norteños* directed the construction of modern Mexico? More currently, why was the north the first region to break the monopoly of one-party rule and become a bastion for political conservatism?

Friedrich Katz theoretically advanced regional history by proposing in his classic work *The Secret War in Mexico* that the origins and outbreak of the Mexican Revolution cannot be properly understood without a close examination of the profound changes that the "frontier to border" transition wrought in northern society. He argued that the incorporation of the north into the capitalist economy and its integration into a centralized political system profoundly transformed the frontier, creating the conditions that provoked the north to violent intervention in the national affairs of 1910–1920. Surprisingly, no other scholar has yet pursued the "frontier to border" approach in a systematic way since Katz first presented it in 1981. Katz also applies this approach in his monumental work *The Life and Times of Pancho Villa,* which explores, among other themes, the creation of a revolutionary society in Chihuahua.

This book attempts to reconceptualize the history of northern Mexico in two ways. First, I argue that the history of northern Mexico needs to be organized by historical periods. I propose that the years between 1848, when the boundary was established, and 1910, when the Mexican Revolution erupted, constitute a defined moment in the history of northern Mexico. Second, I argue that Katz's "frontier to border" approach to the study of northern Mexico offers a clear analytic window for understanding change during a specific period and across a regional space.

The periodization of history is one of the elementary tools of the historian because it establishes time boundaries for the conceptualization of historical themes. Historians do not agree on all periods, as demonstrated in the discussions surrounding the periodization of the Mexican Revolution (for example, 1910–1917, 1910–1920, 1910–1923, 1910–1940, and 1910 to the present), largely because of their differing implications for historical and political analysis. Fortunately, the time boundaries for the early modern history of northern Mexico are fairly well defined. The establishment of the international boundary at the Río Bravo (Grande) in 1848 marks the beginning of the end of the frontier's isolation as well as the initiation of the border as the next stage of territorial development—a process fairly well advanced by 1910. By 1910 the border states had already assumed much of the form they have today: an advanced capitalist economy vis-à-vis the rest of Mexico; the formation of powerful business groups; and a labor market dependent on massive migrations from central Mexico. Moreover, 1910 also marks the north's first contestation of national political power. Northerners later triumphed in the Revolution and thus appropriated the dual roles of constructors of modern Mexico and architects of the governing institutions of one-party rule and the concentration of power in the presidency.

Like other discussions on historical transitions (for example, from "feudalism to capitalism"), the "frontier to border" framework implies a transition from one form of development to another. The combination of state-building, capitalist development, and proximity to the United States transformed the north from a frontier to a border society from 1848 to 1910. The creation of the 1848 boundary initiated this transition, a relatively brief period of forty years dominated by the struggles between the periphery, which sought to maintain its political autonomy, and a central state committed to establishing its authority over every region in Mexico. During this period of transition, federalist caudillos (strongmen) rose, gained political control of their localities, and resisted the integration of their regions into a centralized political system. The transition from frontier to border came to an end around 1890, when the Porfirian state eroded the power of caudillos and forcibly integrated the periphery into a centralized political system.

The northern states began to emerge as the border region with their incorporation into the domestic and world economy. During the second half of the nineteenth century, the dual process of political centralization and capitalist modernization spread throughout all regions in Mexico. The north acquired its own regional and distinctive traits during this period; much of its uniqueness was due to its permanent position as the zone of contact between two nations that were, in many ways, worlds apart.

THE MAKING OF THE MEXICAN BORDER, 1848–1910

David Weber provides a useful starting point for this study with his definition of frontiers as "zones of interaction between two cultures—as places where the cultures of the invader and of the invaded contend with one another and with their physical environment to produce a dynamic that is unique to time and place." [2] To modify Weber's definition, frontiers were also regions with weak ties to centralized political authority and to large-scale economic activity. Extending his definition to its logical conclusion, the frontier essentially became history when the invaders prevailed over the invaded. By 1880 the Native Americans had been defeated on both sides of the boundary.

Although the defeat of the Native Americans came approximately thirty years after the creation of the U.S.–Mexican boundary, 1848 marks the beginning of the end of the frontier era. With 1848 as a starting point, at least for Nuevo León and northeastern Mexico, the plotting of the border needs to be placed within the context of the history of the United States and Mexico. The 1848 redrawing of the U.S. and Mexican maps relocated the frontier from the edge of Mexico and the capitalist economy to the center of two nations on two completely different tracks of historical development, albeit at the periphery of these countries. The early years of border development did not follow any kind of blueprint because neither the Mexican government nor the United States had the capacity to police and administer the societies at the edges of their territories. Even though the United States had not consolidated its political control over most areas west of the Mississippi River, it was well on its way to becoming a continental power as of 1848. By contrast, Mexico was on the verge of disintegrating territorially and would not have a semblance of political stability until after 1876.

All international boundaries are human creations, including the U.S.–Mexican border, a crooked 2,000-mile line that artificially traverses an arid landscape. Therefore, years before cartographers and geographers mapped the flora, fauna, hills, and streams of the border region, *fronterizos* (borderlanders), regardless of ethnicity and nationality, instantly grasped the meaning of the new geography: those who resided north of the boundary were suddenly U.S. citizens living in the southernmost areas of the United States, while those who dwelled on the southern side continued to be Mexican citizens, residing on the northern edges of a Mexico that had just been reduced to half of its former size.

Considering that neither Mexico nor the United States had the ability to enforce its powers fully at its territorial edges, the new boundary at the Río Bravo abruptly put an end to the frontier's geographical isolation. The ending of isolation in the unguarded borderlands created the conditions that altered all established social relations in the northeast. The new boundary had the effect of harming the social position of groups who had wielded power in the confines of frontier isolation (mainly landlords and the independent armed-peasant communities) and improving the position of groups who, by the same token, had been marginalized (mainly indentured laborers and petty merchants). For the former groups, the new border improved their status vis-à-vis the dominant classes and institutions by allowing them a greater degree of freedom. In challenging their subordinate position, they trespassed the boundaries of written and unwritten laws and the established modes of conduct which had marginalized them. For instance, escaping from serfdom to freedom was no longer merely a dream for the thousands of indentured servants but a real alternative because of proximity to the Río Bravo. Servants not only escaped from serfdom by crossing to the "other side," but also undermined the authority of landlords who were losing control of their labor force.

The proposed argument that the Río Bravo created the conditions for human agency might appear to suffer from a heavy dose of geographic determinism. What is proposed here, however, is not that the simple presence of the Río Bravo tipped the scale of conflict in favor of groups which the frontier had assisted in marginalizing, but that the Río Bravo marked the international boundary and a zone of contact between Mexican borderlanders and forces engaged in the "opening of the West" in the United States, as well as with groups who had greater capacities to wage violence (e.g., Apaches, Comanches, and bandits).

The immediate outcomes of this contact between two different societies in this stateless region included a dramatic increase in violence (raids, banditry, filibustering, etc.), mass-scale contraband, and population movements (not only runaway servants, but other Mexicans who crossed the river and built new towns such as Brownsville, Texas). By engaging in all kinds of struggles and often in illegal activities, it was borderlanders, rather than states, who shaped social relations within the Mexican borderlands during the first decades after 1848 — their activities dictated diplomatic matters between the two countries.

"The history of the world is best observed from the frontier," wrote Pierre Vilar, the great historian of Spain.[3] In spite of the distance, one can get a panoramic view of the history of the Mexican state from the borderlands. The strength of Mexico as a territorial organization has largely depended on the degree of absolute authority it has exercised throughout its territory, especially at its boundaries. The presence of the central state was weak in northern Mexico before 1848 and, for all practical purposes, absent from 1855 to 1880, a time when federalist caudillos gained local power. For example, Santiago Vidaurri, the governor of Nuevo León, ruled the northeast with an iron hand from 1855 to 1864.

The Liberals who came to power in 1867 after the defeat of Maximilian considered the north a major obstacle in the unification of the Mexican state. As long as the north enjoyed an autonomous political existence, Mexico could not be unified. Malcolm Anderson argues that "[t]he frontier is the basic political institution: no rule-bound economic, social and political life in complex societies could be organized without them."[4] Mexico had well-defined boundaries but no effective control over them. The Mexican state could not realistically expect to organize society and the economy, especially when caudillos made the unification of Mexico difficult. Liberals were also consumed by the fear that, unless Mexico controlled its boundaries, the United States would enlarge itself at the expense of Mexican territory as it had in 1848.

To avoid this possible scenario and to unify Mexico, Porfirio Díaz made the taming of the north one of his priorities. The Porfirian state imposed its authority over the north by removing caudillos from power and by gaining greater law-enforcement authority, especially along the boundary. It replaced caudillos with imposed governors and (with the help of a loyal army, customs guards, and rural police) also gained a stronger policing presence, reducing illegal activities such as contraband and all-out violence, including Apache raids. The taming of the north coincided with Díaz's successful strategy of improving diplomatic relations with the great powers, especially with the United States. Thus, state-building in Mexico came at the expense of the north's political autonomy; as the Porfirian state gained greater power throughout Mexico, it also made the modernization of the economy its next priority.

All regions in Mexico were incorporated into the central state during the Porfiriato. In spite of this shared episode, modern Mexico has remained from that time to the present a nation composed of "many Mexicos," with at least three distinct regions: the north, center, and south. Each region has its own unique social, political, economic, ethnic, and cultural peculiarities. Among the most important features that distinguished the north from the south and center was its proximity to and evolving economic relationship with the United States.

The United States emerged as the world's leading industrial power during the time frame of this study. Mexico, in contrast, pursued economic development primarily as an exporter of raw materials and tropical goods. According to the best economic estimates, Mexico's total income was approximately 8 percent of U.S. income in 1845, three years before the creation of the international boundary. Notwithstanding the rapid modernization of the Mexican economy during the Porfiriato, the gap had widened to approximately 2 percent of the U.S. economy by 1910.[5] Matías Romero, a diplomat and Mexico's foremost expert on U.S.-Mexican relations during the Porfiriato, noted that the differences in economic histories met at the border, where "two peoples were brought into contact with each other whose economical and commercial condition offered a striking contrast. . . ."[6]

Northern Mexico became a permanent zone in which the economies and cultures of two nations that were in many ways worlds apart engaged each other, creating a unique region different from the interiors of both Mexico and the United States. Substantial foreign (mainly U.S.) investments in railroads and mining sparked the development of capitalism in the north, which spread more rapidly and thoroughly in this region than in the rest of Mexico. Two of the major outcomes of this process were that the northern economy became an extension of the U.S. economy and that the north turned into the new center of Mexican capitalism. Mexico modernized by following an outward (export-led) strategy of economic development: one-third of all exports passed through northern ports of entry by 1911 (over 60 percent if Tampico, a northeastern port, is included), compared to less than 2 percent in 1878.[7]

Emergent capitalism transformed northern society in all aspects, including the creation of fairly new classes. New groups of "self-made" entrepreneurs sprouted up from modest roots, built business empires, and eventually sat on top of the north's economic and political hierarchy: the Terrazas-Creels of Chihuahua, the Maderos of Coahuila, the agrobusiness elites of La Laguna, and Monterrey's industrialists. The Garzas, Sadas, and other Monterrey families were among the best-known industrialists in Mexico, and the city was known as the "Chicago of Mexico."

Concurrent with the emergence of northern entrepreneurs who were among the most powerful business groups in Mexico, the border as a "permanent zone of contact" between two countries molded thousands of uprooted migrants into the large northern working class. "Pushed" out of their localities by the forces of economic modernization, thousands of migrants from Mexico's interior were "pulled" to the north and to the southwestern United States by the prospects of higher wages and employment opportunities. Due to labor shortages and intense competition for unskilled Mexican workers between employers from "el norte" and the "other side," a distinct labor market emerged based upon free wage-labor, where workers sold their labor power to employers who purchased it in market-style relationships, as opposed to the unfree and low-wage labor practices that prevailed in much of the rest of Mexico.

CHAPTER ONE

The Significance of 1848

> Those fantastic forms, fang-sharp, bone-bare, that in
> Byzantine painting were a shorthand for the Unbounded
> beyond the Pale, unpoliced spaces where dragons dwelt and
> demons roamed.
>
> W. H. AUDEN, "CITY WITHOUT WALLS"

The imposition of the Río Bravo (Grande) as the boundary between Mexico and the United States was so extraordinary in its transformative powers that it marked at once an end and a beginning in the history of northern Mexico. It represented the beginning of the end of the frontier's isolation from the rest of both Mexico and the United States, changing almost overnight the life of all people who had been inhabiting and contesting this vast region. The new boundary established a clear line between two societies heading down two completely distinct paths of development. The frontier had not been banished; on the contrary, it now existed at the edge of two territorial states which were far from consolidating their political authority over the region, not to speak of their policing capacities. Considering that neither government had the ability to guard its boundaries, it was the borderlanders (Mexicans, North Americans, and Native Americans), rather than the Mexican and U.S. states, who shaped the structures of society in the region in the first four decades after 1848.

THE REBELLIOUS FRONTIER

On May 13, 1855, Santiago Vidaurri and Juan Zuazua revolted against the dictatorship of Antonio López de Santa Anna. They named their federalist rebellion the Restorer of Liberty Plan and declared that their native state, Nuevo León, appropriated its sovereignty from Mexico until the drafting of a new constitution that was more favorable to the states in the republic. A few days later they and their followers occupied Monterrey, the capital of Nuevo León. After gathering the city's inhabitants, Vidaurri announced the reasons for their mutiny against the Santa Anna government: the central government in Mexico City had violated the basic "rights" of all frontier residents—the rights to life, property, security, and tranquillity. On the following day a committee of civic leaders endorsed the Restorer of Liberty Plan, naming Vidaurri governor of Nuevo León.[1] The Vidaurrista federalist armed-movement was a *fronterizo* mutiny against the central government, adhering conditionally to Juan Alvarez's larger movement, the Ayutla Plan, a loose coalition of Liberal civilians with segments of the Mexican army and local caudillos.

During the next few weeks Juan Zuazua, one of the frontier's most infamous Indian fighters, concentrated on converting the state's dispersed civilian militias into a unified citizens' army, the Ejército del Norte (Army of the North). He shaped it into a powerful army that "liberated" Tamaulipas and Coahuila from Santa Annista control during the summer of 1855. Once these two states (which, along with Nuevo León, composed the Mexican northeast) were freed from the reign of "the center," the Army of the North proceeded to defeat the Mexican army in San Luis Potosí and Zacatecas. Within a matter of a few months the Army of the North elevated Vidaurri from obscurity, making him one of the most powerful and feared caudillos in all of Mexico. Less than a year later, he single-handedly annexed Coahuila to Nuevo León.

The Ayutla coalition ended the political career of General Santa Anna, Mexico's most prominent leader since its independence. As the head of numerous governments, he had often meddled in the northeast's political affairs. Perhaps the *fronterizos* even held him responsible for establishing the Río Bravo as Mexico's northeastern boundary, which split the Gran Chichimeca frontier, making the territory of Baja California and the states of Sonora, Chihuahua, Coahuila, Tamaulipas, and Nuevo León border areas. *Fronterizo* outrage over Mexico's loss of half of its national territory to the United States was not based on strong nationalist sentiment, which hardly existed in the north during this time, but on the profound changes that the 1848 boundary had wrought in the northeast within such a brief period. Most noticeable of all was a relentless increase in violence.

Violence between Indians and *fronterizos* had escalated to a degree unsurpassed in any other period in the 250-year history of warfare between these two parties. Comanche and Lipan Apache raids into Nuevo León increased after 1848, spawning a deep sense of insecurity among the *fronterizos,* especially in the rural communities. Nuevo León's civic militias, made up of civilian volunteers from all municipalities, had been the primary defenders of the frontier, not only against Indians, but also against the North American occupiers of the northeast during the U.S.-Mexican war and against all forces based the "other side" of the Río Bravo: bandits, Texan raiders, and separatist armies. The Santa Anna government had directly contributed to the weakening of the region's defenses by removing and imposing governors, contributing to the disorders wracking this region. Most of all, *fronterizos* resented the government's extraction of their resources. The U.S. consul in Monterrey noted that every "revolution" in Mexico (and there had been many since its independence) was perceived negatively in Nuevo León because it led to the double burden of a "new tax in money and a drain of the population for recruits."[2] By demanding these badly needed resources from the *fronterizos,* the Mexican government had broken one of the historic social contracts between the periphery and the central state—since colonial times the peasant communities had "not paid tribute by virtue of being obligated to sustain the war against the barbarians."[3]

Fronterizos accepted Santiago Vidaurri as their undisputed leader because he articulated their profound resentment against "the center" better than anybody else in the northeast. He targeted the Santa Annista governments as the main source of all evils that had cursed the frontier since the establishment of the 1848 boundary. Vidaurri, a native of Lampazos (a town near the Río Bravo that prided itself on being the first line of defense against Indian incursions), was a product of the frontier. As a member of the Lampazos militias, he had participated in many campaigns against the Apaches and Comanches and had fought against the U.S. occupation of Nuevo León during the U.S.-Mexican war. After serving time in jail for wounding a companion, Vidaurri entered the ranks of the state bureaucracy as a clerk. He later served as Nuevo León's secretary of state for more than a decade and was responsible for organizing the state's defenses against Indian incursions. He established close ties with the commanders of the militias, such as Zuazua, Mariano Escobedo, Ignacio Zaragoza, and others who would later perform heroic deeds for the Liberal cause at the national level. Given the many changes in governors, Vidaurri's long tenure as the highest-ranking nonelected official in Nuevo León provided the *fronterizos* with the only semblance of leadership in an otherwise chaotic political climate.

Once the Vidaurristas removed the Mexican army from the northeast, Vidaurri began to organize the *fronterizos* for the defense of the northeast in 1855. After experiencing thirty-four years of rule under the Mexican flag, *fronterizos* firmly believed that they were better off fending for themselves rather than relying on the "center."[4] Vidaurri warned Juan Alvarez, the leader of the Ayutla rebellion, not "to send us commanders or public employees of any kind because we will resist them with arms."[5] By all accounts, Vidaurri was an extreme federalist—a federalism largely rooted in the frontier's resentment against the center.

Vidaurrista federalism was also ideologically grounded on northern chauvinism toward the rest of Mexico and perhaps even on separatist intentions. He made it a point to define *fronterizos* as a different kind of "Mexican." Vidaurri wrote to Benito Juárez that the Army of the North was made up of property owners who "know their rights" and that they "want to end, once and for all, the discords so that they can dedicate their energies to their work and enjoy a tranquil life with their families."[6] Unlike the "miserable Indians" who, according to Vidaurri, composed the majority of the Mexican population, *fronterizos* were free people who were "conscious of their duties, and, at the same time, their power and rights."[7] Vidaurri, a *fronterizo* chauvinist who believed that the sun only rose and set in the north, was perhaps unaware that Juárez was a Zapotec from Oaxaca, a predominantly Indian state located in Mexico's deep south. At any rate, and despite Vidaurri's chauvinism toward the Mexico south of the tropic of Cancer (i.e., from Durango south), his comments revealed two characteristics of *fronterizo* identity present since colonial times: they own property and are endowed with the rights of "free men," meaning citizens who do not pay taxes.

Fronterizo identity and politics had evolved over a period of 250 years, beginning in 1596 when the first settlers arrived in Nuevo León. Locked into the northeast frontier by geography and distance, *fronterizos* developed a collective identity based on conquering and colonizing a region in which the "other" had been the indigenous population. Mexican independence in 1821 ended the frontier's isolation and coincided with an avalanche of violence (by Apache and Comanche Indians, Texas raiders, and filibusters) provoked by the westward territorial expansion of the United States. The 1848 boundary intensified contact with the violence of the outside world, forcing *fronterizos* to defend a homeland on the verge of disintegration. Their 1855 mutiny against the "center" can best be understood by briefly exploring *fronterizo* history prior to 1848.

THE MAKING OF THE *PATRIA CHICA* IN THE GRAN CHICHIMECA, 1596–1821

After an unsuccessful colonization attempt two decades earlier, the first *pobladores* (settlers) arrived in the present state of Nuevo León in 1596.

Governor Diego de Montemayor, along with a dozen colonizers and their families, founded the village of Nuestra Señora de Monterrey at the eastern foot of the Sierra Madre. From Monterrey the settlers initiated the snail-paced conquest and subsequent colonization of New Spain's northeastern hinterland, christening it the New Kingdom of León. The conquest of Nuevo León and much of the northeastern Gran Chichimeca lasted close to two centuries, ending when the native inhabitants—the Guachinochiles, Bocarros, Borrados, Xanambres, Gualaxises, Zalayas, Pazaltoes, Talahuiches, and other nomadic "Chichimecas"—disappeared from the landscape as identifiable groups due to war, disease, assimilation, and enslavement.

The first settlers' accounts of Nuevo León painted a picture of a landscape that we would not recognize today. According to Alonso de León, one of the early chroniclers, the frontier was ideal for ranching and farming, a northern oasis with abundant supplies of water for farming, green pastures for cattle grazing, trees that could be cut and used for charcoal, and fertile lands that could produce a broad range of crops from watermelons to wheat.[8] Starting with Diego de Montemayor and preceding Juan Bautista Alberdi's famous dictum "gobernar es poblar" (to govern is to populate), Nuevo León's first governors concentrated all energies on populating the frontier by offering any new *poblador,* regardless of ethnicity and class, "free land," water rights, and tax exemptions.[9]

Governor Martín de Zavala, Montemayor's successor and a wealthy miner who had made a fortune in Zacatecas, did everything possible to recruit new settlers. The incentive of "free land," however, attracted only a few Spaniards and Tlaxcalan Indians who received individual *mercedes* (large land grants). "The first conquistadores of the New Kingdom of León," wrote José González, Nuevo León's foremost intellectual of the nineteenth century, "both Spaniard and Tlaxcalan, arrived with all the privileges and responsibilities given to new *pobladores,* that is, they were given land and water, did not pay tribute, and were obligated to sustain the war against the barbarians by their own means. The Nuevoleoneses depended entirely on their own resources to survive; they did not pay any direct taxes, but they were always armed [in order] to defend their properties night and day."[10]

These *pobladores* settled down with their families and brought with them their cattle, work equipment, horses, and weapons (the last two were vital for survival on the frontier). Land ownership entitled male settlers—regardless of parentage, ethnicity, education, wealth, and other categories that defined the status of people in colonial Mexico—to adopt the status of *vecino,* a term analogous to equal, peer, and citizen. All *vecinos,* including Tlaxcalans, were obligated to defend their lands, "pacify" the region, and serve the governor, the only representative of the Spanish monarchy on the frontier.

In his classic work *Land and Society in Colonial Mexico,* François Chevalier pointed out that the northeast's lack of mineral wealth did not attract miners and merchants, the *ricos* who constituted part of the power structure in colonial Mexico.[11] Elites and the religious orders passed over Nuevo León, apparently because the region was too poor in silver, gold, and potential converts. Except for the symbolic presence of a handful of Franciscan missionaries, the religious orders manifested little interest in the conversion of the northeastern native population. The Jesuits built over one hundred churches in Chihuahua and wielded considerable influence over the Yaquis in Sonora. In New Mexico the Franciscans competed with settlers for the souls and labor of the Pueblo Indians.[12]

By all accounts, Nuevo León was a poor person's frontier even though the governors had distributed *mercedes* to wealthy elites from central Mexico. Unlike the frontier settlers, elites did not settle down and instead used their land grants as winter pastures for their flocks of sheep (as discussed later in this chapter). The physical absence of elites and of the church in Nuevo León set the region apart from the rest of the north in at least two key ways. First, it allowed for the concentration of political power in the hands of the governors. Second, because of the absence of the church and elites, the class and ethnic hierarchies of colonial Mexico were not reproduced in Nuevo León, a condition that permitted the development of a more egalitarian society within the *poblador* communities. This was not the case in neighboring Coahuila, where a few landlords established their dominance over the population with their acquisition of most of the land.

Other than appointing governors, the colonial government in Mexico City neglected Nuevo León. As the only representatives of the Spanish monarchy on the frontier, governors ruled with a high degree of autonomy. They exerted complete administrative, judicial, and military authority over the region and wielded an unquestionable authority over the *pobladores.*[13] In this bureaucrat-free environment, the governor's duties included making regular visits to scattered population pockets, granting lands to new settlers, granting larger communities municipal status, settling property disputes, and organizing the defense of the region. More often than not, governors ended as *pobladores* once their tenures were over.[14]

Besides distributing land grants, the first governors awarded settlers *mercedes de indios de encomienda*, the frontier's version of the *encomienda*.[15] In lieu of any real wealth in the form of gold and silver and with the complete absence of sedentary Indians who could provide settlers with agricultural tribute, the enslavement of Indians became the *pobladores'* main means of acquiring labor and wealth. Like the *bandeirantes* of São Paulo, Brazil, settlers recruited neighbors, family members, and friendly Indians with the aim of "punishing," as a settler wrote, "Indians who are in rebellion against the monarchy."[16] Luis Carbajal enslaved 800 to 1,000 Indians during his failed attempt to establish a colony in this region in 1579, selling them to miners from Zacatecas.[17] Two decades later Governor Diego Montemayor and the other leading settlers, the "Diegos," enslaved over 100 Indians each: Diego de Montemayor, 200; his son Diego, 100; Diego Díaz de Berlanga, 150; and Diego Rodríguez, 135.[18] Enslaved Indians furnished settlers with labor or were sold to miners from Zacatecas. In one case, miners purchased a group of twenty-four Indians for 3,120 pesos, approximately 130 pesos each.[19] Indians became a commodity that could be sold, "rented, shared [among settlers], inherited, mortgaged, and given as a dowry."[20] The slave-raiding tradition was passed down over a few generations and was not suppressed until early in the eighteenth century, a meaningless gesture considering that by then only a few Indians remained.

Not much is known about the general history of northeastern Indians. Because they did not survive the conquest of the region and left no written records, the little that is known about them comes mainly from settlers' accounts. Alonso de León, the main chronicler of the northeast frontier, labeled the Indians ignorant "of laws, king, and the lord" and, for this reason, deserving to be enslaved.[21] These accounts also emphasized the Indian resistance to enslavement and the anything but peaceful conquest of the frontier. They reported that Indians escaped from the *congregaciones* and missions, many of them later returning to the site of their enslavement to free their families and friends, to steal goods, and, if the opportunity arose, to attack their tormentors. José González wrote that the Indians' "hatred of the whites multiplied along with their attacks [on settlers], with war being permanent."[22] Periods of peace between *pobladores* and natives were brief. In one of those rare moments, a settler wrote, "now that they [Indians] are quiet and have been pacified, we finally have time to work the land."[23] The condition of *guerra viva*, the lengthy frontier war, dominated the colonial history of Nuevo León as well as most of the history of the northern frontier. Except for the Lampazos presidio and a few other military communities in Texas that were established in the last quarter of the eighteenth century, the "pacification" of the frontier depended primarily on the *vecinos*. During one of the regular inspections of the settlements in 1775, Governor Vidal de Lorea reported that all *vecinos* were armed and enlisted for military services, organized into twenty-two military companies with a total of 1,250 volunteers. Nuevo León had 29,000 inhabitants at the time.[24]

Nuevo León was essentially one large military colony. *Vecinos* were simultaneously soldiers and landowners. They consistently wrote to the governors that with their "arms and horses" they had served "his majesty," the king, in actions against the Indians. As "*poblador[es]* and *conquistador[es]* of the frontier," they were permanently on the alert to defend the region against "the invasions of our enemies."[25] Warfare against the native population was a collective enterprise, also serving as a rite of passage for young males, who often participated in their first military campaigns at an age "when one could reason," meaning from the age of twelve to fifteen.[26] Although the Apaches made a few rare appearances in the northeast around the mid-eighteenth century, the presidios in Texas succeeded in preventing Indian incursions into Nuevo León for the remainder of Spanish rule in Mexico. Thus, the "colonization" and "conquest" of Nuevo León that began in Monterrey in 1596 was completed in the mid-eighteenth century, when almost all the land that constitutes the present state was distributed and when slavery, war, disease, and acculturation had destroyed the local Indian populations.[27] Nuevo León earned the onerous distinction of being the only place in Mexico where the local indigenous population did not survive the colonial era.

Except for the lands governors granted to influential elites from central Mexico, most *mercedes* went only to *pobladores* who had the resources (such as cattle and tools) and the physical capacity to work their lands with relatives and slaves (both Indian and African). True to the meaning of "gobernar es poblar," *vecinos* made the populating of their properties one of their priorities. José Treviño, for example, received a *merced* in 1604, a property equivalent to the current size of the municipalities of Apodaca and Pesquería. He settled with his family, relatives, and slaves, bringing with him 2,000 head of cattle and whatever possessions his ten wagons could carry. Upon Treviño's death, Blas de la Garza inherited his *merced*. De la Garza was one of the leading figures in the "pacification" of the region, well known as an Indian fighter and slave trapper. He once wrote to the governor that he was one of the *vecinos* who had contributed most to the colonization of Nuevo León. Interestingly, he did not emphasize his military deeds, but rather his procreative abilities. He was proud of fathering "eleven sons and daughters who are married," who, in turn, had given him thirty-six grandchildren. His clan had greatly contributed to the "growth of this city [Monterrey] and the kingdom [Nuevo León]."[28]

Unlike the case of neighboring Coahuila, where a few individuals came to monopolize the land and established latifundios, the history of colonial Nuevo León (excluding the southern part of the state) is the story of how the descendants of the first landlords became peasants.[29] The descendants of the first *pobladores,* such as Blas de la Garza, inherited their fathers' *mercedes.* They in turn had more children who would later have more children, and so on, leading to less available land for every new generation of *vecinos.* Like the de la Garza clan, these families were quite large, and landownership diminished with every passing generation. By 1700 most of the original *mercedes* had been subdivided into various haciendas— communities that would later be better known as *comunidades de accionistas.* A case in point is the community of Valle de San Juan Bautista de Pesquería Grande, which was founded by Hernando de Mendiola in the early 1600s. After receiving a *merced,* he settled with fifty people, including his family and slaves. Two hundred years later his *merced* had been subdivided into four hacienda-communities that supported a combined one hundred families. These four communities had organized their own local militia of fifty-six members, built a chapel, and elected a mayor. Each community was a collective of individuals (for the most part family members) who owned a certain percentage of the community's land, albeit an unspecified portion. In other words, individuals knew that they owned a certain amount of land, but it was not specified where the land was within the hacienda-community.

With the passage of time these communities multiplied in membership, while the quantity of land remained fixed. Their growth also gave rise to the political structure of Nuevo León. The municipalities evolved as the governor granted municipal status to the few communities that had enough people and resources to sustain basic services without financial assistance from the governor. Bernabé de las Casas, one of the original settlers, received a *merced* that extended north of Monterrey to the boundary with Coahuila. Within three centuries his descendants had subdivided it into three haciendas of *comunidades de accionistas* that produced the present-day municipalities of Hidalgo, Abasolos, and El Carmen.[30] Most of the present fifty-two municipalities received municipal status from 1825 to 1883.[31] According to the state constitution of 1825, municipal status was given to a community or a group of communities with at least 1,000 inhabitants that had the resources to sustain a chapel, jail, municipal buildings, and school. Elected officials were members of the community who did not receive salaries for their services.

Even though the earlier generations made the clear distinction between themselves and the Indians they enslaved, this distinction ended with the disappearance of the Indians as identifiable groups. Nuevo León did not reproduce the dominant features of Mexico's colonial social structure because it did not produce sufficient wealth to support a rigid class and ethnic hierarchy. As mentioned, colonial elites did not settle in the region because it was poor in minerals. The dominant practice of distributing land to all inheritors prevented the emergence of a landlord class. All *vecinos* were poor in Nuevo León and became poorer in land holdings with each passing generation. In spite of this trend, they were all property-owners who appropriated their ancestors' status of *vecinos,* even after the defeat of the native population. The frontier had democratized status to the point that even the name *vecino* perhaps had been appropriated by the *castas.*[32] According to David Weber, one of the leading scholars of the Spanish and Mexican borderlands: "Inevitably, the frontier population became 'white' as Indians and mulattos declared themselves mestizos, and mestizos described themselves as españoles. As one foreign resident of mid-eighteenth-century Sonora noted, 'practically all those who wish to be considered Spaniards are people of mixed blood.' "[33]

THE ENDING OF THE *PATRIA CHICA*'S ISOLATION

Nuevo León entered the national period of Mexican history with great expectations of a bright future for Mexico and itself. A native son, Fray Servando Teresa de Mier, one of the premier intellectuals of the Latin American enlightenment, represented Nuevo León in Mexico's first congress. In 1825 Nuevo León became a state, and a few years later the Mexican government fulfilled one of the frontier's main demands: the opening of the northeastern port of Matamoros. It was symbolic of the mood that *fronterizos* rechristened most of the municipalities by replacing names of saints with those of insurgents. Villa de San Juan Bautista de Cadereyta became Cadereyta Jiménez, after Mariano Jiménez, and Valle de San Mateo del Pilón became Montemorelos, after the caudillo of the insurgency, José María Morelos.

This frontier euphoria did not last long, however. Between 1821 and 1867 Mexico nearly disintegrated as a nation because of political instability, economic crisis, and foreign invasions. Mexico had three constitutions (1824, 1836, and 1857) during this period and over forty heads of state as Liberals and Conservatives battled for control of the central state. With a weak Mexican state, violence dominated, affecting the economy as mines and haciendas lay in ruin. The United States instigated an expansionist war against its weak neighbor, invading it from 1846 to 1848, as did France from 1862 to 1867. Mexico lost over half of the territory it claimed in 1821: Central America separated from Mexico in 1823, Texas in 1836, and the present southwestern United States in 1848; General Santa Anna sold the Mesilla region of southern Arizona and New Mexico to the United States (the Gadsden Purchase) in 1853.

For over two hundred years geography and political indifference on the part of colonial authorities had isolated the region from the rest of Mexico and the world. Whether the Nuevoleoneses wanted it so or not, their destiny was largely dictated by the increasing contact that their *patria chica* (local homeland) had with the outside world. Three postindependence developments simultaneously occurred which diminished the *patria chica*'s isolation. First, regardless of who held political power in Mexico City, the Mexican state(s), although weak, began to intervene in northeastern affairs. The Mexican army imposed and removed governors at will and arbitrarily taxed *fronterizos* and conscripted them. Second, the northeast's commercial isolation ended with the opening of the port of Matamoros in 1826. Third, Nuevo León was among the first regions in Mexico to come into permanent contact with the overland westward expansion of the U.S. market economy, the population, and, subsequently, the territorial state. As of 1821, Mexico had 1.7 million square miles of land, while the United States had 1.8. For Mexico the cost of the North American "opening of the West" was losing more than half of its territory to its northern neighbor, with the Río Bravo marking its northern boundary in 1848.[34]

Fronterizos were no longer isolated from the world; nor did they have a strong Mexican state to shield them from increasing contact with the outside. Indeed, everything seemed to conspire against the *vecinos* after Mexican independence. In spite of the fact that violence had always been part of their history, the end of the frontier's isolation introduced new forms of violence beside which previous forms of violence paled. In addition to an escalation in Indian raids, *vecinos* confronted filibusters, separatists' armies, the U.S. army, and bandits. In 1841 Antonio Canales, a native of Monterrey and the father of the future caudillo of Tamaulipas, Severano Canales, headed a separatist army which sought to create the Río Grande Republic out of the three northeastern states. In 1851 José María Carbajal led Mexican and U.S. separatists in the ill-fated attempt to establish the Republic of the Sierra Madre. Texan raiders constantly crossed the Río Bravo to terrorize northern communities, while local bandits, like the legendary Agapito Treviño, alias "el Caballo Blanco," did the same.[35] After three days of battle between U.S. and Mexican troops in 1846, Monterrey had the appearance of "a vast cemetery. The unburied bodies, the dead and putrid animals, the silence of the streets, all gave a fearful aspect to the city."[36] *Vecinos* waged guerrilla warfare against the U.S. occupation of their *patria chica* from 1846 to 1847 and paid a heavy price for it. U.S. troops torched communities and ranches that gave "refuge to these bands."[37]

While the *vecinos' patria chica* was collapsing under the weight of the violence emanating from north of the Río Bravo, a sizable minority of the frontier population benefited from Nuevo León's new relationship with the outside world, mainly merchants and the *sirvientes* (debt-peons) of the haciendas. Contact with the outside had the effect of liberating these two classes from their heretofore marginalized status. The opening of Matamoros to international commerce and the overland expansion of the U.S. economy offered merchants their first opportunity to engage in commerce. Meanwhile, the close proximity of the Río Bravo as the international boundary offered *sirvientes* their first opportunity to escape.

In terms of the status of the frontier residents, the new boundary at the Río Bravo was more than a simple line in the middle of a desert. From its inception, the new boundary clearly separated two nations on different paths of development. Years before cartographers and surveyors mapped the border region, troops established forts and barracks, and custom posts opened, the 20,000 or so people who resided along the banks of the Río Bravo from the Gulf of Mexico to Piedras Negras were the first to understand that the new boundary marked the end of one era and the beginning of another. Those who had been residing on the northern banks of the Río Bravo quickly realized that they now resided on the southernmost territory of the United States, while those on the southern side recognized that their properties were located on the northern edge of Mexico.

The new boundary divided communities, shifted population from one side of the Río Bravo to the other, and created new settlements with little government involvement. Mexicans who did not want to live under the U.S. flag, including a good portion of Laredo's residents, crossed the

Río Bravo and founded a new settlement, Laredo-Monterrey, which later became Nuevo Laredo. At the same time, many residents of Matamoros crossed the river and founded Brownsville. On the U.S. side of the Bravo new towns were founded: Eagle Pass, Edinburg, Rio Grande City, and Roma. Their residents built large warehouses to store goods that would be illegally introduced into Mexico. In contrast, the towns on the Mexican side of the Bravo were defensively reinforced with the establishment of five military colonies. For those on the U.S. side of the boundary, the "other side" represented an abundance of commercial opportunities. For most Mexicans on the southern side of the Bravo, the "other side" was the source of violent groups who threatened the existence of their *patria chica*.

The new boundary had different meanings to different people, classes, and communities and to the two national governments. For the government in Mexico City, the border represented nothing but a series of new problems that it was incapable of solving: secessionist movements, Indian and Texan raiders, uncontrolled contraband, and all kinds of threatening diplomatic disputes with Washington. For Washington, D.C., the violence at the boundary was simply another indicator of Mexico's inability to sustain political order. For Matamoros, which had been the most important city between San Luis Potosí and San Antonio, Texas, the new border caused an outflow of commerce and population to Brownsville, Texas. For Comanches and Apaches, increasingly sandwiched between two nations, the unpoliced border provided them with more time to resist subjugation. For frontier merchants, the boundary offered a golden opportunity to engage in large-scale trade, albeit illicit. African-American slaves and Mexican indentured servants crossed paths at the Bravo. For each, crossing to the "other side" represented freedom from one of two different versions of slavery.

Neither the Mexican nor the U.S. government had the capacity to protect its boundary. Given the stateless Hobbesian scenario, it was the borderland residents—Indians, *fronterizos,* and Americans—rather than the national states who set the pace in shaping the economic, social, and political character of the U.S.-Mexican borderlands during the first three decades after 1848. In this stateless region, borderlanders engaged in large-scale contraband, waged violence and defended themselves from it, migrated from one side of the boundary to the other, and ran away from haciendas. If anything, the border intensified the existing contradictions within frontier society, such as those between landlords and *sirvientes* and *vecinos* and Indians. It also accelerated the emerging contradictions, such as those between the periphery and the Mexican state (federalism vs. centralism), manifested by the merchants' illegal commerce, which challenged the Mexican state's custom policies. The following three sections examine these contradictions and the specific impact of the boundary on the hacienda and the merchant and peasant communities.

THE BORDER AND THE HACIENDA

Nuevo León's governors had granted *mercedes* to individuals, including colonial elites, on the condition that they would colonize the region. After they had settled throughout Nuevo León over a few generations, their *mercedes* were subdivided by their descendants, who organized themselves into communities of *vecinos,* with each individual family having shares to the land, albeit unspecified ones. *Vecinos* used their land for subsistence agriculture and cattle ranching. Elites, in contrast, never settled on the frontier and, as absentee-owners, used their lands only as winter pastures for their flocks of sheep. Two patterns of land ownership surfaced from the very beginning of colonization that would dominate the agrarian history of Nuevo León: the privately owned hacienda and community-owned property.

The early history of the Nuevoleonese hacienda can be divided into two periods. The first begins in the early 1600s, when the frontier governors granted large extensions of land to colonial elites from central Mexico, who primarily used their lands for grazing, and ends around the turn of the nineteenth century, when these elites apparently sold their properties to wealthier elites. During the second period, from 1800 to 1848, the haciendas expanded in the southern part of the state when they purchased lands from *vecinos.* Landless peasants were forced into sharecropping, tenancy, and debt-peonage relations with landlords in order to meet their subsistence requirements.

Juan de Espíndola (the 1644 "Treasurer of the Holy Crusade"), Juan Francisco de Bertiz (a Mexico City councilman), the Zúñiga family, and other influential elites from central Mexico received *mercedes* in Nuevo León that averaged between forty to fifty *estancias* for *ganado menor* (sheep) or somewhere between 30,000 and 37,500 hectares. A few individuals received land grants of over 100,000 hectares. Following the model of the Spanish *mesta,* elites used their properties for grazing. Every November their flocks of sheep made an 800-kilometer journey from Querétaro to southern Nuevo León. These flocks (which numbered as many as 30,000 sheep) grazed for five to six months and then returned to Querétaro in late April.[38]

The sheep industry was one of the most secure and profitable enterprises in the Mexican colonial economy. Mutton fed the cities, hides were exported, and wool supplied the woolen industry of Querétaro, a city with 30,000 inhabitants. Mexico City residents consumed 270,000 sheep a year in 1790.[39] Although it is not well acknowledged, Nuevo León played a crucial role in this enterprise. Over a million sheep grazed in Nuevo León during the height of the Mexican *mesta*, and as many as 300,000 sheep were born there every year. If a flock of 30,000 sheep had a value of 15,000 pesos in 1715, then Nuevo León generated 150,000 pesos a year for the sheep owners from the newborn sheep alone.[40]

Even though the northeast's grazing lands tied the region to the domestic economy, Nuevo León did not receive any benefits from this relationship. Despite the value that the pastures had for the elite, most of them had never set foot on their frontier estates; nor did they invest any money in the region. They did not pay taxes on land because as supposed *pobladores* they were exempt. Nor did they pay wages to the local inhabitants, because they recruited most of their shepherds and their crews in central Mexico. "Owners were absentee landlords," according to François Chevalier, "living 800 kilometers away in the capital . . . having no other ties with the region than the income derived from their sheep in winter pastures there."[41] One of the consequences of this enterprise was environmental destruction, as the local flora was replaced by cactus, *matorrales* (thicket), huizache, mesquite, and other plants that flourished in desolate environments.[42]

The history of rural Nuevo León has not been written. There are no in-depth studies on the peasant communities, the haciendas, debt-peonage, and other themes of rural history. From the few sources available, it appears that the hacienda expanded in the first half of the nineteenth century when a new group of landlords purchased properties from older colonial elites and from impoverished *vecinos*. The Querétaro to Nuevo León sheep connection ended in the late eighteenth century due to the collapse of the woolen industry and the depletion of good pasture lands, as happened in other parts of Mexico such as the Valley of the Mezquital. Within this scenario, sheep owners sold their Nuevo León haciendas to other elites during the early years of the nineteenth century.

The haciendas of Potosí and Soledad, for instance, covered much of southern Nuevo León in the early decades of the nineteenth century. Potosí was first owned by the Marqués de Castillo de Aysa and Soledad by the Conde de Casa Rul.[43] By the turn of the nineteenth century, the Conde de

Pérez de Gálvez had acquired Soledad hacienda from his brother-in-law, the Conde de Casa Rul. Both Pérez de Gálvez and Casa Rul were Spanish soldiers who married into the Valenciana mining family. They were among the ten wealthiest individuals in Mexico on the eve of Mexican independence.[44] Just like other sheep owners, the Conde de Pérez de Gálvez was an absentee-owner engaged in many business activities and owned property throughout Mexico, such as Soledad, which supplied the Catorce silver mine in San Luis Potosí with grains, hides, and livestock. He purchased lands from struggling landlords whose fortunes had declined during the war of independence, expanding the size of Soledad so that it stretched throughout southern Nuevo León. Soledad become one of the great latifundios of the northeast. Castillo de Aysa, however, who owned Potosí, died in such dire poverty that his successors could not afford to claim the title of nobility.[45] They probably sold Potosí in order to pay his debts.

John Tutino argues in his book *From Insurrection to Revolution in Mexico* that because of Mexico's economic decline during the decades after independence the agrarian poor and rancheros advanced their economic interests at the expense of struggling hacendados. They gained greater bargaining power over landlords on tenancy rights, resulting in greater production and an overall improvement in their lives.[46] If indeed this was the general case, then southern Nuevo León was one of the exceptions to this development. Besides purchasing lands from struggling landlords, latifundios like Soledad expanded by purchasing plots from *vecinos* whose fortunes had also taken a turn for the worse. In the aftermath of independence, the southern peasantry owed not just their properties but also their personal freedom to landlords. The peasants thus took a path different from their counterparts in the rest of Nuevo León.

Based on limited sources, it appears that in Nuevo León landlords gained ground on the southern peasantry in the isolated confines of the northeast frontier. They did so by procuring control first of land and then of labor. Economic hardships associated with population increases and the decreasing size of family plots forced many peasants to sell their properties to landlords in order to feed their families. Galeana's population increased from 4,567 to 5,726 between 1821 and 1829.[47] Most peasants were either landless or farmed on marginal lands that could not provide a subsistence living. Galeana's mayor reported in 1825 that the "poorest of the *vecinos* farmed only on marginal lands, often on lands without access to water." Three years later he again noted that the poorest of the *vecinos* had been reduced to farming only on hills and in thicket-dominated fields.[48] He did not mention why they farmed on such marginal lands, but it is possible that they had sold their best lands to Soledad (there are no reports of land disputes between the hacienda and peasants).

With their economic security at risk, and in need of additional lands, peasants turned to Soledad as *medieros* (sharecroppers), as *arrendatarios* (tenants), and (the most unfortunate *vecinos*) as *sirvientes*.[49] With the landlords' increasing monopolization of land, *vecinos* had no choice but to offer their services to the hacienda. Landlords profited by collecting crops from sharecroppers, from the cheap labor of *sirvientes,* and especially from the swelling number of tenants. Galeana's mayor noted that "the great majority of the *vecinos* support themselves by paying rents" to Soledad and that rents were "excessively high." [50] Concerned about Soledad's expansion over most of his municipality, the mayor wanted the governor to pressure Conde de Pérez de Gálvez to reduce the rents on properties that he "could not cultivate on his own." [51]

Nuevo León's peasantry took two different paths during the first half of the nineteenth century. All started as *pobladores,* settlers and property-owners who did not pay taxes, in exchange for colonizing and defending the region. The armed northern peasants defended their properties and the region, formed autonomous communities, and maintained the name of *vecinos* for the duration of the nineteenth century. In contrast, the southern peasants sold their properties to the hacienda and thus forfeited the name of *vecinos*. Instead, they became *arrendatarios, medieros,* and *sirvientes,* terms associated with their subservient position *vis-à-vis* landlords.

The new international boundary at the Río Bravo not only changed the fate of the southern peasantry but also blocked the trend of greater hacendado domination over their lives. The most dramatic effect it had on the northeastern hacienda was the notable exodus of *sirvientes* to Texas. Close proximity to the "other side" provided the unfortunate and debt-burdened *sirvientes* the opportunity to escape from a lifetime of bondage for themselves and their descendants. "Among those of the Mexicans who are crossing the Rio Grande for the purpose of protection under the American flag," a Texas newspaper reported on the early exodus of *sirvientes* leaving the northeast in 1848, "are many of those who, being in debt, are held in slavery under the Mexican laws." [52]

The Comisión Pesquisidora, the Mexican government's commission that investigated U.S.-Mexican border problems, especially those in the northeast, reported that 2,812 *sirvientes* (along with 2,572 family members) fled from Coahuila and Nuevo León to Texas from 1848 to 1873. The number of runaways was much higher, given that only half of the municipalities in Nuevo León responded to the Comisión Pesquisidora's request for this kind of information. Considering that Nuevo León had 130,000 inhabitants and Coahuila even fewer and that the population of these two states did not manifest major increases during the mid-nineteenth century, the runaways constituted a large percentage of the frontier's available workforce. On the labor-starved frontier these "fugitives" from Mexican laws easily found employment on south Texas ranches.[53] Nuevo León's hacendados lost 255,995 pesos in wages advanced (this was considered an unpaid debt and also a felony), while their Coahuilan counterparts lost 123,000 pesos, for an average of 135 pesos per *sirviente*.[54] For the hacendados the losses in wage advancements were perhaps not as important as the newly emerging geography, where proximity to the United States undermined "the institution of servants," which "cannot today be sustained."[55] The new boundary strengthened the position of *sirvientes* because they now had the opportunity to escape from the hacienda; even if they did not actually run away, this option more than likely undermined the heretofore absolute authority of the landlord, who would now have difficulty in maintaining a permanent and obedient labor force. Antonio Moreno, a senator from Sonora, understood what the "other side" meant for the most impoverished Mexican borderlanders when he wrote in the late 1870s: "Nobody changes nationalities to assume a worse condition, and it is very dangerous to see just beyond the conventional line prosperity and wealth, and on this side destitution and poverty."[56]

In spite of the discrimination and violence that Mexicans regularly experienced in Texas, the "other side" represented for *peones* not just freedom from landlords but also an improvement in wages and living conditions. A recent U.S. arrival to the border town of Eagle Pass quickly learned that retaining Mexican labor in the labor-starved borderlands depended not just on paying higher wages than could be offered in Mexico but on offering other incentives. She wrote in 1852:

> We have always paid more than twice [the average wage] for our permanent servants, but of late we have repeated proffers of good shepherds and field hands for six and seven dollars a month, with the addition of meat and coffee rations, which the Americans have made a custom, and therefore a social law at Eagle Pass.[57]

Nuevo León's hacendados never learned this lesson.

MONTERREY'S MERCHANTS AND THE BORDER

The *vecinos* and merchants shared one thing in common: an animosity, even though stemming from two completely different historical experiences, toward the central state in Mexico City. After three decades of Mexican rule, the *vecinos* had concluded that the Mexican state was predatory, taxing and otherwise preying on their meager resources. To add insult to injury, the state had conscripted them into the army during the political chaos of the 1830s–1850s and had not provided enough soldiers, resources, or financial assistance to defend the frontier. Merchants were true believers in free trade, an ideological and economic ethos to which they collectively subscribed but one which the Mexican government opposed.

Even though the frontier merchants were nonexistent before independence, their postindependence "freedom of commerce" credo was well grounded in the discourse of officials and intellectuals residing in the northeast during the Bourbon era. Most of these officials, such as Félix Callejas, who later became the Royalists' leading military commander during the early years of the War of Independence, were not natives of the frontier. When they arrived in the region, they noted the extreme conditions of poverty that prevailed throughout the northeast. *Fronterizos* were so poor, according to one of the officials, that they only consumed maize, dry meat, and on occasion beans. They used "hides for clothes, and slept on the floor, using sheepskins as mats." [58] Officials concluded that the *fronterizos* did not choose to be poor: the region's poverty and economic backwardness was the product of the frontier's unfavorable status *vis-à-vis* central Mexico.[59] The center economically dominated the frontier through the *alcabala,* a substantial tax on all goods transported from one place to another, and through the Veracruz and Mexico City merchants' control of foreign and domestic trade.

According to Miguel Ramos Arizpe, Coahuila's representative to the Spanish Cortes of Cádiz in 1811, the *alcabalas* perpetuated on the frontier a "charter of perpetual slavery." [60] To make his point clearer, Ramos Arizpe demonstrated how cotton, one of Coahuila's main products, failed to create wealth for Coahuilans:

> The exterior provinces [central Mexico] receive it in a raw state and return it a year later in the form of manufactured goods which they sell to the same owners, with the added cost of transportation back and forth over more than 520 miles, with two or three sales taxes, due to that many sales and resales, the salary of the manufacturers,

and the profits made by a number of contractors who have handled the cotton. . . ."[61]

Mexico City and Veracruz merchants monopolized foreign trade and controlled much of domestic commerce, a practice the colonial government sanctioned. As long as these merchants had the upper hand in all commercial transactions, the people of the frontier were "destined to be the slaves of four greedy merchants of Querétaro, San Luis, etc."[62] Although they were on opposite sides politically, General Joaquín de Arredondo, the Royalist commander of the northeast during the War of Independence, shared Ramos Arizpe's views of associating "Veracruz and Mexico City's" wealth with the economic subjugation ("servitude") of the frontier, leading to its overall "misery."[63]

According to these officials and intellectuals, the northeast had valuable resources to trade outside of Mexico, in places such as Cuba. For all practical purposes, however, markets were closed off because of distance and the *alcabalas*. Recognizing that the northern periphery carried little political weight, frontier officials acknowledged the futility of attempting to end or reduce the *alcabalas* and to curtail the influence of Mexico City's merchants.

Taking this into account, frontier officials during the Bourbon era began to call for a northeastern port, because it could ease the burden of taxes and merchant abuses while at the same time encouraging economic development and ending the frontier's geographic isolation. A regional port could increase northeastern trade with the outside, lower the cost of transportation, and make frontier goods more competitive by avoiding the numerous *alcabalas* placed on overland commerce. Furthermore, a port could symbolically liberate the northeast from its condition of "perpetual slavery." The need for a port became one of the main frontier demands, one which the Spanish authorities were willing to entertain but not actually grant. The northeast finally acquired the port of Matamoros in 1826, five years after Mexican independence.

Once the Matamoros port (located at the mouth of the Río Bravo) was open, North American and European merchants flocked there, seeing it as the northern doorway to Mexico's internal market. Matamoros immediately became one of the country's main ports, growing to be a dynamic town of 7,000 inhabitants by 1830. Indeed, Matamoros liberated the frontier from the center's commercial domination, forever altering center-periphery trade relations by reversing commercial roles. Two-thirds of all imported goods directed to the region north of Guadalajara and Queré-tero passed through Matamoros.[64] Commercial freedom, however, was far from guaranteed—Mexican custom officials collected high tariffs in Mata-moros from international commerce.

Commercial "liberation" only meant that the frontier no longer had to play a subservient role. The argument that a port could spur economic growth in the northeast proved false because the area produced few goods with which it could trade. The region was poor in minerals, the livestock industry was in the process of decline due to banditry and Indian raids, and any agricultural products, such as sugarcane and cotton, could not com-pete in the larger market. Matamoros served only as a port of entry for imports and exit for exports. Within the northeast, Monterrey was the mid-way point on the Matamoros–central Mexico trade route. Situated at the foot of the Sierra Madre, the city was well positioned as one of the few natu-ral crossings in the mountain range dividing much of the northeast from the interior.

For over two centuries geography had been one of the greatest ob-stacles in the development of capitalism in the northeast. The lack of roads, navigable rivers (other than the Río Bravo), and ports had separated the frontier from the rest of Mexico and isolated it from the world. Then the northeast came into contact with the world of commerce through Mata-moros in 1826. According to Matías Romero, the 1848 boundary at the Río Bravo accelerated this process. It brought two peoples "into contact with each other whose commercial conditions offered a striking contrast." [65] Romero pointed out the two key commercial differences between the coun-tries: the United States at that time had low tariffs on imports and did not levy any taxes on internal trade, while Mexico levied high tariffs on both imports and internal trade, the *alcabala*.[66]

The new boundary established permanent linkages between the northern Mexican states and U.S. overland commerce that would produce "losers" and "winners." Among the losers was Matamoros, which lost most of its population and status as the most important northeastern center immediately after the signing of the Treaty of Guadalupe Hidalgo.[67] Given the commercial differences between the two nations, goods on the Mexi-can side of the boundary cost two to four times more than on the U.S. side, inciting "the inhabitants of the Mexican towns to emigrate to those of the United States." Others simply crossed the Río Bravo to purchase goods in Texas and then "smuggle them over to the Mexican side." [68]

The Matamoros merchant community astutely grasped the significance of the new geography and reacted by abandoning the port. They established their business operations elsewhere along the U.S. side of the long Río Bravo boundary. The reasons for abandoning Matamoros are not difficult to discern: Mexican custom officials could oversee trade at Matamoros, but not everywhere along the long boundary line, where goods could cross undetected, avoiding Mexico's high import tariffs. "Practically every Anglo-American along the line chose the pursuit of a merchant," historian J. Fred Rippy wrote, "and smuggling, ceasing to be blameworthy, soon became meritorious." [69] Charles Stillman, for example, moved his Matamoros trading firm only a few hundred yards across the Río Bravo in 1848. Don Carlos, as he was called in the Bravo region, had resided in Matamoros since 1828. He was one of the founders of Brownsville, a new town facing Matamoros. His son, James Stillman, later made the New York–based National City Bank the first billion-dollar financial institution in the world, an institution with roots in contraband.[70] Other merchants acquired lands opposite Mexican towns on the left bank of Río Bravo where they founded new towns (Roma, Rio Grande City, Edinburg, Eagle Pass, and Brownsville).

William Emory, the first North American commissioned to survey the U.S.-Mexican boundary, visited Roma, Texas, and was puzzled by how this border town, in the middle of nowhere, could sustain such "fine residences and warehouses." As he took a leisurely walk late one night, this naive Yankee unraveled the secret to the existence of Roma: "I encountered a long train of mules, heavily laden, directed towards the Mexican side of the river. . . . the rich burden of contraband goods, intended for the Mexican market, explained the commercial prosperity of the town." [71] Brownsville owed its prosperity "chiefly to the contraband trade with Mexico," while Edinburg, "like all the others in the American side, except Loredo [sic], has been built since the war, and owes its existence chiefly to contraband trade with Mexico." [72] A recent arrival to Brownsville wrote in 1849: "I am told that among the better class of merchants there are those, who will give their oath at the Custom House [at Brownsville], that they paid all the duties as required by law and at the same moment are smuggling in whole cargos." [73]

Although all these descriptions referred to Anglo-American merchants, the new boundary offered an abundance of financial opportunities to any individual with entrepreneurial skills, regardless of nationality. In order for contraband to be so prevalent on the U.S. side of the Río Bravo, participants also must have existed on the Mexican side. While most Anglo-American merchants established their commercial operations on the

U.S. side of the boundary, Europeans and a nascent Mexican merchant class positioned themselves in Monterrey. The city's new merchant community was made up of Spaniards such as Valentín Rivero and Mariano Hernández, Irish like Patricio Milmo (Patrick Mullins), and *fronterizos* such as Gregorio Zambrano, Pedro Calderón, and Evaristo Madero, who formed a tightly knit community connected by both business and marriage ties.[74] They based their operations in Monterrey because most of the overland trade, either legal or illegal, between the United States and Mexico had to pass through this city for reasons of geography, security, and transportation. The Río Bravo thereby "liberated" Monterrey from the hold of Matamoros, making it the northeast's leading city, surpassing Matamoros and Saltillo in population, commercial importance, and prestige.

The Río Bravo also liberated Monterrey from the tariff collectors stationed at Matamoros. Instead of going to Matamoros or Tampico, the only legal commercial ports of entry in the northeast, Monterrey's merchants now crossed the Río Bravo to do their business in Corpus Christi, San Antonio, and any of the half-dozen border towns that came into existence after 1848. Positioning themselves in Monterrey, the most accessible overland crossing point between the Río Bravo and the Mexican interior, Monterrey's merchants formed contraband networks, hired professional smugglers and cart-drivers, and, when necessary, bribed Mexican officials, as a naive American who had recently arrived at the border noted: "There is an immense deal of smuggling—aided and abetted by the Mexican Custom House."[75] The contraband networks had to be sophisticated enough to transport massive quantities of goods into Mexico illegally, such as the caravan reported by a Corpus Christi, Texas, newspaper in 1849:

> A train of over 100 pack mules left our town two days ago, heavily loaded with the merchandise for the interior of Mexico. The party consisted of about thirty well-armed men, who think they are able to defend themselves and their property from the Indians.[76]

Evaristo Madero exemplified the *fronterizo* merchant who, like Stillman, built an empire rooted in contraband. At the age of twenty-one, "Don Evaristo," as he was respectfully called in the northeast, entered the merchant profession in 1849, a year after the establishment of the U.S.-Mexican boundary. Using the border town of Río Grande, Coahuila, as his base of operations, Madero "exported" to Texas silver bullion, wool, and hides and "imported" into Mexico cotton, dry goods, and manufactured goods.

When the dust of the 1848 events had settled, and it became evident to him that Monterrey was the best location for the transit of goods, Don Evaristo moved his business there.

Starting from scratch but with the help of his extended family, Evaristo Madero built one of the largest economic empires in Mexico during the second half of the nineteenth century. Twice married, Don Evaristo fathered fourteen children and had many grandchildren, most of whom played an active part in managing the multimillion-peso family business(es). Madero's oldest son, Francisco (the father of the future "Apostle of the Mexican Revolution," Francisco I. Madero), "was introduced to the business at a young age." He and his sister Prudenciana expanded the Madero family's economic ties by marrying into the González Treviño clan, another upwardly mobile Monterrey merchant family.[77] Jesús Gónzalez Treviño, the family maverick, gained fame in northern Mexico for leading long-distance commercial convoys between the northeast and Chihuahua, journeys that lasted up to two months. He and his *fleteros* (cart-drivers) crossed the dangerous Sierra Mojada and Mapimí deserts, terrains dominated by Apaches.[78]

The impact of contraband in the economic history of nineteenth-century Mexico has not been systematically studied. Smugglers, like those in other professions declared illegal by governments, do not leave many records behind, to protect themselves from the authorities. We do know, however, that contraband was widespread in the northeast and in other peripheral areas such as the Mexican northwest.[79] In the case of the northeast, Mexican custom officials had no effective control over the numerous points of entry along the Río Bravo, other than the port of Matamoros. It was quite easy for any individual to transport goods across the unguarded Río Bravo boundary. By avoiding tariffs and transporting large quantities of goods into the interior, Monterrey's merchants gained the competitive advantage over their rivals in the "center," who had no choice but to deal with Mexican customs at the ports. Now that the north had a decisive commercial advantage over Mexico City and Veracruz, the center loudly protested the commercial offenses committed by the *frontera*. Perhaps some *fronterizos* found this reversal of roles a just retribution for the frontier's many years of economic subjugation to the center.

Contraband emanating from the northeast turned into one of the most alarming problems the post-1848 Mexican governments had to confront. Contrabandists smuggled anything into Mexico for which a demand existed, from coffee to textiles. According to Mexico's minister of economic development, Manuel Payno, contraband goods emanating from the north had inundated Mexico City as early as 1850, causing a significant drop in legal commerce. In Veracruz, Tampico, and Matamoros, three of Mexico's main ports, commercial transactions dwindled after 1848, resulting in the loss of millions of pesos in revenue from uncollected tariffs, money that the Mexican government desperately needed in order to service its foreign debt. Having lived in Matamoros, Payno was well aware of the significance that contraband had on the frontier. In 1850 he declared a war on smugglers with the creation of the custom guards (*contraresguardo*), armed men who patrolled the boundary.[80] The Mexican army, Matamoros's custom officials, and the *contraresguardo* were the only representatives of the central government's presence in the northeast; to the borderlanders, all three were symbols of unwanted domination over the frontier.

The Mexican government had condemned contraband for ruining native industry and for undermining Mexican finances, among other sins originating in the northeast. The government associated the smuggler with a type of criminal activity that harmed Mexico's national interests. *Fronterizos* regarded contraband differently, at least according to Américo Paredes, a leading expert on the border and its popular culture. The residents of the Mexican northeast and south Texas have historically regarded contraband as a "fairly respectable activity," flourishing because "one side of the river always had something that was lacking on the other side."[81] Considering that the Río Bravo's immediate population numbered around 20,000 in 1848 and given the lack of other profitable economic activities, the survival of the few northeastern urban centers depended on contraband. A large part, if not most, of the labor force worked directly in contraband or in professions servicing it (as smugglers, *pistoleros* [contraband protectors], guides, cart-drivers, etc.). The same pattern might have applied to Monterrey, which had 27,000 residents in 1850.

The *fronterizos* proudly subscribed to the central government's equating of smuggling with the northeast. Among the most popular of the border songs are those dealing with contraband, such as "Mariano Reséndez," "Dionisio Maldonado," "Los tequileros," "El contrabando de El Paso," and even today's numerous *norteño* and *ranchera* ballads that laud smugglers, their "underground" culture of fast money and violence, and their struggles against "the law" from both sides of the border: the customs guards, Texas Rangers, and the Mexican federal police.[82] Smuggling continues to capture the imagination of the border population because *contrabandistas* (smugglers) braved many hazards in an extremely dangerous profession. Besides operating in the rough desert terrain, merchants (a respectful term for the smuggling profession during the mid-nineteenth century) confronted the possibility of being robbed by bandits, having their goods confiscated by the custom guards, or being killed by Indians.[83]

Despite the risks involved in illegal commerce, merchants themselves perhaps considered contraband not a crime, but rather an expression of free trade in view of the restrictive trade policies of the Mexican government. By taking advantage of a territorial boundary at the Río Bravo that, in the words of William Emory (the early surveyor of the U.S.-Mexican boundary), "is here only an imaginary line running down the center of the river," Monterrey's merchants dodged tariffs by eluding and bribing custom officers and skillfully avoided paying the *alcabalas* in their entrepreneurial attempts to transport foreign goods into the interior.[84] Emory expressed a view that Monterrey's merchants must have shared:

> As might reasonably be expected in any country where the duties on foreign goods amounted to virtual prohibition, smuggling ceases to be a crime, identifies itself with the best part of the population, and connects itself with romance and legends of the frontier.[85]

Frontier commerce, as it was practiced in Monterrey, was indeed a hazardous profession. The illicit wealth it generated, however, produced great satisfaction for an increasingly confident merchant class. Contraband served as the foundation for amassing great quantities of merchant capital, which over the duration of the nineteenth century were invested in Monterrey's industrialization.

THE *VECINOS* AND THE BORDER

The 1848 boundary created by war and violence would remain unpoliced by both the Mexican and U.S. governments until decades later because of their lack of capacity to control the area. In this vast frontier where the state's "monopoly of the legitimate use of physical force," to use Max Weber's famous phrase, was nearly nonexistent, violence was democratized, if such a word can be used. All groups (Indians, *vecinos,* bandits, merchant-smugglers, mercenaries, secessionists, filibusters, etc.) armed themselves, engaging in and suffering from violence. They used violence to steal, contest territory, protect property, defend themselves, take revenge—in short, to survive. The aura of violence and warfare permeated the northeastern frontier, as depicted by the following Nuevo León government proclamation to the *vecinos:*

The war against the *bárbaros* is a war without mercy, it is a war of extermination and death, and it does not spare sex, age, and physical condition. It is necessary not to view it with indifference, but to wage it with the greatest possible force and at whatever cost.[86]

Many people used violence to contest the Mexican borderlands. Some groups, however, had the edge over others in their capacity to wage violence, mainly because they had better access to the tools of war: weapons, resources, sanctuaries, troops. Occasionally their deeds were sanctioned by government authorities, as was the case with the filibuster armies that enjoyed the unofficial support of Texan authorities.

Of all border groups, the *vecinos* had the least access to the tools of war and received the brunt of the violence, especially from the Comanches and Lipanes. Although the Apaches first appeared in the northeast in the 1750s, they did not pose a serious threat to Nuevo León's inhabitants until after Mexican independence, mainly because the colonial government had financed a network of presidios (military communities) that extended from the Gulf of Mexico to the Gulf of California during the second half of the eighteenth century. Thirty-five hundred soldiers manned twenty presidios strategically located to prevent nomadic Indians from raiding the interior. Moreover, military officials used different strategies to "pacify" the frontier, from peace treaties with different Indian tribes to pitting tribes against each other, as in the case of forging an alliance between the Nations of the North and Lipanes against the Comanches.[87] By all accounts, the Spaniards had been more successful in defending the frontier from Indians and foreigners than the Mexicans. This should not be interpreted as an indicator of the Mexican government's incompetence, because the Spaniards did not yet have to confront the United States' aggressive westward expansion.

At first Mexican officials succeeded in preserving the peace treaties the Spaniards had with "friendly" Indians. In the northeast officials conserved friendly ties with the Kickapoos, Seminoles, Creeks, and especially the Lipan Apaches, who inhabited the area between San Antonio, Texas, and the Río Bravo. Cuelga de Castro, one of the Lipan chiefs, and Guonigne, a Comanche, attended Agustín Iturbide's coronation as emperor of Mexico in 1822.[88] Comanches and Lipanes ended the truce with the Mexicans in the 1830s due to (among many other factors) the dramatic increase of the Anglo-American population in Texas after its independence. Excluding Mexicans and Indians, the population in Texas increased from around 30,000 in 1836 to 125,000 in 1845, 200,000 in 1855, and 600,000 in 1860.[89] Because they were being stripped of their hunting grounds (especially those for buffalo and wild livestock in central and south Texas) and were not going to allow Anglo-Americans to relocate them to other parts of the West, as had happened to other Indians, Comanche and Lipan survival was at risk unless they penetrated into the Mexican borderlands.

The war with the Mexicans began in the early 1830s, when *fronterizos* accused the Lipanes of robbing them of their cattle and horses. The *fronterizo*-Indian war escalated from a "cool" war into a "hot" one after Texas independence in 1836 and came to a boil after 1848 with the establishment of Río Bravo as the boundary. Nuevo León and the border states mobilized their human and meager financial resources for this war, a continuation of the colonial *guerra viva*, the permanent war against the Indians. In spite of the mobilization of troops and resources, *fronterizos* were generally on the losing side of the war throughout most of this period. Indians, especially the Comanches, had become excellent riders, perhaps the best in North America. They also had access to firearms, which they purchased from their sale of stolen horses and livestock.[90]

Bearing in mind that Comanches and Apaches fought two countries with far greater numbers of troops and resources, the horse and rifle allowed them to resist overwhelming odds. The failure of both the Mexican and U.S. governments to carry out a consistent Indian policy, not to mention a bilateral one, also explains the Indians' successful resistance. Moreover, and perhaps more importantly, neither country had the capacity to police its boundaries, a condition that favored the nomadic Indians. Comanche and Apache resistance waned only during the 1870s, when the two governments gained greater control of their boundaries and worked jointly to police them.

Even though the Comanches and Apaches were not native to the Mexican side of the borderlands, they quickly familiarized themselves with its landscape. Tabaquera, a Lipan chief, allegedly had a map of the northeast more precise than any possessed by the Mexicans.[91] Such maps, if widely possessed by Indians, allowed them to escape from their enemies by breaking up into smaller bands, hiding, and meeting again at a designated location; to use the United States as a refuge when pursued by Mexicans and vice versa when pursued by Americans; and to seek sanctuary in Coahuila, because its government had been successful in keeping durable peace treaties with some Indian groups. Coahuila refused to allow the Nuevoleoneses to attack these Indian groups within its boundaries.[92] "Nuevo León demanded punishment and submission," Santiago Vidaurri wrote to President Juan Alvarez in 1855 on the difference between the two states in dealing with the Indians, "while Coahuila protected and paid them off."[93]

The growing Anglo-American population in Texas drove the Comanches and Apaches south and west into Mexico, movements that intensified the *fronterizo*-Indian war. Indian raids in 1839 left eighty *vecinos* dead in three northern municipalities of Nuevo León.[94] Following the signing of the Treaty of Guadalupe Hidalgo in 1848, Apache and Comanche incursions into Nuevo León led to eleven deaths in 1849, twenty-one in 1850, thirty-six in 1851, and sixty-two the following year.[95] Nuevo León's government requested reports from the municipalities regarding the number of *vecinos* who had been killed by Indians. Thirteen municipalities responded that, as of 1851, 760 *vecinos* had been killed, 244 wounded, and 221 held captive. These figures might have been exaggerated to highlight the degree of violence, although hotspots of warfare such as Lampazos and Vallecillo did not submit reports.[96] In any event, Indian raids had the effect of de-populating the countryside, depleting the state's livestock, and creating a state of permanent insecurity and panic among *fronterizos*, as noted by a newspaper:

> The first thing that meets our eyes is always something savage about the Indians. Agriculture, industry, and commerce relapse into insignificance, the revenue ceases, tranquillity is lost by the constant perils which threaten life, honor, and family interests; all, in short, presents the most doleful picture of misfortune and desolation.[97]

Before and after 1848, the Mexican government had done little to defend the frontier against Indian raids, in spite of the large army presence in Monterrey and the fact that Nuevo León was under military rule from 1853 to 1855. Although Nuevo León was leaderless and financially poor, the *vecinos* carried the weight of the war against the Lipanes and Comanches.[98] Precisely because the Mexican government had done so little to defend the frontier, over time it lost whatever credibility it had with the *vecinos*, a point raised by a local newspaper: "Is it just for it to remain indifferent to the killings and exterminations committed by the barbarians?"[99] Even if the Mexican army had made a meaningful commitment to "pacifying" the frontier, local government leaders admitted that conscripted soldiers were practically useless in a war against Indians:

> It is indispensable to know how to mount all kinds of beasts, even the most untamed, to suffer from hunger, thirst, and sleep for four or five continuous days . . . to follow tracks . . . , qualities that are to be found only among a few of the *vecinos*. . . .[100]

In spite of government inertia in dealing with frontier violence, *vecinos* had remained loyal to the central government. The *fronterizos* had rejected a few opportunities to break their bonds with Mexico, at least until the Vidaurrista rebellion in 1855. They had defended the central government against two federalist rebellions that sought to create an independent republic from the three northeastern states. The disenchanted *vecinos* Antonio Canales and Manuel María del Llano sought to create the Republic of the Río Bravo in 1841, and ten years later José María Carbajal, one of the northeast's most notorious and extreme federalists, attempted to establish the Republic of the Sierra Madre. Federalist rebels called for the removal of the federal army from the northeast, the abolishment of taxes and forced conscription into the army, and a major reduction on import duties, among other *fronterizo* demands that later became the anchor of Vidaurri's government.[101] *Fronterizos* might have also welcomed the U.S. occupation of Nuevo León, as Governor Manuel Armijo of New Mexico did. The address that General Stephan Kearney of the U.S. Army gave to the Nuevo Mexicanos in 1846 might also have received a warm reception in Nuevo León:

> From the Mexican government, you have never received protection. The Apaches and Navajos come down from the mountains and carry off your sheep, and even your women, whenever they please. My government will correct all this. It will keep off the Indians, protect you in your persons and property.[102]

Instead of welcoming the North American invaders, *vecinos* fought more effectively against them than did the Mexican army commanded by the incompetent General Pedro de Ampudia. One of the U.S. commanders, William Henry, was infatuated by the courage of a *vecina*, "señorita dos Amades [*sic*], who led a troop of lancers against the Americans."[103]

The *fronterizos* were essentially left on their own to deal with frontier violence. Santiago Vidaurri, the highest-ranking nonelected government official in Nuevo León, organized the *vecinos'* meager physical, financial, and human resources. He regularly visited the municipalities and was in constant contact with the leaders of the state's civilian militias. Along with other northern government officials, Vidaurri promoted the ill-fated attempt to form a northern states coalition to defend the borderlands against the Indians. Delegates from all northern states met in Saltillo in 1852 and agreed on a common Indian policy that involved, among other concerns, creating a small professional army of Indian fighters, establishing military colonies, and pressuring Mexico City to fund part of this cost.[104] Santa Anna's return to national power in 1853 ended this northern coalition.

THE SOCIAL BASES OF THE VIDAURRISTA STATE

Mexican bandits encountered the few surviving members of a U.S. filibuster army that came to conquer northern Mexico in *Blue Meridian,* Cormac McCarthy's novel that highlights violence along the border in the aftermath of 1848. The filibusters had been attacked by Indians at the Bolson de Mapimí, deep in the Coahuilan desert. "When the lambs is lost in the mountains," the leader of the bandit gang warned the filibusters, "they is cry. Sometimes come the mother. Sometimes the wolf." [105]

In the case of the *vecinos,* the central government, "the mother," never came to their rescue. Consequently, they lost all faith in the government's abilities to deal with issues of violence and the protection of the borderlands, especially after the return of General Santa Anna in 1853. Lacking both government aid and the weapons, ammunition, and horses to pursue their many enemies, the *vecinos* were fighting a losing war.[106] During the last political comeback of Santa Anna, the Mexican government was no longer regarded by the *fronterizos* as a "mother" but as the "wolf." Three military generals governed Nuevo León from 1853 to 1855, including the uncelebrated General Ampudia. They taxed *vecinos,* confiscated their horses, and conscripted them into the army. The Santa Annista military government was appropriating the few available resources that the *vecinos* had in order to defend themselves and the region.

Barrington Moore argues in *Injustice: The Social Bases of Obedience and Revolt* that in most societies both rulers and subjects incur mutual obligations, a sort of a social contract:

> Thus the ruler's expected contribution comes down to security: security against foreign and domestic depredation, supernatural, natural, and human threats to the food supply and other material support of customary daily life. In return, the obligations of the subject are obedience to orders that serve these ends, contributions toward the common defense (lacking in those societies where war is unknown), material contributions toward the support of the rulers who do not as a rule engage in straightforward economic production. Finally, subjects are generally expected to make some contributions through their own social arrangements toward keeping the peace.[107]

Fronterizos had done more than their share to keep their end of this un-written social contract. The Mexican government, however, had utterly failed in providing security for the region. Equally importantly, the govern-ment abused a society that had not only remained loyal but had defended it. Perhaps for these two reasons, the Mexican state forfeited its legitimacy to govern over the northeast. The "center" had joined the *fronterizos'* list of enemies.

The Santa Annista nightmare ended in 1855, and a new Vidaurrista regime spread over the northeast. *Fronterizos* recovered from what had ap-peared to be the complete collapse of their *patria chica* during the summer of 1855 when they took the offensive and inflicted a series of defeats on their enemies. In that summer Santiago Vidaurri, their leader, became one of the most powerful figures in Mexico when his Army of the North swept away the Mexican army from the northeast and large parts of Zacatecas and San Luis Potosí.

The rapidity of this surprising recovery needs more in-depth expla-nation. After all, Nuevo León lacked troops and financial resources and had been on the receiving end of the violence for over two decades. Why were the Vidaurristas more successful in defending the borderlands than the Mexican government? How did this impoverished state reorganize itself, take the offensive, and inflict a series of defeats on its enemies in a man-ner of months? Local studies that touch on this question emphasize the leadership of Vidaurri and the fighting abilities of the *fronterizos*—in other words, the Vidaurrista state and the Army of the North, two key elements that need to be better understood.

José Sotero Noriega (a medic in the Mexican army who had partici-pated in the battle of Monterrey) wrote in 1854, a year before Vidaurri's uprising, that the most pressing problem in the northeast was the "pacifi-cation of the frontier." [108] "Pacification" was the code word for ending the violence and instituting a new order. From the point of view of the *fron-terizos,* the Santa Anna military government had lost all legitimacy because it had done so little to pacify the frontier. In effect, it had become one of the five horsemen of the frontier apocalypse—along with Indians, bandits, Mexican filibusters, and Texan raiders—that was dawning on the *patria chica* and threatening the survival of the independent peasant communities. The growing violence faced by the *vecinos* after 1848 had become unbear-able, with no relief in sight.

Barrington Moore's observations again shed some light on this dis-cussion of violence and political legitimacy. Those who are governed detest violent and capricious interference with their daily lives whether it comes from brigands, religious and political fanatics, or agents of the powers to be. People will generally support, even if partly frightened into it, a political leader who promises peace and order, especially when he can do so under some color of legitimacy as defined in that time and place.[109]

Unlike a twentieth-century politician running for an elected office, Vidaurri did not promise the *fronterizos* immediate peace. For Vidaurri and his lieutenants, peace and security could only come from a new political order with the potential to confront violence face-to-face and curtail it. Because the Mexican government was incapable of this, a new state would have to be created, with the potential to impose the "monopoly of the legitimate use of physical force," to cite Max Weber again.

The backbone of the Vidaurrista state was the citizens' army, the civilian militias which Juan Zuazua shaped into the Army of the North. After sweeping the Mexican army from the northeast in 1855, the Army of the North had prepared itself for the defense of the region. In that same year it repelled a large and well-organized Texan filibuster army, but not before it had burned down Piedras Negras, Coahuila. Vidaurri warned the Texans that if they "decide to invade the frontier," he would be "compelled to repel force with force."[110] Bandits, raiders, and cattle rustlers also suffered severe setbacks at the hands of the Vidaurrista army. This army provided the *fronterizos* with a brief respite for the first time since independence.

In 1861 Vidaurri wrote to President Juárez that the Army of the North had maintained "the integrity of the national territory, making [outsiders] respect the national boundary."[111] Although the inhabitants of Nuevo León–Coahuila enjoyed relative "peace and security," the only real problem continued to be "the plague of Indians, who are being combated with all our means."[112] Vidaurri had made the extermination of "that damned race" one of his priorities. After pondering the morality of genocide, he announced to Luis Terrazas, one of the caudillos of Chihuahua, "I have contemplated destroying those tigers with human forms, and I have convinced myself that it is permissible to kill them even with poison."[113] One of his tactics called for selling poisoned liquor to the Indians. The eloquent Evaristo Madero assured Vidaurri that if he ended the Indian menace he would be "showered with an immense glory and we will erect statues to commemorate your glorious merits, and, consequently, you will become immortal to all of us."[114] Needless to say, the Indian wars outlasted

Vidaurri's rule by more than a decade, albeit at a much reduced level of violence.

The embryo of a Vidaurrista state was already historically well rooted in the *patria chica*. *Fronterizos* had immersed themselves in the "commune" since the colonization of Nuevo León. By custom and law, *vecinos* did not pay taxes in exchange for settling and defending the frontier. Each *vecino* owned private property within the community, although in unspecified portions. Larger communities had given birth to the municipalities, and each municipality had a civilian militia, elected nonsalaried officials, and financed the chapel, jail, and school. A passage on peasant communities in *Grundrisse* by Karl Marx is particularly fitting for the *vecinos:*

> The individual relates to himself as proprietor, as master of the conditions of his reality. He relates to the others in the same way and — depending on whether his presupposition is posited as proceeding from the community or from the individual families which constitute the commune — he relates to the others as co-proprietors, as so many incarnations of the common property, or as independent proprietors like himself, independent private proprietors — beside whom the previously all absorbing and all predominant communal property is itself posited as a particular *ager publicus* [state property] alongside the many private landowners.[115]

Nuevo León's civilian militias were not an army of professional soldiers or conscripts but were made up of *vecino* volunteers, the citizens. "Old people, men, and even children volunteer[ed]" in the militias, according to Vidaurri, who had regularly visited the municipalities since 1842.[116] Family heads formed the "sedentary" units that were responsible for defending the settlements. The "mobile" units were composed of single males who were obligated to pursue their enemies far from their home districts. The rank-and-file of militias elected their local commanders, such as Ignacio Zaragoza, the future hero of the "Cinco de Mayo," Juan Zuazua, Mariano Escobedo, José Silvestri Aramberrí, Lázaro Garza Ayala, Francisco Naranjo, and Gerónimo Treviño, all seasoned veterans of the Indian wars. Justo Sierra, the famous educator and diplomat, lauded the *fronterizos* for their "dreadful courage, for their robustness, for the swiftness of their pursuits that they learned in their campaigns against the savages." [117] After the fall of Monterrey in 1846, local commanders of the militias led their followers in guerrilla warfare against the U.S. occupation of their state. Juan Zuazua gained famed for participating in the heist of a U.S. army convoy worth two million pesos.[118]

Private property held in *comunidad* and collective defense of both their property and region were the two elements that unified the *vecinos* and provided them with the substance of their identity. Marx made another pertinent point that fits well with the shaping of the *vecinos'* world-outlook:

> its common character appearing, necessarily, more as a negative unity toward the outside. . . . The commune—as state—is, on one side, the relation of these free and equal private proprietors to one another, their bond against the outside, and is at the same time their safeguard.[119]

Indeed, in this environment where violence had been the norm the attacks by Comanches, Lipanes, filibusters, and Texan raiders had the effect of unifying the *vecinos* in their struggle to preserve their *patria chica*. They "detested" North Americans, according to Justo Sierra.[120] There was no confusion about who their enemies were—they were all outsiders, with the exception of local bandits. It was difficult to erase their parochialism and suspicion of the outside even decades after the "pacification" of the frontier had been completed. In 1914 José Vasconcelos, the distinguished Mexican intellectual, visited Lampazos, the birthplace of Vidaurri and Zuazua, and the town which had given Mexico "*guerrilleros* and generals by the dozens." He noted that the Lampazenses

> are Spaniards and they do not know it, and yet they call themselves Indian because being so close to the influence of Protestant Texas they consider all that is Spanish as a taboo, a symbol of backwardness and obscurity. . . .[121]

Vasconcelos was only half right. Lampazos did produce many military heroes, but it had largely been settled by Tlaxcalan Indians.

THE VIDAURRISTA STATE AND THE EXTREMES OF FEDERALISM

Vidaurri had become one of the champions of Mexican liberalism during the first years of his *cacicazgo* over the northeast, especially of its most radical faction, the *puros*. Unquestionably, he possessed all the credentials of a *puro*. Committed to curbing once and for all the influence of the church and Mexican army, the pillars of national power since independence, he sent the core of the Army of the North into the interior to battle the Conservatives during the War of Reform. He was among the first governors to apply the anticlerical provisions of the Constitution of 1857, expelling the bishop of Monterrey even before the War of Reform had begun.[122]

In spite of Vidaurri's impeccable commitment to the triumph of Mexican liberalism during the first years after the triumph of the Ayutla rebellion, many Liberals and Conservatives feared that he intended to partition Mexico further by creating a "Republic of the Sierra Madre" from the states of Coahuila, Nuevo León, and Tamaulipas. This alarm was proven false only in the sense that no such republic was ever created. The Vidaurristas' Restorer of Liberty Plan had called on Coahuila–Nuevo León to regain its sovereignty only until a new constitution could be drafted. Once the 1857 constitution had been approved throughout Mexico, Vidaurri, for all practical purposes, maintained Coahuila–Nuevo León's sovereignty, ruling over it as if it was a de facto independent nation. The Vidaurrista state had its own army, appropriated complete control over border customs in the areas it governed, and engaged in its own brand of diplomacy (Vidaurri supported the Confederacy during the American Civil War; Benito Juárez, the Union), three key features associated with independent states.

From the outset of his rule, Vidaurri clearly stated to President Juan Alvarez in 1855 the demands for the new relationship that Coahuila–Nuevo León intended to have with the Mexican government: "That the new government give us pecuniary resources or that it at least not take away from us those that we have, nor send us commanders of public employees of any kind because we will resist them with arms." [123] Vidaurri was deeply committed to the triumph of liberalism in Mexico, just as long as the Mexican Liberal state did not interfere in the northeast, undermine his rule, and challenge his two most sacred demands: an independent army under his command and local control of customs. It was precisely the issue of who had command (the national state or the local state government) over the Army of the North and the border customs that positioned Vidaurri on a collision course with the national goals of Mexico's Liberals, especially during the era of Benito Juárez. For Vidaurri these two points were sacred and non-negotiable, and any interference in these affairs would have been considered a declaration of war.

Mexico's Liberal rulers reluctantly conceded to all Vidaurri's demands and conditions, such as the annexation of Coahuila to Nuevo León. It was not in their best interests to challenge Vidaurri, who was simply too powerful and dangerous. Moreover, they needed the support of his mighty army during the War of Reform and the French Intervention. Vidaurri's noncompromising federalism eventually divided the *fronterizo* commanders of Army of the North. Treviño, Aramberrí, Zaragoza, Naranjo, Garza Ayala, and Escobedo left the northeast, dispersing throughout Mexico to fight the Conservatives during the War of Reform and later the French invaders. These commanders believed that in those times of trouble it was in the best interest of Mexico for the Army of the North to be under the auspices of the Liberal state. The commanders led their *fronterizo* followers in distinguished battles. Ignacio Zaragoza became a national hero for his defense of Puebla against the French invaders on May 5, 1862, and Mariano Escobedo organized the second Army of the North, which captured Maximilian at Querétaro in 1867.

Vidaurri eventually broke with Benito Juárez over many issues dealing with diplomacy, customs, and military affairs. He betrayed the republic and the Liberal cause when he chased Juárez out of Monterrey in 1864 and later joined Maximilian's cabinet. Because the history of the split between Juárez and Vidaurri is covered in other sources, the remaining part of this chapter deals with the Vidaurrista state's reorganization of society and economy, a new social order that benefited merchant capital accumulation most of all.[124]

The state government's *Boletín Oficial* reported that the 5,000 soldiers from the Army of the North were combating the Conservatives outside of the northeast during the early months of the War of Reform. They were all "well armed, had ample supplies of ammunition, and were well uniformed. Everything that they have is new, the weapons, uniforms, saddles, etc."[125] Fernando Iglesias Calderón, a minister of war under Juárez, noted that the elite core of the Army of the North, the feared Riflemen of Nuevo León, was well armed with Sharpe and Mississippi rifles. None of the armies that contested national power during the War of Reform even came close to possessing such weapons and resources.[126] The *Boletín Oficial* posed two questions:

From whence has all this money come to pay for these immense costs? How has Mr. Vidaurri built an army that is so respected and powerful from a state that is so small and poor when other states that are larger, wealthier, and more prosperous can not do the same?[127]

The official government newspaper did not answer these questions because they were posed in such a manner that one could only conclude that Vidaurri was the sole cause of all favorable developments in the region since coming to power. Mario Cerutti, a leading historian of the formation of the Monterrey elite during the nineteenth century, argues that the Vidaurrista government organized the region's human and capital resources under a "war economy" policy. Because of permanent warfare conditions, including the War of Reform, the French Intervention, the Indian wars, and the American Civil War, Vidaurri organized the economy and the approximately 150,000 inhabitants for the aims of war.[128] Over 7,500 males, roughly 5 percent of the population, served in the Army of the North, and they needed to be paid, fed, clothed, and armed. The Vidaurrista government purchased agricultural goods, cattle, horses, and other products to feed and supply the army from haciendas, ranches, and peasant communities. Local artisans provided the state with finished goods, such as saddles and leather products, while the eight textile mills in Coahuila and Nuevo León, most built during the Vidaurri era, supplied the army with uniforms.[129]

Nuevo León became the most prosperous state in Mexico because the Army of the North successfully patrolled the northeast–U.S. boundary and because, compared to other regions, the northeast was spared from the violence of the 1855–1867 era. Maintaining a strong army and control of customs, two arms of government that depended on each other, became the cornerstone of Vidaurrista policies. The Vidaurrista state supplied the needs of its army with the revenue it received from border customs, and it could not collect customs unless the army effectively patrolled the boundary. Compared to the pre-Vidaurri average of 50,000 pesos in government revenue a year, it is estimated that Nuevo León's revenue averaged around 660,000 pesos per year between 1855 and 1859, 75 percent of it going directly to the Army of the North.[130]

Vidaurri established a new set of tariffs on international commerce, reducing custom duties to a small fraction of the national tariffs. In light of the Army of the North's patrolling of the boundary, northeastern merchant-smugglers had no other option than to engage in legal commerce and to abide by the new Vidaurrista order. The relationship between Vidaurri and the merchants was a stormy one from beginning to end, mainly because he requested forced loans from them. In spite of the large quantities of revenue collected from customs, it was not enough to sustain the Vidaurrista *cacicazgo* financially. High interest, short-term loans from merchants provided the state with the additional revenue. The government paid its creditors with tariff reductions at the customhouses. In the end, merchants profited from regulated commerce because the northeast was one of the few regions in Mexico to be spared from the violence. The Vidaurrista state provided merchants with the security they needed in order to import large quantities of goods into Mexico and export large quantities of silver and other goods in a period when one of the few secure gateways to the exterior was the northeastern boundary.

Vidaurrista control of the border during the American Civil War (1860–1865) marked a turning point for capital accumulation by the merchants. With the blockade of the Confederate ports by the Union navy, the Mexican northeast became one of the main outlets for the South's cotton trade with Europe. A good portion of all trade between the Confederacy and Europe passed through Vidaurri's customhouses. From the customhouse at Piedras Negras alone, Vidaurri received an average of 50,000 pesos a month due to the "importation" of cotton into Mexico.

While the 1848 boundary had brought on Matamoros's decline, the Civil War made it the largest and most important city between the Río Bravo and the Mexican Bajío, a position it enjoyed as long as the cotton trade passed through. An estimated 7,000 bales of cotton were exchanged every month for weapons, ammunition, food, and other supplies. Some of Europe's largest commercial firms established outposts there, such as Lloyd's of London and the German firm Droege, Oetling and Company.[131] For a few years, Matamoros became the world's third most active port. An estimated eighty vessels were stationed there on any given day during the height of the cotton trade.[132] It was reported that "contraband of war and supplies of all kinds could be bought in New York and Europe and sent to Matamoros, a neutral port."[133]

A Union official stationed at Matamoros seconded that statement: "Matamoros is now the great thoroughfare to the Southern states. They pass their coffee, flour, and in fact all their supplies through there."[134] "Matamoros was to the South," J. Fred Rippy wrote with perhaps some exaggeration, "what New York was to the North."[135] José Morel, a Monterrey merchant, confidently wrote that Matamoros "has been crowded with Gringos lately. Glory be to the father. . . . They all seem to be after the same object, his majesty King Cotton."[136]

José González, one of the state's most prominent civilians, noted that the cotton profits trickled down to all sectors of northeastern society, from the wealthy Monterrey merchants to the "lowest classes of society."[137] Manual workers earned between five and ten pesos a day and the highly demanded cart-drivers up to forty.[138] A small wooden hut in Matamoros could be rented for 500 pesos a month.[139] In their commercial transactions merchants demanded to be paid in cotton rather than the worthless Confederacy currency. Patricio Milmo, Vidaurri's son-in-law, and Everisto Madero received a combined 2,200 bales of cotton in one transaction from the Confederacy for a past service. Merchants speculated in cotton, which sold in Matamoros from twelve to twenty-six cents a pound, making the most astute cotton dealers extremely wealthy. It was reported that "men made or lost a fortune before breakfast buying or selling supplies or cotton."[140] Charles Stillman, for example, netted around 60,000 dollars a month in profits from speculating in cotton.[141]

Besides their speculation in cotton, merchants bought in other parts of Mexico any goods that they could sell to the Confederacy, such as flour, corn, sugar, coffee, salt, pepper, cloth, blankets, shoes, lead, and copper.[142] In one case, the Confederacy purchased from Monterrey's merchants over a million dollars in goods in less than two weeks.[143] Merchants accumulated capital in order to invest it, as the example of the textile industry demonstrates. Eight textile mills, using over 1,500,000 pounds of imported cotton a year, were established in the joint state of Coahuila–Nuevo León during the era of Vidaurri. These mills furnished "all the necessary clothing for the slaves in Texas and could, if necessary, supply the balance of the Confederate states."[144] Don Evaristo Madero, one of the promoters of textile manufacturing, sponsored an 1865 trip for family members to Manchester, England, one of the world's manufacturing centers, so that they could study the most modern advancements in textile production.[145] The Maderos later converted La Estrella into the largest textile mill in the north.

Long after the port's boom days had passed, Antonio Hernández, Evaristo Madero's son-in-law and later one of Monterrey's leading bankers, reflected: "I believed that Matamoros could have become the great commercial center of the frontier, competing with Veracruz."[146] The defeat of the Confederacy in 1865 ended Matamoros's prominence. Scholars who study Monterrey's powerful industrialists underscore the importance of the cotton trade as a key element behind their accumulation of capital, thanks to Vidaurri's control of the northeastern boundary. Notwithstanding Vidaurri's endorsement of Maximilian in 1864 and his "treason" to the republic, he was the guardian of Monterrey's elites, who in turn supported him until the very end. While his government often shook them down for forced loans and harassed them for pursuing profits over loyalty, Vidaurri provided them with the conditions under which they could financially flourish. His army's control of the boundary and region sheltered the

northeast from the violence of the era. No other elite group in Mexico enjoyed such favorable conditions for profiting as Monterrey's merchants did
during this period of crisis.

After being deposed from Nuevo León in 1865 by the second Army
of the North, commanded by Mariano Escobedo, Vidaurri joined Maximilian's cabinet in Mexico City. On July 8, 1867, Vidaurri, the beloved caudillo of the Monterrey merchants, was apprehended in Mexico City by Porfirio Díaz. When Vidaurri was condemned as a traitor of the lowest kind,
Díaz ordered that he be shot by a firing squad to the tune of "Las Can-
grejas" (The Crabs), a popular song of those times. He was reportedly shot
in the back while forced to kneel on a pile of excrement.[147] On a visit by
Díaz to Monterrey in 1899, rumor had it that he stayed in Patricio Milmo's
mansion. Prudencia Vidaurri de Milmo, Vidaurri's daughter and Milmo's
wife, made an "escándalo familiar" (family scandal) due to the presence of
Díaz in the family house.[148]

CHAPTER TWO

The Taming of the Periphery, 1867–1890

A poet described relations between the postindependence Mexican state and society: "mandar no sabe, obedecer no quiere" (the state does not know how to command, and the people do not wish to obey).[1] From the defeat of Maximilian in 1867 until the mid-1880s, the caudillos of northern Mexico represented a major roadblock to the unification of Mexico for two reasons. First, the weakness of the Mexican state had permitted northern caudillos such as Ignacio Pesqueira of Sonora, Luis Terrazas of Chihuahua, Severano Canales of Tamaulipas, and Gerónimo Treviño of Nuevo León to consolidate their *cacicazgos* (local fiefdoms). As long as the Mexican state remained weak, these caudillos successfully resisted the integration of their regions into a centralized government. Second, because neither Mexico nor the United States was able to police its boundary, cross-border violence (banditry and Indian raids) persisted without interruption. As a result, the United States pressured the Mexican government to control its boundaries, a diplomatic threat that soured relations between the two countries to the point of near war in 1878. For these reasons, among others, Liberals like Díaz recognized that Mexico could not become a unified nation unless a strong central state could be created that could secure control of all Mexico, especially its troublesome boundaries.

Operating from a position of weakness in 1876, the Porfirian state (1876–1910) gained complete control of Mexico by 1890, including the north. This chapter examines political relations between Nuevo León and the central state from the defeat of Maximilian in 1867 to 1890. The northeast's political autonomy ended in 1884, when Bernardo Reyes led a loyal army that imposed the "center's" authority in the region for the first time since 1855. During this time Santiago Vidaurri had expelled the Mexican army and custom guards from Nuevo León (the northeastern Liberal armies of the 1855–1884 era were more loyal to their *fronterizo* commanders such as General Treviño than to the Liberal state). The taming of Nuevo León and the north involved the dual processes of replacing these *cacicazgos* by whatever means necessary with state governments more loyal to the Porfirian state and of the central state attaining a greater policing presence in the north. These were indeed difficult tasks, but in the end these types of measures eliminated all competitors and, in doing so, strengthened the power of the Mexican state at the expense of the north's political autonomy.

During this period land served as the foundation for the ascent of new business groupings that emerged in northern Mexico during the 1880s. These groups built large estates from public lands and in some cases by expropriating the properties of peasants, such as the military colonies in Chihuahua and the Yaqui tribal lands in Sonora. Nuevo León was the exception to this development. Monterrey merchants' main source of wealth was economic activities other than land acquisition. After their contrabandist stage ended in the late 1860s, they became "respectable" entrepreneurs engaging primarily in moneylending, commerce, and acquisitions of properties in Coahuila, especially in La Laguna. Nuevo León's hacendados, however, were greatly weakened by the exodus of much of their labor force to Texas. Moreover, they did not carry enough political clout to threaten the peasantry with land expropriations, enabling the peasants to retain the properties which they had owned in community since colonial times.

THE DANGEROUS FRONTIER, 1867–1884

The defeat of Maximilian in 1867 united Nuevo León's Liberal military chieftains under the banner of the Gran Convención Democrática. Political unity rapidly evaporated, however, engulfing the chieftains in a long and bitter power struggle over who would govern Nuevo León. Reflecting the divisions within Mexican liberalism, two factions emerged that tied their political fortunes to the two most prominent national figures, Benito Juárez and Porfirio Díaz. The Treviñistas, headed by Gerónimo Treviño and Francisco Naranjo, supported Díaz, while Mariano Escobedo and Lázaro Garza Ayala, the Escobedistas, backed the civilian governments of Juárez and Lerdo de Tejada. With the exception of the Treviñista interlude of 1876–1885, no individual or political group succeeded in imposing its authority over the region until the ascent of General Bernardo Reyes in the late 1880s. Nuevo León had over twenty governors from 1867 to 1885, reflecting the chaotic political state of affairs.

Dominating this era was the northeast's resistance to the central government's attempts to integrate it within the state-building projects emanating from Mexico City, especially under Porfirio Díaz. These divisions from above filtered down to the bottom, encouraging general instability that was also fanned by more than two decades of economic crisis. The political alliances were not one-sided relationships in which the national leaders dominated local leaders—they were political relations of mutual dependence. Because none of the four presidents who governed Mexico from 1867 to 1884 had their own base of support in the northeast, they needed the support of one of the *fronterizo* factions in order to govern.[2] Juárez, Sebastián Lerdo de Tejada, Díaz, and Manuel González used their political muscle to strengthen the position of their regional allies. Given the periphery-center relationship of interdependence, Nuevo León's political influence on national affairs surpassed that of most states for two reasons. First, because of the prestige that the Nuevo León-based Army of the North gained during the 1855-1867 period and in spite of the divisions among its commanders, three Nuevoleonese chieftains occupied the powerful Ministry of War post: Mariano Escobedo in the Lerdo de Tejada administration, Gerónimo Treviño (1880-1881), and Francisco Naranjo (1881-1884). Second, and more importantly, the northeast chieftains had the capacity to influence national politics significantly. In this period when the Mexican state was weak, with little meaningful authority over the northeast, *fronterizo* chieftains could make governing difficult, if not make or break national governments. Treviño and his political lieutenant Naranjo sided with Porfirio Díaz's 1871 and 1876 military attempts to gain national power, while Escobedo sought to topple Díaz in 1878. Díaz personally operated out of the northeast, using it to acquire arms and resources and to recruit followers during his successful Tuxtepec Rebellion of 1876. Treviño, in contrast, helped sustain the Díaz and González governments (1877-1884) by keeping the frontier as quiet as possible, especially along the troublesome boundary.

Even though the leadership of the Treviñista and Escobedista factions shared common roots in the Army of the North, there was at least one clear difference between the two factions. The Treviñistas ardently advocated states' rights, seeking to keep the frontier as autonomous as possible from the central state, whereas the Escobedistas favored the creation of a civilian-led, centralized republic. Dozens of independent politicians operated outside of the two main factions. For example, twenty-five candidates ran for governor in 1872 and close to seventy in 1879.[3] Within this extremely competitive electoral environment, losers often mobilized their supporters against the victors, especially in municipal elections.

No single leader surfaced capable of challenging the Treviñistas and Escobedistas. José González, an independent who was appointed governor in 1869, attempted to unify Nuevo León along a nonpartisan line. As one of the most distinguished and influential civilians in this state dominated by generals, he had all the credentials to create unity. He had been an educator, philanthropist, doctor, historian, and the teacher of many of the state's political elites. González utterly failed in uniting Nuevo León, however. He described the vicious nature of local politics during his brief gubernatorial term:

> I can assure you that from 1869 to this day there is only one thing that has embittered me and it is the following: I had been highly appreciated by the Nuevoleoneses. However, once I was named constitutional governor I saw the number of my friends reduced to a fourth. The other three-fourths separated from me and looked at me scornfully and censored all my acts, even the most innocent and justifiable ones. . . . Why did they manifest such animosity against me? I do not know, but I can say that I practically saw how the damned politics moves and excites bad passions and drowns the good ones, making individuals fierce enemies of all who are not part of their party and want to run them down and even break all sacred blood ties of friendship and gratitude. . . . What embittered me most was seeing in the opposite party many of my old friends, some of my most beloved disciples, and even close relatives. These people had once needed me as a doctor, as a friend, and as a protector, and now opposed and worked against me whenever they could.[4]

Local politics was not a rewarding occupation for independent politicians like Gonzalitos, as José González was kindly called. When his remaining few friends asked him to run for governor in 1875, he courteously declined their invitation. The consolation for the sensitive Gonzalitos came when a municipality was named after him and he was honored as one of Nuevo León's *beneméritos* (patrons), the highest recognition that local government could give to an individual.

The triumph of the Tuxtepec rebellion ushered in the Treviñista *cacicazgo* as the governing body in Nuevo León, albeit one that could not establish a new political order. The Escobedistas resisted Treviñista rule by consistently running candidates for office and thereby prevented Treviño from establishing political hegemony over the state. In this center-periphery relationship of mutual political dependency, Díaz clearly understood that the stability of his government depended heavily on courting the support of the northern caudillos. In the case of Nuevo León, Díaz did not want to antagonize Treviño and Naranjo, especially during the early years of his fragile rule. Politically astute and knowing quite well the narrow interests that these independent chieftains pursued, Díaz allowed Treviño to govern the region with almost complete autonomy. In 1871 Díaz had asked Treviño for help in securing a seat in one of Nuevo León's congressional districts for a political ally. Treviño refused to help, responding that the *pueblos* of Nuevo León "are accustomed to electing their representatives from among the citizens of their own kind, or at least among those they know. . . ."[5] In the eyes of Díaz, Treviño and Naranjo could be more useful as allies than as enemies, especially in a region where he could not count on any other supporter.

In the aftermath of the Tuxtepec rebellion, relations between the United States and Mexico deteriorated to their lowest point since the U.S.-Mexican War. The United States had not recognized Díaz as the president of Mexico and regarded border violence (Indian raids, cattle rustling, banditry, killings) as the burning issue between the two countries. John Foster, the U.S. ambassador to Mexico, warned Díaz in 1878 that

> the condition of affairs on the Rio Grande frontier is the most serious and present cause of danger of the interruption of peace between the United States and Mexico. . . . When the honor of the American flag is involved, or the lives, liberty, and property of American citizens are concerned, it is difficult to weigh in scales and precisely designate the relative importance of one question of outrage over another.[6]

Foster also made the point that in the last twenty years the Mexican government had for the most part "been more or less impotent to enforce its authority in that region" and that "it had given very little attention to the disordered state of its northern frontier."[7] Blaming Mexico for the state of violence that dominated the boundary area, Foster suggested to Díaz that "a prudent and prominent general should be sent, with a sufficient force, to the Rio Grande, with orders to place himself in direct and friendly communication and co-operation with General Ord."[8] General Edward O. C. Ord commanded the U.S. force in south Texas.

Porfirian officials were apprehensive about future U.S.-Mexican relations and the United States' designs on Mexico. For instance, General Gaspar Sánchez Ochoa, chief of the Department of Engineers of the Mexican Army, opposed the construction of a railroad linking Mexico to the United States in 1877 on the grounds that it might serve the purposes of a U.S. military invasion of Mexico. He warned Mexicans:

> The bloody pages of our modern history will recall to us with bitterness that unjustifiable usurpation on the part of the United States, and this will always be a severe lesson, which will teach us to know with exactness the masked and concealed intentions entertained toward us by our neighbors to the North.[9]

Aware of the deterioration of the relationship with the United States and the possibilities of a confrontation, Díaz attempted to improve relations, acknowledging that a manifestation of Mexico's control of its troublesome boundary was the first step toward that aim. Precisely because Díaz had no allies in the northeast other than the Treviñistas, he depended on Treviño to maintain political order in that region. Moreover, *fronterizos,* including the Treviñistas, were not going to accept an outsider as Díaz's main troubleshooter in the northeast. Treviño's political duties as commander of the Mexican army in the northeast were anything but light. His main responsibility was to make the U.S.-Mexican boundary much safer and to organize defense of the Mexican frontier in view of the possibility of a war with the United States.

Treviño served Díaz well and made the frontier much safer. He launched a major campaign that drove the Lipan and Mescalero Apaches out of the northeast. He also defeated Mariano Escobedo's rebellion of 1878 that sought to restore Lerdo de Tejada to the presidency. After a series of border conflicts involving the U.S. army crossing into Mexico to pursue Indians and bandits that brought the two countries to the brink of another war, Treviño had the responsibility of representing Díaz in the tense negotiations with General Ord. The negotiations turned out better than expected, initiating a long working relationship of joint cooperation in policing the border.[10] In an interview with the *Chicago Times* Díaz made it clear that General Treviño represented him in the northeast and that he had "my instructions to use military force at his command for the suppression of all violence and to co-operate with the American troops in maintaining peace and order on the frontier." [11] The United States recognized the Díaz government in 1879, and as a sign of goodwill the U.S. authorities arrested Mariano Escobedo, one of Díaz's main enemies. General Treviño and General Ord became good friends and later family. Treviño married Ord's daughter, the second of his three wives.

As the new strongman of the northeast, Treviño shared military control of the region with Francisco Naranjo, his faithful friend and second-in-command of the Treviñista *cacicazgo*. When President Manuel González appointed Treviño minister of war, Naranjo became military commander of the northeast. Then they exchanged positions during the second half of González's tenure. Even though both were brigadier generals and had been ministers of war, Naranjo proudly called himself Treviño's "segundo en jefe" (second in command). [12]

Díaz acknowledged that he personally had little influence in the northeast and that his ability to govern Mexico depended to a large degree on maintaining alliances with the northern chieftains. Treviño, Naranjo, and their ally in Coahuila, Governor Evaristo Madero, wielded their greatest influence during the González administration (1880–1884). As the *jefe de jefes* (chief of chiefs), Treviño was more interested in policing the northeast than in the day-to-day business of governing Nuevo León and creating a new order. Instead, he appointed others to run local government. Even though Treviño was not engaged in government affairs, the U.S. consul in Monterrey pointed out who held political power in Nuevo León:

> There is no doubt, that the majority of the inhabitants on this frontier are rather in favor of the present governor, not so much on account of their adherence to Diaz or any political principle—which scarcely exists in the country—but on account of the popularity of the local leaders, especially of General Treviño. [13]

The Treviñistas had done everything within their power to maintain a semblance of regional order during the early years of the Porfiriato. In spite of the alliance, Díaz feared these caudillos, perhaps more than he did any regional leader in Mexico, mainly because of their military and political control over the northeast. Although Díaz had established diplomatic relations with the United States and had negotiated a peaceful solution to the border problems, his central government did not have any type of control over the northeast, including the boundary with the United States. In fact, the central state had not had control of this region since 1855, when Vidaurri removed the Mexican army and the custom guards. Díaz aimed to unify Mexico politically and build a strong central state, a difficult task considering the central government's lack of control over the region and the militant states' rights views of the caudillos who governed it.

Díaz, a skilled politician, was not about to challenge his frontier allies during the early years of his precarious administration. By the beginning of his second administration (1884–1888), two rumors circulated within the upper echelons of Mexico's elites. The first concerned a possible northeastern rebellion against Díaz; the second was that either Treviño or Manuel González would contest the presidency in the elections of 1888. While these might have been only rumors, Díaz did not take matters lightly. Perhaps for precautionary reasons, he immediately took the first steps in integrating the entire north into his state centralization projects in 1884, which served to undermine the political authority of his frontier allies.

NUEVO LEÓN'S LONG ECONOMIC CRISIS, 1867–1890

After the collapse of the Vidaurrista political order in the northeast in 1865, Nuevo León endured a thirty-five-year economic depression that had profound social and political ripple effects. Agriculture, which had never been important in the state except for employing the majority of the labor force, continued to be insignificant as a base for economic growth. Although important in the past, the cattle industry collapsed during this era, mainly due to large-scale cattle rustling, losing half of its value from 1851 to 1872.[14] The most dynamic sector of the economy since 1848 had been international commerce, an activity dominated by merchants. Commerce continued to be the most dynamic sector, but now involved many more people than ever before, including discharged veterans, who introduced a large quantity of illegal goods into Mexico. The massive smuggling of goods into the northeast created insecurity among those sectors that could not compete with foreign goods: artisans, cash-crop producers, and established merchants. Smuggling led to increases in unemployment, migration, and banditry.

The collapse of the cotton trade with the Confederacy ended a golden era for the northeast. José González noted that this paralyzed the northeastern Mexican economy, because "cotton resumed its old and natural course through the American ports" and that, with the exception of a few merchants, most traders who continued to speculate with cotton were "entirely ruined along with many people that they had financial relations with."[15]

Many who had made fortunes in cotton lost them almost overnight. The most dramatic example of the collapse of the economy was Matamoros's commercial and population decline. This unfortunate city witnessed an exodus of capital and people. Its population declined from 40,000 in 1862 to 4,000 in 1890. International trade had so dwindled that on some days customs collected five pesos on import duties. Petty contraband became the leading occupation of those who remained in Matamoros.[16]

A second important reason for the collapse of the economy is that, in complete contrast to the Vidaurri era (1855–1864), the local rulers failed to create a stable political and social order in spite of the consolidation of the Treviñista *cacicazgo*. The Army of the North had sustained the Vidaurrista *cacicazgo,* which in turn was strong enough to curb border violence, force contrabandists to become law-abiding merchants by controlling customs, and organize *fronterizo* society under a permanent war economy. The Vidaurrista state collected all trade customs, including cotton. Revenue strengthened the Vidaurrista state government, while organized trade enriched merchants and employed a large portion of the frontier population. Matamoros, for example, grew from 12,000 people in the 1850s to 40,000, becoming the largest city in the north and, at least for a while, the third busiest port in the world.[17] In contrast, the absence of political order from 1865 to 1885 led to border violence, banditry, and contraband.

The collapse of a regional economy which had largely depended on a strong Vidaurrista state that organized trade displaced thousands of people, who were forced to engage in contraband, banditry, and cattle rustling as a way of weathering the crisis. Thousands of discharged army veterans from both countries settled along the U.S.-Mexican boundary, an area where the weak state could not police effectively. In the absence of legitimate employment, discharged veterans augmented the breakdown of the social order by entering the ranks of the only growing sector of the economy, the "underground" economy of contraband and banditry, two occupations that depended on violence. Francisco Erresuris, for instance, had served in the Mexican army. After being discharged, he stole 210 heads of cattle and 73 horses in Mexico and sold them in Texas. He also killed a North American.[18] Severano Canales, the governor of Tamaulipas (1870–1876), asserted that the striking increases in banditry, "guerrillas," and "insurrectionists" were rooted in the region's high unemployment and poor harvests.[19]

An estimated 5,000 individuals were on the wanted list along the Texas-Mexican border in 1877.[20] General Ord, the commander of the U.S. army in south Texas, told a reporter that on the border "Americans and

Mexicans see the worst type of one another" and that on the Mexican side of the Río Bravo "neither life nor property is safe for an hour together." [21] These outlaws were Mexicans, Americans, Indians, and Mexican-Americans or, as they called themselves, Mexico-Tejanos. William "Tomás el Colorado" Thomas, Victor "el Coyote" González, Rafael "el Cucho" Hinojosa, and Francisco "el Chicheño" González were among the most notorious and dangerous outlaws, leaders of bands "which are famous in the history of banditry." [22] Francisco Naranjo, a military commander of the northeast from 1876 to 1884, noted that the activities of these outlaws were contagious, corrupting other *fronterizos:*

> [The] frontier towns, which had traditionally been known in our country for their notable honesty, had within sight in Texan territory bands of bandits which until then were unknown. . . . Bandits of all nationalities, as I have said, occupy themselves in the infamous commerce which has corrupted the peaceful inhabitants of both sides of the border. . . .[23]

Numbering in the thousands, these outlaws were obviously not the kind of people who would settle down, raise a family, and farm the land, if they had any.

As with any other activity that the government declares illegal, it is difficult to quantify the degree of contraband, mainly because much of it escaped the view of the authorities. Along with the discharged veterans from the Army of the North, many inhabitants of the northern municipalities, such as Lampazos and Marín, actively participated in smuggling into Mexico large quantities of prohibited goods such as cinnamon, tobacco, textiles, and other merchandise. The *Periódico Oficial* of Nuevo León in 1874 described the organizational efficiency of smuggling:

> From the towns of the [Río] Bravo . . . leave the shipments of contraband goods, which are guarded by a considerable number of men who are well armed and are paid by the true smugglers and owners of these goods. And if there are men from Nuevo León involved, we are sure that they are those who were in the state militias [*milicianos*] and have lost the love for work. . . .

Contraband flourished as long as the Treviñistas exercised political and military authority over the northeast. Treviñista army commanders apparently protected smugglers and were engaged in contraband, an accusation made by Bernardo Reyes, the future caudilllo of Nuevo León (1885–1909). He named high-ranking military officials as actively participating in contraband, specifically General Naranjo.[24] Until the arrival of the army commanded by Reyes in 1885, the custom guards had been the only representatives of the central government in the northeast. Operating in a hostile terrain and without much local support, the custom guards could do little to put a halt to smuggling. As the only conspicuous representatives of the central government in the northeast, they were the object of one of Nuevo León's war cries: "¡muera el contraresguardo y viva el contrabando!" (death to the custom guards, long live contraband).[25] Governor Viviano Villareal, a strong proponent of state rights, condemned the presence of the custom guard because the Ministry of Economic Development controlled it. He also questioned Mexico City's association of the northeast with "scandalous contraband."[26]

A third factor contributing to the economic crisis involved the Mexican Free Zone, a policy that Ramón Guerra, the governor of Tamaulipas, initiated in 1858 without the consent of the central state. Thousands of Mexicans from the northeast were "pulled" to the "other side" by higher wages and free labor immediately after 1848.[27] Another attraction was the fact that everyday goods such as sugar, coffee, shoes, and clothing cost two to four times less on the Texas side of the border than on the Mexican side. The legal status of the migrants changed as they became the first Mexican emigrants "pushed" out of Mexico by low wages and, in the case of *sirvientes*, by a life of servitude on the haciendas.

Responding to the "loss of population, which is constantly emigrating to the neighboring country," Governor Ramón Guerra decreed the Free Zone on an emergency basis, "considering that the towns on the northern frontier are really in a state of decay for lack of laws to protect their consumers."[28] As a means of having uniform prices for consumer goods in Tamaulipas and Texas, Guerra's Free Zone authorized a minuscule 2.5 percent duty on imported goods within a twelve-mile radius of the Río Bravo. Benito Juárez's government half-heartedly approved of the Free Zone as a concession to Tamaulipas because of its support of the Liberal cause during the War of Reform. Although the Porfirian government extended the Free Zone to all the border states in 1885, it failed to contain emigration because it could do nothing about the "push" factors that motivated people to migrate: the poor working conditions on haciendas, unemployment, peasants dispossessed of their lands, and low wages.[29]

In the end, the Free Zone produced more negative than positive results, at least for the northeast. Although it was an authentic *fronterizo* response to the loss of population, the Free Zone intensified the northeastern economic crisis. The geographic location of the northeast was not favorable because of its position between two economic walls: an increasingly protectionist U.S. industrial economy and a Mexican economy with various internal economic barriers to the most remote regions of the country, specifically the *alcabalas* (internal taxes) and the cost of transportation. Antonio Hernández, a merchant, understood the disadvantage of geography when he reported that local goods could not compete with foreign products that have "invaded" the northeast; nor could they be sold in Mexico's interior because of the *alcabala* and the high cost of transportation.[30]

Sandwiched between these economic walls, the northeast produced few goods on which it could build a foundation for economic development. Exportable goods, such as cattle, not only were subjected to high tariffs by U.S. customs, but were not competitive in the United States because of higher costs in Mexico. As a state that formally sold cattle to other parts of Mexico, Nuevo León became an importer of Texan cattle as the value of its cattle industry fell by half from 1851 to 1872, from 2.25 million pesos to 1.12 million.[31] Meanwhile, the value of the cattle in nearby Nueces County, Texas, was almost the same as the value of Nuevo León's.[32] It was Nuevo Leon's fate that Texas became world renowned for its commercial ranching, such as the famous King Ranch. More often than not, Nuevoleoneses preferred purchasing cattle in Texas rather than in their own state.[33] "We would like to console our cattle ranchers," a local newspaper commented on the grim prospects for local ranching, "but unfortunately there is nothing that could cheer them. . . ."[34]

The *alcabalas* and the high cost of transportation had historically closed the domestic market for northeastern goods. Unable to compete in the United States and in the domestic economy, Nuevoleonese products were basically restricted to the local market, where they had the onerous challenge of competing with the contraband products which the Free Zone had facilitated. With the low 2.5 percent custom duty, foreign goods entered Mexico legally and then were easily smuggled from the border towns into the interior. Regardless of transportation costs and the bribes given to officials, most contraband goods were still much cheaper in Nuevo León and in Mexico than local goods. Under these conditions (and with few products of value like mineral ores and cattle), Nuevo León's goods did not have a chance of competing in Mexico or the United States. Unable to be integrated into either the domestic or international economy, the state fell into a long depression, leading "our towns into a road of decadence."[35]

Government and business leaders expected the construction of the railroads in 1882 to end Nuevo León's economic nightmare. They believed the railroads would perform works of economic wonder in transporting local "goods to markets where there are more sales and demand. . . ."[36] In anticipation of the expected wealth that the arrival of the Ferrocarril Nacional Mexicano was going to generate, merchants stockpiled their stores with goods and opened hotels and restaurants.

The coming of the railroad addressed two of the region's main problems, unemployment and contraband. Railroad construction employed thousands of people and at the same time introduced legal goods, making a significant dent in the region's high unemployment and large-scale contraband. These achievements quickly wore off, however, as the railroads only aggravated the economic crisis. While the railroad drastically reduced contraband, it introduced manufactured products that competed with local artisan goods.[37] Artisans simply could not compete with U.S. goods. Railroads idled industries, and "everything else also declines due to an abundance of foreign artifacts, which . . . are generally the ones that are purchased here due to their lower prices."[38] Once railroad construction ended, unemployment again rose. With few consumers having money to spend, merchants sold few products and local commerce regressed "day by day."[39] Business confidence reached its lowest point in the years after the railroad arrived in Monterrey in 1882.[40]

Nuevo León's business and government leaders were indeed perturbed by the unanticipated consequences of the railroads in the region. After all, railroads had spurred economic miracles throughout Mexico. Expecting miracles and unable to understand these disappointing results, they hoped that economists could shed light on these "unexplained" effects.[41] With the benefit of hindsight, it is not difficult to understand the failure of the railroad to spark economic growth. Railroads introduced manufactured and finished goods into a region whose economic base was local commerce, small-scale artisan production, and subsistence agriculture. Independent of the railroads, the cost of U.S. goods was much cheaper on the U.S. side of the border than on the Mexican side. A yard of fabric, for example, sold for five cents in Texas but fifteen cents in Mexico.[42] Commerce, as reported earlier, had dwindled to insignificance, a point made by the state government's *Memorias de gobierno*. Commerce had been "reduced to its own [local] consumption. Our commerce is in worse condition than before the arrival of the railroad."[43] Meanwhile, railroads had not contributed at all to increased agricultural production. In 1880, two years before the railroad arrived, the value of agricultural goods was 1,319,024 pesos.

Five years after its arrival, in 1887, the value of agricultural goods stood at 1,308,823 pesos.[44]

The causes of the long economic crisis of 1867 to 1890 were directly connected to the changing role of the border. It had become more than just an international boundary separating two countries. The border was the meeting point between a northern neighbor in the process of becoming an industrial power and a country that, after fifty years of economic chaos and political disorder, was beginning to chart a path of economic development based on exports. Within this emerging economic order, nature had not blessed Nuevo León with a tropical climate, rich deposits of mineral ores, or plentiful farming lands. With or without railroads, Nuevo León had few goods to sell to the world during a period in which Mexico was entering the world's capitalist system as a producer of raw materials, cattle, and tropical goods.

The few benefits that railroads brought quickly evaporated. They greatly reduced contraband, but in doing so left many contrabandists unemployed, as well as the thousands of people unemployed once construction ended.[45] In fact, more people were unemployed after the construction of the Mexican National Railway and International Railway ended. Artisans closed their workshops because they could not compete with cheaper imported goods.[46] One of Monterrey's most successful carpenters complained that his business had virtually collapsed after the arrival of the railroad. Three years after it arrived, he was only able to keep two workers of the more than twenty he had employed in the past. The rest of his workforce was laid off due to the "absolute lack of work."[47]

Adversely affected by the railroads and with no sign of economic recovery, Nuevo León seemed to be condemned to marginality during an era in which the rest of Mexico was blessed by the arrival of the iron horse. Pessimism and insecurity increasingly dominated a society falling ever deeper into poverty. A *regiomontano* (another name for a resident of Monterrey) recalled many years later that the city's inhabitants "were becoming more wretched-looking." They were "losing their jobs, living in more dilapidated houses, and having less money with which to buy the necessities of life."[48] *La Voz de Nuevo León* highlighted the most dramatic effects of a crisis with no end in sight. Monterrey lost

population with the arrival of the railroad; artisans fled to the United States or to the interior of the republic because they said they could not compete with the foreign goods that the trains brought; *jorna-*

leros, attracted by good wages, deserted the haciendas to work in the construction of the iron horse, and, once left without employment, they also migrated from the state. Due to the lack of productive employment many people migrated and, as a consequence, commerce languished. Sadly enough, the unemployed entered the ranks of banditry and vagrancy.[49]

Another local newspaper, *La Defensa,* agonized over Monterrey's slow death, emphasizing that if people continued to flee the city at the current rate it would became a "true desert."[50] The poor, the wealthy, and those in between left the state. Five hotels and restaurants closed their doors within one month in 1883, and 600 houses had been abandoned by 1885.[51]

The Monterrey Chamber of Commerce, the voice of the merchants, called on the federal government to end the Free Zone and strengthen the custom guards in order to halt the commercial decline of Nuevo León. They complained that present custom guards could not contain the flow of contraband and as a result they could not sell any locally produced goods (such as fabrics, sugar, and wheat) and that the "tailors, shoemakers, and carpenters are left without employment because people dress, eat, and purchase all goods from the U.S."[52] The U.S. government joined the anti–Free Zone chorus, using the argument that Mexican goods entered Texas illegally. A report to the U.S. secretary of the treasury emphasized that contraband was largely responsible for the chaos in Mexican finances.[53] One of the demands emanating from Mexico City was "down with the 'Free Zone' and 'long live the national dignity!' "[54] The sole cure for the northeast's economic crisis could have been to end contraband by ending the Free Zone and strengthening the custom guard. These two policies could only be accomplished if the central state gained authority over the northeast.

There were no signs that industry would be the foundation of Monterrey's economic future. As of 1889, a year before Monterrey entered its early stages of industrialization, Nuevo León had thirty-seven enterprises valued at one million pesos with an annual production of 326,360 pesos.[55] Because Monterrey lacked an economic base that could sustain it, the city's boosters futilely promoted tourism. Ailing North Americans could benefit from the city's dry climate and nearby hot spring waters.[56]

MERCHANTS AND THE SURVIVAL OF THE FITTEST

The end of the cotton trade in 1865 bankrupted a lot of commercial firms, bringing financial ruin to many wealthy individuals who had made their fortunes speculating in cotton. Still, a dozen or so merchant families weathered the long economic crisis by engaging in the activities that they knew best (money-lending, the cotton business, and commerce), but far away from Matamoros and Monterrey. The most astute merchants fled Monterrey for greener pastures elsewhere, especially to the La Laguna region of Durango and Coahuila.[57] Evaristo Madero and Patricio Milmo, Monterrey's two wealthiest merchants, moved their businesses during the 1870s to Parras, Coahuila, and Laredo, Texas, respectively. Most merchants retained ties to Monterrey by owning homes and operating small commercial outposts.

The Madero, Milmo, Belden, Armendáriz, González Treviño, Rivera, Zambrano, Calderón, and other families were among the very few merchants in the northeast with sufficient capital to invest, speculate, and lend from 1867 to the 1880s. They established *casas comerciales* (commercial firms) in La Laguna which functioned as commercial stores, investment firms, and banks. It was no coincidence that Monterrey's merchants moved to La Laguna, a northern oasis. They acquired thousands of hectares of public lands in Coahuila after the removal of the Indians in the 1870s. Seven of Coahuila's sixteen largest landlords in 1910 had resided in Monterrey during the Vidaurri years, among them Evaristo Madero, Lorenzo González Treviño, Adolfo Zambrano, and Viviano Villareal.[58]

The coming of the railroad increased the value of these lands, which contained timber, coal (Coahuila had the only known coal deposits in Mexico), ores, guayule, and water for irrigation in La Laguna. With the cultivation of cotton, a commodity with which Monterrey's merchants were quite familiar, La Laguna became one of the most dynamic economic regions in Mexico during the Porfiriato. The merchants were among the early pioneers in exploiting La Laguna's irrigated lands for the cultivation of cotton.

Evaristo Madero, for instance, gained valuable experience in the cotton market during the Vidaurri era that paid off in La Laguna. In 1865 he sent family members to Manchester, England, so that they could gain first-hand experience in cotton manufacturing. After moving to Parras, Madero purchased large estates in Coahuila, including the haciendas El Rosario and San Lorenzo, two former properties of the Marqués de Aguayo. The Maderos cultivated cotton on these and other estates, using it to expand vertically into the fabrication of cotton goods. They purchased La Estrella textile mill, which they converted into the largest mill in the north.[59] By 1900 the Maderos had built one of Mexico's largest economic empires, which included haciendas, ranches, mines, industries, banks, and commercial stores.[60]

Merchants established a dominating presence in La Laguna through their *casas comerciales*. They were instrumental in developing the cotton industry during the early years, when credit was in short supply and banking had not been regulated. Following the lead of the Maderos, merchants purchased estates where they cultivated cotton. They also provided cotton-growers with credit at interest rates that fluctuated from 1 to 1.5 percent a month.[61] These types of contractual arrangements, based on short-term loans, favored moneylenders. In one case, Patricio Milmo loaned Eduardo Avila, a La Laguna hacendado, over 35,000 pesos in 1875 at an interest rate of 1 percent per month. The Milmo-Avila contract also specified that the latter would buy all necessary products for the cultivation of cotton from Milmo and that Milmo would be paid in cotton. Two years later Avila owed Milmo 93,000 pesos.[62] These types of abuses must have been quite common, leading the governor of Durango to accuse moneylenders of speculating at the expense of "citizens of our state."[63]

With one foot in La Laguna and the other in Laredo, Patricio Milmo was one of the most astute merchants of Mexico's northeast. He was already positioned in Laredo a few years before the railroad arrived there. In 1879 he founded Patricio Milmo and Company, whose specialty was to "increase the export-trade of American goods into Mexico," and in 1890 he founded Milmo National Bank in Laredo.[64] This Irish immigrant, who married one of Vidaurri's daughters, had done well on the frontier. By the time of his death in 1899, his personal fortune was estimated to be between ten to fifteen million dollars, making him one of the wealthiest individuals in Mexico.[65]

The Hernández brothers exemplified one of the few frontier merchant families who survived the economic depression. This Spanish family arrived in Mexico in the early 1850s. They settled in Monterrey, where they opened a small commercial store that flourished during the cotton boom years of the American Civil War. Recognizing the end of Monterrey-Matamoros commercial dominance, during the early 1870s they moved their operations to Lerdo, Durango, in La Laguna, where they purchased a 400,000-peso cotton hacienda. Their Lerdo *casa comercial* served as a financial institution for the expanding cotton industry. After almost fifty years of business activities in the northeast, the Hernández brothers retired and left their firm, Hernández Hermanos Sucesores, to Tomás Mendirichaga, their nephew. He used the firm to invest in industrial stock companies in Monterrey, banks, smelting, urban transportation, and the cotton industry of La Laguna.[66]

Gerónimo Treviño and Francisco Naranjo joined the ranks of the small northeastern business elite by enriching themselves with the spoils offered by the Porfirian state. They were two of a handful of individuals who most benefited from the *baldío* (public lands) legislation in Coahuila. Along with Emiterio de la Garza, a Monterrey lawyer who later became one of Mexico's most influential intermediaries for foreign investors, they formed surveying companies which mapped a good portion of Coahuila. Treviño's company surveyed closed to five million hectares in Coahuila and Chihuahua; he received one-third (1,573,649 hectares) as payment for his services according to the Law of Baldíos.[67] Treviño built his hacienda on the ruins of the old presidio of La Babia, one of the centers of colonial defense for the region that was destroyed by Indians and abandoned by settlers. Francisco Naranjo concentrated his economic activities in his hometown of Lampazos, another former presidio, owning more than 850,000 hect-ares of land by 1895.[68] Naranjo and Manuel González, the ex-president of Mexico, sold to the International Railroad the coal-rich La Soledad ha-cienda for 400,000 pesos in 1886.[69]

The merchants moved a significant part of their operations back to Monterrey after 1890. Even though the former frontier merchants were now fewer in number than in the boom period of the American Civil War cotton trade, they appeared to be much more secure economically. They had survived the crisis years of 1867–1890 by expanding into many eco-nomic areas outside of commerce, such as lending money to La Laguna ha-cendados, import-export trade, as in the case of Patricio Milmo and Com-pany, and the acquisition of haciendas and mines, especially in Coahuila. By 1890 this small but consolidated Monterrey merchant group had built its own capital sources and used them to invest in many of the city's industrial enterprises.

THE COUNTRYSIDE

Economic and political developments in Nuevo León's countryside during this era did not follow the same path as in the rest of Mexico. Unlike their counterparts in the rest of the country, the local peasants managed to re-tain their property without major modifications in their organization and land-tenure practices. The haciendas did not expand in size; nor did land-lords gain much in political influence. This development was a fundamen-tal diversion from the rest of Mexico. Why did Nuevo León's countryside move in a direction opposite to the rest of the country, especially during this era marked by the expansion of the hacienda at the expense of peasant communities? How and why did the peasantry survive this era unscathed?

One argument that partially explains why Nuevo León's landlords did not become the dominant class during the Porfiriato, the golden age for the Mexican hacienda, has to do with the lack of available public lands in the state. Landlords could not expand their estates because most of Nuevo León's land had already been distributed legally since the colonial era in the form of *comunidades*, haciendas, and ranches. The state contained few public lands that could be claimed or *ejido* lands that could be broken up, sold, or confiscated. Out of the 12,873,342 hectares of public lands sold during the Porfiriato, Nuevo León lost 120,863 hectares or 1 percent of the total in Mexico.[70]

Moreover, the state had few stretches of good farming lands to inspire much interest in legal or illegal massive land acquisitions. According to José González's estimates, Nuevo León's total land surface equaled 4,216 *sitios* (one *sitio* = 1,755.61 hectares), of which 900 were mountainous and 3,000 were classified as grazing and woodlands. That left only 316 *sitios* that could potentially be used for dry and irrigated farming or approximately 8 percent of the state's land.[71] Even though Nuevo León contained few public lands, this did not deter hungry land speculators from coming. The presence of surveying companies in the state had "caused serious alarm" in 1889.[72] In the southern part of the state, an area that contained some public lands, land sales were not recorded because the "land is of very poor quality" and "for that reason it does not inspire any interest." [73]

Another argument that explains peasants' retention of their properties is that local political and business leaders did not turn against the peasantry as they had throughout Mexico, as in Chihuahua, a state that shared a similar history of close ties between local leaders and *fronterizos*.[74] Instead, Monterrey's merchants and Liberal chieftains acquired properties in neighboring Coahuila, a large state where a handful of families claimed most of the public lands. In 1865 Benito Juárez instructed Mariano Escobedo, the chief of the reorganized Ejército del Norte, to punish Coahuila's landlords who had supported the Conservatives and Maximilian, especially the Sánchez Navarro and Zuloaga families. Landlords could only recoup a small portion of their properties that Escobedo confiscated, making this one of the largest confiscations of private property of the era in Mexico.[75] Juárez believed that this was the opportunity to "destroy the land monopoly." He intended to break these estates into medium-sized lots that could be given to the chiefs and veterans of the Liberal army and to sell the rest at low prices.[76] Although land was either sold or given to veterans and other individuals, in the end Liberal chieftains, politicians, and business leaders acquired most of the lands in Coahuila.[77] Treviño and Naranjo, for instance, bought over two million hectares of public lands in Coahuila during the early 1880s. The Maderos, Milmos, Hernándezes, and other merchants purchased irrigated lands in La Laguna. They became members of the new landowning class of Coahuila, replacing the Sánchez Navarros and Zuloagas.

"In Nuevo León, one of those states which by reason of its great agrarian strengths had managed to retain a certain independence," as Lázaro Gutiérrez de Lara summarized the 250-year history of the peasant-government leader ties, "the local state government endeavored to protect the people in the possession of their lands."[78] Nuevo León does not have a deep-seated history of peasant-landlord conflict. It does, however, have a long history of armed-peasant mobilization in alliance with local government leaders. Under the leadership of local rulers, peasants had been colonizers and defenders of the region. As *pobladores* and defenders of the frontier, the peasant-soldiers received land and did not pay taxes in exchange for defending their property and the state against Indians and other enemies. Santiago Vidaurri established his *cacicazgo* by mobilizing the peasant-based state militias. They became the powerful Army of the North, which was first headed by Juan Zuazua and was reconstructed in 1864 by Mariano Escobedo after Vidaurri betrayed the republic.

Gutiérrez de Lara, one of the first Mexican Marxists, also claimed that Porfirio Díaz "dispatched an overwhelming force into the state, overthrew the authorities, and again accomplished the wholesale eviction of the people and their lands."[79] Gutiérrez de Lara, a native of Nuevo León and an opponent of the Porfirian dictatorship, was only right in that Díaz put an end to the Treviñista *cacicazgo* in 1885. There is no evidence of peasant evictions from their land.[80] The evidence demonstrates that Nuevo León's peasants gained additional lands, a point that needs further discussion.

General Escobedo halted the growth of the hacienda in Nuevo León, which had already been weakened by the exodus of *peones* to Texas that began in 1848. He was an agrarian reformer who advocated the politics of "severely punishing traitors" by confiscating the properties of those who had collaborated with the French invaders.[81] Escobedo, a native of Galeana, a municipality in which the Soledad and Potosí haciendas dominated, began his military career in Galeana's civilian militias in the 1840s and fought against the U.S. occupation of Mexico. He joined the Vidau- rrista rebellion and later became one of Juárez's most trusted commanders as he organized the second Army of the North in 1864. In a move similar to Francisco Villa's actions in 1913, Escobedo and eleven followers formed the core of the Ejército del Norte when they crossed the Río Bravo from Texas in 1864. As a soldier's general, Escobedo demoted himself from brigadier general to captain and Francisco Naranjo from colonel to sergeant during the first stage of rebuilding the army.[82] Escobedo compensated many of his veterans with lands confiscated from the Liberals' enemies. A loyal follower of Escobedo described his aspirations:

> One of his pleasures consisted of discussing politics with his soldiers [*subalternos*], so that he could inculcate in them liberal ideas and ob- ligate them to appreciate the simple life of the citizens more than that of the professional soldier, however, without prejudicing the sacred obligations to the nation. He has repeatedly manifested that his greatest pleasure would be to have his most beloved soldiers turn in their weapons to the Supreme Government and then lead them to the frontier, where they would establish a colony of courageous and hard-working *labradores* [farmers] who could serve as an example to other citizens.[83]

Escobedo fulfilled part of this goal when a few hundred of his veterans founded San Pedro de las Colonias in La Laguna. They received sharecrop- ping rights along the Naza River.[84]

Escobedo confiscated Soledad hacienda, owned by the Pérez Gálvez family and the largest estate in Nuevo León. To retain part of its estate, the Pérez Gálvez family had to cede 256,123 hectares to the government. The confiscated property was to be divided "in an equitable way and for the benefit of the public."[85] Veterans and seven southern municipalities (pueblos and *soldados*) received 122,892 hectares; *jefes* and officers received 75,892; and the remaining 57,338 went to "individuals." Each municipality received 17,556 hectares so that they could be distributed among the "*veci- nos* who might have the greatest needs."[86] Most of the landless were con- centrated in the southern part of the state. *Vecinos* received the land as pri- vate plots rather than in the form of *comunidad*.

According to one of the earliest studies on Mexico's land system, Nuevo León received only 3 of the 3,182 land titles distributed during the Restored Republic era. Out of 4.29 million hectares distributed throughout Mexico, Nuevo León received 152,907 hectares, for a land average of 50,969 hectares per grant—the largest land grants in Mexico.[87] This figure contradicts the expropriation records, which claimed that 256,123 hectares were distributed in three different types of grants (to the municipalities, "chiefs and officers," and individuals), or an average of 85,374 hectares per grant. This confiscation and Escobedista agrarian reform in Nuevo León was unique in Mexico, considering that Coahuila came in a distant second with an average of 3,471 hectares per title.[88]

Instead of expanding as in the rest of Mexico, the largest haciendas in Nuevo León decreased in size, at least in the case of Soledad and Potosí, the only haciendas in the state worth over 200,000 pesos before the Porfiriato. Escobedo confiscated 256,000 hectares from Soledad, the largest estate in Nuevo León, and Potosí's owners partitioned it into smaller haciendas and ranches. Lamenting the turn of events for the larger estates, José E. González wrote that in Nuevo León "property is so divided that it is communism."[89] The breakup of the largest estates, coupled with an unreliable labor force that could always flee to Texas, shaped the making of an insecure class of landlords who could not prosper economically during this period of transition from "frontier" to "border."[90]

Escobedo's land measures awarded the landless southern peasantry with land while at the same time thwarting the growth of the state's largest latifundia. They also marked the ending of the historic ties that had bound local political leaders and *vecinos* since colonial times. The leader-*vecino* "marriage" ended in the 1870s with the removal of Apaches and Comanches from the northeast, the improvement of diplomatic relations between Mexico and the United States, and the assumption by the intrusive Porfirian state of greater responsibilities for the policing of the northeast. Briefly, the central state, for the first time ever, deprived *vecinos* of the duty of defending their *patria chica* from outside forces. Moreover, the state and landlords did not threaten *vecinos*, who did not have to confront the menacing presence of a state that sought to break up their properties or of landlords who sought to enlarge their properties at their expense.

Before the 1870s local government leaders had not had a problem mobilizing *vecinos* in defense of the region, but during these years the state leaders could no longer do so. In 1876 General Naranjo complained that many *vecinos* who had worked in Texas and returned to Nuevo León refused to join the "National Guard, claiming that they are American citizens."[91] Participating in the National Guard had lost its relevance for the *vecinos* because of the constant infighting between the state's leading Liberals, who, in their disputes over regional power, often used them as cannon fodder.

The case of Margarita Garza's family illustrates this point. Her father, Victoriano Garza, commanded a "squadron" that served "the cause of liberty until the French invasion, at which time the fatigue of war obligated him to retire to private life." [92] All four of her brothers participated in Mariano Escobedo's ill-fated takeover of Matamoros in 1878, a rebellion aimed at returning Lerdo de Tejada to the presidency. Margarita Garza's family paid a heavy price for participating in the region's many political upheavals: two of her brothers were left disabled for life and two others were killed. She also had the misfortune of having one of her sons, who had served under Gerónimo Treviño, shot by a firing squad.[93] Three generations of Garzas had participated in armed movements, one against the French and two in local political disputes.

The *vecinos* survived, retaining most of their property during an era when the Mexican peasants lost most of their land, possibly because of the combination of scarce farming lands and ownership of the state's land by many property owners. Finally, and very significantly, the state leaders did not turn against the *vecinos*.

THE TAMING OF NUEVO LEÓN, 1884–1890

In exchange for the support he received from his northeastern allies during the Tuxtepec rebellion, Porfirio Díaz endorsed their quest to gain regional power. Treviño and Naranjo established their *cacicazgo* in Nuevo León, a *cacicazgo* that became stronger during the presidency of Manuel González, their Tamaulipeño ally. Treviño and Naranjo served as ministers of war from 1880 to 1884. Meanwhile, Evaristo Madero, a close ally of Naranjo and Treviño, governed in Coahuila, giving these caudillos complete political control of three border states and considerable influence at the national palace in Mexico City.[94]

Even though they were considered his allies, Díaz was apprehensive of the caudillos' increasing dominance over northern Mexico. As states' rights proponents, these caudillos went against the grain of his goal of creating a strong central state, but Díaz did not move against them during his first administration for two main reasons. First, he feared a frontier rebellion and, second, he needed their support in a region where he lacked other allies. Specifically, he needed them to "pacify" the northeast frontier in light of an increase in border banditry, Indian raids, and conflicts with the United States. Díaz's dependence on the caudillos, however, was only temporary, until he found new allies and the appropriate political conditions to move against his northeastern allies. During his second administration, he considered the creation of a strong state one of his top political priorities, which would lead to a clash with the parochial interests of the caudillos, the champions of states' rights.

During the economic crisis, the Treviñista *cacicazgo* had utterly failed to provide the inhabitants of Nuevo León with political stability. From its status as the wealthiest state in Mexico during the Vidaurri era, Nuevo León had dropped to one of the poorest by 1880. Only the small states of Aguascalientes and Nayarit had a smaller state budget than Nuevo León, with state revenue dwindling to pre-Vidaurri levels. The state government was forced to closed down two of its lower courts, while government employees often went without pay for considerable periods. The same conditions applied to municipal government, where expenditures exceeded revenues from 1881 to 1885.[95] Monterrey had no permanent police force due to lack of funds.[96]

The persistent economic crisis, the deterioration of government services, and the absence of "law and order" added fuel to a growing popular discontent with the workings of local government. The results of the local elections of 1884 provoked violence in Galeana, Villa de Santiago, Sabinas Hidalgo, and other places.[97] In Sabinas Hidalgo two hundred armed residents occupied the municipal building and killed the police chief, the unpopular mayor, and his father. Five rural policemen lost their lives in an ill-fated attempt to dislodge the rebels from the municipal building. Gerónimo Treviño, who had recently returned from a European vacation at the expense of the Mexican government, used his personal influence to mediate a peaceful, but brief, agreement between rebels and local officials.[98]

Much of the discontent continued to be channeled into the political cliques that competed electorally for local offices, especially the self-labeled "independents" (the political "outsiders") and *oficialistas* (the Treviñistas). In spite of being out of power since 1876, Lázaro Garza Ayala led the Club Independiente in electorally challenging the control that Gran Círculo Democrático, the *oficialista* political machine, exercised over state and municipal government.[99] The 1884 local uprisings in Sabinas Hidalgo, Galeana, and Villa de Santiago, for instance, were sparked by the "imposition" of *oficialista* candidates on these municipalities. The Club Independiente voiced its opposition to *oficialista* rule in its newspapers *El Pueblo* and *La Defensa,* accusing the government of many things, including responsibility for the political apathy in the state and poor relations between civilians and rulers. After eight years of electoral defeats, the independents had given up hope of ever winning elections in light of the strong grip that the Treviñista official machine had in the state. The independents' candidate, Lázaro Garza Ayala, lost his bid to be elected governor in the elections of 1885 to the Treviñista, Genaro Garza García. As expected, the Club Independiente's protests of vote fraud went unheeded.[100] Facing a bleak political future, the independent newspaper *La Defensa* presented readers with an obituary of independent and partisan-free elections — "farewell democracy, farewell effective suffrage, farewell forever." [101]

Like Lazarus, the moribund Club Independiente revived. Porfirio Díaz, beginning his second term as president in December 1884, unexpectedly resuscitated the independents by giving them the opportunity to contest and win the upcoming local election of 1885. Garza Ayala, Hipólito Charles, and Pedro Martínez now shared a common cause with Díaz, their former enemy: ending the Treviñista *cacicazgo* and the Gran Círculo Democrático's grip on local government. Each, of course, had different reasons for doing so. On October 2, 1885, two days before Genaro Garza García was sworn in as governor, Díaz appointed General Bernardo Reyes head of the federal army for the northeast.[102] This was a bold move on the part of Díaz, considering that these were not *fronterizo* troops commanded by *fronterizo* commanders. Exactly twenty years had passed since the "center" had stationed troops in Nuevo León.

Díaz had apparently instructed General Reyes to lend the independents a helping hand by whatever means necessary in winning the upcoming municipal elections that were to be held on November 8, 1885. This included, for example, Reyes making a call to the thousands of indentured *sirvientes* (debt-peons) to vote in the upcoming elections and informing them that if they wanted to vote they could go directly to the representatives of "Club Independiente." [103] A week before the statewide municipal election, violence erupted between *oficialistas* and *independientes* in Bustamantes.[104] As a result of this incident, the *independientes* called on the federal army to guarantee their right to participate in the elections because of obstruction by the state government. With the help of the army intimidating the *oficialistas,* ballot stealing, and other irregularities, the *independientes* won the municipal elections.[105] Governor Garza García did not recognize the *oficialista* electoral defeat. He adamantly protested army intervention in the elections as a clear "abuse of the sovereignty of Nuevo León." The independents supported Reyes's intervention in the elections, arguing that "the sovereignty of the pueblo" had already been violated by the *oficialista* party.[106]

Garza García suspended the election results in the municipalities that supported the *independientes,* including Lampazos, a political move that proved to be a tactical mistake in light of the *revoltoso* tradition of the Lampazeses.[107] Given the heated political climate, both *oficialistas* and *independientes* mobilized their supporters for the expected upcoming confrontations. Governor Garza García summoned the Treviñista state legislature to request a leave-of-absence so that he could go to Mexico City to protest to Díaz against the army's interference in the municipal elections. His request was granted, and the state legislature appointed Mauro Sepúlveda interim governor.[108] In the meantime, Manuel Rodríguez, an independent, mobilized an army of Lampazeses which marched to Monterrey to protest the suspension of local elections there. Rodríguez recruited other followers along the way, arriving in Monterrey with eight hundred armed men willing to use force against Sepúlveda and the state government.[109]

General Bernardo Reyes sat on the sidelines as the political crisis deteriorated to the brink of bloodshed, with Rodríguez's army marching into Monterrey. At that point, Governor Sepúlveda unwisely requested that the *oficialista* state legislature, first, dissolve itself and, second, grant him emergency executive and legislative powers so that he could deal with the rebels. After his requests were granted, Sepúlveda left Monterrey to recruit supporters. Lacking political savvy and basic knowledge of the state's constitution, Sepúlveda then temporarily left Nuevo León. This mistake was the great opportunity for which Díaz had waited. Well-trained in jurisprudence, Lázaro Garza Ayala used Sepúlveda's absence from Nuevo León as the legal loophole to end *oficialista* control of the state. He and two hundred followers drafted a petition requesting federal intervention, arguing that whereas the state legislature had granted Sepúlveda full executive and legislative powers, he had left the state without requesting formal permission from the state legislature; therefore no government existed, because the legislature had voted to dissolve itself.[110] The plot could not have been better scripted.

Based on Garza Ayala's constitutional brief, and to prevent a violent confrontation between Sepulvedistas and Rodríguez's forces, the Mexican Senate declared a state of siege in Nuevo León. In the absence of any government, Díaz appointed General Reyes interim governor. Rodríguez disbanded his followers and returned to Lampazos. Sepúlveda, however, had returned to Monterrey with 150 supporters who were not going to go down without a fight. They foolishly barricaded themselves in Sepúlveda's home, where they fired their weapons at the federal army, killing or wounding thirteen soldiers. Reyes was almost killed. The Sepulvedistas surrendered.[111] The U.S. consul in Monterrey reported that the end of the 1885 political controversy had eased tensions in Nuevo León, but also that the *fronterizos* were suspicious of the federal government's intervention in their affairs:

> There is a strong feeling against the appointment of a military governor, and nearly all the prominent men of the border, such as Treviño, Naranjo, and García, are opposed to the administration of Porfirio Díaz and his overthrow of civic power, first in Coahuila and now in Nuevo León, they [*sic*] see their own influence destroyed, and they are not likely to submit quietly. Among the citizens generally it is a cause of congratulations that the strained state of affairs is ended without worse trouble, but at the same time there is much uneasiness as to what will be the result.[112]

Frontier *caudillismo* had been dealt such a severe setback in 1885 that it would not recover. *Compadrazgo* aside (Díaz had baptized one of Treviño's sons and was a good friend of Manuel González), the volatile events of 1885 offered Díaz the political opportunity to end the caudillos' influence in a region that the Porfirians in Mexico City considered dangerous, because the northeast frontier (and the rest of the north) was a center of extreme federalism and states' rights and was controlled by a clique of powerful caudillos who resisted centralization. Moreover, Díaz feared a possible presidential challenge from González, who would have had the support of Treviño in 1888.[113] Without any allies in the region other than the Treviñistas, ending caudillo rule involved siding with the local political "outsiders," such as Garza Ayala in Nuevo León and José María Garza Galán in Coahuila. Díaz later advised Reyes to preserve individuals such as Garza Galán as "political allies, considering that we are operating under the belief that [on the frontier] we are not in the position of acquiring new ones." [114]

Ending caudillo rule and bringing the northeast into the orbit of the central state also involved sending the federal army in the region to guarantee the "outsiders" their victory and to preempt any regional rebellion against the center. As one of Díaz's most trusted troubleshooters, Bernardo Reyes was given this perilous task. It involved weakening the frontier caudillos politically—and, if necessary, militarily—a challenge which Reyes accepted.

Despite his relative youth (he was thirty-four), Reyes was already a seasoned veteran of warfare and politics. He had participated in the 1867 defeat of Maximilian in Querétaro at the age of seventeen and for the next seventeen years had taken part in ending the political careers of caudillos in Zacatecas, Durango, and San Luis Potosí, including the dangerous Manuel Lozada in the Territory of Tepic (Nayarit). Before arriving in Nuevo León, Reyes had been stationed in Sonora, where he helped in the defeat of the Apaches and the *cacicazgo* of Ignacio Pesqueira.[115] Upon his appointment as military commander of the northeast in the summer of 1885, he immediately went to work to erode Evaristo Madero's influence in Coahuila and Treviñismo in Nuevo León. He accomplished all of this by 1886 and then sought to integrate the northeast into Díaz's centralization projects.

Governor Reyes used everything at his disposal, including coercion, to dismantle the last remnants of the Treviñista machine in the state. In August 1886 three *oficialista* deputies to the Mexican congress "resigned" and were replaced by "hard-working and honest" supporters of Reyes and Garza Ayala.[116] Reyes did everything possible to ensure a victory of the "group of General Garza Ayala" in the 1886 gubernatorial elections.[117] Garza Ayala's Club Independiente won the elections and controlled the state government and most of the municipalities. *El Pueblo,* one of the organs of the independents, reported that the 1887 municipal elections were peaceful and free of conflict between "the people and the government."[118] Now that it was on the receiving end of the stick, the Gran Círculo Democrático contradicted this optimistic view, claiming persecution by the "official" group.[119]

Rumors circulated throughout the northeast that the unhappy caudillos, especially Francisco Naranjo, were brewing a *fronterizo* uprising against Díaz.[120] For the most part, the Treviñista leaders accepted their defeat and submitted to the new political order. They had recognized the changing tide and were not about to forfeit their economic gains for a losing cause. Reyes kept a close check on the Treviñistas, however, especially when a good sector of the population continued to be ardent federalists. This federalist sentiment was expressed in *Alcance,* a newspaper that declared itself to be "the voice of the frontier." It denounced Díaz's intervention in local affairs as an assault on the region's autonomy and warned him not to "play with the frontier":

> in the midst of recent oppression and the conditions of slavery that have been created for the free and independent citizens. . . . In all the states of the Mexican confederation an uprising is imminent against

the abusive federal powers which have intervened in the internal affairs of the pueblos.[121]

Vidaurrista thought had not completely faded in Nuevo León, but it was no longer a base for mass action. In 1892 Reyes defeated the Catarino Garza rebellion, the only serious anti-Díaz *fronterizo* armed movement.

No regional rebellion ever matured, and no northern candidate challenged Díaz for the presidency in 1888. In any case, Treviño did not give up all hope of wresting control of the state government from Reyes. In a desperate last attempt to regain regional influence, he even went to Mexico City (a "sin" for a frontier caudillo) to see if Díaz, his *compadre*, could give him a voice in selecting the candidate for governor for the 1887–1889 term. Treviño wanted his ally, Viviano Villareal, a so-called independent politician, to be the candidate. Reyes advised Díaz to reject Treviño's candidate, asserting that this was only a last futile move to regain power after they had lost all hope for a regional uprising.[122] Reyes's opinion carried more weight than Treviño's. Díaz selected Garza Ayala as the *oficialista* candidate for the 1887–1889 term.

THE NEW POLITICAL ORDER IN NUEVO LEÓN

As a native of Jalisco, Reyes had no political roots on the frontier and, in order to consolidate his power in the region, had thwarted the careers of the caudillos. He inevitably accumulated many enemies who did not forget what he had done to them and who would come to haunt him throughout his remaining career. With so many enemies in a region in which he had no political base, Reyes had to depend heavily on Díaz's support. He did not make a major move without first consulting Díaz, his protector. In this sense, Díaz gave Reyes valuable schooling in politics and Reyes, a good pupil, learned his lessons well.

The first and foremost lesson Reyes learned was to exploit the divisions within the opposition. Naranjo and his business partner, Juan Zuazua, one of the reputed leaders of the frontier *gavillas* (gangs) that were to rebel against Díaz, ended their friendship over a land dispute. Zuazua, the son of the infamous Indian fighter and first chieftain of the Ejército del Norte, alleged that Naranjo had swindled land from him. Díaz advised Reyes to take full advantage of this well-known and open conflict by siding with Zuazua, the least threatening opponent.[123] While it is not known how the land dispute ended, it was probably not in favor of Naranjo. The mantle of the Naranjo-Reyes rivalry was handed to Francisco Jr., an engineer and the leader of the Liberal clubs which agitated against the Reyista government throughout the early 1900s.

Díaz taught his pupil a second lesson in his school of political opportunism. As Díaz summarized: "the best benefit that one can receive from weapons is not to kill your enemies, but to make them respect you and even make them serve you at times."[124] Just as Díaz had needed the support of Treviño and Naranjo in his two rebellions against Juárez and Lerdo de Tejada, Reyes needed Garza Ayala's support in the struggle to end the Treviñista *cacicazgo*. In 1890 Reyes accused Garza Ayala of disloyalty, probably over the issue of reelection for governor. General Garza Ayala, the author of Ignacio Zaragoza's famous speech before the heroic defense of Puebla on the "Cinco de Mayo" and an ardent Liberal, broke with Reyes. He became a professor at Monterrey's law school, using his position to influence a new generation of student activists who came close to toppling Reyes in 1903.

A third important lesson Reyes learned from Díaz was never to punish your enemies, just allow them to get rich. Gerónimo Treviño, the wealthiest of Nuevo León's caudillos, recognized his political defeat and retired to his La Babia hacienda. He continued to benefit from the many economic opportunities the Porfiriato offered to individuals of his stature. Although Treviño was an "open" enemy of Reyismo, Díaz encouraged Reyes to help "our common and good friend [Treviño]" get the Matamoros-Monterrey-Tampico railroad concession.[125] While Treviño received the concession, Nuevo León was too small for two caudillos, and the two men never became friends. In the end, Treviño had the last laugh when he eagerly replaced the discredited Reyes as military commander of the northeast in 1909.

By integrating Nuevo León into the network of Porfirian political control and thus helping construct the dictatorship, Bernardo Reyes ascended as one of the new strongmen of the northeast. As Díaz's most trusted ally on the border, he marched to the tune of the dictatorship, governing Nuevo León from 1889 to 1909, a tenure that fitted well within the new political system that Díaz had begun to construct in 1884. Manuel Romero Rubio, Díaz's father-in-law and one of the intellectual authors of "reelection," a polite term for dictatorship, explained to Reyes the essence of the new political system:

I believe that there is no better road that is more proper and patriotic than to frankly initiate the reelection. In part this corresponds to the historic moment and the needs of the Republic, and, on the other hand, it does not break or mock our democratic institutions. . . .[126]

In 1887 Reyes wrote to Romero Rubio that Nuevo León was in strong favor of "reelection," meaning that its population strongly favored Díaz for another presidential term.[127] Two years later the Club Independiente became Reyes's political machine, changing its name to Gran Círculo Unión y Progreso. This Reyista party controlled all elected municipal and state positions for the next twenty years. Unión y Progreso became, in the words of Reyes, "a well organized, strong, and disciplined political association," with chapters in each of the forty-nine municipalities of the state.[128]

The political integration of the frontier into the central state was only one side of the coin of centralization. Securing the boundary and policing the frontier represented the other side, the "law and order" component. The central government had, for the first time since independence, made a serious commitment to enforcing its authority over the disobedient sectors of its periphery—the federalists, dissidents, smugglers, and bandits. The Mexican state employed on the frontier "its monopoly of the legitimate use of physical force," to cite Weber again. Reyes controlled both the army and the custom guard, which joined forces to wage a war on banditry and smugglers. He commanded over 4,400 soldiers in 1893, half of them stationed in northeastern border towns. The northeast had perhaps the highest concentration of troops in Mexico, considering that Díaz had reduced the size of the Mexican army from 33,238 men in 1888 to 8,659 in 1893.[129] Moreover, Reyes increased Nuevo León's urban and rural police from 650 in 1891 to 1,440 by 1896. Within a few years banditry almost came to an end.[130] Dissidents such as Catarino Garza, who waged an ill-fated border rebellion against Díaz, were forced to go into permanent exile.

Reyes reinforced the custom guards, the Gendarmería Fiscal, by appointing new commanders who were loyal to him. Contraband, which (according to Reyes) enjoyed the protection of Naranjo and Manuel González, suffered severe curtailment when Reyes named two sworn enemies of the Treviñistas, Generals Pedro Martínez and Hipólito Charles, to head the custom guards. These two native sons of Nuevo León went on a campaign to arrest the foremost contrabandists, who, according to General Martínez, had been *apadrinados* (protected) by the leadership of the Treviñistas.[131] He aggressively arrested smugglers, whom he considered the "most powerful obstacles to work" and the people who would have ensured a "death to small enterprises." With the elimination of the contrabandists, the most "dangerous" enemies of the country, "Mexico will have its place amongst the nations that find their happiness in labor." [132]

"The support from the state authorities, which could not be counted on in the past," Martínez triumphantly reported, "has been a moral influence that has corrected, for the most part, the vice of clandestine smuggling to which so many inhabitants of this frontier were dedicated. . . ." [133] He called for the abolition of the Free Zone and the strengthening of the custom guard as two solutions to contraband. For his moralizing crusade to purify society of vices and for promoting "law and order" in the frontier, Porfirio Díaz rewarded Martínez with one of Nuevo León's seats in the Mexican Senate. [134] Perhaps more important than the custom guard's role in making a dent in contraband trade was its difficult task of policing the border towns, which had always had the reputation of outlandish independence and of being out of tune with the rest of Mexico. The custom guard represented another aspect of federal intervention in ending the frontier's political independence.

General Martínez, the moralist and corrector of vices, also reported that with the end of the "revolutions" in Mexico and the defeat of "powerful enemies," the smugglers in the northeast, the republic could now pursue the path that the civilized nations had already taken, based on the "happiness of labor." [135] Operating within the same moralistic framework, the Reyista state legislature in 1888 passed laws to correct another social ill, the "vagrancy" problem. The Reyistas had concluded that vagrancy was the result of parental negligence. Parents had simply failed to provide their children with "a useful occupation during their early years, arousing later in them a dislike for work and encouraging the spirit of vagrancy." [136] To the Reyistas, vagrants were individuals who were engaged in all sorts of deviant activities such as banditry and smuggling. With labor shortages dominating the regional labor market after 1890, Reyes's vagrancy legislation would serve to impose labor discipline over the first generation of the nascent working class (see Chapter 5).

CONCLUSION

Within a few years after his arrival in Nuevo León, Reyes had become the most powerful figure in the northeast, a position he held until 1909. Unlike the patterns in the rest of the north, where representatives of one of the local factions came to govern their states and used their power to enrich themselves and their closest associates, Reyes did not use government for personal profit or to enrich one group at the expense of another. In

Nuevo León there was a clear separation between political and economic elites. Reyes, an outsider, governed Nuevo León, commanded the army in the region, and was Díaz's most trusted troubleshooter in the northeast. By 1900 many considered him Díaz's political heir. Díaz, with Reyes as his loyal assistant, had tamed the dangerous northeast frontier. The end of old-style nineteenth-century *caudillismo,* the defeat of the Indians, the decline in contraband and banditry, and the northeast's integration into a centralized political system meant that the "frontier had come to an end," to paraphrase Frederick Jackson Turner, the historian who wrote one of the most (if not the most) important treatises on U.S. history during this period.

The methods that nations employ in policing their boundaries reveal how they perceive both their neighbors and, to a lesser extent, their own border inhabitants. Ever since the Porfiriato the border states have more intensely felt the presence of the federal government, especially through its policing functions, than has the rest of Mexico (with the exception of present-day Chiapas). The state's "monopoly of violence" prevailed in the northeast. Through the use of force, Díaz imposed his authority over the *fronterizos:* the custom guard reduced the volume of contraband; the rural police ended large-scale banditry; and the high concentration of soldiers in the region reminded antigovernment dissidents and deposed caudillos of the cost of rebellion. The region had finally fallen under the grip of the center. To mark the end of the northeastern "frontier" and the beginning of the "border" era, in 1890 the border town of Piedras Negras, Vidaurri's main customhouse, was rechristened Ciudad Porfirio Díaz, in honor of the tamer of caudillos and of the frontier. Perhaps it was symbolic that Piedras Negras was also the town where Gerónimo Treviño, Vidaurri's heir as strongman of Nuevo León, had his famous La Babia hacienda.

CHAPTER THREE

City and Countryside, 1890–1910

En Monterrey, Nuevo León, ciudad de industria pesada
tu gente te hizo crecer y tu industria es respetada.
Es Monterrey cuna de hombres que no tienen miedo a nada
y tenemos un ejemplo: don Eugenio Garza Sada.
[In Monterrey, Nuevo León, city of heavy industry,
Your people made you grow and your industry is respected.
Monterrey, the birthplace of men who fear nothing,
And we have an example: Don Eugenio Garza Sada.]
"MONTERREY COMO HAS CRECIDO"
(POPULAR *NORTEÑO* SONG)

No es mala nuestra tierra, pero el cielo no nos ayuda.
[These are not bad lands, but heaven doesn't help us.]
COUNTRYSIDE EXPRESSION, QUOTED IN
GARZA GUAJARDO CELSO, ED., *NUEVO LEÓN*

No other city in Mexico is more closely identified with industry than the "sultan of the north," as Monterrey came to be known. Monterrey has been the object of many studies, ranging from works examining the origins of industrialization and the formation of capitalists to sociological analyses of modern class relations.[1] The large quantity of literature about Monterrey (compared to studies on the rest of the state) reflects the importance scholars have given to the city. This chapter compares the development of capitalism in Monterrey with the economic stagnation of the countryside from 1890 to 1910 and explores the origins of inequalities between the city and countryside in Nuevo León that are very obvious today but were already apparent by the eve of the Mexican Revolution.

Since 1890 Monterrey has been one of Mexico's most important centers for the accumulation of wealth, population, resources, services, and political power, a development with widespread implications for Nuevo León. Today over 80 percent of Nuevo León's population resides in the Monterrey metropolitan area. In contrast, the countryside failed to keep pace with Mexico's agrarian modernization, lapsing into poverty and losing population and political power.

I approach regional uneven development by focusing on two subjects that have not received adequate attention from historians, including those who study the history of Mexican capitalism: first, the interventionist role that the Porfirian state played from the municipal to the national level in breaking the barriers which had prevented the expansion of the market economy and in ensuring the survival of native industry; second, the role that urban centers played in advancing capitalist relations. Monterrey, a small town with little potential for growth before 1890, emerged as one of the country's most dynamic centers for capital accumulation. No other city in Mexico is more associated with industry. Industry, however, was only one component driving the accumulation of wealth in Monterrey, where the merchants prospered, owning not only the industrial enterprises, the banks, and the large commercial stores, but vast real estate holdings.

While Monterrey prospered, leading Mexico into the twentieth century, the Nuevoleonese countryside languished because of lack of capital to expand subsistence and commercial agriculture and the absence of clear boundaries for private property. Without the capital to expand agricultural production, hacendados failed to modernize their estates even though the lands were suitable for commercial crops like sugar and citruses. They forfeited these cash crops for goods that required little in irrigation and technology, such as *aguardiente* (coarse liquor) and *piloncillos* (brown sugar loaves). The communities faced a crisis of subsistence, as they were no longer able to feed their members, forcing many to emigrate. This type of development created the image of a "progressive" city and a "backward" countryside, which further elevated the status of Monterrey's business community in the region.

MONTERREY AND THE "MAKING" OF THE BORDER

In 1890 a U.S. writer in a travel book on Mexico noted that Monterrey's greatness was "its equable climate and the hot waters of Topo Chico" and its potential for tourism.[2] That same year "Colonel" Joseph A. Robertson, a North American who would later be involved in promoting many of Monterrey's local industries, predicted: "No city of equal size on the north-American [sic] continent shows greater evidence of prosperity and development, than does the city of Monterrey."[3] How were two such different visions of the city's future possible in 1890?

Historians have presented a series of preconditions in Monterrey to explain its rapid industrial development after 1890. Among the most important of these were the strategic location of the city in the broader territory adjoining Mexico and the United States; excellent railroad connections; an "enlightened" state government that favored industry with "progressive" legislation; a merchant class willing to invest in industry; the McKinley tariff of 1890; and an "industrious" tradition among the city's laboring classes. This line of reasoning emphasizes preconditions that were supposedly essential for Monterrey's sudden "takeoff" into the industrial age but does not explain why other parts of Mexico with the same set of preconditions did not industrialize. Equally important, it does not explain why Monterrey did not industrialize prior to 1890 even while exhibiting some of the favorable preconditions.

The arrival of the railroad in the early 1880s did not lead to the expected economic boom but instead intensified Nuevo León's economic crisis: the railroad further accelerated both the decline of Monterrey's commerce sector and the number of bankruptcies; it introduced manufactured goods, leading to a decline of artisan production and thus greater unemployment. The city's overall decline induced population and "capital flight" as the leading merchants concentrated their investments in more profitable regions, such as La Laguna. The argument that a tradition of industriousness characterized Monterrey's population is not borne out, because no working class existed before 1890 and the majority of the population in the state was perhaps not engaged in wage labor at all.

Monterrey's industrialization cannot be examined in isolation from the rest of Mexico, as most histories tend to do, but must be seen as part of larger processes involving the integration of the border region into the Porfirian political system and into the domestic and world economy. The border, which had been an imaginary line in 1848, by midway into the Porfiriato had emerged as a unique region in Mexico linking two countries heading down two different trajectories of economic growth.

By 1890 Porfirio Díaz was midway through his third presidential term. In his attempt to consolidate his dictatorship and create a strong central state, he had eliminated, neutralized, or negotiated with the political actors who had been involved in the political troubles dominating Mexican politics since the defeat of the French: caudillos had been neutralized by economic rewards, the middle classes had been offered jobs with the expansion of the Mexican state, the army had been tamed by corruption and bribes, and friendly relations had been established with its northern neighbor. In the case of the northeast frontier, Díaz instructed Bernardo Reyes to put an end to the *cacicazgos* of Evaristo Madero in Coahuila and Gerónimo Treviño in Nuevo León.

As the Porfirian state gained strength, it passed a series of laws aimed at modernizing the Mexican economy. After the state defeated the no-madic Indians and quelled peasant unrest over the expropriation of lands, it passed the *baldío* laws, which allowed individuals to accumulate large tracts of "public" lands. Madero, Treviño, Naranjo, Manuel González, and friends carved up much of the northeast, especially Coahuila. The new mining codes revived the mining industry, which received heavy infusions of foreign capital. Again the northern states benefited from the new ex-ploitation. During the second half of the dictatorship, the Porfirian state ended the *alcabalas* (internal taxes) in 1896 and gradually eliminated the Free Zone, two measures aimed at integrating the north into the domestic economy.

The Porfiriato falls into the period of world history that Eric Hobs-bawm calls the "Age of Empire," when the great powers, including the United States, expanded their economic activities throughout Latin Amer-ica, Asia, and Africa. During this period, with the help of foreign invest-ments, Díaz moved Mexico into the ranks of the "civilized" nations of the world, a process that involved the integration of the Mexican economy into the world capitalist system. Mexico's economic growth, fueled by an exten-sive railroad network, depended largely on its exports of natural resources and tropical goods: from mineral ores in northern and central Mexico to oil from the Tampico area to henequen in the Yucatán peninsula. Foreigners, mainly North Americans, invested over a billion dollars in Mexico during the Porfiriato.[4]

Capitalism had spread more extensively in the north than in other parts of Mexico by the turn of twentieth century. The defeat of the nomadic Indians freed millions of hectares of land for economic development, while the heavy concentration of foreign investments in the north spurred the spread of capitalism. Four border states received 25.3 percent of total U.S. investments by 1902, with Coahuila receiving 9.5 percent; Sonora, 7.3 per-cent; Chihuahua, 6.3 percent; and Nuevo León, 2.2 percent.[5] The high con-centration of foreign investments in the north transformed the border states from some of the most "backward" areas into Mexico's fastest-growing economic region. Chihuahua, for instance, produced 4,820,000 pesos in mineral ores and cattle products in 1883. By 1908 the value of these mostly exportable goods had increased to 48.5 million pesos.[6] La Laguna, a region hardly populated before the Porfiriato, produced 90 percent of Mexico's cotton by 1910.[7] The north was also home to some of the wealthiest families in Mexico who made their wealth during this period: the Terrazas of Chihuahua, the Maderos of Coahuila and Monterrey, and Monterrey's industrialists such as Francisco Sada and Vicente Ferrara.

The need for labor attracted thousands of migrants from the interior. By 1910, 270,000 migrants resided in the border states, where they worked in smelting, ranching, agriculture, railroads, mining, and industry. The need for labor also shaped a labor market different from the rest of Mexico in terms of high concentrations of foreign skilled and semiskilled workers and highly paid and mobile workers in comparison with the rest of Mexico. The competition for labor among northern states and the United States entirely dominated the market during this period.

In Nuevo León, as in other parts of the north, foreign investments were concentrated in the export sectors of the economy, specifically railroads and smelting. Monterrey, strategically located in the corridor between central Mexico and the northeast border with the United States, became Mexico's leading railroad hub after Mexico City, with connections to the border towns of Nuevo Laredo, Ciudad Porfirio Díaz (Piedras Negras), and Matamoros and to the interior, through Tampico, San Luis Potosí, and Torreón. While in the long run railroads were instrumental in Monterrey's overall industrial development, it was governmental policies (a factor often neglected in the historiography of Porfirian Mexico) that initially sparked the city's industrialization. Once the Porfirian state secured the political integration of all regions, it then sought to break the barriers that had prevented the growth of a domestic economy. It ended the *alcabalas* and the border Free Zone, which had hampered local industries because of the massive smuggling of foreign goods into Mexico, two issues of extreme importance for the north.

In many ways Monterrey's fate was indirectly decided in the halls of power in Washington, D.C., Mexico City, and Monterrey. A series of binational and local government measures provided the conditions for the industrialization of the city. The most important measures included the McKinley tariff of 1890, the state government's tax-free concessions of 1888 and 1889, and the Porfirian government's protectionist policies concerning native industries (the ending of the *alcabalas* and Free Trade zone). The combination of these government initiatives facilitated the industrialization of Monterrey.

During the Lázaro Garza Ayala administration (1887–1889) the state legislation passed two key pro-business legislative bills that spurred local economic recovery. The 1888 bill exempted new enterprises with a value over one thousand pesos from both state and municipal taxes for up to seven years. A year later Governor Bernardo Reyes modified this bill by extending the tax exemption for up to twenty years to new industries that were considered of "public utility." The second bill of 1889 granted municipal and state tax exemptions for up to five years to new urban houses worth over five thousand pesos.[8] These two bills initiated a lasting and fruitful partnership between business and the Reyista state government.

In 1890 the U.S. Congress passed the Sherman Silver Purchase Act, which forced the Treasury to purchase 4,500,000 ounces of silver each month, raising the price of this ore to $1.25 an ounce.[9] The Sherman Silver Purchase Act benefited U.S. mining and the smelting companies and would also have benefited Mexican mining firms which exported large quantities of ores to the United States. In this age of growing protectionism in the world economy, however, Congress also passed the McKinley tariff in 1890, which taxed foreign imports an average of 49.5 percent, one of the highest import duties in the industrial world.[10] The McKinley tariff would have had a pernicious effect on Mexican mining because Mexico was an exporter of mineral ores and did not have much of a smelting industry— its unrefined ores had to pay the tariff of one and a half cents a pound.[11] The tariff threatened the future development of Mexican mining, one of the cornerstones of the nation's economy. But a few enlightened entrepreneurs in Monterrey and in the United States (specifically, the Guggenheim family—the owners of the Philadelphia Smelting and Refining Company, which operated a large smelter in Pueblo, Colorado, that depended heavily on imported Mexican ores) recognized that they could minimize the impact of the McKinley tariff by smelting ores in Mexico. "But why give up on Mexico?" insisted Meyer Guggenheim, the patriarch of the Guggenheim family. "If we can't bring Mexican ores to Pueblo, let us take a smelter to Mexico."[12]

Despite its remoteness from the mining centers, Monterrey's excellent railroad connections, its proximity to the border, and the state government's tax exemption convinced the Guggenheims and other entrepreneurs to build their smelters in the city. Three smelters were established there within a year after the passage of the McKinley tariff. Railroads facilitated the transportation of minerals, as Monterrey received ores from throughout the country.[13] Monterrey smelted close to one-fourth of Mexico's ores, even though it was an insignificant mineral-producing state (see Table

Table 3.1. MINING AND SMELTING VALUES IN MEXICO,
1897–1900 (IN PESOS)

State	Mining Value	State	Smelting Value
Chihuahua	42,723,406	Nuevo León	68,948,271
Durango	38,947,909	Aguascalientes	30,000,862
Sonora	26,441,398	San Luis Potosí	25,503,284
Sinaloa	24,876,783	Sonora	23,022,454
Zacatecas	23,007,783	Hidalgo	21,435,647
Hidalgo	22,089,652	Baja California	20,554,406
Coahuila	19,805,374	Durango	20,073,877
Guanajuato	18,665,219	Sinaloa	19,200,405
San Luis Potosí	15,492,843	Chihuahua	18,969,882
Baja California	13,898,693	Zacatecas	18,961,401
Total	245,949,060	Total	266,670,489

Source: Antonio Peñafiel, *Anuario estadístico de la República Mexicana, 1900*, pp. 311–315.

3.1).[14] While the McKinley tariff was a blessing in disguise that contributed to Monterrey's early stage of industrialization, the Windom custom decision of 1895 appeared to have solidified Monterrey's position as one of the world's leading smelting centers. Based on limited available evidence, this decision apparently lowered the tax on refined silver exported from Mexico to the United States.

In appreciation of the Windom custom decision, Joaquín Maíz, a Monterrey mining and smelting entrepreneur, said, "We ought to raise a silver statue to the memory of Secretary Windom for his decision in regard to the admission of silver ores." [15] Maíz had a personal motive for his veneration of Secretary Windom—he was grossing a thousand pesos a day from his San Pedro mine in 1896.[16]

The convergence of the McKinley tariff and state government's pro-business legislation invigorated Monterrey's economy. Between 1887 and 1897 entrepreneurs "claimed" (*denunciaron*) fifty-four mines, most of them within a thirty-mile radius of Monterrey.[17] In addition to the three smelters, twenty new industries received concessions between 1890 and 1891. Meanwhile, by 1891 the state and municipal government had given tax-free concessions to three hundred new houses in Monterrey, each valued at five thousand pesos or more.[18] Housing construction and the operation of enterprises subsequently launched a dash to acquire real estate in Monterrey and on its outskirts. Indeed, the city recovered economically in the 1890s, and its future looked promising.

FROM "FRONTIER" MERCHANTS TO
THE MONTERREY "BOURGEOISIE"

In 1900 Monterrey smelted close to 25 percent of the ores in Mexico, even though it only mined 1 percent of the nation's mineral wealth. Considering that Nuevo León did not produce steel and lumber for railroad construction or mineral ores for the smelting industry, one of the most important spillover effects of the export-oriented industries was job creation. Thousands of migrants came to Monterrey to work in foreign-owned smelters and railroads. These industries generated thousands of pesos in wages, which in turn contributed to the economic revival of the city, because workers needed to eat, drink, dress, and shelter themselves.[19] Monterrey's perceptive merchants never passed up an opportunity to make a profit, recognizing that they had a captive population and that money could be made from the city's population growth. They invested in small firms that catered to the needs for food, drink, clothing, and construction materials. The state government granted dozens of tax-free concessions throughout the 1890s to enterprises that produced a variety of goods such as cement, bricks, beer, soft-drinks, flour, and furniture.[20]

Merchants invested in small firms that catered to the city's needs. They had accumulated their capital from frontier commerce, especially the prosperous cotton trade during the Vidaurri era. Merchants had created large family-owned *casas comerciales,* such as Casa de Valentín Rivera Sucursales, Casa Calderón, and Sucursales de Hernández Hermanos, which diversified their operations during the economic crisis of 1867 to 1890 and engaged in financing and in land speculation.[21] La Reinera, founded by the Hernández brothers in the 1850s and managed by their nephew, Tomás Mendirichaga, in the 1900s served as a commercial store, an import-export house, a financial institution, and an investment firm with stakes in La Laguna cotton estates, mining enterprises in the northeast, and many of Monterrey's industrial firms.[22]

The family-owned commercial houses provided much of the original capital for Monterrey's early industrialization. These merchant families, which numbered around twenty or so, pooled their resources into *sociedades anónimas,* the stock companies. Investing in firms through stocks, instead of individual family investments, reduced the financial risks in general and the risk of bankruptcy in particular.[23] Investments in stock companies allowed families to invest in numerous firms. Key individuals, such as

"Colonel" Robertson and Vicente Ferrara, sold the idea of new enterprises to potential investors, raised the required capital, and then organized the firm after its incorporation as a stock company.[24]

The creation of stock companies allowed the merchant families to invest in firms that required large capital, such as Compañía Minera, Fundidora y Afinadora de Monterrey, the second largest smelter in the city. In 1890 the Ferraras, Maderos, Milmos, and Zambranos owned 73.3 percent of this 300,000-peso smelter. Ten years later these families possessed only 46.5 percent of the stocks, but the firm's value had increased to three million pesos.[25] Moreover, these families owned many of the mines in the northeast that fed the smelter with ores. By 1904 the smelter's value had increased to eight million pesos.[26]

Monterrey's merchants were keenly aware of Mexico's growing integration into the world economic system and of the expansion of the domestic market for food, drink, clothing, and construction materials. In the case of the domestic market, the Porfirian state was strong enough by the 1890s to eliminate two of the chief obstacles that had hindered the economic expansion of the frontier. Porfirio Díaz wanted to end the *alcabalas,* the internal taxes which had prevented frontier goods from entering markets in the interior due to multiple taxation. In 1879 he told a U.S. reporter that he wanted to end the *alcabalas,* "but it is impossible to do everything at once. My government will do all in its power to make the custom houses uniform and avoid any system that might lead to the imposition of double duties."[27] In 1896 Congress finally abolished the *alcabalas,* while at same time imposing a 18.5 percent duty on imported goods entering the Free Zone. Foreign goods had entered the border towns duty-free since the creation of the Free Zone in 1858. These goods were then smuggled into the interior. Congress finally abolished the Free Zone in 1905.[28]

The ending of the Free Zone and *alcabalas* allowed Monterrey's industrial goods to enter the domestic market without any restrictions. The expansion of the market presented the merchants with many opportunities to invest in enterprises that catered to domestic demands. Consequently, they concentrated their investments in an early form of "import-substitution-industrialization" that evolved due to the growth of the domestic market and the high cost of imports. By setting high tariffs on foreign goods, the federal government protected domestic enterprises.[29] In spite of the early importance of the export industries, Monterrey's domestic-oriented industries had become the dynamic sectors of the local economy by 1900.[30]

Before the establishment of Monterrey's nail and wire enterprises in 1899, for instance, these two products were imported from the United States. Nail and wire imports increased due to the growing trend of fencing private property and the scarcity of timber in Mexico.[31] The growing domestic market for nail and barbed wire led to the establishment of an enterprise in Monterrey. Within a few years after being founded, this company claimed close to 50 percent of the Mexican wire and nail market.[32] *Regiomontano* entrepreneurs aimed to curtail foreign imports, especially those involving food, clothing, drink, and construction materials. They were convinced that selective enterprises could compete with foreign imports and thus gain a greater share of the domestic market.

A few of Monterrey's enterprises succeeded in curbing foreign imports during the Porfiriato (specifically beer, nails, and barbed wire). These firms expanded their markets beyond Monterrey and a few, such as the Cervecería Cuauhtémoc, competed for the domestic market. If there was a "model" firm that started with modest capital investments and expanded to become a major firm, it was the Cuauhtémoc Brewery (see Chapter 7). It started operations in 1890 with an investment of 125,000 pesos. By 1910 it was worth between five to eight million pesos and had expanded vertically into other divisions such as packaging and glass. Meanwhile, the value of the Compañía Minera, Fundidora y Afinadora de Monterrey increased from 300,000 pesos in 1890 to eight million pesos in 1904. Table 3.2 shows the industrial expansion of the largest firms during the 1890–1911 era.

The founding of the Compañía Fundidora de Fierro y Acero de Monterrey in 1900 represented a new stage in the formation of Monterrey's capitalists. Vicente Ferrara, a prominent *regiomontano* businessman, undertook the large task of raising the capital and organizing this firm, also called the Fundidora de Monterrey, the first integrated steel mill in Latin America. This company represented the first attempt by Monterrey's capitalists to establish a firm with enormous capital requirements, which could have been considered a risk mainly because it was not viewed as a "safe" investment like food and textiles. The creation of the 10-million-peso steel mill meant that local business leaders had the capacity to raise large amounts of capital within the city and from the outside. Ferrara pulled most of Monterrey's leading families and some major investors in Mexico City into this project to gain control of Mexico's expanding steel and iron market. His venture was received "favorably," and "we were able to raise ten million pesos for this project."[33]

The establishment of Fundidora de Monterrey led to new patterns of investments: the creation of firms that required large amounts of capital to

Table 3.2. INDUSTRIAL EXPANSION OF MONTERREY'S MAJOR FIRMS
(IN PESOS)

Firms	Original Investment	Value, 1910
Gran Fundación Nacional	300,000 (1890)	10,000,000
CMFA de Monterrey	300,000 (1890)	8,000,000
Cervecería Cuauhtémoc	125,000 (1890)	5,000,000–8,000,000
Fundidora de Monterrey	10,000,000 (1900)	16,000,000 (1911)
Fabricas de Vidrios[a]	100,000 (1899)	1,200,000 (1911)
Cementos Hidalgo	1,000,000 (1906)	2,000,000
	11,825,000	42,200,000–45,200,000

Source: Compiled from data in Isidro Viscaya Canales, Los orígenes de la industrialización de Monterrey, pp. 80–96; Caja de Préstamos–Fundidora de Monterrey loan contract, AGN, Caja de Préstamos.
[a] Closed in 1904 and reopened in 1909 as the Vidriera de Monterrey.

navigate the new industrial waters of coke, coal, cement, steel, iron, and glass production. As students of trends within the domestic market, Monterrey's capitalists firmly believed that they could profitably engage in this new sector of the economy, which, for the most part, had not been explored yet by domestic capitalists in spite of the fact that Mexico had the raw material to produce these goods. They sought to satisfy the nation's growing demands for these goods, a goal that required curbing the importation of these products. Alberto Cárdenas, the founder of a cement factory, rationalized the need for a new cement enterprise, "because this product is imported, and because it would give value to our natural resources that have not been exploited in spite of the wealth that they represent."[34]

The Porfirian government highly valued these new types of enterprises, such as Cementos Hidalgo. In fact, members of the government shared the views of Monterrey's entrepreneurs concerning the restriction of foreign imports. José Limantour, the minister of economic development, applauded the creation of Cementos Hidalgos because it was an example "of what could be done in this country in replacing the importation of foreign goods with the production of domestic ones."[35] In an age in which foreign domination of the economy was seen as a growing danger, the Porfirian state attempted to protect almost all the Mexican-owned industries.[36] The government ensured the survival of these new firms by placing high tariffs on steel, iron, and cement, among other products that were spearheading the industrialization of Mexico.

The creation of the Monterrey-based Compañía Carbonífera de Coahuila, a firm with a value of a million pesos in 1897, illustrates this new industrial ethos of investment. This firm was founded to exploit the discovery of coal and coke deposits in Coahuila and Nuevo León at the turn of the century. "For Nuevo León as for Coahuila," *El Espectador* reported, "these are new sources of wealth which will help Mexico escape from this terrible shadow which has preoccupied all the great businessmen of this country. . . ."[37] The "terrible shadow" was a reference to Mexico's dependence on expensive imported coal and coke that fueled industries and railroads. Merchant families and *regiomontano* firms purchased the 10,000 stocks at one hundred pesos each in creating the Compañía Carbonífera de Coahuila. At least in the case of this enterprise, a new pattern of investments surfaced. Nine Monterrey companies, rather than individuals, purchased the majority of the stock, including the Cuauhtémoc Brewery and the Fundidora de Monterrey, with the first owning 10 percent of the stock and the second almost 20 percent. Firms accounted for 75 percent of the total shares of the new company, while individuals owned the remaining 25 percent.[38] Although we do not have a study on the nature of investments after 1910, it is probable that company investments in new enterprises became the norm instead of family and individual investments.

Joint investments, besides serving economic aims through the *sociedades anónimas,* also fulfilled social purposes. Joint investments in enterprises fostered elite group identities with the rise of noncompetitive industrial groups, such as the Cuauhtémoc and Fundidora. Even though Monterrey's economic elite was composed of only fifteen to twenty families, they all participated in each other's economic activities. Most families tended to be large. Evaristo Madero had fourteen children from two marriages. The males ran the businesses, and the females married other businessmen. Unlike La Laguna's divided elites, joint investments consolidated group unity. Moreover, the lack of interelite rivalries in Monterrey helped to shape the industrial bourgeoisie into a coherent and dominant class in Nuevo León and perhaps even the northeast. Joint economic activities were also linked to another social function: elite intermarriage, a pattern begun in the post-1848 expansion of border trade, which attracted *fronterizo,* European, and U.S. merchants to the northeast. The Maderos were tied by marriage to the Zambranos, Sada Muguerzas, and González Treviños.[39] These merchants established their economic headquarters in Monterrey, where they formed a tightly knit group through business deals and intermarriage. By 1910 Monterrey's leading families were tied in one way or another through marriage and business. Marriage was a way to ensure the reproduction of elites within a socially enclosed and exclusive upper-class system.[40]

THE "COMMODIFICATION" OF THE CITY

During the last twenty years of the Porfiriato, Monterrey gained the reputation as one of the most "progressive" cities in Mexico. "Progress," the economic code word of the Porfiriato, was measured by the amount of industrial and commercial activity and by improvements in Monterrey's infrastructure (such as those in housing and urban transportation). From its position as one of the cities least likely to industrialize in 1890, Monterrey had become Mexico's most important industrial center by 1910, producing 13.5 percent of the country's total industrial output.[41] During this period, 342 enterprises had been established in Nuevo León, most of them concentrated in Monterrey and its surrounding municipalities, ranging from small firms worth a few thousand pesos that employed less than a dozen workers to a 10-million-peso modern steel plant that employed over a thousand workers. An estimated 56 million pesos had been invested, excluding firm improvements and expansion.[42]

Mexico's small but growing domestic market was vital for Monterrey's overall industrial expansion. Industry shaped the destiny of Monterrey, one of Mexico's few industrial centers, but represented only part of a broader portfolio of economic interests for *regiomontano* capitalists. They were also engaged in all of the important sectors of Monterrey's economy, especially banking, real estate, and commerce.

The "sultan of the north" became Mexico's fourth largest city and by far the most important northern one, jumping from 14,000 inhabitants in 1877 to 78,528 by 1910. Thousands of migrants from throughout Mexico flowed into Monterrey in search of work and "were one of the principal causes" for the city's demographic growth.[43] Monterrey based its early industrialization on the production of beer, soft drinks, flour, textiles, and furniture, among other goods that helped to feed, dress, and house its growing population. The city's industrialists highly valued migrants as potential wage earners who were needed for the expansion of industry. As owners of the large commercial stores, these industrialists also valued city dwellers as consumers. Monterrey's capitalists owned not only the enterprises that produced the goods that were consumed by the inhabitants, but also the large commercial establishments that supplied and sold those products, as well as others that they did not produce, to the city's

Table 3.3. URBAN GROWTH IN MONTERREY, 1885–1903

	1885	1903
Population	30,000	80,000
Housing (units)	6,000	13,000
Municipal rent (in pesos)	70,000	300,000
Urban rail line (kilometers)	10	40
Telephones	0	1,000
Municipal buildings	1	7
Banks	0	5
Other financial institutions [a]	0	3
Hotels	1	9
Newspapers	4	12
Timber sales (in pesos)	80,000	1,000,000
Mining investments (in pesos)	60,000	5,550,000
Industrial enterprises	3	29
Industrial investments (in pesos)	80,000	21,000,000

Source: La Voz de Nuevo León, March 28, 1903.
[a] Commercial firms that functioned as financial institutions.

consumers. Within the dynamic of industrial expansion, job creation, and urban growth, real estate became another economic activity where business owners were major players. In short, entrepreneurs were engaged in the most profitable sectors of Monterrey's economy.

In 1885, before the smelters' smokestacks poured out the black smoke that darkened the city's landscape, Monterrey contained approximately 30,000 inhabitants. The city's only sign of "modernity" was the recently constructed railroad yards. By 1903 the "old" Monterrey was unrecognizable: the population had more than doubled along with the number of housing units, urban rail lines had quadrupled, the number of hotels had increased from one to nine, and the number of telephones had increased from 0 to 1,000 (see Table 3.3). Monterrey's urban advancements continued from 1903 to 1907, with major improvements in the tramway and sewage and water system.[44] In 1907 the U.S. consul summarized the correlation of Monterrey's industrial expansion, wage earners, consumers, and urban improvements:

The smelters, steel plant, mills, and factories produced more than the usual amount, old industrial plants were enlarged, and numerous small factories were established, increasing the demand for labor, with a visible increase in the wages of nearly all laborers; the pay-rolls were unusually large, and the people had money to spend. As a result, the general business conditions of the city was [*sic*] never more prosperous, and merchants purchase and sell more goods because the local demand was greater. . . . The city of Monterrey saw more general improvements last year than in any other in its history. A complex sewage system, a modern water system, a well-equipped electric-car system, a new union station for all railroads entering the city, and the paving of the streets are near completion, and will tend to give Monterrey a more substantial and modern appearance.[45]

Within this scenario, the acquisition of urban properties and development of industry turned into the most lucrative investments for the city's capitalists. The city's real estate market boomed after 1890, thanks to the state government's five-year exemption of municipal and state taxes on new houses and buildings worth over 5,000 pesos. Over three hundred houses and buildings were constructed within a few years, mainly in the central zone. The price of urban property soared near the railroad lines and in the central part of the city, especially along Unión and Progreso, the main commercial streets. In 1895 the state government continued to facilitate the expansion of the profitable real estate market in the central zone by granting tax exemptions to new housing and buildings worth over 8,000 pesos.[46]

In addition to granting tax concessions to new housing, the Reyista state and city government further encouraged the acquisition of real estate properties. Because of "the overall growth in the state's capital and in other towns" the state legislature passed a "public domain" law in 1890.[47] Based on the concept of population and economic growth in urban centers, the new legislation granted the state government the right to expropriate lands, with just compensation, in the best interest of "progress" and the public good. The impact of this law has not been studied, but the association of "progress" and "public domain" tended to serve the needs of the business community.

Perhaps more important than the public domain law was the privatization of Monterrey's *ejidos* (community lands), which the municipality had owned communally since the 1600s. The colonial government had granted municipalities enough land to sustain the community with water, farming land, and pasture. The new era called for the privatization of the *ejidos* either by *denuncio* (claim) or in public auctions. For example, "Colonel" Robertson, one of the leading land speculators in the city, "acquired [*denunció*]" seven hectares of *ejido* lands that were adjacent to his brick factory.[48] Meanwhile, Samuel Fisk outbid his competitors for 34,915 *varas* (24,518.84 square meters) that the city government offered in a public auction. These *ejido* lands were located on the north side next to a railroad line. Fisk later sold them to Patricio Milmo.[49] No systematic study has yet been done on the privatization of Monterrey's *ejidos*, but the municipal archives contain many cases of such "claims" and "auctioning."

From its core in the central zone Monterrey expanded north, along the emerging industrial corridor. "There are no intermediate lands that have not been claimed," a newspaper reported in 1893 on Monterrey's northward expansion; "this capital is uniting with the essentially manufacturing [textile] northern towns."[50] Three years later the same newspaper noted that the north side, which was previously covered with bushes, was now "occupied by manufacturing plants, buildings, and street railways, the same progress being noted, though in less degree, in the other quarters of the city. . . ."[51] Monterrey also expanded south of the Santa Catarina River, home of the famous "San Luisito" working-class neighborhood. By 1909 San Luisito contained 9,000 residents, mainly from San Luis Potosí, who lived in small *jacales* and *chozas* (shacks).[52]

While the role of entrepreneurs in the Monterrey real estate market has not been studied, real estate ventures and speculations apparently became activities in which most of the leading entrepreneurs were heavily engaged.[53] Without a doubt, purchasing, selling, and speculating in land yielded high returns. "Colonel" Robertson purchased 69 *manzanas* (each *manzana* was equivalent to a city block) on the north side that he used to develop Bellavista, the first planned residential neighborhood in Monterrey. He sold one part of this property as individual plots for residential homes and the other to the Cuauhtémoc Brewery.[54] Such was the real estate craze that even some established *comunidades de accionistas* near Monterrey fell victim to the great land grab of the era. San Bernabé de Topo Chico, one of the oldest communities in the state and located eight kilometers north of Monterrey, owned only 4,518 hectares of "poor quality" land by 1910. Land speculators, among them Francisco Armendáriz and Santiago Belden, had confiscated its lands under the guise of *baldíos* (public lands) and by other means "that cannot be known from the documentation."[55]

A foreign student of Porfirian Mexico noted that urban property in Monterrey was "one of the most stable investments, continuously improving in value," a point that the *regiomontano* press confirmed.[56] An interesting article in *El Trueno* illustrates the striking rise in property values in Monterrey. Individuals who purchased a *manzana* for 80 to 100 pesos in 1890 could sell the same property for 4,000 to 6,000 pesos in 1903. Meanwhile, plots that were purchased for 30 pesos a *vara* (approximately a square yard) sold for 100 pesos two years later. This newspaper estimated that it cost 4,000 pesos to build a new house in 1901, 2,000 for construction and another 2,000 for the plot (*solar*). Within a few years that same house could be sold for 6,000 to 8,000 pesos.[57] With the completion of sewage and water systems in 1906, urban property escalated to three to four times its earlier price.[58] In one real estate case, a plot was bought for 4,000 pesos in the 1880s; in 1906 it was sold for 300,000 pesos.

The booming real estate market dictated the shape the city assumed. The central zone, the most expensive part, contained the government buildings, commercial stores, and the wealthy residential neighborhoods of the upper middle class and elites. The northern part of the city contained the industrial enterprises and residential neighborhoods of the middle class, such as Bellavista. Increasingly, the working class concentrated south of the Santa Catarina River in overcrowded neighborhoods like San Luisito. The highest bidders, who tended to be individuals with financial means, did not purchase all the city's *ejidos*. In public auctions some workers purchased lands from the city's *ejidos* that were reserved only for the "vecinos pobres" (poor residents). That was the case of Manuel Cortés, a blacksmith, who bought a plot from the city to "build a *jacalito*" in the San Luisito neighborhood.[59]

Just as industry fueled the boom in the real estate market, it also revitalized the city's commercial activity, which had been on the decline since 1867. Over 30 million pesos were invested in commercial enterprises between 1890 and 1910.[60] The city's growing population once again provided the base for the expansion of commerce. As with real estate, commerce became another major urban activity which involved a good portion of the city's elites—capitalists such as the Holcks, Cantú Treviños, Riveras, and Hernándezes owned the large retail stores. The five largest commercial stores reported over five million pesos in sales in 1904, a considerable sum for a provincial city.[61]

Monterrey's strategic location and important railroad outlets propelled the city to regain its status as the commercial hub of Nuevo León and the northeastern states of Tamaulipas and Coahuila. Monterrey's capitalists, through their ownership of the large commercial and retail stores, profited from the purchasing, processing, and circulation of goods that entered the city. Agricultural products, cattle, mineral ores, and raw materials were purchased, processed, and later sold to local consumers or "exported" to "the rest of the border, the interior of Mexico, and the exterior."[62] The best example is the smelting industry and to a lesser degree the leather and hide industry. Although Nuevo León was not known for its cattle industry, it was the third largest producer of hides and leathers in Mexico after Mexico City and Chihuahua.[63]

As early as 1896 *La Voz de Nuevo León* predicted that "before long" Monterrey "will constitute a complete commercial and industrial organism."[64] Elites held a similar view of Monterrey as a single economic unit in which money was continually recycled. Francisco Sada, one of the leaders of the business community, emphasized that his enterprise, the Cuauhtémoc Brewery, bettered the city because it paid wages to its labor force, who spent their salaries in the city, helping to generate new businesses and thus create more demand for industrial and consumer goods.[65] The Fundidora de Monterrey paid a monthly *raya* (salary) to its labor force of 60,000 pesos.[66]

Entrepreneurs were developing an important component of their ideology during the 1890–1910 era. Before envisioning Mexico as a nation of millions of consumers, merchants first conceived of Monterrey as an organic economic and social unit. Involved in many business activities throughout the city, merchants developed a holistic view of Monterrey as an orderly economic community potentially generating wealth for all members: entrepreneurs owned the enterprises employing thousands of wage-earners; workers were also consumers who spent their salaries on food, drink, housing, and clothing; Monterrey's factories produced many of these consumer goods, which were sold in large stores owned by the same entrepreneurs who owned the factories. The logic was that what was good for business was good for Monterrey, because money was recycled within the city, which kept growing economically and in population—more money meant that new investments could be made in new enterprises that would employ new workers who in turn would become consumers. This cycle would be repeated over and over for the benefit of all.

Indeed, this holistic view of Monterrey was the basis for an emerging vision and ideology of a merchant elite in the process of becoming Mexico's leading industrialists. Tied by marriage and joint investments, Monterrey's business leaders began to conceive of Mexico as a nation of millions of potential consumers in the last decade of the Porfiriato. Unlike other business groupings in Mexico and Latin America of this age, they initiated the production of steel, coal, cement, iron, glass, and other goods essential to the modernization of industry that Mexico otherwise had to import in large quantities.

RICH CITY AND POOR COUNTRYSIDE

The development of capitalism in Nuevo León was partial and uneven. Capitalism was highly developed in Monterrey, but it lagged far behind in the countryside. Monterrey yielded over 80 percent of the state's entire physical output. By all indications Nuevo León's unequal development originated around 1890 with Monterrey's industrialization. A few years earlier the value of agriculture had been four times greater than the value of the state's industrial production.[67] In 1908 the state produced a total value of 78 million pesos in industrial, mining, and agricultural products. Agriculture accounted for around 6 percent of the total of 4.3 million pesos, however.[68]

The industrialization of Monterrey instituted a pattern that would dominate Nuevo León's modern history—the high concentration of population, services, and wealth in the city and the relative economic decline of the countryside. This decline was manifested not only economically, but also by the loss of population and political influence. From the beginning of the Porfiriato in 1877 to its end in 1910 Nuevo León's population increased by 92 percent, while Monterrey's grew by 460 percent—much of the state's population increase was in fact due to Monterrey's demographic growth. During that same period, the city's share of the state population grew from 7 percent to 21 percent.[69] Monterrey's urbanization encouraged the centralization of such services as health and education in the city. By 1900 Monterrey contained 38 percent of the teachers in the state, 75 percent of the lawyers, over 50 percent of the doctors, and 83 percent of 1,950 foreigners in the state.[70]

Adolfo Duclos-Salinas, a *regiomontano* intellectual, noted this economic divergence between city and countryside as early as 1904: "it is an established fact that this city has notably progressed; however, the entire state has remained almost stagnant . . . three-fourths of its villas and towns have lamentably regressed."[71] Numerous obstacles prevented the full development of capitalism in the countryside, including a state government that neglected the rural areas, the unclear property status of the agrarian communities, and the lack of credit for irrigation, machinery, and other resources that were needed to improve agriculture. To understand this growing gap between city and countryside, two issues must be examined. First, it is important to define land ownership by stressing that Nuevo León con-

Table 3.4. RURAL HOLDINGS IN NORTHERN MEXICO, 1905

State	Haciendas	Ranchos	Unclassified
Baja California	42	860	565
Coahuila	247	569	60
Chihuahua	147	182	72
Durango	214	1,445	248
Nuevo León	508	1,436	3,327
San Luis Potosí	272	948	193
Sinaloa	113	1,091	542
Sonora	175	571	572
Tamaulipas	114	756	131
Zacatecas	147	1,210	2,125

Source: *México Industrial*, December 15, 1905.

tained few *baldío* (public) lands. Second, the state's land area had historically been much divided into *comunidades,* ranchos, and haciendas, in the
words of José González.[72] The *comunidades* owned approximately one-
third of the land by 1910.[73]

Statistical data demonstrate that the Nuevoleonese countryside underwent profound land tenure changes during the Porfiriato. The haciendas
more than doubled in number, from 247 in 1876 to 508 in 1903 and 600
in 1910. The number of ranchos increased from 1,436 in 1903 to 1,994 in
1910. "Unclassified" properties, however, declined from 3,327 in 1903 to
2,115 in 1910.[74] Table 3.4 compares the number of haciendas, ranchos, and
"unclassified" properties in Nuevo León and the rest of northern Mexico.
Nuevo León, the smallest of all the northern states, had the largest number
of properties classified as haciendas, the second largest number of ranches,
and the most properties without classification. The data indicate that haciendas and ranchos were growing at the expense of so-called unclassified
entities (the *comunidades*) and that Nuevo León had the largest number of
properties that defined private property in rural Mexico, the haciendas and
ranchos.

The statistical data lead to erroneous conclusions, however, because
Porfirian definitions of hacienda, rancho, and unclassified properties do not
apply to Nuevo León. In general a hacienda was defined as a large estate
that produced grains or allocated the land for cattle, while a rancho was a
smaller portion of land operated by independent farmers. By all accounts
Nuevo León had the smallest ranchos and haciendas in northern Mexico.

The problem of using the labels "hacienda" and "rancho" in Nuevo León is that many *comunidades* called their properties haciendas and ranchos. Of the twenty-eight haciendas in the municipality of General Terán, for example, eight were owned by individuals and eighteen were *comuneros,* another name for *comunidad.* In Rayones all four haciendas were owned by *comuneros,* while in Cadereyta Jiménez individuals owned all the haciendas. In Galeana all ten haciendas were owned by individuals, most of whom lived outside the state.[75] It is also probable that the same rule applied to the ranchos, based on the example of a *comunidad* in Hualahuises. That *comunidad* was made up of 213 members whose property was organized into four ranches, each with numerous members.[76] The growth of haciendas and ranchos in the state by these accounts was simply due to the renaming of some *comunidades* as haciendas and ranchos without any major modification in land tenure practices or transfers of land. Thus, in general, the traditional haciendas were concentrated in the southern part of the state, the *comunidades* in the center and north, and the "ranchos" (individual and *comunidad*) throughout the state.

Ironically, the only entity with a clear definition in Nuevo León was the one that Porfirian statisticians labeled "sin clasificación" (unclassified) —the *comunidad,* which the state government defined "as a union of people who are owners of property [*cosa raíz*] by virtue of a title that assigns them proportional parts and not specific portions of it." [77] In any case, all this indicates that Nuevo León's countryside assumed a different form of development than the rest of Mexico: the state contained few public lands, and much of its land area by 1910 was divided into many small properties called haciendas, ranchos, and *comunidades.*

Although the land was divided among these three entities, the amount of good land that could be used for agriculture was quite limited. According to José González's rough 1873 estimates, only 8 percent of the state's land could be used for either dry and irrigated farming (*labor temporal* and *riego*), because the rest was grazing land, hills, and mountains.[78] His estimates were mostly correct, because in 1910 only 201,996 hectares were used for farming out of a total of 4,552,336 hectares classified as farming, grazing, and woodlands (*bosques*), approximately 4.5 percent.[79] Of the 201,996 hectares used for farming, less than half (77,359 hectares) were irrigated, although one must be careful in using this term.[80]

Nuevo León is not blessed with plentiful water resources; people irrigated their fields only during the rainy season, lasting just a few months, when creeks and rivers carried water. More often than not, the region weathered long droughts with distressful effects on rural society.[81] Scarce river and well water was divided among the *comunidades,* haciendas, and ranchos in proportion to individual *porciones* and *derechos* (precise water rights) by days, hours, and even minutes. Each *accionista* was forced to irrigate his or her plot for the "precise time that he has a right to it and then he hands it to the next shareholder." [82]

The structure and usage of the land in the state had led to one of the more egalitarian rural societies in Mexico. Bernardo Reyes outlined rural property ownership to Manuel Fernández Leal, the minister of economic development: "in Nuevo León there are no large properties, but, on the contrary, land is distributed into small holdings. . . . [Consequently] there are no rich potentates, and, yes, there are many poor people. On the other hand, there are no miserable people who lack the means on which to live." [83] Indeed, with the exception of a handful of *hacendados,* rural society was more or less egalitarian: the great majority were poor, but had land.

THE ORGANIC *COMUNIDADES*

For three hundred years the frontier had shaped Nuevo León's rural population and the way it organized itself. Geographically isolated from central Mexico and the world, the *comunidades de accionistas* survived the Porfiriato without radically altering land ownership. These peasant communities of self-sufficient producers had confronted many obstacles that challenged their survival as economic and social entities. For almost three centuries the *comunidades* were threatened by weather, Indians, banditry, and, after independence, a central government that sought to intrude in their lives. Except for the weather, those threats ceased during the Porfiriato. The Porfiriato presented new threats to their survival, however, the most serious of which was the fact that the amount of land and access to water had remained the same while the communities had grown in membership. These problems led to a new development: an increasing trend within the communities to divide communal property into private properties, a process initiated during the Porfiriato but never completed.

The *comunidades de accionistas* were descendants of the original *pobladores* of the northeast frontier. Colonial governors gave individual settlers *mercedes* (land grants) with the aim of colonizing the region. For instance, sergeant major Carlos Cantú, a *poblador,* received a large individual *merced* of 334,966 hectares (around 191 *sitios de ganado mayor*) in the late 1600s. Second lieutenant José Cantú received a medium-sized grant of 7,800 hectares (10 *sitios de ganado menor*) in 1699; the mission of Lampazos had received four *sitios* of grazing lands by 1714, in addition to farming lands.[84] Beginning with Diego de Montemayor, the colonial governors' basic policy was to colonize, giving each *poblador* "land and water," which were necessities for the "public good, such as the creation of new *pueblos* [communities]." To ensure colonization, the governors granted each *poblador* more than enough *labores* (farming land), *solares* (pasture lands), and water.[85] The postindependence governors followed the same tradition of prioritizing settlement by granting each new municipality *ejido* and grazing lands (*dehesa común*), as in the case of the founding of the municipality of Aldama.[86] As late as the 1880s each new municipality continued to receive *ejido* lands.

The *herederos* (descendants) inherited the land grants, but not as they were originally surveyed. In the case of Carlos Cantú's land grant, he sold Captain Diego González around 50,000 hectares in 1704; and in 1765 his grandson, an *heredero,* petitioned the colonial authorities to partition the land among his new *herederos.* The colonial authorities surveyed the land and divided it among the new *herederos,* according to the *testimonio* (will) of Cantú's grandson. Thus, each *heredero* received a new title that demarcated his or her property's boundaries. Throughout the colonial era the authorities partitioned the land upon request by way of *testimonios* and *hijuelas* (partition by will).[87] Clearly, each new generation of *herederos* received less land than the previous generation; if the practice of legal partition had continued, Nuevo León might have been dotted with thousands of ranches, each subdivided among the new *herederos* upon the death of the owner.

After independence the legal partition of land among the *herederos* ceased for all practical purposes, because it was too costly and impractical (each property becoming smaller and smaller) and because of the instability of governments, the only authority that could partition property based on wills. The practice of *herederos* inheriting the land continued throughout the nineteenth century, but without proper titles that specified the exact portion of land. The *herederos* had become *accionistas* of a common property, with each owning an unspecified *porción* (portion). The only legal title with reference to land ownership was the last survey done by the colonial authorities by way of *hijuela.* José Cantú's 7,800-hectare *merced* that he received in 1699 led to the formation of two *comunidades de accionistas,* Atongo and Capellanía, each with fifty families who held precise titles that were more than one hundred years old, this being the last time the authorities partitioned the property based on wills.[88]

These *comunidades* functioned as true organic communities throughout the nineteenth century. Communities identified a member—the so-called *vecino, comunero, heredero,* or *accionista*—as someone who inherited a portion of the community land, but did not specify a defined, definite portion. The *comuneros* of the Benavídez Olivárez community in Cerralvo proudly stated that they inherited their "possessions" from "our fore-fathers." [89] *Herederos* had the right to farm their own land and build a house, had grazing rights to pasture lands, and had access to the "resources of the land" such as water and wood.[90] The *vecinos* of the San Juan de Ocampo community of Montemorelos owned "their own homes as well as lands for farming and pastures, and have lived on this land peacefully [*pacífica*] and continuously since time immemorial, and they live a life that is independent and proper." [91] The Pilón Viejo community of Montemorelos defined itself as "peaceful [*pacífica*] since time immemorial" and said that its members were *herederos* and others who purchased membership rights. There were a few community members

> who, although they do not have documentation [for the property], have peacefully lived here for a long time. All the individuals have their own houses and their land for farming that they have worked on their own and have improved by constructing fences, wells, etc.[92]

From these descriptions of what constituted a typical *comunidad de accionistas* one perceives the communities as historical entities ("since time immemorial"), with continuous land ownership across many generations, collective labor to improve the land, and an autonomous formation ("an independent way of life"). Besides having rights to home, land, water, and other resources, *accionistas* were also responsible for the internal improvements within the community, such as roads, fences, and irrigation structures. After a flood destroyed the irrigation structures of a community in Cadereyta Jiménez, an *accionista* described his responsibilities to the *comunidad*: "to help as one of the many *accionistas* of the Escondida hacienda to construct the ditches for the irrigation canal and other repairs within the property." [93]

Each of these organic communities was autonomous, and it appears that the members regulated water and land usage through collective consensus. "An independent way of life" perhaps meant that the communities had their own unwritten internal laws and were not regulated by the state government. In spite of the large number of *herederos* who had proportional rights to these resources that were not exactly and clearly specified, the communities regulated land and water usage by their own means, a complicated process. In Agueleguas a person who enjoyed the trust ("merecía confianza") of all the *herederos* regulated water usage within the community. This individual apparently knew the exact amount of water rights to which each community member was entitled in terms of days, hours, and minutes.[94] José González wrote that the general practice was for *accionistas* to water their fields according to the precise time allotted by their rights and then pass the circulation of water "to the next one."[95] In Los Herreras "our forefathers always maintained a perfect order in the usage of land" between *ganado mayor* and *menor,* while in Garza García the communal road since "time immemorial" had served for the transit of all the *vecinos.*[96] These examples indicate a strong sense of community autonomy, an orderly framework for the use of resources, and a collective memory of who had more rights to the resources, especially water.

"CON EL ALAMBRE VIENE EL HAMBRE": THE *COMUNIDADES* AND THE DISPUTE BETWEEN PUBLIC AND PRIVATE USE OF RESOURCES

The preceding discussion has painted a portrait of organic communities that enjoyed a high degree of internal cohesion. This was the history of these communities of small producers for most of the nineteenth century. The great majority of *comunidades de accionistas* survived the Porfiriato without radically altering land ownership. Although landlords and the state did not threaten the communities, they were not static and immune to change. The communities were transformed not by the threats of external forces such as landlords, but by the combined pressures of weather, the increase in new *herederos,* and the lack of credit, which challenged the self-sufficiency of the communities. Those pressures, coupled with the fact that community property and resources remained the same, led to an escalation of intra- and intercommunity conflicts over *derechos* (rights to resources), boundary disputes, land, and water usage. These conflicts undermined the internal cohesion of these organic communities and altered the relations between their members. By the end of the Porfiriato many *accionistas* were pushing for the dissolution of their communities into private properties.

"Our land is not bad, but heaven does not help us" was a common expression of the Nuevoleonese countryside. Although the area had a consistent history of regular droughts and severe water shortages, these never threatened the survival of the communities more than during the Porfiriato, owing to the fact that the number of *comuneros* had increased but the size of their properties had remained the same. Droughts affected all rural areas throughout the state. In arid Mina, a northern municipality, the lack of rains in 1904 brought about the "loss of cattle and harvests, and the town in its entirety is entering a state of desperation."[97] Cadereyta Jiménez, a municipality in the central part of the state, had a history of droughts. Ten years of prolonged droughts had forced many *comuneros* to forfeit their community water shares in 1905 because the harvests were so meager that they did not "compensate for the expenses that are needed to sustain the well and canal."[98] In Doctor Coss the 1890–1892 drought contributed directly to the complete loss of the early and late harvests, besides causing the death of both *menor* and *mayor* animals. The mayor of this southern municipality presented a grim picture:

> the inhabitants of this town find themselves in a situation that is so critical that they cannot occupy themselves in any kind of enterprise because there are no prospects of any type and many of them have been forced to seek other means just to ensure the bare subsistence for their families.[99]

If droughts did not wreak havoc in the countryside, then heat waves or floods did. The heat wave of 1909, the worst recorded in thirty years, led to the death of most of the cattle in Galeana.[100] Nature punished the countryside not only with the heat wave, but also with torrential rains of July 1 and 2 of that year, which led to major flooding of rivers and creeks. The floods killed many people in the state and destroyed animals and crops. The flooding of the Sabinas River in Bustamante caused the death of 700 head of cattle and destroyed the crops; Villaldama reported damages of 60,000 pesos, while Sabinas Hidalgo reported a loss of 25,000 pesos.[101] These natural disasters depleted the meager wealth of the communities.

Most communities remained poor during the Porfiriato, with most of their members engaged in self-sufficient agriculture and ranching. In the absence of irrigation, José González wrote that Nuevo León's peasants of the mid-nineteenth century "prefer to farm on large expanses of land," which resulted "in inferior harvests."[102] He also noted that in 1853:

> A considerable majority of the population only eat maize, *chile piquín,* and on occasions meat. Having only these substances, the sober inhabitants of these towns live happily. Because of their poverty, or their lack of foresight, they do not save sufficient amounts of maize

for the remainder of the year and frequently purchase it at twice the cost as in the period of the harvest.[103]

Not much had changed in the living conditions of the peasantry since González's reports. A community of dry farmers in Hualahuises provides an example of the degree of poverty that dominated the countryside. This community was organized into four ranchos owned by thirty-six families. In 1907 it contained 213 people and reported a total wealth in crops and animals of 9,424 pesos or approximately 44 pesos per person. Most families owned a few head of cattle and goats and a horse and produced just enough corn to feed themselves.[104]

In 1896 Bernardo Reyes pointed out one of the chief barriers affecting most rural communities: although they owned one-third of the state's land, the *accionistas* could not better their lot because of the "scarcity of resources," especially credit to improve their properties.[105] Nuevo León, the smallest and most populous state in the north, did not have large stretches of good land and sufficient supplies of water for commercial farming—and because of the division of the state into many properties it did not have large open ranges that could be used for ranching. Credit could have been used to pump spring water or build wells, aqueducts, canals, and other irrigation projects necessary to expand agricultural production and thus secure the survival of the communities. But the lack of capital for improvements, combined with the growth of membership in the communities, reduced the portion of available land and water per family. With the survival of many communities at stake, *herederos* and *comunidades* fought over land and water usage and land ownership. In some ways the internal conflicts revolved around the disputes between private versus community need for resources.

Conflicts between neighboring communities dealt with legal claims to a specific portion of land. Often both communities had legal documentation for the same contested land. In Cadereyta Jiménez the communities of San Nicolás de Atongo and Capellanía emerged from the same *merced* given to José Cantú in 1680. Apparently, the two communities were heirs of Cantú but developed autonomously from each other. The *apoderado* (legal representative) of Atongo took his case directly to Porfirio Díaz, arguing it on the basis of titles and historical possession of the contested property:

. . . we have protected this land with proper titles that are old and we have been in quiet possession of this land for more than a century. This litigation affects the interests of a community of more than one hundred families, almost a town, which has been established in Atongo for over a century and with improvements and possessions that are numerous and valuable.[106]

In this litigation, Atongo refused to acknowledge the legitimacy of Capellanía and sought its removal from the disputed territory. Capellanía, however, claimed to have "equal rights" (*derechos iguales*) to the land. While both had proper titles to the land, Atongo argued that the *vecinos* of Capellanía were not *herederos* of Cantú.[107]

The dispute between Capellanía and Atongo was not solved during the Porfiriato or by the Comisión Nacional Agraria of the 1920s because both communities had proper titles and shared a common history of "possession" of the contested property; neither could prove which one was the legitimate "heir" of Cantú.[108] This was not an isolated case of contesting claims to the original *mercedes*. Litigation over land became part of the norm during the Porfiriato.[109] As in the conflict between Capellanía and Atongo, however, these litigations could not be resolved because the communities had proper titles to the last land will and claimed common "possession" of land.[110]

Four communities that contested access to 4,019 hectares of land in Montemorelos illustrate this problem. These communities had their origin in the Viejo Pilón *merced* and, at least in the case of two communities, had been in "peaceful possession of the land since time immemorial."[111] These conflicts could not be resolved by the state courts, because most communities could claim legal ownership, or by the federal government, because no *baldío* lands were involved. The impasses in these conflicts between communities sometimes ended in negotiations between the involved parties. The communities of Mamuliqui and Villa Higueras, which had "for many years been in litigation," finally settled, with Mamuliqui selling the disputed land for 2,172 pesos.[112]

The second type of conflict within the *comunidad de accionistas* revolved around the internal use of land. Intercommunity conflicts did not involve usage of lands destined for farming; apparently those rights were well defined according to inheritance.[113] Conflicts evolved over the *agostaderos* (the pastureland). With the increase in *herederos* while the land remained fixed, many communities experienced a breakdown of the traditional division of the *agostaderos* between *ganado mayor* (mainly cattle and horses) and *ganado menor* (primarily sheep and goats). The partition of the *agostaderos* lost its meaning as both *mayor* and *menor* animals competed over pasturelands. *Mayor* and *menor* beasts were incompatible with each other. While cattle grazed on the surface grass, sheep burrowed under the surface to eat the roots and thus "destroy everything on their path, converting the land into an empty plain." [114] The orderly use of *agostaderos* had broken down in many communities, and their use was "without order, rule, or method." [115] Some *vecinos* of Los Herreras captured the sense of this breakdown:

> Our forefathers always maintained a perfect order in this disputed land, reserving a portion of the land for *ganado mayor*. Because of the increase in the number of *herederos,* the land is completely disorganized, due to the whim of some people who do not respect that harmony that our forefathers kept and prejudicing those who seek to maintain that order. . . .[116]

These types of grazing conflicts became more urgent during the last years of the Porfiriato, as growing membership in the communities outstripped the supply of available *agostaderos*. This issue divided communities into two opposing camps, those who wanted to use the *agostaderos* only for *ganado mayor* and ban less profitable animals such as goats and sheep from community lands and those who opposed such measures. Some communities continued to solve grazing preferences by consensus. The majority of the *comuneros* of Hacienda Horcones in Lampazos voted to allow only cattle and horses in the communal pastures.[117]

At any rate, these examples indicated that the communities were undergoing profound changes that in some ways were eroding the traditional order. Equally important, many communities could no longer solve their internal problems by consensus, not to mention the erosion of the influence of the traditional authority figures who regulated the use of resources such as the *agostaderos* and water. One group of *comuneros* in Los Aldamas "solved" a grazing conflict by cunningly outmaneuvering the other faction. The group claimed to represent the majority of the *accionistas* in the community and adopted measures that banned *ganado menor* from community lands. It gave shepherds of the community ten days to remove their flocks or else face a fine.[118] The deputy mayor, representing another faction of shareholders within the same community, opposed that severe measure, first, because other *accionistas* were not present at the meeting where the decision was made and, second, because it was "a violation of my rights, and in my opinion I don't believe it is just that they reserve all the land for their cattle by virtue of the fact that not all the land is their property."[119] In another case, the Board of Directors that managed the supply of water for the communities of Agueleguas had invaded "el derecho ajeno" (the right to private property) of the *herederos*,[120] using Benito Juárez's famous phrase. The *vecinos* claimed that while the majority of the community was away, the Board of Directors had tampered with the flow of water from a well.[121]

These examples of conflict between *comuneros* embodied the increasing "commodification" of community resources of pasturelands and water. In Los Herreras a minority in a community favored greater regulation of pasture lands by arguing along lines of wealth: "it is cattle that prosper the most, because it is an important source of wealth in the state and the main source of wealth in this municipality."[122] In 1897 the state had 119,285 head of cattle valued at 1,658,051 pesos (approximately 14 pesos per head), and 1,064,942 goats and sheep with a value of 803,514 pesos.[123] The owners of both *mayor* and *menor* animals contested the *agostaderos*. Water, the most precious of the resources, had also become "commodified" and was sold just like any other product. In Cadereyta Jiménez some *vecinos* sold their allotted water rights for twenty-five to fifty centavos a night to intermediaries who later sold it to others at a much higher price.[124]

The old *norteño* idiom "con el alambre viene el hambre" (with barbed wire comes hunger) has quite a bit of validity, at least for the majority of the communities in Nuevo León where the use of land and water was contested. Barbed wire fences were symbolic of this dispute between community members over control of these two resources. The construction of fences symbolized the growing desire within the communities to privatize property and, along this course, to restructure rural society along individual lines and away from community needs. Fences embodied private property, challenging the traditional order by enclosing access to water sources, communal roads, and pasturelands.

The *vecinos* of Huilahuises unsuccessfully petitioned Governor Reyes to stop an individual from constructing a fence because it "threatened" to "deprive" them of a creek "that since time immemorial" constituted the "life" of their ranchos. Without access to the creek, "they will be left without water even for the personal consumption of the inhabitants."[125] In Cerralvo another *vecino* with means constructed a large fence around what he considered to be his *derecho* (share) in the communal pastures. The community opposed the construction of the fence because it enclosed a creek that "since immemorial times" had served the needs of the community, especially as a watering hole for their animals. The *vecinos* asserted that the individual with means was not an *accionista* and therefore had no right to construct the fence. Citing the traditional use of the creek to legitimate their claim, they also argued that public needs superseded private needs: "it is not right, nor fair, that just because of one individual so many people have to suffer," "just because an individual who has the resources and takes advantage of them to acquire land only to not cultivate it." [126] The fence builder responded by asserting that he was an *accionista* and property owner and that he had the right to built his fence within his share of the *agostadero*. He also stated that he built the fence to "prepare the land for cultivation." [127]

The construction of fences, as in these cases, represented a trend in which wealthier individuals sought to carve out private ranchos within community lands.[128] In General Terán another individual claiming to be an *accionista* built a fence within the community. The *vecinos* opposed that measure, first, by doubting his *accionista* claim and, second, by alleging that the real motive behind the fence was to annex community lands to expand his ranch.[129] Besides restricting movement, fences also abolished traditional roads, which, as in Garza García, "since time immemorial have served and, in those areas that have not yet been enclosed, continue to serve the transit of the *vecinos*." [130] In the Garza García case, the road had served the needs of the community since 1833. The *vecinos* demanded that the communal road remain open and that "things stay the same as they were [in the past]" because the closing harmed their interests, benefiting only the "private interests of a few *vecinos*." [131] In this contest between private and public needs, the private interests of individuals gained ground during the Porfiriato.

THE NUEVO LEÓN HACIENDA

The Mexican hacienda had a golden era during the Porfiriato, the era that included the greatest expansion of landlords in the history of Mexico. Northern Mexico became associated with the large hacienda and well-known hacendados. The best-known hacendado families included the Maderos of Coahuila and Terrazas of Chihuahua. The Terrazas built their empire from the export of cattle to the United States, earning from 500,000 to a million dollars a year between 1883 and 1889. The earnings from cattle exports provided the Terrazas with the revenue needed to build their economic empire.[132] The Maderos had a long history of accumulating capital in frontier commerce and pioneering the cotton industry in La Laguna.

They also used their earnings to build one of the largest economic empires in Mexico.

The northern haciendas prospered due to the growing world and domestic demands for raw materials and food products. La Laguna, one of the showcases of Porfirian progress, produced 90 percent of Mexico's cotton, half of the country's demand. With major irrigation works in the Mayo and Yaqui districts, Sonora become one of Mexico's leading commercial agricultural centers.[133] The Maderos and Terrazas founded their own banks to finance their economic operations. The Terrazas' Banco Minero de Chihuahua had become one of the most (if not the most) important provincial banks in Mexico.[134] The Maderos used the Bank of Nuevo León as the "center" of the family's many businesses.[135] Meanwhile, hacendados in the Yaqui Valley received credit from the Caja de Préstamos, a lending institution financed by both banks and the government.[136]

Nuevo León was one of the few locations in Mexico where landlords did not prosper. The typical Nuevoleonese hacienda differed from the ordinary Porfirian hacienda in three ways: it was smaller and had lower amounts of capital invested and lower production capacities. Among the key obstacles that prevented the Nuevo León hacienda from developing at a pace similar to that of its counterparts in other parts of Mexico were the lack of credit for hacienda improvements and a state government whose policy priorities concentrated on the development of Monterrey. Although the Nuevoleonese hacienda played a less significant role than its counterpart in the rest of Mexico, the hacienda was nonetheless important to Nuevo León as the main source of food production and the largest employer of labor. By 1910 thirty thousand *jornaleros* toiled on haciendas, a labor force far greater than Monterrey's industrial proletariat.

The lack of credit largely explained the failure of the Nuevo León hacienda to modernize during the Porfiriato. The church had traditionally been the main source of credit for Nuevo León's hacendados prior to the Laws of Reform. Once the church ceased to provide that service, hacendados had few possibilities of acquiring credit, forcing them to sell their harvests early, "under disadvantageous conditions, sacrificing all their profits in the usury." [137] At least within the state, the only sources of credit were the Monterrey business leaders, who "employed their capital in financial, industrial, and mining enterprises" rather than agriculture.[138] For the most part, Monterrey's investors neglected the Nuevoleonese countryside, preferring to invest in the profitable cotton industry of La Laguna. The Banco de Nuevo León, for example, had twelve branches throughout the largest cities of the northeast, but none in Nuevo León other than its Monterrey headquarters.[139]

One can only speculate that creditors considered hacendados credit risks because they did not have enough collateral. Porfirio Ballesteros, one of the wealthiest hacendados in Montemorelos, was worth 23,168 pesos in 1900–1910. Water rights from four different sites constituted half of his net worth, however, while his animals were valued at 4,846 pesos, with 5,384 pesos from five different properties, and 1,171 pesos in tools and machinery.[140] In spite of his stature as one of central Nuevo León's wealthiest hacendados, he was a credit risk because his properties were small and scattered throughout the municipality. Moreover, he only had a few days' worth of water rights. At most he could get a small loan of a few thousand pesos, using his animals and property as collateral. Established creditors tended to favor short-term loans of six months, preferably to commercial enterprises.[141]

As early as 1892 Bernardo Reyes proposed to Porfirio Díaz the formation of a government-sponsored rural bank to aid hacendados who had difficulty procuring credit.[142] It was not until 1908 that the federal government and domestic banks established the Caja de Préstamos to provide credit to hacendados. Nuevo León's hacendados did not benefit from Caja de Préstamos, however, which favored large-scale agricultural estates. Tamaulipan and Coahuilan hacendados received over 10 million pesos in loans from the Caja de Préstamos between 1908 and 1912.[143] Nuevo León received close to 4 million pesos, but the Fundidora de Monterrey, an industrial enterprise, received 2.9 million pesos of the total from this credit institution that was established to promote large-scale agriculture. The rest went to the Fuentes Hermanos, a large Saltillo-based firm with landholdings in southern Nuevo León, and to Jesús González Treviño, a Monterrey capitalist tied to the Madero family.[144]

The lack of credit hindered the development of large-scale agriculture in Nuevo León. Landlords could not produce on a broad scale products such as sugarcane and citrus fruits, two crops that prospered in Nuevo León later in the twentieth century. Sugarcane, a traditional cash crop of the state, was mainly used to make *piloncillos* (unrefined sugar loaves).[145] During the nineteenth century small-scale producers "exported" their *piloncillos* to Coahuila, San Luis Potosí, Durango, and Chihuahua.[146] *Piloncillo* consumption dropped during the Porfiriato owing to the rise of sugar, a mass-produced product whose price gradually fell. Unable to afford to modernize their estates, Nuevo León's hacendados lost an opportunity to shift from *piloncillos* to sugar, a process that required the complete upgrading of all aspects of production, from better grades of sugarcane to milling. *La Voz de Nuevo León* lamented the fact that hacendados could not take advantage of this opportunity to upgrade their estates:

> hacendados concentrate on the production of *piloncillos,* using the most primitive means and with mills of low capacity and energy. They have never produced the quantity of *piloncillos* that their lands and waters are capable of giving them.[147]

In 1896 hacendados produced 155,512 pesos in *piloncillos* and only 17,444 in sugar, figures that indicate their failure to make the necessary transition.[148] Many hacendados took the easiest route available after failing to produce sugar by switching to *aguardiente,* a hard liquor consumed only by the poorest sectors of society.[149]

Nuevo León lost the opportunity to produce sugarcane on a large scale. Morelos and Veracruz planters, the two leading producers of sugar in Mexico, had all the advantages that their rivals in Nuevo León lacked. The sugar planters had access to credit, an abundant and cheap labor force, and a state government sympathetic to their interests and, perhaps more importantly, were constantly acquiring new fields at the expense of the free villages. Morelos's largest planters spent over 100,000 pesos each on irrigation and as much as 350,000 pesos to purchase modern machinery. They converted Morelos into a rural sugar factory, the most productive sugar region in the world after Hawaii and Puerto Rico.[150]

Nuevo León's lands were also good for citrus crops, especially oranges. But the lack of credit once again forced hacendados to forfeit this profitable crop to U.S. investors. In the 1890s U.S. investors arrived in Montemorelos, where they purchased lands, invested in irrigation, and then brought the orange trees from California. The state's 1910 orange crop sold for 100,000 pesos and was expanding to other regions in Nuevo León.[151] Native hacendados could have also exploited this crop if they had the credit that was needed to supply the orchards with plenty of water and to attend the orchards for three to eight years until the trees matured. Once this was done, each hectare could bring in as much as 8,400 pesos a year, leaving a generous profit, considering that the only major cost was providing water and paying a *jornalero* to tend the orchard and to harvest the oranges.[152]

The lack of credit only partially explains the failure of the modernization of the Nuevoleonese hacienda. Hacendados had to confront another dilemma: the state had few *baldío* lands available to expand their estates, while private property was highly divided among haciendas, ranchos, and communities. Governor Reyes wrote to Porfirio Díaz that "property is highly divided and the people who engage in agriculture do so on small parcels of land and with scarce resources."[153]

As mentioned in Chapter 2, Liberal leaders did not attack the *vecinos'* properties, as had happened to the peasantry in other parts of Mexico. Instead, they broke up Soledad hacienda, the largest estate in the state, distributing 256,123 hectares among the southern municipalities, soldiers, and officers. Even though still one of the largest estates in Nuevo León by 1920, Soledad was merely a skeleton of its former self by 1920, containing only 35,177 hectares.[154] By all accounts, the Nuevoleonese hacienda was small and without many possibilities to expand. Even the most modern haciendas, some of which were owned by Monterrey business leaders, also tended to be small. Jesús González Treviño's hacienda contained only 11,046 hectares, while Francisco Armendáriz's property was 3,682 hectares.[155] Meanwhile, González Treviño operated a 5-million-peso hacienda in Coahuila with 191,161 hectares.[156] Nuevo León's estates were modest compared to the size of most northern haciendas, such as the numerous haciendas of the Terrazas family, who owned 4,767,833 hectares of Chihuahua's land.[157]

Restricted by size and encircled by many properties, haciendas had to share nature's resources, especially water, with its neighbors. Montemorelos, one of the breadbaskets of the state and the center of the nascent citrus industry, contained 60 haciendas, 163 ranchos, and 119 properties classified as "agricultural." The hacendados, just like the *vecinos* of the communities, had inherited or purchased *derechos* to water. Porfirio Ballesteros, one of the wealthiest hacendados in the area, had to share water with many of his neighbors. He had the right to four different water sources in Montemorelos, with the smallest *derecho* accounting for one day a month and the largest for eight days. Once the allotted time ended, he had to turn the water over to the next person. Another "wealthy" hacendado from Montemorelos, Jesús Echeverría, had *derecho* to three different water sources, the largest being for three days and twenty-two hours. Water rights became the most valuable asset that hacendados had, even more valuable than land, animals, housing, and tools.[158] *La Voz de Nuevo León* summarized the problem for landlords in sharing limited water supplies:

> the majority of the hacendados are owners of a small *derecho* of water, and this resource is co-owned by fifteen to thirty or more owners.

Each one only has access to a little bit of water, and their harvests are limited.[159]

Jules Randle, a Monterrey capitalist, said: "Both the state and the federal government give due protection to manufacturing enterprises, which, it may be said, do not [always] succeed in satisfying the numerous demands made upon it [*sic*]."[160] The Porfirian and Reyista governments responded proactively to the demands of the industrialists: tax concessions, import-duty free technology, ending the *alcabalas* and Free Zone, and high protectionist tariffs that shielded native enterprises from foreign competition. These government actions helped in promoting the development of Monterrey into Mexico's most important industrial center and one of the showcases of Porfirian "progress."

Many of Monterrey's industries, such as the Fundidora de Monterrey, would almost certainly have failed without the intervention of the Mexican state. Fearing that Mexico would become an economic colony of the United States, Díaz regarded Monterrey as one of the few places where Mexicans could resist foreign domination of the economy. Consequently Monterrey, as the industrial center of Mexico, played a crucial role in the formulation of the Porfirian industrial policy of protecting native industry with high tariffs and other measures associated with an early form of import-substitution-industrialization (a policy that the postrevolutionary government also adopted).

In addition to the government policies that favored industry and the city, Monterrey's capitalists could always count on Governor Reyes's personal influence. In general there was little or no distinction in Mexico between economic and political elites at the regional and national level. From the Terrazas of Chihuahua to the Molinas of Yucatán to the Científicos in Mexico City, elites throughout Mexico used their political positions to advance economically. Bernardo Reyes was one of the few exceptions to this rule. His critics and political enemies—and he had many—accused him of being authoritarian, power hungry, and repressive. But they did not accuse him of corruption, of poor administration, or of profiting from government.

Monterrey's business community benefited more than any class in Nuevo León from Reyes's rule. He played the intermediary role of connecting key industries to high government officials in Mexico City, especially

Cementos Hidalgo and the Fundidora de Monterrey. The federal government constituted the largest market for the Fundidora de Monterrey's steel and iron products, especially rails for the "Mexicanization" of railroads. Cemento Hidalgo's cement products were used for the drainage works at Xochimilco.[161]

Almost every enterprise had received some kind of "favor" from Reyes. He renewed tax concessions to industries whose exemption had ended, as in the case of the Monterrey Tramway, Light, and Power Company, whose concession was renewed in 1898, 1904, and 1909, and La Reynera soap company in 1900, in order to "help enterprises so that they won't collapse."[162] Using his personal influence, he also was instrumental in the merging of two competing soft-drink enterprises in 1908.[163] During the economic depression of 1907–1908, José Limantour, the minister of finance, ordered the Banco Nacional de México to ease up on its collection of loans from Monterrey's business leaders, "not only to please you [Reyes], but also for the benefit that it could bring to commerce and the industrialists of that important city. . . ."[164]

It is safe to argue that the Reyista state was more interested in satisfying the needs of both industry and the overall development of Monterrey than in the countryside. A case in point deals with the role the cement industry played during the construction of water and sewage works in Monterrey in 1905 and 1906. Using his influence with the federal government, Reyes requested that cement imports that were needed for Monterrey be exempt from taxes. After local capitalists failed on two occasions to create a cement firm that could supply the city's infrastructure projects with quality products, Cementos Hidalgo was finally established. This company produced cement whose quality was "equal" or "better" than Portland Cement, the main exporter of cement to Mexico. To protect Cementos Hidalgo, a high tariff was once again imposed on foreign imports.[165]

By comparison, government policy toward the economic development of the countryside was one of indifference. Government "favors" to the countryside are almost completely absent, at least in the archives— not that this represented a diabolical plot to keep the countryside backward. The state government did not have the financial means to provide the much-needed credit to hacendados and the *comunidades* to improve their properties. Nevertheless, government had the legislative power to help the countryside. It could have provided tax concessions to hacendados and other small producers, just as it did to industrialists. It could also have clarified property relations within the *comunidades de accionistas*.

Unlike Monterrey's industrial enterprises, the countryside did not receive tax concessions. The Reyista state, for example, rejected the request from hacendados to classify the shift from *pilloncillo* to *aguardiente* as a new industry so that it could be exempted from taxes.[166] Moreover, haciendas paid taxes on both the value of their estates and the amount invested in them, as opposed to industry. Galeana hacendados had invested 93,900 pesos in ixtle estates by 1908 and paid 2,550 pesos in taxes every year, regardless of the value of production. In contrast, Van Voorghis y Sandford, a Monterrey commercial store, paid around the same amount in taxes, even though it sold 358,520 pesos' worth of goods.[167] It is plausible that the countryside paid the great bulk of state taxes because most industrial enterprises were exempted from them. Industrial and commercial enterprises paid 87,566 pesos in 1908, compared to 35,871 in 1886.[168] In essence, the countryside was subsidizing a state government whose foremost policies concentrated on developing Monterrey and its industries. More importantly, the government was removing scarce capital from the countryside, which desperately needed it to modernize the state, while at the same time allowing capitalists to accumulate wealth by not being taxed.

In 1903 *La Voz de Nuevo León,* the Reyista state's mouthpiece, proudly reported that Nuevo León had the lowest taxation policies in Mexico.[169] Reyes inherited a state government that did not believe in heavily taxing its population and economic entities. Reyes was a firm believer in low taxation and associated it with the freedom of commerce. The state government received the bulk of its revenue from taxes on the reported value of urban and rural property, which, for taxation purposes, was always undervalued by the owners. Industry, the most dynamic sector of the economy, was almost entirely exempt from taxation due to the state's long-term, taxation-free concession policies. The state did not have a tax on the value of production or individual incomes. Due to these conservative taxation policies, Nuevo León, the state with the fewest potential sources of revenue in Mexico, lagged behind other states in revenue to provide services. Chihuahua, a state with more or less the same population as Nuevo León's, had a revenue of 1,321,317 pesos in 1908.[170] Nuevo León's revenue, by contrast, was only 332,861 pesos, approximately one-fourth of Chihuahua's.[171]

The state's taxation policies contributed to the growing division between a prosperous city and a poor countryside. Operating under a fiscally conservative state government, Nuevo León's forty-eight municipalities had to be self-sufficient entities, as in the past. Municipal revenue came mainly from sales taxes on commercial activity. By law and tradition the municipalities sustained local government, police, jails, and schools, among other municipal services, with their own resources. Most municipalities did not have the revenue to maintain adequate services due to the low level of commercial activity that generated sales taxes. Cadereyta Jiménez illustrates this point: its mayor complained in 1893 that the budget was too small to maintain a good educational system. The municipality had too many students in need of an education and not enough schools and teachers. Many parents had to pay schoolteachers from their own incomes in order to guarantee their children a basic education. As a result, parents indebted themselves to hacendados in their quest to give their children an education.[172] With a touch of Social Darwinism's most basic principle of survival of the fittest, Governor Reyes explained his philosophy of fiscal conservatism to the mayor of San Nicolás de los Garza, who, like his counterpart in Cadereyta Jiménez, petitioned the state government for financial assistance:

> The state government is the central power that directs the administrative and political progress of all the municipalities. These entities should sustain themselves and should help sustain the state government. . . . when a *municipio* can no longer cover its most essential expenditures, the logical step is to incorporate itself into another *municipio*.[173]

Allowing commercial activity to dictate municipal revenue and expenditures only accelerated the further development of Monterrey. Even taking the state's low taxation policies into account, the city's heavy commercial activity generated large revenues for Monterrey. In 1904 the five largest commercial stores in the city sold 5,109,296 pesos in goods, while the total value of agricultural production was 4,144,154 pesos.[174] Jules Randle, the owner of Monterrey's tramway system, captured the feeling of this era of economic expansion: "Here money is abundant, not a single failure has occurred, and the merchants are doing good business."[175] Monterrey's share of revenue exceeded that of all the municipalities in the state combined, even though it had less than 25 percent of the state's population. While the municipalities appealed to the state for aid in solving their budget deficits, Monterrey in 1910 had a surplus of 127,478 pesos in its treasury.[176] By 1905 Monterrey collected over half of all the state's municipal tax revenue, and the percentage kept increasing. In fact, Monterrey's revenue was much larger than the state government's revenue.[177]

The Reyista state government was essentially the manager of a few available financial resources. As the administrator of state revenue, the Reyista legislature devoted most of the revenue to Monterrey, the state capital. In this way the countryside subsidized Monterrey, because government spent most of its revenue in the city. In addition to the large number of government employees who lived and spent their salaries there, Monterrey had the only public hospital in the state, the state penitentiary, the Colegio Civil, the only high school in the state, and the law, medical, and workers' technical schools and teachers' schools. The state government provided the budget for these institutions. By investing much revenue in the capital, the Reyista state contributed to the centralization of the most important government services in Monterrey. Apparently, Bernardo Reyes consciously sought to concentrate state expenditures in Monterrey. Alfonso Reyes, his son, and later one of Mexico's foremost literary figures, recalled his father's words on government expenditures:

> I ensure that this government always has pending enterprises, projects that need to be done. When there are none, I plan new ones because this is the only way not to let the machinery of government rust. Because there is always pending work, all are always working and do not have the obligation of sitting down in their offices as it happens in Mexico City. . . . In this way I provide work to a multitude of workers and always maintain an equilibrium where these government projects function as an escape valve: if the projects are too excessive, I lessen them; if they are too scarce, I multiply them and develop new ones.[178]

Of course, these projects were located in Monterrey.

CONCLUSION

By the turn of the century Monterrey had attained a reputation as one of Mexico's leading centers of "progress." This "progress" meant different things to different kinds of people: for migrants from Mexico's interior, it meant a city where industrial employment could be found; for middle-class nationalists, the city's native-owned enterprises represented one of the few centers of resistance in the losing battle against foreign domination of the economy; for the political elite, Monterrey embodied the success of Porfirian "progress and civilization" policies. In 1898 Porfirio Díaz advised his financial advisor José Limantour to visit Monterrey, not only because it was a "center of progress," but also because it "was capturing the attention of all those people interested in the advancement of the nation."[179] Young nationalist officers of the Mexican Army, such as Felipe Angeles, a future Villista revolutionary general, applauded the Monterrey elites' investments in "coal, the great source of energy, and steel that is abundantly needed in the present [development of Mexican] civilization."[180] Those officers, who represented the growing nationalist views, believed that these kinds of enterprises would soon manufacture weapons and thus end Mexico's dependence on the United States and Europe in these areas.[181] In neighboring San Luis Potosí the newspaper *El Contemporáneo* scolded the state's business leaders for not taking advantage of the many economic opportunities that the era offered. It advised them to emulate the Monterrey elites' vigorous "spirit of enterprise" ethos, which had brought great "progress" to the city.[182]

All these images of Monterrey served to enhance the reputation of the city's captains of industry. As the *norteño* song "Monterrey como has crecido" stresses, the "sultan of the north" became associated with native-owned industry and with capitalists who were not afraid to enter the uncharted industries of coal, steel, cement, and glass. The image of the city as "progressive" and as a "pacesetter" contrasted completely with the image of the countryside as "poor" and "backward." For Monterrey's elites, intellectuals, and press, the Nuevo León countryside represented poverty, labor bondage, and inefficient use of land, labor, and resources, among other negative connotations. As *La Voz de Nuevo León* editorialized:

> It is sad to see the emptiness of some areas of the state, almost deserts, without trees and forests, which have been destroyed without being replanted due to laziness and abandonment by their owners. It is even sadder to see how our virgin mountains have been devastated by the ax of the woodsman and how the ebony, live oak, brazil, and chapote trees are used for fuel. . . .[183]

Alfonso Reyes captured this image when he recalled a common expression of the region: a traveler went to a home of rural dweller and asked the housewife, "What do you have here to eat?" She responded, "Whatever you brought with you, sir."[184]

CHAPTER FOUR

Nuevo León and the Making of the Border Labor Market, 1890–1910

Governor Bernardo Reyes claimed that he did not know much about economics except that labor and capital constituted two of the basic elements for economic development.[1] In general, historical studies on Nuevo León have traditionally focused on the capital side of this equation, implicitly giving the captains of industry credit for the emergence of Monterrey as the industrial capital of Mexico. For the most part, historians have neglected the labor side of the equation, including relations between laborers and employers.[2] This chapter attempts to fill in some of the gaps in these accounts by concentrating on the interactions between labor and business in Monterrey and rural workers and landlords in the Nuevoleonese countryside from 1890 to 1910. In these years industrialists and hacendados, the two largest employers of labor in Nuevo León, used different labor strategies in order to compete for workers in a regional labor market with great labor scarcities.

In 1889 *La Voz de Nuevo León,* Bernardo Reyes's mouthpiece, confidently editorialized that "an absolute truth that is acquired from political economy is that free labor is more productive than forced labor."[3] At least in Nuevo León, this political-economic ethos of the nineteenth century was validated during the last twenty years of the Porfiriato. In 1889 the total value of agricultural goods in Nuevo León was four times greater than the value of manufactured products. This figure was more reflective of the poverty of the state than of the wealth of the countryside.[4] By 1908, however, agricultural goods accounted for only about 6 percent (4.3 million pesos) of the state's total value in industrial, mining, and agricultural goods (78 million pesos). There are many reasons for the disparity between the prosperous city of Monterrey and the poor countryside, but among the most important was the emergence of a dual labor market in Nuevo León— one based on free labor in the city, and the other on labor bondage (debt-peonage and other forms of unfree labor) in the countryside.

During the Porfiriato, a labor market emerged in the northern Mexican states, set apart from the rest of Mexico by free labor. In this era of great demographic restructuring, thousands of migrants from central Mexico settled in the Mexican and U.S. border states. Lured to the north by employment opportunities and higher wages, migrants constituted an important component of the workforce, if not the majority, in this emerging labor market, where labor was scarce and employment abounded. High rates of labor mobility prevailed as workers moved from one location to another, creating high turnover rates in all enterprises, from mines to haciendas. Given the scarcity of labor and high turnover rates, the fundamental problem that all employers confronted during this period was to gain control of the workforce. This process included first recruiting workers then retaining and disciplining them into a permanent and efficient workforce.

Employers did not have much difficulty recruiting labor as long as they paid competitive wages because workers, as uprooted wage earners, had no option other than to work in order to subsist. The real challenge for employers involved what E. P. Thompson called "time-discipline," the methods used for retaining and disciplining labor into a permanent workforce. Retaining labor was a difficult task due to the intense competition from both sides of the border for scarce Mexican unskilled workers. Discipline was an equally difficult task, considering that the first generation of workers had virtually no experience with wage-labor and the capitalist "work ethos" based on time, discipline, and efficiency.

Monterrey's industrialists were catalysts in the making of this emerging labor market. In order to recruit workers, they raised wages and engaged in a variety of labor practices aimed at retaining and disciplining labor, including offering wage bonuses, housing, and schooling and promoting Mexican unskilled labor to higher skills. They behaved no differently than other industrialists in the world, who, according to Thompson, used various mechanisms to discipline labor:

> In all these ways—by the division of labor, the supervision of labour; fines; bells and clocks; money incentives; preachings and schoolings;

the suppression of fairs and sports—new labour habits were formed, and a new time-discipline was imposed. It sometimes took several generations. . . .[5]

While the success of "time-discipline" methods is hard to evaluate for the first generation of industrial workers in Monterrey (1890–1910), the methods that industrialists employed in disciplining labor gradually did become institutionalized into an increasingly paternalistic labor system. The clear imposition of this system became obvious among the largest firms in the aftermath of the Mexican Revolution.

In contrast to the great majority of the employers in northern Mexico, Nuevo León's landlords went against the grain of this emerging labor market based on free labor. Landlords would have ceased being landlords if they had depended entirely on free labor because they did not have the financial resources to retain a permanent labor force. Landlords recruited laborers by advancing wages and bound them to the hacienda by ensuring that these money advances could never be repaid. The landlords held rural workers in bondage by means of low wages and indebtedness to the hacienda and, most importantly, with the help of the local authorities, who used their powers to ensure that laborers did not abandon the hacienda. Even though they were successful in holding onto a large portion of the rural population, the hacendados utterly failed to create a loyal labor force.

THE MAKING OF THE BORDER LABOR MARKET

One of the most striking developments in Latin America in the last half of the nineteenth century involved the massive availability of land that would be used for the expansion of capitalism. Land, the source of raw materials, tropical products, and meat products for export, served as the foundation for the capitalist development of Latin America from 1870 to 1945. The largest Latin American countries—Mexico, Argentina, and Brazil—shared at least three features as they modernized their economies.

First, a great portion of the land that became available for economic development was acquired through the "closing of the frontier." In Brazil this process led to an economic and population shift from the coast to the interior, especially to the São Paulo region. The taming of the north in Mexico and the "Conquest of the Desert" in Argentina, two events that involved the defeat of the nomadic Indians, freed millions of hectares of land for economic development. Mexican hacendados also confiscated on a massive scale properties belonging to peasants throughout Mexico, including those in the north.

Second, because these countries did not have the financial resources to develop their economies, foreign investments, mainly from Great Britain and the United States, played a crucial part in developing the key economic sectors such as transportation. These three countries received the major share of all foreign investments in Latin America. Except for the competition they received from U.S. investors in Mexico, British investors dominated in the largest Latin American countries. The key difference between these countries was that the Atlantic Ocean separated Brazil and Argentina from greater economic integration with Europe, while Mexico shared a land boundary with the United States that had tied the two countries economically since 1848.

Finally, because the largest nations of the hemisphere—Argentina, Brazil, Mexico, Canada, and the United States—lacked a labor force sufficiently large for economic expansion, government leaders sought to recruit European immigrants to fill their labor shortages. In contrast to these nations that successfully recruited millions of European immigrants, Mexico utterly failed. In fact, Mexico was the only country in the Americas where large numbers of its population emigrated, at least until the 1960s. Over 100,000 Mexican immigrants resided in the United States in 1900, increasing to over 600,000 in 1930. Part of the new economic relationship that integrated the Mexican economy with the U.S. economy included the migration of Mexican laborers north of the Río Bravo.

Mexico became integrated into the global economy during the Porfiriato as an exporter of raw materials, tropical products, agricultural goods, and labor. One of the most important developments of this period involved landlords dispossessing peasants of their lands, leaving them landless and prone to migration. While the peasants lost their lands, other sectors were uprooted because they could not compete within the new capitalist economy: rancheros (medium-size farmers and ranchers) lost out to haciendas and cattle estates; artisans to imported and domestic manufactured goods; and arrieros (mule-herders) to railroads. Displaced by the market economy, these individuals joined landless peasants in forming the growing ranks of potential migratory wage earners. David Montgomery, the leading historian on the U.S. working class, best summarized the worldwide human movements of that period in an analysis also applicable to Mexico:

In the periphery, nineteenth-century capitalism destroyed established patterns of bondage and commercial life that had tied much of the population to the land, made the quest for money wages imperative, intensified national and religious persecution, and provided the railroads and steamships the means by which tens of millions of men and women could engage in what Frank Thistlethwaite has graphically called "proletariat globe-hopping."[6]

By 1910 approximately half a million people from central Mexico had settled in the U.S.-Mexican border states.

One of the explicit assumptions in the literature of Mexican migration is that Mexico had a surplus of labor and as a result could afford to release workers to the United States. This "escape-valve" premise only holds true for the post-1910 era, when the turmoil of the Mexican Revolution and other forms of social conflict disrupted the economy, leading to high levels of unemployment. During the Porfiriato, the labor shortages were so severe that landlords and other employers in the central and southern part of the country used various methods to retain scarce labor and keep wages low, including debt-peonage, sharecropping, company stores, and the suppression of unions. These measures were sanctioned by the Porfirian state.

Railroads played the dual role of integrating Mexico's export-oriented economy into the industrial world while at the same time facilitating the massive movements of people within Mexico and to the United States. Nuevo León and the border states, the region that sustained the greatest rates of economic growth in Mexico during the Porfiriato, competed not only with each other for the thousands of unskilled Mexican laborers, but also with the southwestern United States. The coming of the railroad to Mexico did not initially lure large numbers of migrants to the north. Mexican laborers were "pulled" by labor agents who went into central Mexico with the sole objective of recruiting potential workers.[7] Employers from northern Mexico and the United States hired professional labor contractors, also known as *enganchadores,* who recruited workers with offers of free transportation to the north and wage advances.[8] By 1907, however, labor recruitment in central Mexico had ended as the tide of human movement turned in the opposite direction—migrants on their own now sought labor recruiters in the northern states and at U.S. border towns or went directly to the centers of employment.[9]

"We desire that our brothers from the interior . . . settle in this [part of the] *frontera,*" a Saltillo newspaper declared, because the border states offered laborers, among other enticements, a salary two to three times greater than their former salary.[10] Migrant labor was indispensable for the growth of northern Mexico's economy. In Coahuila, the state manifesting the greatest rate of economic growth in the north, out-of-state migrants,

Table 4.1. MIGRANTS IN NORTHERN STATES, 1895–1910

State	Percentage of Out-of-State Migrants	State Population	Rate of Growth
Coahuila			
1895	26.43	241,026	131.46[a]
1900	25.75	296,938	50.23[b]
1910	31.30	362,092	247.73[c]
Chihuahua			
1895	4.67	262,772	45.75
1900	8.36	327,784	50.40
1910	12.12	405,707	24.75
Nuevo León			
1895	15.45	309,252	63.00
1900	13.56	327,937	18.08
1910	12.43	365,150	92.47
Sonora			
1895	4.88	191,281	72.62
1900	7.68	221,682	38.74
1910	12.65	265,383	139.50
Tamaulipas			
1895	15.54	206,502	47.50
1900	13.70	218,948	20.89
1910	13.15	249,640	78.32

Source: El Colegio de México, Estadísticas sociales del porfiriato, 1877–1910, pp. 68, 73–74, 107.
[a] 1877–1895.
[b] 1895–1910.
[c] 1877–1910.

heavily concentrated in urban centers, composed close to one-third of the state's population in 1910 (see Table 4.1). By 1900 migrants constituted over 50 percent of the inhabitants in Torreón and San Pedro de las Colonias, Coahuila's two largest cities, and 35 percent of Monterrey's 62,266 residents (in all likelihood an undercount). An estimated 270,000 migrants, or 15 percent of the total population, had settled in the five northern border states by 1910 (excluding the territory of Baja California).[11]

The north attracted a large labor pool from the interior by offering the highest wages in Mexico. Many arrived penniless in Chihuahua, Torreón, or Monterrey, often dressed in the typical garb of the *campesino*, "huaraches [sandals], *el calzón blanco* [white pants], and *el chilapeño* [white shirt]." [12] Most of them did not have any difficulty finding employment. In spite of the thousands of migrants who arrived in northern Mexico, however, employers continued to suffer from labor shortages throughout the Porfiriato. In part this was due to the fact that they had to compete for labor with U.S. employers, mostly those based in the southwestern border states, who paid significantly higher wages than in northern Mexico.

Upon arrival in the north, migrant workers quickly learned about the geography of wages in the two countries and that it was not difficult to find employment "on the other side," especially given the open border and labor shortages. Through the different migrant networks and contacts with other workers, they obtained "the exact information regarding what they should do on the other side, then they learned one or two English words. After that they leave." The decision to go north of the Río Bravo was not difficult to make. Wages in Texas were twice as high as in northern Mexico for unskilled labor, while the cost of living was not that much higher.[13] The Guggenheim operations, with smelters in Monterrey, Aguascalientes, and Pueblo, Colorado, provide an example of the difference in wages along national and regional lines. These operations paid their smelter workers in Pueblo two dollars (gold) a day. Meanwhile, their Monterrey workers earned a peso (silver) or forty cents in U.S. currency and their Aguascalientes workers sixty-two centavos (silver).[14]

Those who decided to try their fate on the "other side" usually worked for a short period in the northern Mexican mines, industries, and agricultural enterprises in order to earn enough money for a train ticket to one of the border towns. A third-class train ticket from Chihuahua City to Ciudad Juárez cost five pesos in 1907 or a week's wages.[15] Many of those who left for the United States were laborers who had been contracted to work for Mexican employers. *El Nuevo Mundo* reported on the motives that drove the migrant to crossing the border to the United States:

> Because of the close proximity to the United States, the recent arrivals hear about the good salaries. They learn that instead of a silver peso that they would earn on this side [of the boundary], they could earn a gold peso on the other side. On the day least expected, they leave without paying the hacendado who contracted them, gave them wage advancements, and paid for transportation fare.[16]

Northern employers, including Monterrey's industrialists, were constantly reminded that in the nearby border towns, such as Laredo, U.S.

labor agents, the so-called *enganchadores,* patiently waited for every passenger train to arrive from Mexico and caught their prey, the *enganchados* (the hooked ones). From the border towns *enganchadores* shipped newly arrived Mexican laborers to the cotton fields of Texas, to the sugar beet fields of Colorado, and, after 1910, to the industrial Midwest.[17] Labor agents and employers from north of the Río Bravo could always count on a continuous stream of Mexican laborers, one which a Laredo newspaper aptly described in 1904:

> During all the months of this year we have noted that many Mexicans, in numbers that have averaged more than 500 souls, cross daily to the United States. They emigrate in groups of five, seven, and up to twelve people. The groups are made up of men, women, and children who are dressed in the clothing of rural workers from Mexico's interior and who carry on their backs the few possessions they had in their miserable homes.[18]

The Mexican press attempted to counter the view of the United States as a nation of economic opportunity for Mexican immigrants. It highlighted the discrimination, unemployment, and the poor living and working conditions of the Mexican *braceros* in the United States. *El Monterrey News,* for example, reported that in the midst of the economic crisis of 1908–1909 more than 2,000 Mexicans walked the streets of El Paso, Texas, searching for work.[19] Such reporting did not deter the flow of immigrants. By 1910 the Mexican consuls were reporting that most immigrants were staying permanently in the United States and that they were bringing their families and friends with them.[20] According to the U.S. census, between 1900 and 1910 the Mexico-born population grew from 103,393 to 221,915, a figure that was probably much higher because many Mexicans did not register at the U.S. customs offices due to the open border.[21] Half of the Mexican immigrants settled in Texas, only a few hours away from Monterrey by train.[22] In 1910 the northern border states and the United States contained over half a million migrants from Mexico's interior.[23]

MONTERREY: A PORT OF ENTRY FOR THE NORTH

Monterrey's many industries operated within the context of a highly competitive border labor market. Unlike the northern haciendas, railroads, and mining enterprises, however, Monterrey's industrialists did not depend on *enganchadores* to recruit workers from Mexico's interior. *Regiomontano*

Table 4.2. OUT-OF-STATE MIGRANT FLOWS IN NUEVO LEÓN AND
MONTERREY FROM SELECTED STATES, 1895–1900

	Numbers of Migrants in Nuevo León		Numbers of Migrants in Monterrey		Percent of Migrants in Monterrey	
	(1895)	*(1900)*	*(1895)*	*(1900)*	*(1895)*	*(1900)*
Aguascalientes	557	662	387	473	69	71
Coahuila	7,364	6,639	3,881	4,165	53	63
Durango	754	561	406	439	54	78
Guanajuato	1,110	1,156	729	750	66	65
Jalisco	940	939	588	653	63	70
S. L. Potosí	22,941	21,600	8,735	11,253	38	52
Tamaulipas	6,036	5,520	1,364	2,037	23	37
Zacatecas	3,440	3,616	2,130	2,781	62	77
Total	43,142	40,693	18,220	22,551	42	55

Source: AGENL, Censos nacionales de 1895 y 1900.

employers counted on the trains to bring in many workers, who "arrived
from many states of the interior in search of employment."[24] Although
many migrants initially came to Monterrey, the leading railroad hub of
northern Mexico, it was the few who permanently stayed on who formed
the core of the first generation of the *regiomontano* industrial proletariat.

In 1891 the Nuevo León Smelting, Refining, and Manufacturing
Company and the Guggenheims' Gran Fundación Nacional initiated large-
scale smelting operations, thus launching Monterrey's industrialization.
In the neighboring states, especially in San Luis Potosí, Monterrey gained
a reputation as a center with vast employment opportunities and better
wages. Accordingly, thousands of migrants poured into the city in search of
the work readily available in the smelters, railroad yards, industries, workshops, and construction sites. In May 1901 *El Trueno* stated that "there
has been a large migration from the interior. There are many workers who
come in search of employment."[25] In that year over one-third of the city's
population consisted of out-of-state migrants, mainly from the neighboring
states of Coahuila, Zacatecas, Tamaulipas, and especially San Luis Potosí
(see Table 4.2).

Between 1895 and 1896 Monterrey's population increased from
40,765 to 56,674.[26] Given this rate of demographic growth, Monterrey

should have reached the 100,000 inhabitant mark by 1900. Instead, the city recorded 62,000 inhabitants in 1900 and would not reach 100,000 until 1920. Like a magnet, Monterrey attracted large numbers of migrants. But conditions in the city had the effect of propelling migrants to other parts. Monterrey, a major railroad center with outlets to the border towns of Piedras Negras, Nuevo Laredo, and Matamoros, attracted a large floating population of migrants who worked in the city for a period to earn enough money to carry them to other locations in northern Mexico and the United States. During their brief stay in the city, migrants acquired vital information about wages and working conditions in other parts of northern Mexico and in Texas.

In spite of the city's need for laborers, Monterrey was not an attractive place in which to settle. Not only did it have one of the worst climates in Mexico, with suffocatingly hot summers and extremely cold winters, but the city could not accommodate the constant flow of people. It suffered from severe housing shortages and a cost of living much higher than in the rest of the country.[27] Furthermore, Monterrey was struck by two disasters which led to population losses in the thousands. The yellow fever epidemic struck Nuevo León in 1903, claiming the lives of over 1,000 people, including 424 Monterrey residents. Over 15,000 panic-stricken people left the city.[28] Six years later, on August 29, 1909, the Santa Catarina River flooded and destroyed part of the working-class neighborhood of San Luisito. It is estimated that the flood killed anywhere from 1,300 to over 4,000 people in Nuevo León.[29]

Monterrey's industrialists benefited from the city's geographic location as the railroad hub of northern Mexico and as a port of entry to the north, including the United States. In a country with severe labor shortages, the advantage of location offered the opportunity to recruit among the thousands of potential workers who arrived in Monterrey in any given year. The large concentration of potential workers attracted labor recruiters from other areas. The Gran Fundación Nacional's manager complained to Reyes that a labor recruiter from Yucatán was recruiting his own labor force outside of the smelter plant and its mines.[30] The Sonora-based Moctezuma Copper Company solicited Bernardo Reyes's aid in securing workers from Nuevo León. Reyes rejected its request for local labor, responding that not only did Nuevo León also have labor shortages but Monterrey needed additional workers who could propel the "great expansion of its industries."[31] North Americans were also interested in recruiting in Monterrey. In 1907 Victor Clark, a labor economist for the U.S. Department of Commerce, went to Mexico to study Mexican immigration to the United States. *El Monterrey News* remarked on his investigative trip to Monterrey:

> He came to Mexico or, better stated, they sent him with the purpose of studying Mexican immigration to the United States. He said that they [Mexican workers] are well esteemed and liked [by employers] because of their satisfactory work and good behavior from California in the west, to Illinois in the east, and even in Wyoming and farther away where they are employed in ranching during the winter. In Texas, Louisiana, and Mississippi they are urgently solicited for labor in the cotton fields, in which they are irreplaceable. On the Santa Fe rail line they have replaced the Greeks, Japanese, and Italians. . . .[32]

LABOR RECRUITMENT IN MONTERREY

Despite the large mobile population residing in Monterrey at any given time and despite the relatively higher wages paid there compared to the rest of Mexico, city employers (including industrial, railroad, and building contractors) suffered from labor shortages throughout the 1890–1910 period. The "lack of workers" forced the managers of the Guggenheims to close some of their works in 1897.[33] Building contractors needed several thousand workers for Monterrey's vast infrastructural construction projects from 1906 to 1908, while railroad companies were "extremely affected in some direction for lack of workmen; labor never being so scarce as in the present. Placards and announcements are placed everywhere announcing the need for mechanics."[34]

Given the large mobile population and the labor shortages, employers had the difficult task of recruiting a permanent workforce. City employers, especially the large companies, had to experiment with different methods for recruiting and retaining labor. They first raised Monterrey's minimum wage and succeeded in attracting a steady flow of laborers into the factories. Managers quickly learned that a higher wage did not guarantee a dependable and permanent labor force, however, because other employers in the north and in the United States could at the very least match the salary or possibly double it. They had to provide labor with other incentives if they were to maintain a permanent labor force.

With the opening of the smelters in 1891, firms ranging from the Guggenheims' Gran Fundación Nacional to the smaller, independently operated Nuevo León Smelting, Refining, and Manufacturing Company transformed the overall local labor market in Monterrey. When these firms raised wages to three or even four times Monterrey's average of twenty-five centavos daily (as did the Guggenheims), other employers were forced to do the same if they were to retain their labor force. The Guggenheims did not have problems raising the minimum wage when it was necessary because the cost of labor in Mexico was much lower than in the United States. They expanded their Monterrey smelter to match the size of their Philadelphia Smelter Company in Pueblo, Colorado. The two smelters had a similar number of workers, and each plant processed 3,600 tons of ores each day.[35] The critical difference between the two smelters was that the Monterrey smelter was more profitable. Workers at the Pueblo plant earned two dollars (gold) a day while their Mexican counterparts in Monterrey were paid a peso (silver) a day or forty cents in U.S. currency. The weekly payroll for the Pueblo plant was 19,200 dollars, compared to 3,840 dollars for Monterrey.[36]

Almost overnight Monterrey surged from having one of the lowest urban wages in Mexico to one of the highest. Wages started in the smelters at seventy-five centavos to a peso a day for unskilled workers and three to six pesos for the skilled laborers, who were usually North Americans. In order to prevent their workforce from deserting to the smelters, other *regiomontano* employers had to raise salaries. Monterrey's wage scale for unskilled labor was considered high compared to the central or southern part of the country, where workers were paid fifty centavos per day or less, even as late as 1910 (see Table 4.3).

When the Gran Fundación Nacional's managers elevated Monterrey's average daily wage from twenty-five centavos a day to seventy-five centavos to one peso in 1891, they were shocked to discover that the promise of a higher wage was not a sure guarantee for sustaining a stable labor force. A fourfold wage increase simply meant that a local worker, long accustomed to the minimum wage of twenty-five centavos, could now earn it in one day rather than four and thus could not be relied upon to go to work every day.[37] Monterrey's employers shared with the Guggenheims' managers the problem of how to make a large and undisciplined labor force into a permanent and efficient working class. This was indeed a difficult task, considering that most workers were not born in the city and many with rural backgrounds lacked an understanding of the notions of punctuality, work "ethics," and even wage labor.

In addition to higher wages, employers had to experiment with dif-

Table 4.3. MINIMUM WAGES IN LEADING INDUSTRIAL FIRMS,
1902–1906 (IN PESOS)

Firm	1902	1906
Gran Fundación Nacional (ASARCO)	1.25	1.61
CMC y Afinadora de Monterrey	1.00	1.92
CF de Fierro y Manufacturera	3.00	3.00
Ladrillera de Monterrey	0.62	1.00
Cervecería Cuauhtémoc	0.81	1.00
Fábricas Apolo	0.75	1.00
Fundidora de Monterrey	0.75	3.73
Compañía Industrial de Monterrey	1.50	1.37
Fábrica de Azucar	0.50	—
La Leona	1.00	1.00
La Fama de Nuevo León	0.62	—

Source: AGENL, Correspondencia del Gobierno de Nuevo León con la Secretaría de Fomento 1896–1910, 1902–1906, and 1902–1907; Nuevo León, *Memoria de gobierno del Estado de Nuevo León 1903-1907*, 2 vols. (Monterrey: Imprenta de Gobierno, 1907), 2:806–814.

ferent methods aimed at maintaining, disciplining, and "socializing" the first generation of *regiomontano* workers, a generation of unskilled workers who had never had any previous experience in industrial environments. Besides pioneering the new minimum wage scale in Monterrey, the managers of the smelters quickly learned that in order to keep their workers and make them into efficient employees they had to offer other incentives. They recognized that housing shortages (especially in low-rent dwellings) plagued Monterrey.[38] Although all industrial firms in Monterrey had to keep up with the average seventy-five centavo to one peso daily wage, only the larger enterprises had the resources to provide subsidized or free housing. According to *La Voz de Nuevo León*, the Nuevo León Smelting, Refining, and Manufacturing Company secured a labor force by offering housing and "investing in accessories which are costly, but, in the end, lead to a reduction of its labor cost." The larger enterprises were aware that an incentive, such as reduced housing rents, was the necessary price to pay for a "reduction" in the "labor cost," meaning reducing the high labor turnover rate that plagued most industries in the city.[39]

Typical of larger firms in Monterrey that offered incentives was the Compañía Manufacturera de Monterrey, a brick factory that employed 240 workers in 1897, some of whom were children. Like many industries, it was located on the outskirts of the city. The wage scale ranged from thirty-three centavos per day for children to twice that amount for adults, which was below the city's unregulated minimum wage of seventy-five centavos to one peso. Lower wages were offset by the company's policy of providing housing for ninety-six families.[40] This firm also commissioned a merchant to establish a store on company property, hired a company guard for security, operated a school and a drugstore, and employed a doctor in residence. According to *El Espectador,* this was a model firm in spite of its lower wages because the company store sold goods much more cheaply than any other commercial establishment. Thus, "the real wage is superior to the gross wage, and not lower, as occurs in other enterprises, especially in some mining companies, which are truly well-organized *tiendas de raya* [company stores]."[41]

The Compañía Manufacturera de Monterrey fits the description of a typical company town: the firm provided housing, medical services, education, and the store where workers purchased their necessities through contract. Because of the company's monopoly powers, workers' wages returned directly to the company. Monterrey's "company towns," however, did differ from others in Mexico because of the open competition for labor—if company abuses displeased workers, they could easily find employment in other firms. Selecting employers was one of the benefits that workers had in a labor environment characterized by labor shortages, free labor, and labor mobility, including migrating to the United States.

Labor shortages, high labor turnover rates, proximity to the United States, and a region dominated by a free labor market forced Monterrey's employers to offer incentives which made them appear to be more benevolent than others. Without these constraints, the city's entrepreneurs would have behaved just like any other employer. For example, Monterrey capitalists owned the Compañía Carbonífera de Coahuila. The company essentially owned the coal-mining border town of Colombia, Nuevo León. As the main source of employment in Colombia and the owner of the major store, the firm paid the workers monthly in company chips, instead of the customary weekly pay in cash.[42] Moreover, the company discriminated against local residents by hiring mainly outside workers who, according to the locals, were *tributarios* (tributaries) of the firms.[43] Perhaps this firm preferred outside workers, because in 1901 the town miners threatened a rebellion against the abusive practices of the company. The town's *jefe político* called for troops, fearing a surprise assault against the town by the local coal workers.[44]

THE PROLETARIANIZATION OF THE
REGIOMONTANO WORKING CLASS

Industrialists attempted to inculcate in the first generation of industrial workers the principle of work efficiency. Capitalists like Pablo González Garza, Mexico's "king of the corn mills," especially wanted to instill the work ethic in the nascent working class. González Garza, who owned over a hundred corn mills in Mexico, was fond of providing the following advice: "the best charity you can give to people is to teach them how to work."[45] This was also the philosophy that Monterrey's entrepreneurs attempted to put into practice. Labor discipline and efficiency were important to firms like the Compañía Minera, Fundidora y Afinadora de Monterrey, which, at least until 1907, had not stopped its operations for one day since its founding in 1890.[46]

From an industrial proletariat of just 571 workers in 1890, the *regiomontano* working class had grown to over ten thousand by the eve of the Revolution.[47] By 1906 twelve industrial firms employed over one hundred workers each, with three enterprises employing over 1,000 workers (see Table 4.4). Higher wages and a series of other incentives (such as free or low-rent housing) lured workers into the factories, but they did not always guarantee the creation of permanent and efficient employees, largely due to the managers' early and uncompromising methods. They attempted to create disciplined workers by force, requiring them to work ten to twelve hours a day, without a day of rest during the week. Because workers usually got paid on Sunday nights, they often failed to report to work on Mondays. Without a rest day, *san lunes* (saint Monday) became the unofficial day of "rest" for the *regiomontano* working class, with drinking its favorite pastime.

An editorial in *La Defensa del Pueblo* condemned *san lunes* and drinking:

The custom of the great majority of our workers has become to consecrate Monday as a day of rest, if the state of drunkenness to which they have surrendered could be called rest. Because of their state of intoxication they fail to go to work for two or three days and sometimes, when this vice has entirely dominated them, the entire week. It has been the custom of the *patrón* [boss] to force workers to toil on Saturday nights, Sunday mornings, and sometimes the entire day. From then on they enter a state of drunkenness. They do so because

Table 4.4. COMPANIES WITH 100 OR MORE EMPLOYEES, 1906

Company	Production Value (in pesos)	Employees
Fundidora de Monterrey	5,000,000	1,700
Gran Fundación Nacional	11,438,007	1,485
Cervecería Cuauhtémoc	1,920,000	1,000
CMF Afinadora de Monterrey	8,727,608	700
El Porvenir	623,283	470
CF de Fierro de Monterrey	200,000	200
Ladrillera de Monterrey	400,000	175–200
CM de Cerillos de Monterrey	200,000	140–150
Compañía Industrial de Monterrey	169,000	128
La Fama	179,000	120
Ladrillera Unión	200,000	100
Fábrica de Cementos	350,000	100
Total	29,406,898	6,318–6,353

Source: Compiled from La Voz de Nuevo León, March 30, 1907.

of the workers' low level of organization, poor nutrition, and an imperfect moral education. It is within their nature to search for a way of resting, seeking to restore strength to their tired bodies. And following the instincts of their own nature, they enter into a state of intoxication in the absence of an honest form of distraction that could enlighten their spirit.

The worker who gets drunk on Mondays harms the employer who knows that on that day and the following, he cannot make a commitment to take on any kind of work because he would not have the laborers and thus fails to make a profit.[48]

La Defensa del Pueblo pinpointed one of the major labor relation problems of Monterrey's early industrialization: the tensions between managements' harsh methods as they sought to create a permanent and efficient workforce and workers' resistance (e.g., san lunes) to those methods. The experience of labor shortages and high turnover rates within a large labor market of "drifters," as well as san lunes, forced managers (especially those of the smelters) to devise new incentives. The smelters offered wage bonuses to those who would work for twenty-five consecutive days. In 1903 metal workers earned a minimum wage of seventy-five centavos to one peso daily. The additional fifty-centavo daily bonus was given to workers who worked for twenty-five consecutive days: 12.50 pesos could be collected at the end of the required twenty-five-day stint.

In the long run, metal workers had to pay a high price for the benefits of this incentive: a twelve- to fourteen-hour working day and a seven-day work week, conditions that quickly undermined workers' health. Because workers would lose their entire bonus of 12.50 pesos if they missed just one day, they often hired another worker to substitute for them on days when they were absent or recuperating from exhaustion.[49] *El Trueno* reported on the human cost of the bonus practice:

> The daily salary of 1.50 pesos to the worker is meager, especially when the worker has to perform such hard, unpleasant, and dangerous work. During his daily task the worker absorbs metallic and deadly gases through his skin and lungs. And if he continues poisoning himself for thirty consecutive days, he could be on the verge of entering the grave, especially when the worker does not follow the required hygienic guidelines of the profession due to his ignorance, poverty, or other circumstances. It is for these reasons that somewhere between the tenth and fifteenth day since beginning his stint, the worker almost always gets sick. He then has to find another individual who can substitute for him while he recovers physically, so that he won't lose his bonus.[50]

Certainly, that pace of work must have led to many work-related accidents. Records of accidents in Monterrey's smelters are not available. If the Guggenheim plant in Pueblo, Colorado, is any indicator, however, one can surmise that there were many. In 1913, for instance, one out of every four workers there suffered a disabling accident.[51] The wage bonus incentive shortened the lives of many workers, but it greatly profited the owners of companies like the Compañía Minera, Fundidora y Afinadora de Monterrey, which was able to operate continuously after opening its doors in 1890. Not all workers were willing to risk their health for an additional fifty centavos a day, however.

Choosing their employer was one of the benefits that workers had in a free labor environment. The manager of one of the smelters complained that the railroad labor agent from Yucatán was succeeding in recruiting workers outside of his plant even though his labor competitor "only offers our workers fifty centavos a day, while we pay six *reales* [seventy-five centavos] and some even get a peso."[52] With the expansion of Monterrey's infrastructure in 1907–1908, hundreds of workers "deserted the factories," including the American Smelting and Refining Company (ASARCO) plant, for less strenuous employment in construction. These enterprises suffered from the "lack of workers." [53] To prevent more "desertions" and to recruit additional workers, the American Smelting and Refining Company once again took the lead in raising the city's minimum wage. According to *El Monterrey News,* this increase in the minimum wage was due "to the lack of workers here in Mexico, obligating [the company] to retain its employees with all kinds of benefits." [54] The minimum wage had stabilized at one peso at the smaller firms and more at the larger enterprises by 1906 (see Table 4.3).

After ten years of experience in large-scale employment and industrial organization, management at best had lukewarm results in creating a disciplined and permanent labor force from a working class composed predominantly of out-of-state migrants. Records of the Compañía Aurífera del Pánuco provide one of the few sources of information about wages and the number of days laborers worked. Thirty-eight workers were employed during the month of April in 1900, earning from a minimum of thirty-seven centavos a day (probably children) to a maximum of two pesos. Some workers worked the thirty days, while others worked only for a few days. One can infer from this either that employment was irregular (because workers averaged only fifteen and a half days that month) or that they worked whenever they wanted. The probable explanation for the lower than expected monthly payroll of 591.50 pesos is that workers continued to resist the seven-day work week. [55]

Management's attempts to produce a more efficient and disciplined working class faced other obstacles, especially those created by the abusive and hated *mayordomos* (foremen), many of whom were North American. In the absence of natively trained personnel and skilled workers, Monterrey's industrialists recruited them from Europe and the United States. It is possible, therefore, that foremen in Monterrey's industries, like foremen in the United States, had tremendous powers within the firms and over workers. Daniel Nelson, a labor historian, discusses the role of the foreman before the era of scientific management in the United States (pre-1910):

The foreman performed several important functions relative to the workers. First, and most important, he "got the work out," a job that varied from industry to industry, depending on the degree of management participation in production decisions. A second function was to interpret the management's policies to the worker, a much less onerous task. Finally the foreman hired, trained, motivated, and disciplined the workers.[56]

Indeed, the workplace was the "foreman's empire," where he often abused his powers. In Monterrey it was not uncommon for the foreman to lay off the worker a day or two before the bonus period ended and employ someone else—the foreman could then collect the bonus belonging to the worker.[57] Other abuses included accepting bribes from workers desiring a transfer to another department within the firm and fining employees for tardiness or for the production of faulty goods. Foremen often earned an extra 60 to 80 pesos a month, in addition to the company salary, from fines on workers.[58] As in the United States, Monterrey's management later sought to reduce the power of the foreman, including the elimination of these abusive practices.

THE "MEXICANIZATION" OF THE LABOR FORCE

A large urban working class emerged from virtually nothing over a twenty-year period. From less than 1,000 in 1890, the working class in Monterrey and the surrounding municipalities had grown to well over 10,000 by 1910, laboring in various occupations in industry, mining, construction, commerce, transportation, and domestic services. In 1907 the four largest industrial enterprises employed close to 5,000 workers, while 3,000 labored in the construction of Monterrey's water and sewage systems and electric urban rail lines.[59] According to the 1900 municipal census, the city also contained large concentrations of nonindustrial workers: 1,067 miners; 1,044 *albañiles* (construction workers); 1,043 carpenters; 1,106 tailors and shoemakers; and close to 6,000 domestic workers. Monterrey's labor hierarchy had been fairly well established by 1900, ranging from management on top of the wage scale to women and children at the bottom. Managers, foremen, and semiskilled and skilled workers, almost all foreigners, held the highest and mid-level positions. Mexican unskilled workers held the bottom positions. The labor composition of the workforce employed by the Monterrey Water Works, a Canadian-owned enterprise, illustrates this hierarchy. At the height of construction in 1907, the company hired between 2,000 to 3,000 workers, most of them unskilled laborers. Foremen earned 6 to 10 pesos daily; crane men, 6; cast-iron pipe joiners, 4.50. Most of these skilled workers were North Americans. Mexican masons and bricklayers earned 3 to 4 pesos; carpenters, 2 to 2.50; unskilled workers, 1 to 1.25; and children, 37½ to 50 centavos.

The working class was composed of unskilled Mexican and skilled foreign workers. Women and children were also heavily represented. The textile, hat, and food manufacturers employed large numbers of women workers. Women composed one-third of the 200 workers of El Porvenir textile mill in 1891 and held 20 of the 25 positions at the Compañía Manufacturera de Monterrey. Even though they performed the same work, women earned from two-thirds to three-fourths the wage of males.[60] Outside of the industrial firms, women were concentrated in different types of "domestic" occupations. Women occupied 717 of the 759 laundress positions and dominated the seamstress profession (500 in all). Among the most exploited workers were the 1,700 women *criadas* (maids).[61] A cook in an elite household earned ten pesos a month working sixteen hours a day, from seven in the morning to eleven at night. Many domestic workers supplemented their incomes by sewing for twenty-five centavos a day.[62]

Through different labor strategies (ranging from raising the 25-centavo minimum wage three- or fourfold to wage bonuses), management had secured a large enough labor force, which at least in the smelters and "under American and European supervision" operated "some of the largest plants in the world."[63] Producing over 18 million dollars in metals by 1900, Monterrey had become one of the leading smelting centers in the world, smelting over one-fourth of the total ores in Mexico.[64] In the smelters, management had not overcome labor turnover rates and *san lunes*, but had made significant gains with wage bonuses. George Conway, the chief engineer of Monterrey's massive water and sewage works of 1907–1908, reflected what might have been management's attitude toward Mexican labor in the waning days of the Porfiriato:

> For the ordinary skilled and low-skilled labor, Mexicans were employed exclusively, and, on the work, which was quite new to them, they proved entirely efficient and satisfactory; throughout the work, on which at some periods between 2,000 to 3,000 men were employed, chiefly under the Company's direct administration, they were very tractable and willing to do their best, and no trouble was experienced at any time. The Mexican "peon" and also the ordinary skilled workman in the north of Mexico, is intelligent, and is excellent for purely routine work, but he is not adaptable or resourceful in the case of an emergency. Under intelligent and careful supervision, however, it is quite possible to get as good results as could be obtained anywhere.[65]

Chauvinism aside, Conway's evaluation of Mexican labor was representative of an attitude shared by other managers. After more than ten years of struggling to discipline labor, management had developed sufficient confidence in Mexican workers' abilities to engage them in more challenging tasks. Monterrey's workers had apparently reached a level that distinguished them from their counterparts in other parts of Mexico. A student of Mexican labor noted that "peasants" made up the majority of the smelter workers at Aguascalientes and that they "usually leave work in July to put in their crops. There is a constant labor shortage, though the manager said his best laborers did not migrate." [66] Laborers in Monterrey did not have the same options as those in Aguascalientes. It was almost impossible for Monterrey's workers to return to their original homes to farm the land, if they had any, because the city was a long way from their original home. They had become dependent on wage labor for their subsistence.

Management's next step in its enduring struggle to create more efficient and disciplined native workers was to "Mexicanize" the labor force. This process involved training a considerable portion of the unskilled labor force to be the semiskilled and skilled workers who could perform the full range of complex tasks involved in industrial production. The ever growing need for more semiskilled and skilled workers and the fact that foreign workers were becoming too expensive—not altruism—forced the cost-minded managers to reevaluate the role of native workers. The need to produce a native working class with greater skills was noted by *La Unión*, a Monterrey newspaper:

> The severe lack of workers who understand the operations of different machines that are being employed with the growth of our businesses is becoming more and more notable every day. Some businesses have never gotten off the ground because of this.[67]

One of the aims of "Mexicanizing" the labor force involved reducing the dependence on high-priced foreign workers who had been recruited during the early phases of Monterrey's industrialization to do indispensable jobs for which the native laborers were poorly equipped.

All of the equipment and machinery for new enterprises in Monterrey (and the rest of Mexico) was imported from abroad, along with most of the semiskilled and skilled workers and managers. Foreign workers made up 5 percent of Mexico's total industrial working class by 1910, a proportion that might have been higher in Monterrey.[68] Mexico's largest enterprises, including those in Monterrey, depended on foreign workers for all phases of production, from supervision to machine repair. The Cuauhtémoc Brewery recruited most of its skilled personnel, from the foremen to the brewmaster, in Germany, as did Fábrica de Vidrios y Cristales de Monterrey. North Americans held all of the mechanic positions in these two firms.[69]

To attract foreign workers to Monterrey, managers had to offer them higher wages than those they had received in their native countries, in addition to free housing and other incentives. The Guggenheims, for instance, offered their foreign workers comfortable living quarters, a recreation hall with an auditorium, and a sports field with a bowling alley.[70] The Fundidora de Monterrey built the Colonia Acero for its key personnel. This neighborhood of skilled and semiskilled workers contained a hotel with 55 rooms, 120 houses, a company store, and a hospital.[71] Without these attractions industries would have had to close, because native labor did not have the necessary skills to run the enterprises.

By virtue of their skills and their trade unions, foreign workers commanded great leverage over management. They brought with them their organizational practices and traditions. German glassblowers arrived in Monterrey already organized into a craft guild, while North American railroad workers had their own union. Foreign workers used their trade unions to bargain with management over wages, working, and living conditions. While very little research has been done on the role of foreign trade unions in Mexico, U.S. craft unions apparently operated differently than the German ones. For the most part, Americans, primarily railroad workers, used their craft unions to exclude native workers from the skilled and semiskilled occupations.[72] German glassblowers, however, accepted Mexican apprentices.[73]

After a decade of "proletarianization" many managers believed that many unskilled Mexican workers were ready to move upward into the ranks of the semiskilled and skilled craftsmen. To upgrade the skills of their Mexican labor force, management offered apprenticeships, the experience of "trial and error," and technical education. At the Fábrica de Vidrios y Cristales de Monterrey skilled German glassblowers trained Mexican apprentices. After a few years of training, these Mexican apprentices had acquired many of the intricate skills of glassmaking.[74] The Fundidora de Monterrey founded the Escuelas Acero in 1912, the Cuauhtémoc Brewery established the Escuela Politécnica Cuauhtémoc in 1911, and the Reyista government opened a technical school which mainly catered to railroad workers. The Fundidora was also known as "La Maestranza" (the teacher) because it produced the first generation of native steelworkers.

Through the use of apprenticeships, technical schools, and sheer trial and error, Monterrey's managers had successfully upgraded the skills of many of the common workers to the point that by the mid-1900s Mexicans began to displace many of the foreign skilled workers. At one of the foundries management raised the occupational status "of the Mexican artisan to theirs [Americans'], in salary, rights, and guarantees." [75] Some native workers were even promoted to the position of department supervisors within this firm. The Cuauhtémoc Brewery promoted a Mexican to foreman of the ice plant.[76] Along with the occupational promotion of native labor came an increase in wages. At the above-mentioned foundry, the Mexican workers' daily wage was raised to the scale of foreign workers at 5 to 7.5 pesos per day. In the accounting department of the Canadian-owned Monterrey Water Works two Mexicans earned 225 pesos a month, while a few were employed in the engineering department, earning from a low of 35 pesos a month to a high of 250.[77]

Given the trend of replacing foreign workers with Mexicans, a considerable number of common laborers benefited from occupational mobility. One of these workers, who rose through the ranks of the *regiomontano* working class, remembered: "After I finished school, I began working in a smelter. . . . It did not take long to get into work which required some skill and I was paid ten dollars a day. This was good pay for a young man at that time." [78] Upward mobility, however, did not guarantee that the worker would make a commitment to the enterprise. In the case of this worker, he saved enough money to abandon the smelter and open a grocery store in Monterrey.[79] Nor did it mean that Mexican semiskilled and skilled workers were sufficiently trained to take over all aspects of production. Trained Mexican glassblowers replaced all the German workers after they went on strike at the Fábrica de Vidrios y Cristales de Monterrey. But the quality of their work was not as good, forcing management to close down the plant in 1904.

From the foundries to the Cuauhtémoc Brewery, the cost-minded managers made a strong push to promote Mexican laborers to the skilled positions in the final years of the Porfiriato. Management's policies supporting occupational mobility for Mexican workers emerged in the midst of growing labor unrest in the last five years of the Porfiriato, mainly from native railroad workers, and middle-class nationalist agitation. Railroad workers agitated foremost against U.S. workers who controlled the key semiskilled and skilled positions within this industry. Nonetheless, it is possible that Monterrey's working-class occupational mobility was independent of those political activities. Evidently, enough Mexicans had reached the semiskilled and skilled levels that foreign workers were expendable. U.S. craft workers demanded "American wages," while the unorganized semiskilled and skilled Mexican workers could be paid "Mexican wages." U.S. machinists were paid 125 dollars a month, which was double the pay of a Mexican with the same skills.[80]

U.S. workers used their unions to oppose management's efforts to weaken their privileged position in Mexico, especially those policies aimed at promoting native workers to the semiskilled or skilled level. In 1898 a U.S. railroad worker physically attacked a Mexican worker who had been promoted. Fifty-one of the U.S. workers went on strike, perhaps in solidarity with their colleague, who was arrested by the Reyista authorities. The authorities used the "vagrancy" law to end the strike. In all likelihood these workers were deported, just like the German glass workers who waged a strike in 1904.[81]

U.S. railroad workers continued to agitate against Mexican occupational mobility throughout the 1900s, but they were not the only U.S. workers to challenge management over the promotion of Mexicans.[82] American foundry workers belonged to a "well-organized union" which opposed both wage increases and the promotions of native labor. The foundry's manager, James Feeney, feared a violent reprisal from the union members because they were

> a resentful group, who for a long time have challenged me, because I have not placed them in the special category of "distinción" [distinction] that would benefit them and be used against the interest of the Mexican workers, whom I pledge to grant an opportunity by teaching and educating them so that they can move up within this enterprise. I have the great satisfaction that this goal has been accomplished. I have not only been limited to teaching them, but I have also steadily raised the salary of the Mexicans from 50 and 75 centavos a day to the superior salaries of $5, $6 and $7.50.[83]

For these actions, the U.S. workers called the manager "a Mexican lover." Not all foreign craft opposition to management was based on Mexican upward mobility, however. The glassblowers' strike of 1904 was provoked by working conditions, not by the occupational advancement of the Mexican workers. This strike also ended in defeat when the government authorities deported all of the German workers. In any event, management used the promotion of Mexican workers to weaken the bargaining power of foreign workers, who were well organized in trade unions.

By the end of the Porfiriato the major industries of Monterrey had successfully created the first generation of industrial workers—a relatively permanent, reliable, and efficient workforce. This workforce, however, was no longer a homogeneous mass of unskilled workers, as in the early years. By 1910 Mexican skilled and semiskilled workers, who were paid two to three times more, labored next to the unskilled workers, who in turn were paid twice as much as women workers and three times more than children. A household could thus have a father who earned a peso a day, the mother fifty centavos, a boy thirty-three centavos, and a girl twenty-five centavos. These wages, however low or stratified, were among the highest in the country, paid by industrialists who were anxious to secure (in the midst of labor scarcity) a dependable, hard-working labor force for Monterrey's burgeoning companies. Because wages alone could not guarantee or maintain employee stability, the industries offered the additional incentives of wage bonuses and in some cases upward mobility. All these conditions not only shaped the first generation of *regiomontano* workers but transformed Monterrey from a declining commercial center into the "Chicago of Mexico"—the largest and most diverse industrial center, home to one of the most powerful regional elites in Mexico and to one of the nation's largest concentrations of workers.

THE CHILDREN OF THE *REGIOMONTANO* WORKING CLASS

"The trains that have arrived in the city are loaded with families who are migrating to Monterrey," *La Voz de Nuevo León* reported in 1903; "the city like an immense sea receives these contingents of population and working people." [84] More precisely, Monterrey's employers welcomed these migrants as indispensable sources of labor, considering that the city itself was not producing the labor force required for the continuation of its economic expansion. This is highlighted by the city's demographic growth. It boomed from 40,765 people in 1895 to 56,674 in 1896, an increase of almost 16,000. Monterrey registered 2,446 births and 1,996 deaths, for a population gain of 500, during the first six months (January 1–June 30) of 1895 and 1896. [85]

The fact that Monterrey registered more births than deaths in 1895 and 1896 was a rare feat. Monterrey recorded 23,107 births and 25,592 deaths during the entire 1903–1910 period, for a shocking population loss of 2,485. In contrast, the entire state, including Monterrey, registered 35,485 more births than deaths during this same period.[86] According to *Estadísticas sociales del porfiriato*, the best collection of statistics on Mexican society during the Porfiriato, migrants from other states made up 35 percent of the 62,266 residents in Monterrey.[87] The data on births and deaths in Monterrey strongly suggest that the city's growth depended entirely on migrants.

As has been mentioned, Monterrey attracted thousands of people in any given year. Nonetheless, the city retained only a small percentage of them. Thus, in this labor-starved environment with high labor turnover rates, management experimented with various incentives to create a permanent and disciplined labor force, including wage bonuses in the smelters, upward mobility in railroads and the foundries, schooling (the Cuauhtémoc Brewery and the Fundidora de Monterrey), reducing the hours of the work day (the brewery), subsidized or free housing, and, when necessary, raising the minimum wage (ASARCO). Another experiment involved the recruitment of children with the aim of molding them into a disciplined and permanent workforce for the future.

It was difficult being a child of a *regiomontano* working-class family for two major reasons. As in the rest of Mexico, children entered the labor force in large numbers and at an early age. Few of them went to school, and they had no option but to mature quickly into adulthood. Second, Monterrey had very high death rates among children, much higher than in the countryside. Children who did not live past their first birthday composed 10,000 of the 25,592 deaths registered in Monterrey from 1903 to 1910, around 39 percent.[88] In addition to receiving poor medical treatment, the working class lived in overcrowded living quarters, while their neighborhoods lacked potable water and raw sewage drained in open sewers, conditions that caused the spread of disease among children.[89]

If the working-class child was one of the fortunate half to reach the age of five (over 50 percent of children in Monterrey died before that age), then it was quite likely that she or he did not attend school. In 1900 Monterrey contained close to 18,000 children between the ages of five and fifteen. Of these, 8,644 were classified as "escolares," students who attended private and public schools.[90] The great majority of the working-class children did not go to school, a point confirmed by data collected from five working-class neighborhoods outside of Monterrey's city limits, where only 26 out of 773 school-age children attended school.[91]

Economic necessity compelled working-class children to mature quickly in the city. The labor of children or teenagers (twelve years and older) constituted one of the main features in the formation of the *regiomontano* working class during its formative period. In the absence of company records to analyze, one can only speculate on the basis of scattered evidence and the history of other countries, including the United States, that Monterrey's firms employed large numbers of children. In a city with an early industrial history of high labor-turnover rates, the desperate search for labor propelled many of the firms to employ children, especially boys. In what might have appeared to be a long struggle to "discipline" adults into permanent laborers, children represented a future investment for capitalists. They perhaps considered children to be more reliable employees, because children had families and could not simply pack their bags and leave like the adult "drifters" who made up a large portion of the working class. Employing children allowed management to "socialize" them into a permanent labor force, including "schooling" them for the higher tasks of semiskilled and skilled labor. The Cuauhtémoc Brewery, for instance, employed "young Mexican men" as apprentices to German skilled glassblowers.[92] Children might have also represented an opportunity to correct at an early age what management might have deemed to be deviant working-class behavior: absenteeism, low levels of "ambition," and *san lunes*. Work conceivably also had its advantages for children. It gave them a sense of pride and self-worth to help their families with an extra income. Work quickly opened the cultural doors into adulthood—because they earned money, children could drink and smoke and socialize with adults. Work gave them a certain degree of control over their destiny, an awareness expressed by a young man who secured a job at the ASARCO smelter: "I was very happy when I started working and I did not regret going back to school because for the first time I had something secure that was mine. I was happy, I felt like a complete man." [93]

Young workers had greater opportunities for upward mobility within the firms than older workers, especially in enterprises seeking to "Mexicanize" their labor force, such as the Fundidora de Monterrey and the Cuauhtémoc Brewery. Perhaps the reason for this was that management believed that youths could learn the necessary skills faster than older workers. Most workers acquired their skills as apprentices or through on-the-job experience. This was the case of Dámaso Martínez, a native of Guanajuato, who arrived in Monterrey in 1901 at the age of nine. At twelve he started working for the railroad as an assistant to a mechanic while attending a public school. This ambitious young worker moved up the skills ranks, and by the time he was eighteen he was a fireman (*encendedor de máquina*).[94] In another case, a woman recounted that her father started working at the Fundidora de Monterrey in 1905 at the age of twelve, the same age at which Martínez began working for the railroad.[95]

In the absence of reliable records, it is difficult to ascertain labor turnover rates among younger workers. The few pieces of evidence suggest that children started working at a firm and remained as permanent employees until age or illness forced them into retirement. A woman recalled that the labor force of the Fundidora de Monterrey was made up of "generations and generations" of family members: "my father worked in *la maestranza,* as it was called then. So did the father of my husband." Not only did her husband work at the steel mill, but so did her four sons.[96] If not for the closure of the steel mill in 1986, her grandchildren might also have followed in the same footsteps. At any rate, this family with three generations of steel workers was not unique—the "generations and generations" of families appeared to be the rule in other enterprises.[97] This same pattern holds true for the Cuauhtémoc Brewery, which had a policy of favoring the employment of the sons of its workers. In another case, Braulio and Daniel Colchado, the leaders of the 1914 metal workers' strike, had worked at the Compañía Fundidora y Afinadora de Monterrey "since they were children."[98]

RURAL NUEVO LEÓN IN THE MAKING OF THE BORDER LABOR MARKET

In 1893 Guillermo Leaske requested from Governor Reyes information pertaining to Nuevo León's labor conditions. Leaske, a representative of British investors in southern Mexico, asked Reyes if it was true that Nuevo León was burdened with unemployment, poverty, and overall misery. He was basically proposing that Reyes could help Nuevo León escape from these dreadful conditions by allowing him to recruit laborers who could be used for the plantations in Veracruz, Chiapas, and Oaxaca.[99] The typecasting of Nuevo León as a poor state annoyed Reyes, who, from the outset of his rule in Nuevo León, wanted to cultivate the overall image of "progress" for his adopted state. Politely but bluntly, he responded to Leaske that in Nuevo León "there is no misery and unemployment" and that "there is no need for people to migrate." Moreover, Reyes emphasized that Nuevo León attracted migrants from other states, who could easily find plenty of employment opportunities.[100]

Perhaps Reyes was just responding to conditions in Monterrey, a city with a migrant majority and vast employment opportunities, because wages and labor conditions in the Nuevoleonese countryside were a world apart from those in the city. The only important feature shared by city and countryside was that both suffered from labor shortages. In contrast to Nuevo León's rural employers, who shared with Aguascalientes the dubious distinction of paying the lowest rural wages in Mexico (an average daily wage of 18¾ centavos), Monterrey's employers paid from 75 centavos to a peso a day.[101]

If both the Nuevoleonese city and countryside operated within the context of an emerging border labor market largely based on intense employer competition for scarce labor, why did Monterrey employers pay two to three times more for common laborers than hacendados, the largest employers of rural workers? A simple geographic and economic answer to this question would emphasize the importance of location in determining wages within this emerging border labor market. Higher wages were determined by proximity to Monterrey and the U.S. boundary (see Table 4.4). This type of answer, however, cannot explain why southern Nuevo León, where most rural workers resided, paid among the lowest wages in Mexico as late as 1910.

At the time, some argued that rural people were satisfied staying at home, living in poverty. A newspaper took this point of view in commenting on the reasons why people prefer exploitation by landlords rather than searching for a better life in Monterrey:

> There is no explanation as to why in the ranches, haciendas, and small towns there are *domésticos* [rural workers] who earn ten to twelve *reales* a month working up a "good sweat under the holy sun," as their *amos* [employers] like to say, when in Monterrey they could earn such good salaries. . . . In the villages men earn 25 centavos a day to 31 centavos at most or, better stated, between 4 and 6 pesos each month and a weekly ration of 16 liters of corn and do so by *sudando la gota gorda* [working hard]. Meanwhile, in Monterrey there is a need for men to perform hard work in the Gran Fundación Nacional, in the factories, etc., where the daily wages range from 75 centavos a day to 1.50 and up to 2 pesos. Love for the NATIVE SOIL [*amor al terruño*]! That is what makes the Mexican poor. We die, even of hunger, exactly in the same place where we were born, without ever leaving it.[102]

Unlike most rural people in southern and central Mexico, Nuevo León's rural laboring population—from the landowning *vecinos* struggling to subsist on their plots of land to the landless indebted peons and sharecroppers—had the option of migrating to Texas, where wages were significantly higher than in northern Mexico. Nuevo León is not known in the literature on Mexican immigration as a "sender" of labor. Yet Nuevoleonese migrations to the "other side" preceded the mass migration of Mexicans of the twentieth century. In fact, along with Coahuila and Tamaulipas, Nuevo León has the longest history of Mexican immigration to the United States, a history that began with the creation of the 1848 boundary.

Between 1848 and the coming of the railroad in the 1880s, rural people primarily left northeastern Mexico for two reasons: either because they had accumulated large debts to hacendados or because of Mexico's political instability and economic collapse. An 1873 Mexican government study reported on these two types of immigrants who had settled in Texas. The first was made up of *jornaleros* (hacienda laborers), "who, due to the labor shortages and the nature of work in these states [the northeast], are given large advances for their future work." They fled to Texas so that they could escape from the debts they had incurred with landlords. The second group was "made up of honest and hard working people who fled the revolutions in their country." [103] Juan Salazar, a runaway peon, typified the migrant who sought freedom from a life of servitude in Nuevo León's haciendas. He fled far away from the hacienda in 1866, settling in Montana, where he stayed for thirty-nine years.[104] Ramón and Diego Sánchez exemplified the second type of immigrants, who left for reasons related to Mexico's political and economic instability. In 1874 both settled in Dimmit County, Texas, where they worked in ranching, one of the main employers of Mexican labor in Texas.[105]

During the Porfiriato, Mexican immigrant labor was instrumental in Texas's economic shift from ranching to commercial agriculture, especially in south Texas.[106] Attracted by higher wages than those paid in their municipalities, many Nuevoleoneses left for Texas, one because he "heard that there was work and good wages on the tracks and picking cotton." [107] While no quantitative data are available on the origins of Mexican natives who emigrated to the United States, migration patterns to Dimmit County indicate that Nuevoleoneses formed one of the largest groups of Mexicans residing in south Texas. Of the 793 residents of Dimmit County in the early 1930s who were baptized in Mexico, 70 percent came from Coahuila and Nuevo León.[108] More importantly, the Texas–northeastern Mexico migrant network, in existence since 1848, was firmly grounded by the turn of the twentieth century as people migrated back and forth.[109]

Between 1858 and 1910 wages for a Mexican cowboy in Texas increased from six dollars a month to twenty-five. One immigrant in Texas saved six thousand dollars between 1908 and 1917.[110] Once settled, this immigrant brought his family, just as the Sánchez family had been doing since 1874. By 1930 the Sánchez family numbered sixty in Dimmit County.[111] Juan Salazar, the runaway peon who had settled in Montana, later returned to Nuevo León with over sixteen thousand pesos that he had saved in his thirty-nine-year stay in the United States.[112] With wages ranging from thirty-seven Mexican centavos in southern municipalities to seventy-five in the northern part of Nuevo León in 1910, no rural worker in Nuevo León, or for that matter in Mexico, could have saved such large sums of money. Despite discrimination, poor treatment, and lower wages than native workers, Mexican immigrants poured into the United States after 1900.

Monterrey, as a port of entry for migrants heading to northern Mexico and the United States, and the countryside were fertile ground for the recruitment of labor. With the lowest wages in Mexico in 1891 (an average monthly salary of 5.63 pesos), the countryside was ripe with recruitment prospects. Hacendados from Cadereyta Jiménez went to Doctor Arroyo to recruit labor because

> it has been more and more difficult to attend [our fields] with care due to the lack of field hands, and this is a grave disadvantage not only for us but for the entire town in which we live. To remedy this inconvenience, I have adopted the means of going personally, or through a labor agent, to recruit laborers to the city of Doctor Arroyo.[113]

In-state hacendados competed not only with each other for laborers, but also with out-of-state labor recruiters. Labor *enganchadores,* especially those from neighboring Coahuila, lured rural labor away from the state. A Coahuilan *enganchador,* for example, recruited sharecroppers in Galeana, paying for half of the transportation fare and providing land, seeds, and mules. The *medieros,* in return, were to give the landlord half of their cotton, maize, and bean production.[114]

Throughout most parts of northern Mexico hacendados maintained a labor force by offering the highest rural wages in Mexico or through a "paternalistic" system of labor relations (or both).[115] Unlike the situation in many parts of central and southern Mexico, the hacendados of the border states of Coahuila, Chihuahua, and Sonora did not rely on indentured labor as the primary means for securing labor.[116] Coahuilan hacendados like the Madero family raised wages, which—coupled with employer paternalism—secured the permanent hacienda workforce needed to build their large empire. Besides offering competitive wages, the Maderos offered their rural workers schools and, in times of economic insecurity, food. The paternalism characteristic of that form of northern labor relations is best expressed in a letter that Francisco I. Madero wrote to Evaristo Madero, the patriarch of the family:

> You will also have the satisfaction of seeing the manifestations of harmony and affection from all the workers in your haciendas, people who, in great part, owe you their education and well-being because you have been one of those individuals who has distinguished yourself by a desire to promote public education. . . . in the periods of droughts that bring to this region unemployment and its subsequent misery, you have been one who has turned charity into a salary. In these periods of misfortune you have promoted great works with the goal of feeding these poor wretches, but fed them in an honest way, although at the lowest level.[117]

Hacendados of the Yaqui Valley in Sonora secured a labor force, composed mainly of the rebellious Yaquis, by offering them the highest rural wages in Mexico or through practices that could be defined as paternalistic, like those of the Maderos, or through some combination of the two. Wages for rural workers in the Yaqui Valley more than doubled in less than ten years, from a daily wage of sixty-two centavos to 1.50 pesos in 1911.[118] In addition to offering higher wages, some hacendados, like José María Maytorena, protected the rebellious Yaqui Indians from the political authorities by giving them refuge on their estates.[119]

NUEVO LEÓN'S SECOND SERFDOM: LABOR CONDITIONS ON THE HACIENDAS

Unlike their counterparts in the north, Nuevo León's hacendados depended on coercive labor practices more in tune with the labor retention methods used in southern Mexico (in places such as Yucatán) than with those commonly used in the north. How did the Nuevo León hacienda secure a large labor force through coercive means in an environment increasingly dominated by labor mobility and free labor? Why did Nuevo León's hacendados go against the grain of this trend?

As discussed in Chapter 3, Nuevo León's landlords were financially poor compared to other hacendados in Mexico. Their dependence on debt-peonage was based entirely on necessity rather than on a preference for labor coercion over free labor. They simply did not have the financial resources to pay higher wages and provide their labor force with medical services and schooling. Hacendados increasingly relied on debt-peonage, used at least since the turn of the nineteenth century, as the only means of retaining a labor pool within an emerging border labor market based on mobility and the freedom of labor. Because of proximity to Texas and northern Mexican centers of employment, the landlords could only maintain labor in bondage with the help of the local government authorities. Without the support landlords received from the authorities, Nuevo León would not have had a second serfdom. The local authorities, from the municipal mayor to the local police, sustained debt-peonage as the labor system in the countryside. They did everything in their power to ensure that the indebted peon stayed attached to the hacienda and did not question the authority of the landlord.

Nuevo León's second serfdom coincides in time with the political order Bernardo Reyes established from 1885 to 1909. Even though Reyes, a *laissez-faire* Liberal, opposed the use of unfree labor for ideological reasons, he quietly accepted it. He did not have the political muscle to suppress debt-peonage, at least not until 1908. More interested in Monterrey's development and national politics, Reyes ignored the debt-peonage question in order to avoid challenging his political base in the countryside, which energetically sustained this labor system. He allowed his political allies complete freedom to run local affairs, and debt-peonage was considered a local concern. These local Reyista despots used and abused their powers to maintain the system of debt-peonage. They arrested *jornaleros* who questioned the authority of hacendados, kidnapped relatives of runaway peons, and threatened those who refused to work on the haciendas with conscription into the army.

Most of the Reyistas in the countryside shared a common history. The Bernardinos, as they were also called, had belonged to the Garza Ayalista Club Democrático, the political "outsiders" of the 1867–1884 era. They gained control of the municipalities when Reyes ended the Treviñista *cacicazgo* in 1885. In the rural municipalities they formed the core of the Reyista party, the Gran Círculo Unión y Progreso, holding all elected and nonelected positions in government at least until 1909, when Reyes went into exile in Europe. As of 1903, the Bernardinos in Linares had been in charge of "la cosa pública" (local government) for eighteen years and in Galeana and Mier y Noriega for the duration of Reyes's tenure.[120]

United by political, economic, and kinship ties, the Bernardinos established *cacicazgos* in each of the municipalities. As members of the Gran Círculo Unión y Progreso, they formed part of the local political and economic elite. For instance, Abraham Buentello headed a local *cacicazgo,* serving as the Reyista mayor of Bustamante for fourteen years (and four years as alternative mayor). He owned a drug and general store, bought and sold maize and *piloncillo,* owned transportation carts, and was a moneylender. In spite of his many business activities, he only paid a meager bimonthly tax of two pesos. For taxation purposes, he and the other local merchants "regularly report lower sales than what they actually sell." [121] Bustamante's *cacicazgo* was composed of twenty-five Reyistas who were "united by family and *compadrazgo* [friendship] ties," and it practiced "nepotism to the detriment of justice." [122]

The despotic *cacicazgos* of Cruz Estrello (Mier and Noriega), Abraham Buentello (Bustamante), Antonio Peña (Colombia), Cosme Peña (Los Aldamas), José Noriega (Linares), Santos Cavazos (China), and Luis Cortés (Galeana), and others were associated with nepotism, profiteering, corruption, and, above all, abusing their powers. Antonio Peña, the political boss of the border town of Colombia, headed a *cacicazgo* which secured for itself much of the wealth of this impoverished town and exerted his influence in all areas. A *vecino* arbitrarily jailed by Peña petitioned the governor for a trial outside of Colombia because "here Señor Peña holds a powerful influence over all the local officials so that all matters are settled to his complete satisfaction. . . ." [123] The authorities used the charge of "falta a la autoridad" (disrespect for the authorities) as the most common offense for jailing individuals.[124]

In contrast to the rest of northern Mexico, Nuevo León had close to fifty municipalities, all governed by *cacicazgos* except for Monterrey, which was Reyes's domain. Each *cacicazgo* ran its municipality with relative autonomy from Reyes, most often governing in a despotic fashion. A resident of Galeana pointed out how the system of justice operated in his municipality:

> The guarantees that the laws concede to citizens are absent in these places, and, moreover, all the hacendados are protected by the authorities, who never attend the poor even when justice is on their side. [The authorities] always intimidate [people] with imprisonment . . . resulting in people never complaining.[125]

Unlike the Terrazas oligarchy, which covered all of Chihuahua, Nuevo León's many municipalities involved numerous hacendados. Within this decentralized political system landlords were strong only at the municipal level, especially in southern Nuevo León, where "local politics is the burning issue," as an individual wrote.[126] As an economic group, they were not unified politically at a statewide level.

Connected by family relations, politics, and economics, these municipal *cacicazgos* protected their labor pool from outside competition. They prevented outside labor agents from recruiting workers in their municipalities. For example, Galeana's mayor fined a Coahuilan *enganchador* for "illegally" recruiting ten families.[127] Doctor Arroyo's mayor prevented a labor agent from recruiting rural workers in his municipality. Ironically, he justified his action on humanitarian grounds, intending to prevent "the exodus of people who might be recruited to work in the United States of America, where our proletariat class suffers so much."[128]

How did an individual become an indentured servant in such an environment surrounded by free labor? Sickness in the family, a poor harvest, a prolonged drought, economic destitution, and other hardships forced poor people to migrate or to enlist in the service of landlords who did not have great difficulty in recruiting workers. In the absence of banks which could lend small quantities of money, poor people turned to the landlords, the only ones who could advance them money. Landlords used wage advancements as the incentive for recruiting most of their labor force and, conversely, owing money to the landlord was the most common way one became a *peon*. For example, a Mina landlord advanced 100 pesos to a poor family in 1890. To pay off their debt, the family sent their sixteen-year-old daughter to work for the landlord at a salary of 1.50 pesos a month.[129] Given this wage, it would have taken her over five years to pay back the cash advance.

Yet not all individuals who ended up as indentured laborers entered this condition voluntarily. Hacendados often used the local authorities to force free workers to labor on their estates for free or for low wages. If free workers refused to work, Reyista officials threatened them with imprisonment or conscription into the army, nearly a prison sentence. One of Rafael Dávila's *mayordomos* conscripted three *jornaleros* into the army. Dávila, Bernardo Reyes's son-in-law, promised to release them from the army only under the condition that they work on his estate, without wages, for two years.[130] Meanwhile, Galeana's hacendados often called on the mayor to conscript into the army individuals who refused to work on their estates. In the army they were to "be purged of their fleas. I forget for how long [they had been kept in the army], but I never saw anyone come back until the Revolution emancipated them."[131]

Table 4.5. DAILY RURAL WAGES FOR SELECTED MUNICIPALITIES,
1899 AND 1910 (IN PESOS)

Municipio	1899	1910	Number of Jornaleros, 1910
Abasolos	.37	.50	70
Agueleguas	.37	.50	175
Allende	.23	.50	650
Apodaca	.37	.50	160
Aramberrí	.23	.37	2,350
Cadereyta Jiménez	.40	.60	1,050
Cerralvo	.50	.60	550
Doctor Arroyo	.18	.30	2,674
Galeana	.26	.50	2,800
García	.40	.50	530
Garza García	.37	.75	70
General Terán	.37	.50	1,600
Guadalupe	.37	.50	500
Juárez	.25	.37	500
Lampazos	.40	.50	500
Linares	.25	.50	4,000
Mier y Noriega	.31	.31	900
Mina	.37	.50	460
Montemorelos	.18	.50	2,300
Monterrey	.40	.75	321
Sabinas Hidalgo	.37	.75	673
S. N. de los Garza	.37	.75	220
Santa Catarina	.37	.75	216
Santiago	.25	.50	1,850
Vallecillo	.23	.50	200
Villaldama	.39	.62	300

Source: Nuevo León, Memorias de Bernardo Reyes, 1895–1899, 2 vols. (Monterrey: Imprenta de Gobierno, 1900), 2:2, p. 885; AGENL, Correspondencia del Gobierno del Estado de Nuevo León con la Secretaría de Fomento 1907–1911 and 1911–1912.

All landlords in Nuevo León depended on indentured labor, although geography determined the degree of dependence as well as rural wages. Municipalities near the United States and Monterrey paid the highest rural wages and depended less on unfree labor than the southern municipalities, a large debt-peonage enclave. Rural wages in 1910 ranged from 11.25 pesos a month in Aramberrí, a southern municipality, to 22.50 pesos in Monterrey and other northern localities (see Table 4.5).

Hacendados in northern and central Nuevo León engaged in a wider variety of labor practices, using a combination of higher wages, wage advancements, and sharecropping. This was the case in San Antonio y Anexas hacienda, located in the central municipalities of Mina and García. The hacienda, owned by Jesús González Treviño, a prominent Monterrey businessman and a relative of the Maderos, was part of his large network of investments in commerce, industry, and rural holdings, including a 2.4-million-peso land company in Piedras Negras, Coahuila. San Antonio y Anexas employed fifty *peones acasillados* (hacienda residents), fifteen *eventuales* (free laborers), and twenty-five *aparceros* (sharecroppers). The daily wage for its workforce was seventy-five centavos a day, twice as high as in the southern municipalities, in which laborers were only paid an average of thirty-seven centavos in 1910. Even though this hacienda paid higher wages than most haciendas in the state, it offered advance wages to its *peones acasillados,* the majority of the labor force, for reasons that were "strictly economic."[132]

Landlords who had fewer resources for recruiting labor depended more on wage advancements and other incentives, such as free housing. La Soledad de la Mota hacienda of General Terán in central Nuevo León employed forty *jornaleros,* each paid eight pesos a month in 1908, less than thirty centavos a day. The hacienda compensated for the low wages by offering its peons a daily ration of three liters of maize, free housing, and access to a small plot of land which they could use to supplement their meager incomes. The hacendado also advanced 4,000 pesos in wages to their workers, an average of 100 pesos per person, as a device for retaining the labor force. This hacendado asserted that advanced wages were "indispensable for securing labor."[133] In Cadereyta Jiménez, near Monterrey, debt-peonage coexisted alongside the nearby free labor market. Hacendados recruited *jornaleros* by paying for the transportation from the peon's last residence, a daily salary of fifty centavos, and housing.[134]

Even though the hacienda was present in all rural areas in Nuevo León, it only played a dominant role in the southern municipalities, the traditional stronghold of the hacendados since colonial times, where conditions resembled those in southern Mexico more than those in the north. The *comunidad de accionistas* overshadowed the haciendas in the northern and central parts of the state. In the southern municipalities (geographically isolated by mountains and poor means of transportation) a low-wage, debt-labor enclave emerged during the Porfiriato. Landlords from Galeana, Linares, Aramberrí, and Doctor Arroyo held close to 12,000 rural workers in bondage, a labor force larger than Monterrey's industrial working class (see Table 4.5). Most of the hacendados in this part of the state were absentee owners who lived in the cities of Matehuala, San Luis Potosí, and Saltillo. They left the day-to-day operations of the haciendas to administrators and *mayordomos*. After the 1848–1885 decline during which landlords lost a good portion of their labor force to the United States and Soledad, the largest estate in Nuevo León, was expropriated by Mariano Escobedo, the southern haciendas flourished again during the Porfiriato, a period of economic growth and political stability. The haciendas' second life was due to the cultivation of two highly profitable export products (guayule and ixtle) and the support of the local authorities, who helped the landlords to maintain a permanent labor force earning the lowest wages in Nuevo León and northern Mexico.[135]

The ability to retain a large labor pool and the export of ixtle and guayule were crucial for the resurgence of the landlords as the dominant class in southern Nuevo León. Once *jornaleros* received wage advancements, the hacienda's administrators and *mayordomos* kept them in bondage by paying such low wages that the debts could never be paid. With a daily wage of thirty-seven centavos in 1910, one-half lower than the wage in other parts of the state, *jornaleros* continually "request wage advancements from their employers, and they in turn give it to them."[136]

Requesting wage advances represented an individual decision, with the probable understanding that perpetual debt to the landlord would result. The *jornaleros* recognized that wage advancements were essentially a charter for their enslavement. Once *jornaleros* received an advance, regardless of the amount, landlords regarded them as their property, as in the case of Teodoro Cepeda's sixteen-year-old daughter, who went to work to pay off a 100-peso advancement given to her family. The landlord prohibited her from leaving the hacienda and from having any communications with her family.[137]

To ensure that they would never pay off their debts, landlords used faulty accounting methods to keep the *jornaleros* always in debt. The case of Santa-Ana Martínez, a peon from Galeana, arrested by the mayor for not paying off a debt, typifies this condition. After five years of laboring on a hacienda, Martínez had accumulated a debt of 130 pesos, largely through his "rudeza" (ignorance). Evidently he did not know his exact debt, because "he is a man who does not know how to count and because they did not give him the liberty of having another person who could verify his accounts."[138] After abandoning the hacienda, Martínez acquired a new *amo* (hacendado) who paid off only 90 pesos of his 130-peso debt. Galeana's mayor jailed him for the remaining 40 pesos.[139]

As long as *jornaleros* owed the landlord money, they were considered the property of the landlord. Not even sickness, injury, or death excused them from their debts. In another Galeana case, Miguel Mireles, also a hacienda peon, suffered a work-related accident which left him without an arm and unable to work. His father was forced to seek employment on a hacienda and request a two-year wage advancement to pay for his son's medical expenses. In addition to this loan, Mireles's father also owed the debt of his brother and therefore virtually owed his life to the *amo*.[140]

There were only three ways in which indentured laborers could terminate their relationship of perpetual bondage to the hacienda. The most difficult one was to save enough money to pay off the wage advancement, an almost impossible task, bearing in mind the low wages that prevailed in the countryside. The second most difficult choice was fleeing to the United States or other parts of Mexico. Although many individuals fled, they did so at a cost: their families were held responsible for their debts. Thus, the family served as a sort of insurance policy for landlords. The third choice involved a landlord purchasing the debt of an indentured *peon* from another landlord, a common practice among landlords from the same locality. This was the case of Nacario Román, whose 86.50-peso debt was purchased by his new *amo*, and of Santa-Ana Martínez, who owed 130 pesos.[141]

The system of labor bondage in Nuevo León almost guaranteed that landlords would retain a large pool of labor. Given the circumstances of perpetual bondage, the only real choice that *jornaleros* had was to flee the hacienda. Hacendados used the local authorities to prevent their workers from leaving their estates. Indentured laborers often escaped from the hacienda, as Sebastián Rodríguez did, settling in Monterrey. Mina's authorities arrested the five members of his family as a means of forcing Rodríguez to return to the hacienda.[142] This was not an isolated case. In China an hacendado kept a family in bondage after the father left without paying his debts, while Galeana's mayor held three children responsible for a 50-peso debt their father, Pedro Salas, had incurred with Soledad hacienda. The father complained that he was "old, decrepit, and sick" and that his children had not been released after working for "one year, three months, and nineteen days." Too poor to afford transportation, Salas had walked from Galeana to Monterrey to present his complaint directly to the governor, arguing that he could not get any justice in his municipality.[143]

CONCLUSION

By the end of the Porfiriato Monterrey had emerged as the industrial center of Mexico, dominated by an economically and politically powerful regional bourgeoisie, with a disciplined and permanent wage-labor working class. In stark contrast to the city, Nuevo Leon's countryside, with an economy based on debt-peonage and sharecropping, entered a period of long-term decline, which began even before the Revolution and from which it never recovered.

Labor conditions in the Nuevoleonese hacienda mirrored those in southern Mexico, where landlords treated their workforce as private property. In complete contrast to their northern counterparts, who maintained a permanent labor force through paternalistic measures and higher wages, hacendados in Nuevo León could only recruit a labor force with wage advancements and keep them attached to the hacienda by ensuring that these advances would never be paid off. In the end, the methods that landlords employed in recruiting and maintaining a permanent workforce never created a loyal laboring population.

The evidence reveals the laboring population's profound discontent with their indentured condition and the poor treatment they received from landlords. A *jornalero* argued that just because of the money owed to a landlord, "we are obligated to suffer all types of abuses and poor treatment, instead of [him] having pity for our miserable situation."[144] Indeed, this landlord "had the habit of beating the people that work for him."[145] Another landlord threatened to jail a bed-ridden *jornalero* who was too sick to work and could not afford medical care. Jail was the best place to "get cured" quickly, according to the landlord.[146] As the following chapter shows, the *jornaleros* did not wait passively for the Mexican Revolution to liberate them. By escaping en masse, waging strikes, and questioning the authority of both landlords and local officials, *jornaleros* increasingly undermined debt-peonage and the existence of the hacienda in the years leading up to the eruption of the Revolution.

CHAPTER FIVE

The Crisis of the Countryside and Public Policy in the Late Porfiriato

> Peasant life is a life committed completely to survival.
> Perhaps this is the only characteristic fully shared by
> peasants everywhere.
> JOHN BERGER, *PIG EARTH*

Capitalism had evolved unevenly in Nuevo León from 1890 to 1910. It triumphed in Monterrey but, in contrast, made only minor headway in the countryside. Monterrey, also known as the *sultana del norte,* held less than one-fourth of Nuevo León's population, but produced over 80 percent of the state's physical output. A first impression of the Nuevoleonese countryside would have suggested social stability and economic growth, albeit at a slower pace than in the city. The many peasant communities coexisted with haciendas. The value of agricultural products increased from 4.5 million pesos to almost 6 million pesos from 1903 to 1906.[1] A closer examination, however, would have revealed a profound crisis in the communities and the haciendas. Peasants retained their lands during the Porfiriato, but the land could no longer sustain them. The absence of credit, insufficient good lands for expansion, a small rural labor force, and a state government inimical to hacendado interests undermined the power of the hacienda and impeded its complete dominion over the countryside. Meanwhile, *jornaleros* witnessed the ending of a period dominated by debt-peonage and the emergence of an era in which the state government, combined with *jornalero* resistance to oppressive conditions, almost entirely eliminated labor bondage.

    This chapter examines the social crisis that prevailed in the countryside during the last ten years of the Porfiriato, in particular the effects of the subsistence crisis on the *vecino* communities and the conflicts between *jornaleros* and hacendados. The crisis of subsistence did not receive the attention of government leaders, forcing the *vecinos* increasingly to abandon their lands. In the case of *jornalero*-hacendado conflicts rooted in the poor working and living conditions on the haciendas, however, the government passed proactive legislation aimed at modernizing labor relations in the countryside and abolishing debt-peonage.

THE COMMUNITIES, THE STATE, AND
THE CRISIS OF SUBSISTENCE

In the years from 1900 to 1910 all of the state's forty municipalities except nine, including Monterrey, either maintained or lost population without any major increases. These nine municipalities contained close to two-thirds of the state's population by 1910, had 45 percent of all the rural workers, and produced over 60 percent of the state's total agricultural output.[2] The *comunidades de accionistas,* however, were concentrated in the forty municipalities that declined economically.

The members of the *comunidades de accionistas* faced a profound social, demographic, and economic crisis during the last decade of the Porfiriato that threatened the existence of the communities because it affected peasant subsistence. The *comuneros* did not have the credit needed to expand agricultural production and were consequently at the mercy of nature, which punished them with severe droughts. Moreover, population pressures diminished the amount of land available for each new generation of *comuneros*. Two movements emerged within the communities, which were unable to subsist on the land. The first involved growing internal pressures within the communities to break up into private property (see Chapter 3). The second movement involved the migration of many *comuneros* to other locations, mainly Texas.

One of the effects of this crisis of subsistence was to change the meaning of equality as previously understood by the members of the communities, the *vecinos*. Before the Porfiriato all *vecinos* regarded each other as equals, regardless of wealth and ethnicity. Equality had been based on the defense of the *patria chica,* the self-sufficient homeland, uniting all *vecinos* against outside threats such as Indian and bandit raids. The meaning of *vecino* radically changed during the Porfiriato, however, when the threats to the communities ceased and market relations predominated. Wealth became a determinant of status, as manifested by a community in Hualahuises. By 1907 the *vecinos* there had formed 4 ranches with 36 heads of family for a total population of 213. In total the community owned 185 head of cattle, 43 horses, 290 goats, and 197 hogs and produced 2,830 hectoliters of corn for a total community wealth of 9,426 pesos in crops and animals or an average of 261.70 pesos per family. Economic inequalities within the community were well advanced by this time: fairly well-off "entrepreneurial" peasants, Nuevo León's poorer version of the Russian kulaks, emerged alongside dirt-poor *campesinos* who could no longer subsist off the land. The wealthiest peasant family in this community had a total wealth of 709 pesos, while the poorest had 15.75 pesos.[3] The meaning of *vecino*, which for close to three centuries had been synonymous with equality on the frontier, was redefined during the area's transition into a "border" region based on new conditions of wealth and poverty. A passage about European peasants by John Berger, the well-known English cultural critic and novelist, also describes those in Nuevo León:

> The nineteenth-century peasantry was still a class of survivors, with the difference that those who disappeared were no longer those who ran away but were forced to abandon the village and become wage earners. One should add that under these new conditions a few peasants become rich, but in doing so they also ceased, within a generation or two, to be peasants.[4]

The communities could no longer sustain most of their members during this age. Population pressures led to a crisis of subsistence, accelerating intracommunity conflicts over boundaries and intercommunity conflicts over membership, water, and grazing. A Cadereyta Jiménez *comunero*'s complaint typified the problems besieging the poorest of the shareholders of community lands. He could no longer sustain his family because his plot produced only small amounts of maize and *piloncillo:* "this is not enough because, year after year, I am obligated to buy maize to meet the most urgent needs of my family. . . . I can assure you that instead of benefiting from my plot I am getting into more problems."[5] Another *comunero* from Bustamantes seconded this bleak view, noting that

> agriculture is completely unstable and more so this year because eight months have passed without any rain and the water in the well has diminished considerably, and I can sincerely tell you that if we have not abandoned our plots it is because we do not want to lose the land we inherited from our grandfathers. . . .[6]

The plots that *vecinos* inherited could no longer sustain them. Many of them forfeited their plots and migrated. In Bustamantes conditions had became so desperate for the *vecinos* that they only had two alternatives in order to survive—to continue working on their plots and enlist their services at the nearby haciendas as *jornaleros* to make ends meet or to abandon their property. Those who chose the former earned fifty centavos a day on the hacienda, toiling in the maize and sugarcane fields from sunset to sundown. These wages were barely enough "to poorly feed our large families."[7]

Given this alternative, most *comuneros* preferred to abandon their community plots or leave them to an *apoderado* (proxy) within the community. For this group, Bustamante's subsistence crisis led to an "exodus of laborers to Texas" and an "alarming" local labor shortage.[8] One individual claimed that 2,000 residents of the municipality had migrated to Texas.[9] The mayor of Bustamantes said that the exodus of residents was rooted in the poor working conditions of the haciendas, which "pay our poor *jornaleros* a monthly wage of six to eight pesos." With these low wages, and in order to feed their "large families," laborers received wage advancements, accumulating debts of two to three hundred pesos from their *patrones*. As a result, "they lose all hope of improving their condition" and "are forced to go to Texas."[10]

Bustamantes, a "sender" of migrant labor, lost many of its residents, mainly to Texas. According to the census, Bustamantes lost 294 males and 400 women from 1900 to 1910 as its population dwindled from 4,190 to 3,496.[11] The fact that women outnumbered males indicates that whole families migrated instead of the typical male-only pattern that dominated Mexican migration to the United States during this period. Family migration also indicates that most emigrants had little hope of returning. Other municipalities in central and northern Nuevo León, where the *comunidad de accionistas* predominated, did not fare any better than Bustamantes. Fifteen of Nuevo León's forty-nine municipalities lost population from 1900 to 1910.[12] Rural "sender" communities in Nuevo León established a pattern of sending inhabitants to Texas, a "receiver" of Mexican immigrants.

Nuevo León's economic development during the Porfiriato exhibited contradictory patterns. While Monterrey was in the vanguard of Mexico's attempted leap into the twentieth century, the countryside clearly remained far behind, manifesting no signs of keeping pace with the rest of the nation's rural economic development, not to speak of Monterrey's. For the "enlightened" sectors of the city the countryside represented only backwardness: most *comuneros* were not involved in large-scale agricultural production, and perhaps an even larger number were not involved in the market economy at all; debt-peonage represented the main form of labor on the haciendas; and the inefficient haciendas produced little wealth.

The state governments did not have any clear and direct proactive policies to solve the many problems affecting the *comunidades* similar to the energetic policies that benefited the city and industry or the new legislation of 1908, which was intended to end debt-peonage as it had existed for generations. The affairs of the communities should have been a major concern considering that *comuneros* made up a large part of the state's population, if not the majority. The federal government did not intervene in Nuevo León's countryside because it did not contain many "lands that could be classified as national [public]" and thus it did not affect the "interest of the federation." [13] The Porfirian government considered Nuevo León's community lands to be under the legal jurisdiction of the state government.

The Reyista government mostly remained indifferent to the many problems that the communities faced because it had no legal jurisdiction over community affairs. This political indifference favored the *comuneros*, who opposed the privatization of the communities, and allowed for the legal continuation of the communities.

The government had no legal basis for making clear policy concerning the key problems of the *comuneros*. The first settlers, according to a 1910 study, passed their lands to their successors without documenting or delineating precise boundaries. Through this process "an indefinite number of *accionistas*" owned the community's properties—"each one owns this or that portion of property, and if they work the land, they do it however it pleases them." [14]

Without modern private property legislation, it was difficult for the state government to determine who was a legitimate *heredero* (descendant) of the original colonizer because the communities had grown in membership over time. The only basis for determining the precise number of shares of land a *comunero* had was the title to the original *merced* or the last *higuela* (will). These two documents had not been modified since colonial times. If the community itself was private property owned in common, how could it solve the problems created by the growing tendency to fence property within a community? Was erecting a fence a crime against the community or an indication of an individual claim to private property? Could the individuals who destroyed a fence be brought up on criminal charges for the destruction of private property? [15] The state government did not have legal answers to these questions precisely because it did not have legislation that specifically applied to the *comunidades*. Moreover, any genuine attempt to solve the community's problem would have required an investment of vast amounts of money to train a professional staff who could deal with community boundary disputes, wills, and genealogies, among other issues. To determine what was specific private property within a collective setting, the exact farming, pasture, and water portions owned by each *comunero* would have to be determined. These decisions would have required a study of genealogies and wills over long periods.

In one of the few cases in which the state government intervened in the affairs of the communities, it created turmoil. Governor Reyes intervened in a factional community dispute in China by naively ordering that it be broken up "according to the proportion that corresponds to each individual."[16] His resolution met resistance from one of the opposing factions, led by the mayor. They argued that dividing community lands into equal portions was unfeasible because:

> it breaks with the past practice that has been established in settling these kind of disputes; because it harms, damages, and injures our rights and it excludes us from participating in defense of our concerns. It seizes our property and possessions without our adversaries proving legally that they have greater rights. . . . the land can not be divided proportionally because not everybody has the same equal portions and because the authorities are not qualified to value the rights of each. . . .[17]

China's mayor clearly stated the difficulties of dividing the communities into private property: the process broke with the traditional method of settling internal conflicts; specific ownership of exact portions could not easily be determined; and the state did not have the qualified personnel to carry out these kinds of projects. The state government simply did not have clear criteria for dealing with the many complicated problems evolving within the communities. Moreover, it did not have the money and had not provided any legal basis for reforming the communities. Finally, it might not even have had an interest in dealing with problems of communities which had been autonomous for almost three centuries. This was not just a problem for the Reyista authorities. The revolutionaries also failed to provide a clear policy for "those who called themselves *accionistas* and whose only titles to property in the majority of cases are the ancient *higuelas* that their forefathers left them."[18]

In spite of the state government's passivity in dealing with the problems of the communities, Monterrey's intellectuals and the press called on the Reyista authorities to deal with the problems that communities faced, which were considered "unresolvable" without state government intervention. Using *laissez-faire* arguments, *La Voz de Nuevo León* editorialized in 1908 that one-third of the state's land could not be used for "ordinary purchase and sale transactions" because it was owned in community.[19] As early as 1892 this newspaper called for the dissolution of the communities because "these lands could be used for individual gain and for the expansion of agriculture, if each individual had his own plot."[20] José Noriega, an agronomist, wrote in 1931 that "in [this part of] the frontier, where there are no Indians, it is well known that the communities have been a complete failure, especially those that [could have access to] water." He noted that none of the communities had been able to construct a dam.[21]

According to this line of reasoning, the lands would continue to be unproductive in the hands of *comuneros*.[22] The division of the communities into private property was the only salvation for the *comuneros* and the only solution for the modernization of agriculture, as Pablo Livas, a Monterrey educator, argued.[23] Armed ideologically with Adam Smith's economic principles espousing the beneficent "invisible hand" of the market, Porfirian forces called for reforms whose end result would be to strengthen the privatization of land and its resources. The communities' management of their resources was regarded as obsolete in this new era.

Free from state pressures and left on their own to deal with their internal problems, some communities sought to adjust independently of the state. Throughout the Reyes era, the state legislature passed only two laws concerning the communities. In 1894 it passed the Law Project on the Communities in the State of Nuevo León, which essentially confirmed the communities' right to own land in commune as they had for close to three centuries. The law reaffirmed the community as a legal entity composed of members who owned portions of the community's land and resources, without specifying exact portions. As a legal unit, the community was obligated to establish its own internal rules of governance as a legitimate legal entity.[24]

The Hacienda Horcones, owned by a Lampazos community, illustrates the case of a self-regulating community. In order to "remedy the wrongs and disorders and to prevent new ones," the *accionistas* voted "unanimously" on the rules for the "internal regime," a new social and legal contract. The *comuneros* agreed on a series of measures that regulated the daily activities of members, including water usage, types of animals allowed in communal pasture lands, and the rights of the non-*herederos* who resided in the community, specifically the *arrimados* (squatters) and *arrendatarios* (tenants). The most important measures specified that only cattle and horses could graze on pasture lands (outlawing goats and sheep); that each *accionista* had the right to have up to three non-*comuneros* and their families without having to pay rent to the community; and that *arrimados* had to provide three days of free labor per month on the canal, in addition to a day of labor on the community fence. Other rules stipulated that if one-third of the *accionistas* decided that *arrendatarios* were "prejudicial" to the community they had to leave the hacienda; that each individual was responsible for his or her stock; that all rents and fines collected at the end of the year would be distributed among the *accionistas;* and that no liquor could be sold on community property—if any was sold, a twenty-five-peso fine was imposed that would be used for the public school.[25]

In 1908 the Reyista government passed Article 689, the first law aimed at dissolving the communities. According to this law, a community could be divided into private property only when the *accionistas* who held 67 percent of all shares of the land agreed to do so.[26] This article apparently led to the breakup of Icamole, one of the oldest communities in the state, located near Monterrey, where the value of property was much higher than in the rest of the state. The *comuneros* agreed to divide Icamole into individually owned ranchos a year after the passage of Article 689. Each property was enclosed with barbed wire fences, creating a series of new problems, the most pressing of which was the closure of the communal road due to the many fences.[27] In this case, the individual needs superseded the community ones.

Although Article 689 was the first government act aimed at dividing the communities into private property, it left that decision to the *accionistas*. In 1912 Viviano Villareal, the Maderista governor of Nuevo León and President Francisco Madero's uncle, reinitiated the discussion on dissolving the communities. He proposed to the state legislature drastic measures that would divide the communities once and for all. According to Villareal, the dissolution was necessary because the existence of communities did not "correspond to the reality" of the era and they were "notoriously anti-economical [*sic*] and highly harmful to public and private wealth." He also pointed out that growing community membership would only create a multitude of legally based problems if the matter was not immediately resolved.[28] Victoriano Huerta's overthrow of the Maderista government postponed this attempt to put an end to the *comunidad de accionistas*.

The revolutionaries (regardless of their labels as Maderistas, Carranzistas, Obregonistas, or Cardenistas) as well as other political forces also shared the views of the Porfirians. Along the same line of argument used by the Porfirians, a Monterrey law professor called for the immediate break-up of the communities in 1933 because land owned in community was economically backward and inefficient. He also concluded that the privatization of land was of the essence because history demonstrated that these communities "were a complete failure."[29]

The dissolution of the communities finally occurred in 1949, when the state government passed the Law Pertaining to the Dissolution of the Rural Communities of Nuevo León, by means of which all of the communities were divided into private property. Indeed, no political leader from the Porfiriato to the postrevolutionary age defended the right of *comuneros* to own property in community. Perhaps the closest "ally" the *comuneros* had throughout this period was the state government, which remained passive on the issue of privatization because of lack of concern for the affairs of the *comuneros,* the inheritors of Nuevo León's colonization, which began in 1596.

JORNALERO RESISTANCE AND THE BREAKDOWN OF HACENDADO AUTHORITY

Unlike the rest of Mexico, Nuevo León did not produce a strong class of landlords during the Porfiriato. Landlords lacked credit to expand agricultural production, owned only limited amounts of good lands, and had to share scarce resources (such as water) with ranchos and communities. Furthermore, they wielded little political influence within the state government. Economically poor and politically weak by the standards of their class throughout Mexico, hacendados confronted the fundamental problem of securing a large permanent and stable labor force. Unable to compete for laborers within the highly competitive border labor market, they could only retain labor through debt-peonage, a mechanism that required the assistance of the municipal authorities.

Their inability to create a system of paternalistic "consent" based on free labor and "humane" treatment of their laborers, as in the rest of the north, finally caught up with the hacendados in the waning years of the Porfiriato. *Jornaleros* rebelled against the repressive methods that hacendados employed on their estates. They waged strikes and deserted en masse from the estates. Hacendados lost whatever authority they had over their *peones;* in the last years before the Revolution, the hacienda was on the verge of collapse.

Hacendados in southern Nuevo León treated their *sirvientes* no differently than their counterparts in Yucatán or the Valle Nacional of

Oaxaca. Isolated by geography from the rest of Nuevo León and the free labor market of the border region, landlords held a large number of workers under bondage, including sharecroppers. They created a debt-peonage enclave by advancing wages to thousands of impoverished rural workers. These advances were large enough to ensure the impossibility of repayment, given the low wages that prevailed in these localities (between twenty-five and thirty-five centavos a day). The local authorities ensured that the indentured servants stayed on the hacienda through different forms of punishment, including imprisonment. Keeping large numbers of *jornaleros* in bondage provided hacendados with a temporary sense of security.

In Galeana hacendados and their *mayordomos* were notorious for "terrorizing" their workforce. A native of this municipality recalled that the *peones* of Potosí hacienda, one of the largest estates in Nuevo León, "complained that their *amo* [master] was not too kind. It has been said that on more than one occasion he whipped some of them." [30] Potosí was a hotbed of *jornalero* unrest in 1907 and 1908. Meanwhile, at neighboring Soledad, perhaps Nuevo León's largest and most important hacienda, the *mayordomos* awoke their workers at three in the morning so that the day's tasks could be completed before sundown. [31] Tied to the hacienda by debt, *jornaleros* tolerated these types of abuses for a wage of twenty-five centavos or less a day, one of the lowest wages in Mexico.

This coercive system of labor retention worked until the last five years of the Porfiriato because hacendados had at their disposal the support of local authorities. Local officials sustained the labor system in various ways, from returning runaway peons to the landlords to maintaining "order" in the haciendas. Aramberrí's local police raided areas where the so-called vagabonds concentrated, forcing them to work on the haciendas, while those at Doctor Arroyo "lent a decisive hand to the hacendados when the *sirvientes* abandoned their work." [32]

Notwithstanding key similarities between landlords in Nuevo León and Yucatán in maintaining a large labor force in bondage, Nuevo León was not Yucatán. *Jornaleros* there possessed one major advantage over other *peones* in the rest of Mexico: proximity to the U.S. border. Escaping from the hacienda had been within the reach of those *jornaleros* since the creation of the international boundary in 1848. Before the Porfiriato unknown numbers of *jornaleros* escaped to the "other side," a courageous act whose final aim was freedom from a life of modern slavery. The Comisión Pesquisidora, a Mexican government commission, reported in 1873 that the number of runaways was so great that this "matter deserves consideration." It proposed laws which "would close the door on the system of roaming, which is indulged in by the people of the states of Nuevo León, Coahuila, and Tamaulipas, toward the frontier of Texas."[33] No legislation was necessary, as the strengthening of the Porfirian state and establishment of strong local *cacicazgos* after 1890 made fleeing extremely difficult, although not containing it entirely.

After 1890 escape was an individual act of courage. Rarely did it involve groups of *jornaleros,* because the risks of capture were greater. In any event, fleeing was at most the personal act of a small minority among the mass of discontented. Even though it might have involved hundreds of "fugitives" over many decades, it did not endanger the existence of the hacienda because the remaining families of the escapees served as an insurance policy. Landlords recovered the cost of the runaways by transferring their debts to family members, who were then forced to work.

Jornaleros and sharecroppers waged strikes after 1905, a tactic of resistance unheard of for indentured laborers and sharecroppers, two groups whose class distinction was blurred in Nuevo León. The number of sharecroppers in Nuevo León is unknown. The Caja de Préstamos, a government financial institution, calculated in 1909 that *medieros* made up 60 percent of *agricultores en pequeño* (small farmers) in Mexico.[34] Sharecroppers provided hacendados with a portion of their harvest as a rent for land usage. According to the Caja de Préstamos, landlords had the upper hand in this relationship. They advanced money, corn, beans, and other goods to the sharecroppers, at the shocking rate of 25 percent interest a year. Sharecroppers then paid the landlords with their crops, which were sold below the market price. Sharecroppers ended up owing the landlords great quantities of money impossible to repay, given this relationship.[35]

The historical literature on debt-peonage argues that indentured laborers for the most part were passive actors compared to free laborers because the hacienda secured their basic subsistence needs. If so, then in Nuevo León the hacienda apparently no longer met the subsistence needs of the *jornaleros,* who used the proletarian tactic of the strike to further their aims of higher wages, less work, and a reduction in the price of food from the hacienda store. Strikes in the haciendas marked the beginnings of *jornalero* collective action. They increasingly took bolder measures in the last years of the Porfiriato, including escaping en masse from the haciendas, eroding the landlord's authority.

In 1906 a "crew of laborers" from Hacienda de Raices, a guayule-producing estate in Galeana, went on strike. Led by strike leaders Reyes Mendoza and Antonio Gutiérrez, the *jornaleros* refused to work because the guayule, a fiber used in the making of rubber, was too hard to cut. They demanded higher wages and a "reduction of work." The hacienda administrators refused to negotiate with the strikers, forcing them to abandon the hacienda in protest. On orders from the hacienda's manager, Galeana's authorities arrested the two strike leaders—not for leading the strike but for owing the hacienda a combined total of 174 pesos in wage advances.[36] Each owed the hacienda about a year of free labor at the prevailing wage of 25 centavos a day.

This was not an isolated strike, but the beginning of a wave of *jornalero* unrest in southern Nuevo León. Another strike erupted at San Jorge, a hacienda in Galeana, in 1907 when five *sirvientes* refused to work. Luis Cortés, the mayor of Galeana, arrested them on the grounds that they owed the hacienda a combined sum of 500 pesos in advance wages, an average of 100 pesos each or four hundred days of free labor each at the going daily wage of twenty-five centavos. The imprisoned *jornaleros* were willing to return to work "as in the past," according to Cortés, who did not mention the motives behind the strike. He nevertheless assured Governor Reyes that these types of incidents "would not occur again" and that he was going to let all of Galeana's "laboring people" know about "the inconveniences and responsibilities that such disorders bring to oneself and to warn them of the consequence [strikes] that these incidents bear." [37] Cortés failed to keep his promise, not because he was inept in his utilization of force, but because he had no control over the external forces that had given birth to these labor disturbances.

At the turn of the twentieth century haciendas in southern Nuevo León had prospered when they switched from grains and cattle to ixtle and guayule, two export products. While Nuevo León ranked almost at the bottom of food production in Mexico, it was among the highest producers of ixtle and guayule, producing close to one-third of all the ixtle in Mexico.[38]

Eugenio Ortiz, a Spanish immigrant, purchased Soledad Hacienda for 165,000 pesos during the 1890s. Within ten years Soledad had produced 230,000 pesos in guayule, while ixtle had brought similar returns. In addition, the hacienda produced the traditional commodities such as corn, wheat, fruits, lumber, and cattle.[39] The rate of profit was high, considering that guayule and ixtle were two of nature's gifts to the region. Although machinery was available for the harvest of these crops, landlords did not invest in it because labor was much cheaper than technology. Indentured laborers earned twenty-five centavos a day, one of the lowest wages in rural Mexico.

The demand for ixtle and guayule fell during the 1907–1908 economic crisis, affecting many estates in southern Nuevo León. As a result, the price of ixtle dropped from fifteen centavos a kilo in 1906 to five centavos in 1907, making it unprofitable to continue producing it, even with a poorly paid labor force. Yet all but a few haciendas continued to produce guayule and ixtle.[40] Why continue to produce goods that were not returning profits? Were the hacendados bad entrepreneurs?

The mining and industrial enterprises at best laid off a good portion of their labor force during the 1907–1908 crisis and at worst closed their doors. But most hacendados in Nuevo León could not opt for either of these choices. Their dependence on debt-peonage and sharecropping finally caught up with them, tying them in a straitjacket from which they could not escape. Hacendados had advanced thousands of pesos in wages and credit to *jornaleros* and sharecroppers, amounts that could never be recovered at the prevailing wages. Advancing credit and wages was necessary to conserve a permanent labor force in a competitive border labor market.

Given the economic crisis, hacendados had only two clear choices regarding their labor force. First, they could release their employees from bondage by forfeiting their debts, a decision that would have benefited the *jornaleros* but would have cost landlords thousands of pesos in advanced wages. Second, they could weather the storm by burdening their labor force with additional hardships, including wage reductions, a lengthened workday, reduced food rations, and higher food prices at the hacienda store. Disregarding the cost of maintaining their permanent labor force, landlords opted for the second choice. They kept thousands of *jornaleros* in bondage, a decision that involved a greater exploitation of an already highly exploited labor force.

Hacendados who continued to concentrate on ixtle and guayule did so not because it was profitable, but in order to provide their "*braceros* [field hands] with work when they have no other work in agriculture" and "so that they would not be idle" in the absence of any real work.[41] This line of reasoning has a paternalistic aspect. But hacendados made the decision to employ their entire labor force not because they felt responsible for the well-being of their *jornaleros,* but because they had invested thousands of pesos in wage advancements. Although the cost of keeping labor employed was higher than the profits generated from ixtle and guayule production, hacendados had to keep *jornaleros* attached to the hacienda.

This persistence in producing ixtle and guayule in a period when the price and demand of these goods fell dramatically illustrates the great cost of labor in operating haciendas. Hacendados had spent more on maintaining a labor force with wage and credit advancements than on machinery and irrigation. It is difficult to calculate their investment in labor, but surely it must have been in the hundreds of thousands of pesos. Galeana's hacendados, for instance, reported investing 93,000 pesos on ixtle production in 1908, most of it in advanced wages. Wage advancements ranged from 125 pesos for small ixtle producers (who employed one or two laborers) to 22,500 pesos (with perhaps a few hundred workers). Galeana had 2,800 jornaleros, according to the 1910 census of Nuevo León.[42] In this enclave of low wages (not only by northern Mexico standards but also for Mexico in general, regardless of the region), debt-peonage had become the costliest component in operating haciendas.

Pressured by the economic crisis and having advanced thousands of pesos in wages, landlords made greater demands on their labor force and thus fanned the flames of jornalero discontent. Hacendados tightened the screws on their labor force to the point that it became unbearable for the jornaleros and medieros, as manifested at Potosí, where thirty people went on a "peaceful strike" in the summer of 1908. Potosí's managers had reduced their labor force's wages from thirty-seven to thirty centavos and increased the price of food sold to them, especially maize, their basic staple. Jornaleros' conditions had deteriorated to the "point that you can not live." Thus, when the striking sharecroppers attempted to "settle their [hacienda financial] accounts, they were notified that they did not have any claim to their upcoming harvest." That was the straw that broke the camel's back in hacendado-jornalero relations. Other jornaleros on the hacienda, either in solidarity with the strikers or because of "not having any claim" to their harvest, refused to "lend their services" to Potosí.[43] Bernardo Reyes, who was by then very worried about the wave of jornalero unrest in Galeana, urged Cortés to solve the conflict at Potosí. Cortés sought to solve the strike by forcing the jornaleros who were "discontent" to settle their accounts with the estate. They had eight days to leave the hacienda and could return to collect their share of the harvest later. Jornaleros had two months to pay their wage advancements to the hacendados.[44] This type of solution was a no-win situation for the hacendados and the local officials, who lost control and authority over jornaleros. Hacendados could no longer "win" because the economic changes had altered the rules of the game in favor of the labor force.

The rebellion of the peones was not just confined to Galeana. Like a contagious virus it had spread throughout southern Nuevo León, alarming Governor Reyes, who had never demonstrated much concern about the development of the countryside. The trouble spot was not Galeana but neighboring Doctor Arroyo. Reyes had perhaps lost confidence in the ability of the local authorities to curb *jornalero* unrest. In early 1907 he sent one of his top aides, Emilio Hinojosa, to Doctor Arroyo to assist hacendados in dealing with "the abuses of their *sirvientes,* who are abandoning the work that they are engaged in."[45] Landlords were apparently on the defensive as *jornaleros* deserted the haciendas in large numbers. It is probable that mass desertions had become an organized and collective endeavor for *jornaleros.* Mass escapes may have been the form of *jornalero* resistance most threatening to the hacienda because of their effects: the loss of great quantities of money in advances and the erosion of the hacendados' and *caciques'* authority, which seriously threatened the survival of the hacienda, especially its abilities to retain a large labor force.

As an insider in the *jornalero*-hacendado conflicts, Hinojosa was abhorred by the landlords, the cause of this unrest. Hinojosa, a graduate of the state's law school and later its director, provided Reyes with an analysis of the "origins of the differences between property owner and *sirvientes.*" He blamed the hacendados for the disturbances that had led to mass desertions. According to Hinojosa, the discontent was rooted in the exploitation of the *peones.* He argued that although landlords in Doctor Arroyo operated the most profitable estates in Nuevo León, they paid their *jornaleros* twenty-five centavos a day, a wage that was not enough to "live by." Therefore *jornaleros* were compelled to solicit wage advances, while others "go to other parts in search of better wages."[46] Hinojosa made two recommendations aimed at reducing social tensions: first, for hacendados to suspend the practice of wage advancements and, second, to double the daily wage from twenty-five to fifty centavos so that *jornaleros'* salaries could be uniform throughout Nuevo León.

Hinojosa's analysis of *jornalero* unrest and policy recommendations helped educate Bernardo Reyes, who changed his views on *jornalero*-hacendado relations and the meaning of servitude. Possibly based on the information fed to him by local officials, Reyes at first judged the *jornaleros* to be the belligerent party. Hinojosa's eye-opening report encouraged Reyes to reform labor conditions on the haciendas. With that pressing goal of reform in mind, and given the critical situation of a possible complete collapse of order in Doctor Arroyo and perhaps all of the southern municipalities, Reyes ordered Hinojosa to collect more information on labor conditions on the haciendas. Moreover, he appointed Hinojosa as his personal representative in the south and asked him to do everything possible to prevent more *jornalero* desertions from the estates.

Hinojosa responded to this request by saying that he would "do everything within my legal powers to stop the emigration of the *peones* from this district."[47] He did not elaborate on how he intended to stop the flow of desertions. Reyes advised him to proceed with "the due confidence that this matter deserves" in the gathering of information:

> considering that if the proletariat group or the group that employs them finds out the motives behind this [the collection of facts], it would awaken in them immoral pretensions, with consequent disorders that should be avoided at any cost.[48]

Hinojosa was to collect his information as discreetly as possible, considering that the type of questions he might ask could accelerate the intensity of the already heated conflict between landlords and *jornaleros*. Hacendados might not like anybody asking questions about *jornalero* conditions and wages, while rural workers might interpret their own growing resistance to their social conditions as receiving a sympathetic ear from the state government. He had to ensure that the *jornaleros* did not acquire any "seditious ideas that would bring them to their own ruin" and thus end whatever aid the state government could give.[49] Reyes warned that order had to be restored at any cost, however, and any further intensification of *jornalero* unrest had to be avoided. Otherwise "it could lead us to the excesses that in other parts have been found necessary to repress, even if the execution [*fusilamiento*] of some wretched ones [is necessary]."[50]

Reyes needed the information so that he could be equipped to go directly to the hacendados and convince them to change their evil ways. Previously he had believed that it was the *jornaleros* who had provoked the unrest. Perhaps based on Hinojosa's reports, he changed his opinion about the cause of rural unrest. Nevertheless, he thought that hacendados were receptive to the voice of reason, as he sought to approach them with the "tact, discretion, and caution that this case demands." Reyes hoped to persuade them to raise the minimum wage from twenty-five centavos a day to fifty and to end the practice of wage advances, two of Hinojosa's original recommendations.[51]

It was Reyes's political style to use cordial persuasion to convince employers to change practices that had caused unrest within their workforce. In an earlier case involving mine workers in Coahuila who protested being paid bimonthly and in company chips, Reyes believed that the workers' complaints had been justified. He advised Miguel Cárdenas, the governor of Coahuila, to use his "influence" with the mine owners so they could put an end to those practices.[52] It is not known whether Reyes approached landlords in Nuevo León with the recommendation to raise the minimum wage and end wage advancements. If he did, then he apparently failed to convince them that it was in their best interest to take the initiative in reforming labor relations. It would be up to the state government to carry out the reforms.

THE JORNALERO LAW OF 1908

By 1907 an antiservitude consensus had emerged in Monterrey, coalescing around the city's business community, the press, and state government. These city circles perceived debt-peonage bondage as the antithesis to enlightenment and progress because it held thousands of workers under the oppression of bondage. Their views on labor had been shaped in Monterrey, the industrial center of Mexico, where free labor was the rule. Moreover, debt-peonage went against the grain of the emerging border labor market, where the competition for scarce labor was intense. Underneath the consensus also lay a certain contempt for the hacendados, who, while not contributing greatly to Nuevo León's economic development, held in bondage around 30,000 jornaleros, a figure much larger than the number of Monterrey's industrial proletariat. This antibondage consensus coalesced in the midst of the escalation in jornalero unrest, an indication that the rural workers played a significant role in forcing the city to intervene in the countryside through the formulation of social policy.

While Emilio Hinojosa was busy collecting information on jornalero-hacendado relations and attempting to maintain order in the countryside, a group of entrepreneurs formed the Centro Agrícola de Nuevo León in January 1907. The Centro Agrícola promoted "the development of agriculture and its associated branches" in more efficient ways. It called, for example, for more "scientific" approaches to agriculture and for implementation of "large-scale" efficient farming.[53] Improving rural workers' living and working conditions was necessary for the modernization of agriculture so that the pueblo agricultor would not be "subjected to social unrest" rooted in the "absorption of wealth in a few hands." [54] Basing their views on their own experiences with urban labor and a strong belief in a liberal political economy, these industrialists, who had neglected the countryside in terms of investments and finances, claimed to be part of the moral consciousness of the northeast countryside. Business leaders aimed to redirect its development, especially the ending of debt-peonage. The formation of a core group of reformers was another example of the extension of the city's influence over the countryside.

Bernardo Reyes, who held ceremonial posts in the leading organizations of Monterrey, from the elitist Casino de Monterrey to the Gran Círculo de Obreros de Monterrey, presided over the Centro Agrícola de Nuevo León. Adolfo Zambrano (president), Constantino de Tarnava (vice-president), Miguel Ferrara (treasurer), and Gustavo Dresel (*primer vocal*), all prominent members of the Monterrey's business community, held the leading positions in this organization. Reyes was perhaps convinced that hacendados would not reform labor relations on their own initiative. Therefore, he used the Centro Agrícola's recommendations on reforming *jornalero*-landlord relations. They were essentially presented to the state legislature, which passed the *jornalero* law of 1908. Hacendados did not have a political organization that could represent their interests, perhaps an indication that they did not carry much political weight outside of the southern part of Nuevo León.

These 1908 laws originated when the Centro Agrícola de Nuevo León, a year and a half after its founding in 1907, introduced in the state legislature an article directed at abolishing debt-peonage. Reyes strongly endorsed this measure because he wanted to end the "servitude" which kept people "tied for life to the services of the moneylender." Labor bondage had to end because it was "harmful to the peon" and because its continued existence was an act of "immoral manifestations." [55] Labor reformers perceived debt-peonage to be a regressive system of labor retention because the *jornalero*

> accepts unconditionally servitude [*servidumbre*] of many years, a period in which, for various reasons, other areas are improving their wages.... In a certain way these debts even become an obligatory inheritance of payments from fathers to sons, damaging and restricting the progress that should be realized by free people.[56]

To correct these wrongs the state legislature passed the *jornalero* law in August 1908. The law had four basic points, all aimed at ending bondage: to eliminate the practice of advancing wages to rural workers; to set a minimum wage of fifty centavos a day for all rural workers; to set contracts that stipulated the legal obligations between hacendados and *jornaleros;* and, in order to compensate landlords for the advanced wages already in effect and once the first three conditions were met, to allow hacendados to deduct one-third of the *jornaleros'* wages a year until the debt was paid off.[57] The first two points of the law were exactly the recommendations that Emilio Hinojosa had proposed to Bernardo Reyes in February 1907, suggesting that his analysis of the turmoil in the southern haciendas established the base for the new state policy. Although the Centro Agrícola de Nuevo León sponsored this law and it was passed by the Reyista legislature, it would be erroneous to consider this type of reform to be "state-centered" or emerging from "above." This legislation was also passed as a reaction to *jornalero* resistance, mass desertions from haciendas, and strikes. The combination of *jornalero* unrest and elite influence, in both political and ideological articulation of the "immorality" behind the meaning of servitude, suggests that the law was a "society-centered" initiative.

Labor reformers expected the *jornalero* law of 1908 to replace servitude with free labor. The legislation abolished salary advances and raised the rural minimum wage as the solution to rural unrest and mass desertions. In spite of the desired goals of this legislation, it does raise a few questions. Did the state government have the power to enforce it? Did the hacendados abide by the law? Did it lead to new social relationships between landlord and *jornalero*? The Mexican Revolution of 1910–1920 makes it difficult to appraise the impact of the law over a long period. Nevertheless, the passage of the law gave rise to some new developments.

The *jornalero* law of 1908 sent a strong message to other landlords outside of Nuevo León, especially in Tamaulipas, where it was "difficult to find an hacendado who had not invested a considerable amount of capital in [wage] advancements to *jornaleros* and sharecroppers." [58] A few months after the passage of Nuevo León's landmark legislation, the members of the Cámara Agrícola y Ganadera de Tamaulipas met privately. In Tamaulipas, unlike Nuevo León, the voice of reason prevailed: landlords, without external pressures, agreed to end the practice of advancing wages to laborers as the main mechanism for labor recruitment. [59] Moreover, they confessed that the "principal cause, and we can call it the only one," behind the rise of *jornalero*-hacendado conflicts in Tamaulipas was the wage advances, which, in the end, kept thousands of *peones* in bondage.

In addition to the ripple effect of the *jornalero* law in Tamaulipas, a good portion of Nuevo León's many hacendados apparently adhered to the legislation. What Reyes wanted was not to eliminate the hacendados as an economic force but to push them in the direction of "progress." Contracts, minimum wages, and the elimination of debt-peonage were means toward that end. Most of the twenty-six municipalities in Table 4.5 complied with the wage requirements, including eight that paid above the minimum. Landlords from Cadereyta Jiménez abided by the new order: they offered contracts (stipulating the wages along with access to hacienda housing) to their laborers and raised the wage to fifty centavos a day.[60] In Bustamantes conditions for *jornaleros* improved and "and would improve even more the day that all know about that enlightened law of our state."[61]

Landlords from the southern municipalities, the heart of servitude, resisted the *jornalero* law of 1908, however. Old habits died hard. In 1910 close to 6,000 *jornaleros* in Aramberrí, Doctor Arroyo, and Mier y Noriega, all southern municipalities, earned between thirty and thirty-seven centavos a day. Galeana, which contained close to 3,000 *jornaleros*, was the only southern municipality that complied with the minimum wage of fifty centavos. Landlords maintained their old habits without taking into consideration that the *jornalero* laws were aimed at eliminating debt-peonage. They violated the laws by continuing to advance wages to their *jornaleros* and by not raising the minimum wage.[62] A Cadereyta Jiménez hacendado, for instance, hired a labor agent to recruit *jornaleros* in Doctor Arroyo only to be blocked by the mayor, who did not allow him to "take out the people" from this municipality.[63] Meanwhile, others adhered to the practice of buying and selling *jornaleros'* debts as if it was simply another business transaction. For example, the owners of Ciénega de Toros Hacienda in Galeana purchased a 300-peso debt that two *jornaleros* had accumulated.

The landlords manifested their resistance to the legislation by advancing wages to recruit labor, maintaining the minimum rural wage below fifty centavos, and purchasing *jornaleros'* debts. The fact that they carried on with their old ways was also an indication that the state government did not have the means to enforce the law through inspectors, fines, and courts. But why did some hacendados, especially those in the south, continue to go against the grain of reform? Was the law a simple exercise of Liberal ideology, lacking real consequences? Hidden beneath the hacendados' resistance to the law was the fear of losing complete control of their labor force, composed of indentured *jornaleros* and sharecroppers.

Unlike Monterrey's capitalists, who had invested more in technology than in labor, hacendados lacked the credit to invest in technology, relying more on low-wage labor and labor-intensive farming. Skills and the availability of labor determined Monterrey's wages. Hacendados, in complete contrast, regarded wage advances as a necessary investment to maintain a present and future labor force. B. Traven, the eccentric novelist (who among his many novels wrote six on the Mexican southeast), examined the differences between free and unfree labor during the Porfiriato in *The Carreta*. He compared the relationships between *carreteros* (cart drivers), who were free, and the unfree *peones* who labored in the plantations of Chiapas:

The *carreteros* knew that they were free and could go when and where they pleased. The peons knew that they were not free and had no right to go when and where they pleased. . . . The *finqueros* [planters] made a higher profit by maintaining the peonage system, and the others made more by having free men to work for them.[64]

Close to 30,000 *jornaleros* labored on the Nuevoleonese haciendas of 1910, most of them under conditions of debt-peonage. More than anything, hacendados were afraid of losing their labor force to the free labor market, where they could not compete as employers because they lacked the financial resources to pay competitive wages. Losing workers also meant losing the large amounts of money that they had already advanced to secure a labor force. The evidence suggests that *jornaleros'* debts to the landlords ranged between 100 to 150 pesos per person. The Soledad de la Mota hacienda, for instance, employed forty *jornaleros* who had accumulated a combined debt of 4,000 pesos. This hacienda belonged to Sucesores de Mauro Salazar, an agricultural company which operated five other properties, and had advanced another 15,000 pesos in wages to the *jornaleros* it employed.[65] If they obeyed the new antidebt peonage legislation, hacendados stood to lose thousands of pesos they had invested in labor, not to mention their labor force, to the free market. Taken together, the loss amounted to a few million pesos (30,000 *jornaleros* times 100–150 pesos in wage advancements equals 3,000,000 to 4,500,0000 pesos), money that was impossible to recover.

Because of the difficulty of recruiting rural workers, labor had historically represented the highest cost in operating the Nuevoleonese hacienda. Hacendados panicked over the possibility of losing thousands of *jornaleros* and their wage advances. The 1848 boundary had a similar debilitating effect on landlords, as Comisión Pesquisidora reported in 1873. The commission claimed, perhaps with a degree of exaggeration, that the departure of indentured laborers cost landlords "over one million [pesos] a year." What perturbed pre-Porfirian landlords most, however, was not "so much the loss of money," but the loss of "labor to places where the population is sparse, the loss of men being a loss of capital to the country, considered, as they are, instruments of labor."[66]

By Mexican standards, most landlords in Nuevo León were poor. They did not own large estates, suffered from lack of credit, and could only sustain the hacienda through labor peonage. Many had borrowed money from moneylenders so that they could advance wages to their workers.

Mexican small landlords "have to submit themselves to the yoke of the local *agiotistas*" (moneylenders), who charged interest rates of 25 percent on loans, according to the Caja de Préstamos.[67] The Sucesores de Mauro Salazar borrowed 54,000 pesos from Hernández Hermanos, a Monterrey commercial and financial house. Of this, 15,000 pesos had been destined for wages advanced to its *peones*.[68] The potential loss of 15,000 pesos would have ruined this hacienda, which would have been unable to pay its creditor at such a high interest rate.

The law of 1908 also had the effect of helping erode the authority that hacendados and local officials held over *jornaleros,* even before the Mexican Revolution began. Indebted peons could not be held against their will on the hacienda, according to the law. Therefore, the law provided *jornaleros* with new choices that directly challenged hacendados. The choices ranged from simply "ignoring their debts" to paying their debts on their own terms (such as with "monthly payments of one peso") to fleeing from the hacienda with the "tools, wares, household goods, and other utilities for which they had responsibility." [69]

Thus, the mass desertions continued. Three months after the passage of the law, Galeana's mayor reported an increased number of "cases that have been presented [to me] in which some *sirvientes* and *medieros* have left the haciendas to which they have commitments to work." [70] In 1910 another mayor reported that the hacendados "had for some time complained that they have been swindled and robbed of their interests by laborers, share-croppers, and *contratistas* [contract workers] that furtively escape from the haciendas." [71] Each defector cost landlords money, as in the case of Hacienda Ciénega de Toros. The hacienda lost 366 pesos in advances to two runaways.[72]

The new laws empowered *jornaleros,* who through their many actions eroded the authority hacendados and local officials held over them. Now that the local *caciques* could no longer legally keep *jornaleros* in jail or tied to the estate, they requested guidance from the state leaders on dealing with *jornalero* assertiveness. Given the laws of 1908, and in view of the new attitude of *jornaleros,* they wanted to know what could be done to provide hacendados with "ayuda moral" (moral help).[73] Although Bernardo Reyes sympathized with the "plight" of the hacendados, he advised the mayor of Galeana, and, perhaps all other local officials, that the legislation of 1908 was the law of the land and that failure to pay debts could not constitutionally force a *jornalero* to go to jail. His advice was to "conciliate the private and general interests" of both "servant and served" by guiding them in the direction of the new "constitutional prescriptions."[74] In spite of the law *caciques* continued to jail *jornaleros,* however, under the charge of "falta a la autoridad" (lack of respect for the authorities), rather than for failure to pay debts or for desertions from the estates.[75]

RURAL NUEVO LEÓN ON THE EVE OF THE REVOLUTION

Under the new post-1908 conditions, the economic fortunes of haciendas still depended largely on their ability to retain a labor force. The evidence indicates that on the eve of the Revolution haciendas tended to recruit labor through sharecropping. The case of the Ciénega de Toros hacienda illustrates this point. The Fuentes Hermanos purchased this hacienda, a large Saltillo land company, in 1902. Ciénega de Toros initially cultivated a modest 400 to 500 hectares of wheat, expanding to 4,000 hectares by 1904 and to 8,000 hectares by 1912. In 1912 this enterprise received a long-term, low-interest loan of 454,000 pesos from the Caja de Préstamos, the lending institution funded by banks and the government. With this new loan from the Caja de Préstamos, the hacienda planned to open up an additional 4,000 hectares of wheat lands.[76] As one of the few modern haciendas in the state, it invested in machinery, including the reaper, which "does the work of seventy who use the sickle."[77]

As much as this "modern" agrarian enterprise wanted to encourage and expand wheat cultivation by its own means, resources, and technology, it was limited by labor shortages. The collapse of the system of debt-peonage led to mass migrations to Texas, causing severe labor shortages on the haciendas. Because it was almost impossible to secure wage laborers, hacendados concentrated on sharecropping as the device for recruiting labor. Apparently, haciendas had no other option except to offer *medieros* half of the production and *tercieros* two-thirds of all production.[78] Often the hacienda gave a daily wage advance of thirty-seven centavos a day, to be paid back with the crops that were to be harvested. As the owners of Ciénega de Toros, the Fuentes family, contended:

> We would have preferred to cultivate all this land by our own means; however, it would be impossible to care for it and in no way would we have the labor force needed to work it, even when we pay high wages. With the sharecropping system that we operate of *medieros* and *tercieros* it is not difficult to assemble the necessary workers that are needed because, naturally, there are more advantages [for the sharecropper] than in working as peons, even if the wages are high.[79]

In 1909 the Ciénega de Toros had under contract 600 sharecroppers, distributed throughout the different ranches that made up this enterprise. To open up the additional 4,000 hectares of wheat, Ciénega de Toros needed to recruit a labor force of 200 to 250 persons, all under *terciero* and *mediero* contracts.[80] According to the contracts, they were obligated to work for the hacienda in the "dead" period between planting and harvest for a wage of between thirty-seven and seventy-five centavos a day.[81] An auditor for the Caja de Préstamos evaluated the future prospects of Ciénega de Toros:

Perhaps with the sharecropping system that has recently been adopted the number of field hands could increase. If it weren't for the plowing machines that open up for cultivation 8 to 15 hectares of land a day, the harvest would be very limited.[82]

For the *jornaleros* the sharecropping system was a lesser evil compared to debt-peonage because sharecroppers had more independence and did not have to be burdened by the *mayordomo,* the hated hacienda overseer. The hacienda had no choice other than sharecropping if it sought to secure a labor force. Even with the adopted sharecropping system, however, retaining a permanent labor system was not guaranteed. In one case at Ciénega de Toros, two *medieros* left the hacienda after their first harvest failed. Only one returned; the other permanently deserted, leaving a considerable debt to the hacienda—an increasingly typical pattern. "There are a growing number of cases in which some *sirvientes* and *medieros* leave the estates," Galeana's mayor noted, "and then renounce their debts or offer to pay them in installments of a peso a month, thus covering their debt obligations."[83]

In summary, the hacienda did not emerge as the dominant institution in the region. While the hacienda played a more important role in the Porfiriato than it had in the past, it faced many obstacles that impeded the development of a competitive, market-oriented hacendado class. Because the hacienda could not overcome these obstacles, an insecure hacendado class emerged that adopted coercive labor practices just to maintain a stable labor force. Access to the international boundary and a state government which did not regard the hacendados as a major cornerstone of the overall economic development weakened the landlords. In the end, the hacienda developed as a weak institution compared to the role it played in the rest of Porfirian Mexico.

Of all the rural problems, the issue of indentured labor best places the growing city-countryside divisions into perspective. The haciendas controlled 30,000 *jornaleros,* a total larger than the number of Monterrey's industrial proletariat, through the coercive means of advance payments. By the 1900s *jornaleros* had begun to resist the conditions tying them to the haciendas by running away to other parts or by challenging the hacendados on the issue of declining wages. In a period dominated by the emerging border labor market of free labor and competition for scarce labor, the Reyista state, in alliance with Monterrey's business community, challenged the hacendados on the issue of indentured labor. The state imposed legislation which outlawed indentured labor by setting a minimum wage of fifty centavos a day and banning advance payments. The purpose of the law was to release a large sector of Nuevo León's workforce for the free labor market.

For 250 years the countryside had sustained the region economically and militarily. Since the origins of colonization at the turn of the seventeenth century, the peasant-soldier had defended the region in exchange for free land. The integration of Nuevo León into the Porfirian central state, coupled with the defeat of the Indians in the 1870s, ended the long-established peasant-state alliance. Unlike its actions in other parts of Mexico, the state did not turn against the peasants. The *comunidad de accionistas* continued to enjoy an autonomous existence for the duration of the Porfiriato.

The combined force of the market economy, droughts, and poor harvests weakened the communities as many internal conflicts emerged over land and water usage. By the end of the Porfiriato it was becoming clear that the once autonomous, self-sustaining *comunidades de accionistas* could no longer economically support their members. The Nuevoleonese peasantry suffered a profound crisis of subsistence and was at the mercy of the market economy.

The countryside emerged in a relatively weak and powerless position *vis-à-vis* the city. Monterrey's industrialization and urbanization established a pattern that continues to the present—the centralization of population, industry, services, education, and government in the city. This process contributed to the image of the city as progressive and the countryside as backward, an image that also served the ideological purposes of identifying "progress" with the urban bourgeoisie and thus legitimized the urban bourgeoisie's economic and ideological dominion over the region.

If immigration to the United States can be used as an indicator of the effects of the social and economic crisis in the countryside, then immigration records indicate that the crisis was severe. Between July 1, 1910, and June 30, 1911, Nuevo León ranked fourth, after the Federal District, Chihuahua, and Coahuila, as the place of residence for persons migrating to the United States. During that year 7,295 people registered with border authorities as having Nuevo León as their last residence, surely an undercount considering that many people did not register. Furthermore, of those who returned to Mexico in the period of July 31–December 31, 1910, Nuevo León ranked fourteenth as a destination, with only 781 returning to the state.[84] In the end, the Nuevoleonese countryside was an exporter of labor to the emerging border labor market.

Class, Culture, and Politics in Monterrey, 1890–1910

Las distancias apartan las ciudades,
Las ciudades destruyen los costumbres . . .
Y estuve al punto de cambiar tu mundo,
De cambiar tu mundo por el mundo mío.
[Distances separate cities,
Cities destroy customs . . .
And I was ready to change your world,
To change your world for mine.]

"LAS CIUDADES" (*RANCHERA* SONG)

Tengo orgullo de ser del norte
de mero San Luisito,
porque de allí es Monterrey.
De los barrios, el más querido,
por se el más reinero,
sí señor, barrio donde nací.
[I am proud of being from the north,
from the heart of San Luisito,
because it is in Monterrey.
Of all the neighborhoods, the most beloved,
because it is the most royal,
yes, sir, the neighborhood in which I was born.]

"EL CORRIDO DE MONTERREY" (*RANCHERA* SONG)

Although Monterrey had a three-hundred-year history by the turn of the twentieth century, the city had outworn its ancient rags, having been transformed from a declining commercial town after 1890 into the industrial center of Mexico and producing 13.5 percent of the total industrial output of the nation on the eve of the Mexican Revolution. The operation of the smelters, textile factories, steel mill, brewery, and the many other enterprises at the base of this industrial output required a complex organization of technological, human, and capital resources. Ores from the mining centers of Mexico were needed to operate the smelters; cotton from La Laguna and Texas for the textile mills; hops from Europe and malt from the United States for the brewing industry; oil from Tampico and coal from Coahuila to fuel industries. Capitalists like "Colonel" J. A. Robertson from Tennessee, Vicente Ferrara from Italy, and Tomás Mendirichaga from Spain as well as native capitalist families like the Sadas, Zambranos, Calderóns, and Maderos invested in these industries while consolidating themselves as the dominant class through business deals and marriages. Industrialists recruited European and U.S. managers and hundreds of skilled workers to build and operate the industries; glassblowers and beer brewers from Germany; and steel experts, carpenters, bricklayers, and mechanics from the United States. As skilled and semiskilled labor, hundreds of U.S. workers toiled in the smelters, factories, and railroad yards along with the thousands of unskilled recent arrivals from Zacatecas, San Luis Potosí, and other parts of Mexico's interior. The Sultan of the North, as Monterrey is called, could have staked a claim as the flagship steering Mexico into the twentieth century.

Workers' overalls and business suits symbolized Monterrey's transformation into a center of work and capital accumulation, a point *La Voz de Nuevo León* constantly made from 1890 to 1910. In 1904 it editorialized that Monterrey was a place where "workers provide capital with the valuable contingent of their labors" and receive in exchange "wages that are determined by the skill that they have developed in their respective employment, as is well known."[1] The newspaper presented the view of an evolving business-labor partnership in the making of modern Monterrey, a view that local intellectuals and the press have continued to promote even to the present. This outlook has contributed to one of the prevailing narratives about Monterrey: the absence of class conflict. Proponents of this point of view do not negate the existence of classes, asserting only that conflict based on classes has not been part of the overall history of Monterrey. This interpretation is based on the premise that capitalists, the middle classes, and workers have worked harmoniously for the betterment of Monterrey— all for one and one for all. Capitalists became capitalists by working hard and by treating workers with dignity.[2]

This understanding presents class harmony as one of the driving forces of Monterrey's modern history, assuming that capitalists have acted as the anchors of society and minimizing any active role for the subordinate classes other than as economic actors whose needs were satisfied by well-paid employment. This conception of society has had a powerful influence on much of the historical writing on the region, in which the history of the subaltern groups, for all practical purposes, has been ignored.

This chapter challenges the interpretations of Monterrey's history based on class harmony. Monterrey served as the arena in which the collective identities of classes were formed by the specific relationship between these classes and the Reyista state, which was consistently building the institutional framework in which society operated, and by their relationship with each other. Classes interacted inside and outside the workplace, and class conflict decisively shaped class interests and political activity during Monterrey's formative years of industrialization.

THE IDEOLOGY OF THE "PROGRESSIVE" CITY

From 1890 to 1910 literally thousands of migrants from Zacatecas, San Luis Potosí, and other states arrived by the trainload in Monterrey. These migrants came because the city had a reputation as a place where employment abounded and, as a newspaper reported in 1903, "they immediately find work."[3] After their arrival, if they did not have any family in Monterrey, migrants rested in hotels, in boardinghouses, and in the streets. Depending on the amount of money that they had, they could either stay at the expensive Windsor Hotel or at the less expensive Sol Naciente and Monterrey Hotels. The Sol Naciente Hotel offered rooms and meals for 1.25 pesos a day per person in 1907. It provided small rooms for twenty-five centavos a day, although without any services. Boardinghouses also accepted families.[4] Those without any money and family slept in the streets, the plazas, and the railroad station.

After resting, the migrants explored Monterrey, a city that did not resemble anywhere they had ever been unless they had worked in the United States or visited a big city like Mexico City or Torreón. Even though Monterrey had celebrated its 300th anniversary in 1896, industry and rapid urban growth had transformed the city beyond recognition. The number of housing units had more than doubled between 1890 and 1903.[5] The newly arrived migrants may have felt a combination of curiosity and apprehension at their first view of the city: smoke-stacked factories, the seven-story Cuauhtémoc Brewery building (the tallest building in Mexico), large commercial stores stacked with a variety of imported and domestic products, urban rail lines, paved streets, telephones, and a few automobiles.

Perhaps unobtrusively, the city immediately began to work its influence on the migrants. They would have had a difficult time finding *pulque* to quench their thirst. Monterrey's inhabitants consumed ice-cold beers and soft drinks instead, two products that were unfamiliar to the tastes of most Mexicans at the turn of the twentieth century. They could select from various internationally acclaimed beers, such as Carta Blanca, which the Cuauhtémoc Brewery so cleverly advertised to encourage consumption, or Moctezuma Brewery products. They could choose between soft drinks made by the Topo Chico Company or Las Fuentes de San Bernabé. Perhaps Monterrey's beers and soft drinks were associated with progress because of their newness to Mexicans and because they were mass-produced. *Pulque*, in contrast, was relegated to the old Mexico of the past and its countryside.

The local press, government, and business leaders promoted Monterrey as a "progressive" city, a code word for industry, urban development, high culture, schools, consumption, and new social attitudes, among other traits. Progress was also defined in contrast to "backwardness," its supposed opposite. For example, hard work and savings were considered progressive human qualities, in contrast to idleness, wasteful spending, and heavy drinking. *Regiomontanos* were constantly reminded of "progress," and the word entered the vernacular. One of the main thoroughfares of the city was named Progreso Street, and the Reyista party that governed Nuevo León was called the Gran Círculo Unión y Progreso.

Monterrey attracted people from all walks of life, but government officials and entrepreneurs mainly wanted workers, people who would labor and establish permanent roots in the city as wage earners. They did not want drifters, vagrants, beggars, and other people associated with "backward" attitudes toward work and individual advancement. *La Voz de Nuevo León* welcomed newcomers to Monterrey as long as they met certain criteria:

the capital of Nuevo León is an enclave of employment where the wealthy can profitably invest their money and the poor can find employment. This is what is actually taking place in Monterrey, but by no means is it a place where the lazy can find bread. It is lunacy to think that the lazy have a right to life when it is not nourished with labor. It truly pleases us to see a large number of individuals who come to help us with their labor. They are the ones who help in the actual and constant development of our sources of wealth. It saddens us to see that some [people] settle here hoping to find charity wherever it is to be found. Comfort is only given to men who submit to work. It is the hardworking migrants that we need: they bring the goodwill that is needed to advance our progressive condition and they will receive, in return, all the required protection from the authorities and all the considerations of citizenship.[6]

Monterrey welcomed migrants with open arms, but only if they were hardworking and energetic, two progressive individual qualities. The lazy did not deserve the "considerations of citizenship."

Recent arrivals would have also noticed the disparities between wealth and poverty in Monterrey. The city contained quite a few people of means but also the shocking presence, at least to a U.S. tourist, of "such distressing numbers of cripples" who spent the day begging.[7] People were responsible for their social condition, according to the ideology of progress. Poor people were poor because they did not want to work or spent their wages unwisely (for example, by drinking). The only people who deserved charity were those who were totally helpless, such as orphans. Monterrey's business leaders raised the funds for the Melitón Villareal Orphanage, "which is so necessary to mitigate the disgraces that are caused by the helplessness that misery creates, especially among children who by their own efforts can not free themselves from it."[8]

At least for the Reyista press, the Catholic church was considered backward and unhealthy for the minds of *regiomontano* society. As a center of "progress," Monterrey's press was on guard against the spread of backwardness, occasionally warning society with alarmist headlines such as "The Clerical Plague Threatens the Republic."[9] San Francisco Street, one of the major thoroughfares in the city, was ironically and arbitrarily renamed Ocampo, after Melchor Ocampo, one of the leading anticleric ideologues of the La Reforma era. The renaming of the street was necessary because this "street does not deserve that name in a progressive city."[10]

Newly arrived migrants quickly discovered that Monterrey did not have many churches and that priests were not part of the city's power structure. Their lack of influence was manifested not only in the arbitrary renaming of streets but in the number of priests. In 1910 the city had more lawyers (one for each 737 people) and teachers (one for each 330)—two "progressive" professions—than priests. Twenty-nine overworked priests serviced the spiritual needs of 73,000 people, or one priest for 2,517 people.[11]

Recent arrivals would immediately have recognized that they were empowered with many choices, from choosing employers and a variety of consumer goods to attending church. In contrast to the social pressures in Mexican villages, towns, and some large cities, such as Puebla and Guadalajara, where priests wielded considerable influence, Monterrey's residents could choose to attend church or not. This choice involved a different type of social pressure, however. The city's "progressive" aura perhaps most influenced their decision. Males refused to enter churches for fear of being called "fanatics" or "retarded." Women were the only consistent worshipers.[12]

In addition to being identified with progress, Monterrey was emerging as one of the centers of Mexico's new nationalism. This nationalism was deeply rooted in the growing fear that foreigners, especially North Americans, were gaining greater control of the Mexican economy. *Renacimiento*, an independent local newspaper and a proponent of the new nationalism, argued that "the progress of Mexico is not national progress, but progress of the foreigner."[13] According to this argument, foreigners were gaining economic "ownership of the nation," which, in the end, translated into political "ownership of the republic."[14] Nationalists regarded Monterrey, a city in which Mexicans owned most of the industrial enterprises, as one of the few centers where Mexicans resisted foreign domination of the economy. They praised the owners of the Fundidora de Monterrey, the only steel mill in Latin America until the 1940s, for "their patriotism."[15]

A U.S. reporter asked Bernardo Reyes a series of questions, among them: "Is it true, as it is said in the United States, that you belong to the political tendency of 'Mexico para los mexicanos?' "[16] Reyes, a Porfirian nationalist, denied that assertion. In any event, Monterrey emerged as one of the leading centers of the new "México para los mexicanos" nationalism, which found many forms of expression among *regiomontanos* (including those from the working class, as discussed later in this chapter). Although the press and the middle class produced much of the nationalist discourse, Monterrey's business leaders also articulated their own brand of nationalism, albeit less alarmist.

As a small and tightly knit class, *regiomontano* industrialists not only considered Monterrey home but also articulated their own conception of the city as a center of capital accumulation. According to their evolving view, Mexican entrepreneurs owned the enterprises and employed laborers, who performed work for a wage. These workers, along with the other city residents, were also consumers who spent their salaries on food, drink, clothing, and other goods that entrepreneurs produced and sold in stores, the largest of which they owned. What was good for business was good for the city because money was recycled—more money meant new investments, and thus more employment. The cycle repeated itself. Francisco Sada, one of the most prominent industrialists, articulated this outlook in explaining the role that the Cuauhtémoc Brewery played in the betterment of Monterrey and Mexico:

> [The brewery] directly benefits the city and the state because it distributes a great part of its utilities by way of salaries and wages in this locality, and these [wages] favor the creation of small businesses that produce . . . new sources of wealth from the point of view of taxation. . . . it also contributes to the reduction of imports, the patriotic aim to which all important enterprises aspire.[17]

From an economic perspective, the growth of Monterrey went hand in hand with the growing prosperity of this small but influential elite: they owned most of the large and medium industries, the banks, and large commercial stores and were very involved in the booming real estate business. Monterrey's urban growth ensured a secure source of profits at a local level; Mexico's expanding domestic market, in turn, ensured a growing market of consumers for their manufactured goods.

A MIGRANT'S WALK IN THE CITY

Newly arrived migrants explored the city with the goal of mapping areas for employment and affordable housing. Given the city's notorious history of high labor-turnover rates in industry, migrants quickly found jobs. In fact, they could select the firm for which they wished to work, a decision that required some contemplation of the benefits and drawbacks of laboring for each specific enterprise. *El Trueno* estimated that unskilled workers earned between 20 and 40 pesos per month in 1903, an estimate supported by other data.[18]

Metalworkers earned a minimum of 1 peso a day, plus an additional 50-centavo bonus that could be collected only if they worked a stint of twenty-five consecutive days at the smelters. This could total 37.50 pesos per month, a good salary for unskilled workers.[19] The other option was to work for a minimum wage of 75 centavos to 1 peso a day, but under less stressful and dangerous conditions. Because of the dangerous nature of the smelting industry, smelters had a notorious reputation for high labor turnover. Workers who stayed at the smelters did so because of the bonus. Some workers preferred to work for other enterprises, such as the Cuauhtémoc

Brewery. The wage difference between working for the smelters and the brewery was great: the latter only paid a minimum wage of 81 centavos or 20.25 pesos for working at least twenty-five days a month in 1903. In spite of the low wages, the brewery did offer some advantages: a shorter workday and employment that was a lot less dangerous. Many migrants left Monterrey for other destinations in northern Mexico and the southwestern United States. Labor mobility was one of the privileges of laboring in the emerging border labor market.

Besides searching for work, migrants also sought affordable housing, which was more difficult to find. This search would have taken the newcomers into different neighborhoods. The dynamics of the real estate market and the specific needs of industry had dictated the location of working-class neighborhoods. Most industrial firms (some of which provided housing for workers) and the large middle-class community of Bellavista (the first planned residential neighborhood in Monterrey) were located on the north side of the city. Middle and upper-class housing clustered in the central zone, the most expensive part of the city, along with the large commercial stores, public plazas, and government buildings. The large, unskilled migrant working class increasingly concentrated south of the Santa Catarina River.

The bulk of the working class lived in neighborhoods far from the centers of employment. This was the case of San Luisito, the largest working class *colonia* in Monterrey. Located at the south end of the city, across from the Santa Catarina River, San Luisito, as the name implies, was mainly made up of natives of San Luis Potosí. San Luisito exhibited many of the features of an unplanned urban neighborhood: overcrowded housing, unpaved streets, open sewers, and no running water, conditions that invited the spread of disease. Nine thousand people resided in San Luisito, living in *jacales* and *chozas,* two names for the kind of housing that differs little from Monterrey's shantytowns today.[20] *Jacales* were poorly constructed one-room dwellings assembled with any cheap or readily available material: tin, cardboard, scraps of lumber, and *sillar* (stone). On August 29, 1909, after a few days of torrential rains, the Santa Catarina River flooded, washing away a good part of San Luisito's *jacales* and population. It is estimated that the flood killed anywhere from 1,280 to over 4,000 people in Nuevo León.[21] San Luisito, which today is called Colonia Libertad, was rebuilt.

In spite of the city's hunger for workers, Monterrey was not an attractive place in which to settle. Newcomers came by the thousands but also left the city in large numbers. Not only did Monterrey have one of the worst climates in Mexico, with hot summers and cold winters, but it could not accommodate the constant flow of people, suffering from severe housing shortages.[22] While the majority of the "drifters" could have adjusted to the weather, the lack of affordable housing forced many to leave. Monterrey had over 600 vacant houses in 1885, an indication of the city's commercial decline and loss of population. Even though the number of housing units had more than doubled from 1890 to 1903, Monterrey could not provide the "necessary facilities for housing the people that form our floating population."[23]

The ability of workers to secure housing—purchasing it, paying rent, or having it provided by the firm—determined not only whether they remained in the city, but also the location where they lived. The post-1890 construction boom increased the value of real estate, preventing most workers from purchasing property. *El Trueno* estimated in 1901 that it cost 4,000 pesos to build a new home in Monterrey, half for the plot and the other half for the construction of the house. While the newspaper did not specify the location and type of housing, the cost of a new home was beyond the means of the great majority of the working class, bearing in mind that unskilled workers earned between 20 and 40 pesos a month in 1903. Most workers paid an average of 12 pesos per month in rents, according to *El Trueno*. This meant that workers spent between 30 to 60 percent of their wages on housing. Evidently the high rents drove many migrants out of city.[24]

A DAY WITH THE BOURGEOISIE

Monterrey's "bourgeoisie" was composed of *fronterizos,* such as the Madero, Calderón, and Zambrano families, and foreigners, such as the Riveros, Mendirichagas, and the Maíz family from Spain, the Ferraras and Benardis from Italy, the Beldens and Milmos from Ireland, the Moebiuses, Holks, Bremers, and Crams from Germany, and "Colonel" Robertson and Roberto Law from the United States. The first generation of foreign entrepreneurs retained their loyalties to their homelands, often returning to their native lands after retiring, as in the case of the Hernández-Mendirichaga group. Foreigners formed their own social clubs, such as the Club Alemán and Club Español, while North Americans had their own schools and newspapers, the *Monterrey Daily News* and the *Monterrey News*. Of the 1,252 Americans, Spaniards, and Germans residing in Monterrey in 1900, only seventeen had become Mexican citizens.[25] They also represented their nations as consuls and vice-consuls in Monterrey: Pablo Buchard (Germany); John Sanford (England); José Armendáriz (Spain); Miguel Ferrara (Italy); "Colonel" Robertson (United States); and Pedro Lambreton (France). Curiously enough, Antonio Hernández, a Mexican native and member of the Madero clan, was the consul of—of all countries—Belgium.[26]

In spite of retaining their loyalties to their homeland (or perhaps imagined homelands, as in the case of Antonio Hernández), foreigners cohered with their Mexican counterparts economically through joint business activities, socially by intermarriage, and culturally by participating in many of the elite's cultural activities. Because most entrepreneurs owned large commercial enterprises, the Monterrey Chamber of Commerce grouped together all the leading capitalists of the city. Much of the elite's "socialization" occurred in the Casino de Monterrey. Founded in 1870, the casino was the place "where the most select elements of society meet,"[27] as El Monterrey News noted. The city's elite held many exclusive events at the casino, including balls, weddings, and birthday parties. It contained a bar, a billiard room, a game room, a library, a dining room, and a ballroom that could hold four hundred people, enough room for the most "select" of society.[28]

Business leaders met at Casino de Monterrey for drinks, relaxation, gossip, and political and business deals.[29] They also mingled in other environments that catered to the wealthy, such as Salvator, which offered its customers fine liquors and served "lunch" from 10 A.M. to 4 A.M. They dined, smoked cigars, and played pool at the Jockey Club.[30] When not at the gentlemen's clubs that stayed open until the early hours of the morning, the elite also held social events in their residences and at the elegant Juárez Theater, where they enjoyed the opera and plays. Isaac Garza, of the Cuauhtémoc Brewery, celebrated his saint's day in high fashion. The invitees dressed as eighteenth-century French aristocrats and waltzed to classical music.[31]

It was the second generation of business leaders who boldly redirected bourgeois culture in Monterrey. They came to maturity from 1890 to 1910, an era in which they established a new set of cultural traits. Unlike their parents, who were self-made entrepreneurs, members of the second generation not only were born to wealth, but were highly educated, graduating from foreign universities such as the Massachusetts Institute of Technology and the University of Michigan. Having studied abroad, young members of the elite returned to Monterrey with a new set of cultural influences that were more in tune with the tastes of their generation. They founded the Club Atlético de Monterrey in 1895 to "promote and foment sporting activities that make a great contribution to the physical development of men, such as horse and human [foot] races, ball games, baseball games, 'lawn tennis,' and other similar sports that are quite common in Europe and do not yet have a name in our language."[32] One of high society's misfits, Francisco I. Madero, not only started the Revolution in 1910 but also introduced "spiritualism," an eccentric philosophical movement with some influence in Europe. Madero, the "apostle" of the Mexican Revolution, was the vice-president of the Monterrey-based Círculo Espiritista Fraternidad.[33]

Those who were too young to be *socios* (members) of the Casino de Monterrey formed the Club Terpsicore in 1897. José Calderón, the son of the Cuauhtémoc Brewery patriarch, became its first president. It sponsored cycling, horseback riding, and automobile shows. The Club Terpsicore later purchased its own building, which contained a bar, dining room, and ballroom. These young men became members of the Casino de Monterrey once they met the age requirement and other qualifications.[34]

As promoters of new sporting activities which did not "yet have a name in our language," the second generation formed the new vanguard of "high culture" for the first decades of the twentieth century, albeit an imported culture. They introduced a series of new words from abroad that would become part of the elite's vocabulary, such as "cocktail," "lunch," and "surprise," often distorting the spelling. For example, the bars that advertised lunch as part of their services spelled it "lunch," "lunche," "lonchee," and "lonche."[35]

On March 7, 1905, the elite celebrated the first "masquerade dance" in the history of the city at the Casino de Monterrey. Consuelo Garza Sada was costumed to represent *art nouveau;* María Belden dressed as a shedevil (*diablesa*); Bernardo Reyes's daughter Amalia as an Italian contrabandist; Rosa Zambrano as a gypsy; Ricardo Paz Sada as a Moor; and Joaquín Belden as a Louis XVI aristocrat. By sponsoring these types of events, the casino earned a reputation as one of the trendsetters of "bourgeois" culture in Mexico. According to *El Imparcial,* a Mexico City newspaper, the Casino de Monterrey acquired "fame for being the most elegant, best attended, and best received in material of good taste of all the existing ones [casinos] in the Republic."[36] Impressed by the "Monterrey aristocracy," especially the single women, a reporter for this newspaper attended an event at the Casino de Monterrey in 1898. He reported: "With great pleasure I noticed the great illustration of the beautiful opposite sex. All the *señoritas* speak English with admirable correctness, and some of them speak French and German."[37]

With the exception of a few ardent Reyistas, such as Manuel Rivero and Adolfo Zambrano, both of whom served as deputies to Nuevo León's congress, Monterrey's business leaders did not hold public offices in either state or municipal government. Nevertheless, they actively and visibly participated in the civic affairs of the city. Four of the best-known businessmen chaired four of the city government's thirteen commissions in 1910.[38] Francisco Sada, Adolfo Zambrano, Manuel Cantú Treviño, and Manuel Rivero formed part of the select committee of business and government leaders that organized Monterrey's centennial of Mexican independence, an event Bernardo Reyes supervised before his departure to Europe. They also organized the activities surrounding Porfirio Díaz's visit to Monterrey in 1883 and 1898. On both occasions business leaders gave Díaz a royal treatment, spending great quantities of money on balls, receptions, and dinners.[39]

As the self-proclaimed cultural and civic anchors of Monterrey, industrialists were also involved in philanthropic projects aimed at uplifting the city's subordinate classes, from sponsoring mutual-aid societies at the workplace to supporting orphanages. Florentino Cantú Treviño sponsored a worker mutual-aid society in his La Fama textile mill.[40] Antonio V. Hernández, Alfonso de Tarnava, and "other employees of commerce" founded the Círculo Mercantil Mutualista de Monterrey in 1901. This mutual-aid society catered to middle-class professionals and small business owners. It became the largest mutual-aid society in Mexico and perhaps in all of the Americas.[41] Francisco Sada of the Cuauhtémoc Brewery established one of the first chapters of the Boy Scouts in Mexico in 1911, if not the first, while Valentín Rivero and Francisco Belden served as board members of the Melitón Villareal Orphanage.[42]

Even though not involved politically in governing Monterrey and Nuevo León, Monterrey's business leaders strongly endorsed the Reyista government, a pro-business regime. The great majority of the capitalists were Reyistas because they considered Reyes a businessman's politician. Moreover, he had done them many "favors" without requesting financial payoffs. Unlike most governors in Mexico, such as the Terrazas of Chihuahua or the Molina-Montes clique of Yucatán, who used their control of the state government to create economic empires, Reyes did not use his power for personal enrichment.[43] Moreover, he was an honest politician and an excellent administrator, two qualities that business leaders re-

spected. Even Reyes's most outspoken critics, and he had many of all political shades, had some kind words to say about his management of state
resources. Francisco Madero stated that Reyes had "great administrative
qualities" and "is among the most honest politicians of the current administration."[44] A North American writer who was not too fond of Reyes wrote:
"It was rumored that no peso of his money need have any shame about its
origins. . . ."[45]

Reyes, in fact, had numerous opportunities to acquire wealth in a
business climate conducive to profiteering, especially in the real estate sector. The Hernández Hermanos firm, for example, invited him to participate
in a business partnership. Reyes courteously refused what could perhaps
have been a profitable venture, explaining that "I am entirely separated
from business, with the exception of the public duties that I perform and
for which I barely have time."[46] Well aware of his national status, Reyes
cultivated a reputation for personal honesty in the financial and administrative affairs of Nuevo León. His fatherly advice to his son Rodolfo was
that "as long as it is not believed that we are thieves, insensitive, or cowards,
everything else is tolerable."[47]

Reyes believed that "honest" government was the best rule, a practice he personally followed and often tried to instill in his subordinates.
Few Reyistas, however, heeded their leader's pleas for a corruption-free
government. Anti-Reyista critics considered Pedro Martínez, the mayor of
Monterrey, "from all points of view one of the most corrupt people who
has lived on the frontier."[48] Reyes tolerated the corruption in his followers
just as long as it did not involve "shakedowns" of the business community.

A DAY WITH THE WORKING CLASS

Not much is known about the Monterrey working class during its formative period because thus far no study has thoroughly examined it. One
of the difficulties in reconstructing the history of Monterrey's working
class is the paucity of available sources, especially sources emerging from
the working class itself, such as newspapers, pamphlets, and organizational records. In part this was due to the nature of the Reyista state,
one that many Liberals considered the most authoritarian in Mexico. The
Reyista rulers censored all literature deemed subversive, including the Liberal press, and consequently limited workers' abilities to express their political concerns. Meanwhile, the Reyista press tended to report only on
Monterrey's industrial progress and class harmony and never on social
conflict.

The foreign press occasionally provided accounts on Monterrey that were quite different from the picture painted by the Reyista press. For instance, the Reyista press's coverage of the yellow fever epidemic of 1903 did not mention casualties in Monterrey, only the effect of the epidemic on the economy, particularly the poor sales at stores. A communication from a member of the U.S. Marine Hospital Service to the *San Antonio Daily Express News* gives a different image of the effects of the epidemic. This newspaper reported:

> The death rate among the peon class must be very high, but the authorities have succeeded in hiding pretty well the true conditions of the affair. The Board of Health has finally let it be known that they only wanted the grave forms of the disease reported. The public report is simply ridiculous, for they are having more deaths than cases reported . . . we will never know anything like the true figures of the epidemic. . . . Every portion of the city, including smelters and steel mill, is infected.[49]

The Reyistas also "succeeded in hiding pretty well" the history of the working class from later historians by reporting only on those subjects deemed favorable to Reyismo and censoring others. Given these constraints, one can offer only a fragmentary account of working-class history and culture.

The first working-class organization in Nuevo León, the Gran Círculo de Obreros de Monterrey, was formed in 1874, following the program of the Gran Círculo de Obreros de México. This organization, whose members were mainly artisans, followed the self-help, mutual-aid tradition. Workers formed mutual-aid societies to alleviate "the most pressing contingencies of life, such as sickness, and lack of work."[50] These groups provided members with payments for work-related accidents, relief from unemployment, medical expenses, and funeral costs. In 1886 Alberto Sada noted that membership in the Gran Círculo had increased noticeably as the organization had "awakened" the interests of workers, transforming their "weak" forces into a "powerful and robust one."[51] Unlike the Gran Círculo de Obreros de México, which later adopted a more radical ideology, the Gran Círculo de Obreros de Monterrey remained a self-help organization, at least until the dawn of the Revolution.

Members paid the Gran Círculo a portion of their wages, placed in a general fund designated for the members' most dire needs. The Gran Círculo de Obreros de Monterrey, for example, provided moral and financial support to Concepción Uno de Gracia, whose husband was bedridden. The members visited her husband everyday, purchased the needed medicine, ensured that the doctor made regular visits, and provided her with fifty centavos a day. After her husband died, the Gran Círculo not only paid the entire cost of the funeral, but attended en masse. She also received an additional thirty pesos for her needs.[52]

Mutual-aid organizations flourished in Monterrey. By 1905 the Gran Círculo de Obreros de Monterrey counted 563 members and 61 honorary members, among them Bernardo Reyes and other leading entrepreneurs. It had 32,000 pesos invested in urban property, sponsored English classes, founded the Casino Obrero de Monterrey for recreational purposes, and participated in the Liga Anti-alcohólica.[53] Workers' organizations that remained within the mutual-aid framework did not directly evolve into militant organizations. On the contrary, the state government and some enterprises encouraged the formation of mutual-aid groupings. For instance, workers from La Fama textile mill formed a mutual-aid group that was sponsored by the mill owner, Florentino Cantú Treviño, who brought workers together at his home.[54]

Despite the "conservative" tendencies in mutual-aid societies, such as investing in real estate, participating in the sobriety movement, and sponsoring English classes, these organizations arose from the working class itself and provided crucial support to the membership. The Sociedad Cooperativa El Porvenir de la Unión was formed by "poor" textile workers who "for some time, and on a monthly basis, have deposited insignificant amounts of money into our credit institution."[55] In the absence of financial institutions that provided loans to the working class, this cooperative loaned money to its members. Mutual-aid societies were manifestations of workers' solidarity and collective intervention in aiding members, especially in times of economic duress.

With the emergence of industry after 1890, Monterrey attracted large numbers of workers, many of whom organized *gremios* or occupation-based unions. The Hermandad de Ferrocarrileros appeared in 1898, the first *gremio* in Monterrey.[56] By 1903 Monterrey had over twenty workers' organizations, ranging from the Gran Círculo de Obreros de Monterrey to occupation-oriented *gremios,* such as those for bakers, teachers, tailors, bricklayers, and miners.[57] Almost all the workers who specialized belonged to a *gremio.* The bricklayers' *gremio* had 1,300 members and the tailors' 530 members.[58]

In this formative period the working class and its organizations could not escape the shadow of Reyista authoritarian rule, which largely defined the political space in which workers could operate. Based on the available sources, and with the exception of the 1903 metalworkers' strike and the 1906–1907 railroad workers' unrest, Monterrey was not a center of working-class militant activism. In 1885 the state passed a "vagrancy" law under Article 806 of the Penal Code. It defined a vagrant as an individual who was not gainfully employed and lacked the means of subsistence.[59] A "vagabond" could be arrested or forced to work for an employer under this law. "Vagrancy" laws in other parts of the world often appeared in labor-scarce regions to facilitate the recruitment of workers. It is difficult to determine how the law was implemented in Nuevo León, given Monterrey's labor shortages and a large mobile population. Yet in at least one case the "vagrancy" law was used against workers from the rail line Monterrey al Golfo who went on strike in 1898. *La Voz de Nuevo León* reported that "the Municipal President called in the strikers, letting them know that, according to the articles of the Penal Code, they had ten days to look for other work or prove that they had the means to sustain themselves."[60] He also notified the workers that if they did not meet those conditions within the allotted time they were going to be classified as vagrants. Perhaps workers feared expressing their demands openly or striking because of this repressive law.

The business elite and upper middle classes socialized at the Casino de Monterrey, dined at the Jockey Club, attended the opera at the Teatro Juárez, and played lawn tennis. These were exclusive activities that distinguished them as a class from the lower middle and working classes of Monterrey. Members of the working class also created their own organizations, cultural expressions, and forms of spending the scarce leisure time which shaped their identities as a class.

After working a long week, for ten to twelve hours a day, laborers often attended the circus and bullfights in two of the city's arenas.[61] Following payday on Sunday, *san lunes* (Monday)—with its main activity, drinking—became the workers' unofficial "holiday." In the beer capital of Mexico, in terms of both production and consumption, Monterrey's enterprises could count on a low worker turnout on *san lunes*. Workers consumed their Monterrey, Carta Blanca, and Saturno cold beers in bars, outside the factory gates, and in other locations that the working class frequented. The Londres cantina, located in the central district of the city, appeared to be a popular bar for the lower classes. It served "cold beer and hot cheese and meat tacos at all hours."[62]

The most important cultural contribution that arose among the popular classes was *norteño* music, sometimes also called *conjunto*. *Norteño* as a musical style is dominated by the accordion and *bajo sexto*. Although the origin of the music is a topic of some debate among musicologists, *norteño* became associated with Monterrey just as the blues are with Chicago, jazz with New Orleans, country music with Nashville, and *mariachi* with Guadalajara. A scholar emphasized that Monterrey evolved into the center of a "vast hinterland in the north of the country" where *norteño* spread in the 1920s and gained tremendous popularity, as it did in Mexican communities in the United States.[63] *Norteño* deals with *frontera* themes such as migration, work, contraband, imprisonment, violence, heroes, and outlaws, not to mention love, farewells, and heartbreaks. The music acquired a broad working-class and rural following as people danced to it in dance halls and listened to it in bars and other places where the working classes concentrated.[64] The first *conjuntos* appeared in Monterrey in the 1920s.

SEGREGATION AND ZONES OF INTERACTION

In 1909 the bridge that crossed over the Santa Catarina River and united San Luisito with the rest of the city burned. Alfonso Reyes, the son of Bernardo Reyes, wrote to one of his literary mentors that this bridge "served to unite the aristocratic and *plebeya* [plebeian] parts of this city."[65] The bridge served as a metaphor for the residential segregation of the city, manifested most clearly in the quality of housing. Of the 11,667 housing units in Monterrey in 1900, 5,125 were classified as *jacales* and 6,328 as houses.[66] One can speculate that the city's elites lived in the remaining 184 dwellings, which contained two or more floors. A U.S. visitor to Monterrey noted the services that a typical elite household enjoyed:

> a *portero* [doorkeeper], *cochero* [coachman], *recamarera* [chambermaid], *lavandera* [laundress], *planchadora* [ironing woman], *caballengo* [hostler], *mozo* [errand boy], *cocinera* [cook], *molendera* [woman who grinds corn], and a *lacayo* [footman].[67]

Upper middle class households only had four or five servants to attend to their needs. With cooks earning 10 pesos per month, working from seven in the morning to eleven at night and fed only tortillas and beans, the upper classes in Monterrey enjoyed a luxurious life comparable to that of any elite group in Mexico.[68] It can be assumed that the middle classes, semiskilled, and skilled workers lived in one-story houses constructed with wood and bricks. The poor "mobile population" and unskilled workers lived in one-room *jacales*, with housing made of whatever material was available.

The city's business community established its own exclusive neighborhood in the middle of the city during the 1890s when the Reyista government exempted new housing with a value of at least 5,000 pesos from state and municipal taxes. Governor Reyes planned to convert the city's main avenues of Progreso, Unión, and Cuauhtémoc into the exclusive neighborhood of the city, like Mexico City's Reforma Avenue district.[69] But Reyes and the elites failed in their ambitious project to create an exclusive neighborhood that separated them from the encroaching working- and middle-class neighborhoods. J. Cram, a native of Germany and the owner of one of the largest stores in the city, claimed that one of the reasons for this failure was that some owners of this highly valued property stopped construction because less-expensive wood houses were being built in this rich neighborhood, which "offended" upper-class sensibilities: ". . . who wants to invest and live in modern houses when at their sides they have the *poblacho* [plebeians] who lodge in the *casuchas* and *chozas* [shacks]?"[70]

Perhaps recognizing the losing battle to maintain an exclusive and segregated neighborhood, Cram urged the governor to prohibit the construction of wood houses and, in spite of the antitaxation beliefs of Monterrey's business community, believed that property in this exclusive zone should be taxed so that those who could not afford to develop it would "sell it to those with means."[71] In the end, the idea of an exclusive neighborhood in the center of the city failed, as the poorer elements slowly moved in. "Mansion" and "adobe hut" had to share the same space.[72] Elites, however, did not give up their hopes for exclusive neighborhoods. Years later, they abandoned the central zone for the "exclusivity" of the city's outskirts and suburbs, far away from the *poblacho*, who, along with the middle classes, came to inherit the city.

Workers and capitalists did not have much contact even within the factories. Workers had more direct contact with foreign managers, *mayordomos*, and skilled workers than with the native owners of enterprises. With the exception of Francisco Sada, Isaac Garza, and Vicente Ferrara and a few others, most business owners were investors. They recruited highly paid foreign managers and skilled personnel to operate their enterprises on a daily basis. After working ten to twelve hours a day, workers, managers, *mayordomos*, and business owners went to their own neighborhoods or places of relaxation, with no further contact until the next work day.

The public plazas were apparently the only places where all the city's classes gathered. But even the customary afternoon walk in the plazas re-minded the inhabitants of their class backgrounds and the hierarchical makeup of the city. The outer parts of the walkway were reserved for the rich, including all North Americans, the middle part for the middle classes, and the inner part for the "peons," meaning the working and poor classes. To ensure that no class strayed onto the walkway of another, a policeman was stationed in the public plaza.[73]

The public plazas were also becoming hazardous for polite society. A carnival was held at Zaragoza Plaza in 1907, but a confetti riot erupted when the *poblacho,* who "lacked culture and a good education," began to throw it in the faces of other people, forcing polite society to leave the plaza. *La Unión* recommended more policing for the next city festivities.[74] In the end, the upper classes forfeited the plazas and other public spaces to the lower and middle classes, including the large mobile population, a danger-ous crowd when not allowed to move freely.

During the height of the yellow fever epidemic of 1903, Bernardo Reyes was forced to quarantine Monterrey, prohibiting all rail transporta-tion for a month. Trapped in Monterrey and panic-stricken, the restless drifters rioted. Monterrey, a foreign journalist reported,

> earned some unenviable distinction by reason of the popular riots which have taken place there; and on one occasion, when the govern-ment found it necessary to impose certain restrictions on account of the outbreak of fever, something like a general insurrection occurred, the troops had to be called out.[75]

While management labored hard to create a permanent and disci-plined labor force inside the factories, the press and "reform-oriented" movements (such as the sobriety groups) worked tirelessly to instruct work-ing people on the proper conduct outside of the workplace, especially on the ways workers spent their wages and leisure time. These reform-ers of working-class behavior professed that the circus, bullfights, drink-ing, and other leisure activities morally corrupted workers. Workers spent their money unwisely in these activities, money that could best be used for savings and for feeding their families. *Renacimiento,* for example, scolded working people for wastefully spending their money at the circus: "In the fifteen to twenty days that it [the circus] is set up, it extracts forty to fifty thousand pesos from the *pueblo* [people], who, in turn, . . . leave all their valuable possessions in the pawnshops."[76]

The Anti-Alcoholic League was formed primarily to educate workers on the evils of drinking and *san lunes,* the Mondays when workers, small shopkeepers, and artisans did not show up for work. Workers were paid on Sunday afternoons and often reserved Mondays for heavy drinking. According to reformers, drinking deprived families of "food, because their wages barely cover [the cost of food]."[77] They considered abstinence from drinking and saving money a "progressive" deed. Drinking and careless spending were regarded as regressive and deviant, evidence of two working-class character faults that needed to be reformed.

El Trueno lumped all the unredeemable disciples of *san lunes* into the group of those who could not be saved for the crusade of progress. It also lamented that shopkeepers did not advertise their businesses in newspapers, "because they do not have the money and because of their lack of business acumen. On the other hand, a *san lunes* costs them more than a good announcement."[78] *El Trueno* provided a list of reasons why shopkeepers did not advertise in newspapers: "Why should I advertise when I'm not going to sell more; nobody reads the advertisements; I sell a lot."[79] Small shopkeepers were apparently not in tune with Monterrey's progressive march. These remnants of the past were "martyrs in the terrible struggle for life, without any aspirations and goals other than to survive the day."[80]

The struggle over *san lunes* and drinking did gain some popular following, however. Residents of a working-class community outside of Monterrey petitioned the governor to close the taverns and billiard rooms because the "proletariat class" wasted their money on liquor. They wrote that alcohol deprived workers of their senses and set "bad examples" for the youth and that drinking did not provide any benefits, only hard work did.[81] Another convert to sobriety later recalled: "When I became older, and the young men with whom I associated offered me wine or beer, I always thought of these unfortunate creatures and resisted. I am now more than fifty years old and liquor has never crossed my lips."[82]

Workers and others resisted all these social pressures to change their "holiday," and *san lunes* remained a day away from the workplace for the working class. After all, they resided in Monterrey, where the Cuauhtémoc Brewery advertised its products in newspapers. One of its advertisements claimed: "The good health that Germans and Americans generally enjoy is proof that beer is good nutrition. Consume the exclusive, best beers in America, brewed by the Monterrey Brewery."[83]

THE STRIKE OF 1903

Porfirio Díaz visited Monterrey in 1898 for the first time since 1883, when he had come specifically to baptize the son of General Gerónimo Treviño, his *compadre* and one of his main allies from La Noria and Tuxtepec rebellion days. His second visit was the great event of 1898 in Monterrey, which had recently celebrated the 300th anniversary of its founding in 1896. In spite of its age, Monterrey had an aura of newness. Its industrial facelift impressed Díaz and his entourage, which included José I. Limantour, the new head of the Científicos after the death of Romero Rubio, and General Mariano Escobedo, one of Nuevo León's favorite sons. At a banquet organized by business leaders, Díaz gave a toast: "General Reyes, that is the way to govern! That is the way to follow the sovereign mandate of the people [*pueblo*]." [84] Two years later, Díaz promoted Reyes to minister of war. Reyes could see the National Palace from his office in Mexico City.

Reyes, who turned fifty years old in 1900, was much younger than most of the generals in the Mexican army, many of them veterans of the 1854–1867 struggles. Reyes labored to modernize the military and to energize a sluggish and notoriously corrupt army. He replaced the *ley leva* (forced conscription) with volunteers and created the Second Reserve, a reserve army of citizens. These and other military reforms strengthened the army at the expense of the Científicos. While in Mexico City Reyes headed the anti-Científico wing of the Porfirian elites who were positioning themselves to succeed the aging dictator. Reyes and Limantour emerged as the two leading successor candidates.

After 20,000 volunteers from the Second Reserve marched in Mexico City on the orders of Reyes, Díaz suddenly felt the presence of a potential rival to head the nation. On December 22, 1902, Díaz gave Reyes his Christmas gift two days early, asking him to resign from the cabinet. In his letter of resignation, Reyes expressed his desire to avert "dissidence [within] the sound politics of the government." [85] The Científicos celebrated the departure of their main enemy.

Four days after resigning, Reyes arrived in Monterrey to resume his position as the constitutional governor of Nuevo León. On December 31 he attended the New Year's party at the elegant Casino de Monterrey, where he was the center of attention among the "best elements of Monterrey's society." [86] Reyes, the president of the casino, left the party early because he needed to rest in order to oversee the administrative events of the following day, mainly the ceremonial oaths of the municipal mayors, who assumed their duties on January 1. Everything appeared to be the same as it had been when he took a leave-of-absence as governor in 1900 to be minister of war.

Reyes's falling-out with Díaz initiated one of the first (if not the first) political crises of the late Porfiriato, one with profound political repercussions in Nuevo León. With the help of modern communications (specifically the telegram), *regiomontanos* received the news of Reyes's removal from the cabinet almost immediately after the fact. "The first news that we received in Monterrey was that General Reyes had fallen out of favor with the President," wrote Adolfo Duclos-Salinas, an anti-Reyes critic and writer who captured the euphoric mood that a good portion of the Nuevoleoneses felt, and "a wave of hope reached all social classes within three days."[87] With little information except that Reyes had resigned, a series of rumors spread throughout Monterrey, including one that Reyes was going into exile.[88] These rumors offered hope to those sectors of *regiomontano* society who could not express their political concerns openly for fear of repression.

"[T]he fact that no one complained" between 1890 to 1902, according to a newspaper that appeared in 1903, was interpreted throughout Mexico "as an evident sign that the entire state enjoyed an unmatched well-being."[89] The removal of Reyes unleashed a wave of complaints that had been concealed for fear of Reyista repression. The long political silence that had overshadowed Monterrey and Nuevo León had unexpectedly ended.

But it was the workers who were the first to test the extent of the changing political climate. A workers' strike on January 1, 1903, began Reyes's most difficult year, which would test his abilities to navigate in the turbulent waters of Mexican politics. On that first day of the year Monterrey woke up to a metalworkers' strike at the Guggenheims' smelter, the first major strike in the city's history and one which spread quickly to other industries in the city during that year. Soon after the strikes ended, a broad civil rights and electoral movement emerged that challenged Reyista rule. Spurred into action by the prevailing view that Reyes's political career was over, and blessed by the Científicos and the deposed caudillos of the region, the middle class came fairly close to deposing one of the strongest men in Mexican politics.

On January 1, nearly 1,000 metalworkers from the Guggenheims' smelter went on strike. The smelter provoked the strike when it attempted to "increase the amount of work, while reducing wages."[90] Due to the decline in the price of silver during the 1902–1903 recession, the Guggenheim managers sought to reduce labor cost by curtailing the bonus. They eliminated the 50-centavo a day bonus for workers who worked for twenty-five consecutive days. Instead, management set a flat 10-peso bonus for workers who worked thirty consecutive days. They also eliminated the practice of workers hiring other workers as substitutes for the days when they were absent from work. This was a common practice for workers who wanted to keep their bonus. Workers made the calculations: 37.50 pesos for twenty-five days of work as opposed to 40 pesos for thirty days, or five extra days for 2.50 pesos more—they lost both wages and rest days.[91] The wages for furnace and roster workers, two semiskilled occupations, were reduced from 50 to 40 pesos a month.[92]

The new labor policy called for more work for less pay. Metalworkers rejected the new policy, given that the cost of living had increased throughout Mexico because of a severe drought. The value of agricultural production fell by more than half in Nuevo León, from 6,746,319 pesos in 1901 to 3,267,978 pesos in 1902. The cost of food, especially grain, increased dramatically.[93] The price for a *carga* of maize, the main staple of the lower classes, doubled from 1893 to 1903, from five to eleven pesos, while sweet corn sold for twenty pesos.[94] Urban consumers felt the increase in the price of food. *La Voz de Nuevo León* reported on the difficult "situation" that the working class faced in affording basic goods, calling on the Reyista municipal government to publish price lists for goods so that consumers could compare prices at different stores. Informed consumers could then punish "the abuses committed by commerce of bad faith."[95] Wages had not kept up with increases in the cost of staples and rents as of 1903, not to mention other expenses like meat, clothing, shoes, and transportation to and from work.[96]

The reduction of wages at the smelters would have made life more difficult for all workers in Monterrey. The Guggenheim smelter had set the wage structure for the rest of the industries. In 1890 it set the wage for unskilled workers at one peso, forcing the other enterprises to do the same for fear of losing their labor force to the smelter. It raised wages again in 1907, when metalworkers fled to work at different construction sites. Other enterprises could have followed the smelter's lead in reducing wages in 1903, but the metalworkers' strike preempted that scenario.

Instead of demanding that the old bonus system be restored, metalworkers insisted on wage increases, ranging from 1.25 to 3 pesos above their former daily pay.[97] It is possible that they demanded wage increases not only to keep up with inflation, but also to reach pay parity with U.S. metalworkers, who earned three to four times more than the Mexican workers did. *El Trueno,* the first newspaper in Monterrey to break the Reyista monopoly of the press, reported on the differences between native and foreign workers at the smelter:

No company has treasured the work of the Mexican as much as Smelter Number Three. Here hundreds of corpses have been exchanged for gold. Frequently workers are burned, horribly crushed, mutilated, etc., without counting those who have died by being poisoned by the metallic gasses. The curious thing is that foreigners do the same work as the Mexican workers, who earn a peso and their bonus. Foreign workers, we repeat, do the same work and never earn less than five, six, and even seven pesos a day. Why is the good and honest labor of our national workers despised? Because we are not *gueros* [blonds]![98]

The smelter's managers planned to continue production with strikebreakers. When the police and army were sent to the plant to escort the strikebreakers, violence erupted as striking workers attempted to block the entrance to the smelter. Even though two workers were seriously injured, the metalworkers succeeded in closing the smelter, forcing management to call Governor Reyes. Through threats (perhaps involving the vagrancy law), persuasion, or a combination of both, Reyes advised workers to accept the new offer made by management: work under the old salary and bonus terms. The *San Antonio Daily Express News* reported that workers "would not have resumed work until the demand for an increase had been complied with" and only did so on account of Reyes's "influence and intervention."[99]

About 100 workers continued to strike, rejecting the agreement and insisting on the wage increases. Reyes told the strikers that they had the "perfect right to strike" just as long as they did not interfere with those who wanted to return to work.[100] After a week on strike, metalworkers did not "abandon their demands" for higher wages. According to *El Trueno,* these workers enjoyed "tremendous support" in Monterrey; however, "we do not know of anybody of value who could effectively intervene on their behalf. The powerful will always triumph."[101] Workers praised Colonel Ignacio Morelos Zaragoza, the recently appointed chief of the Monterrey police, as a way of appeasing him.[102] But their warm gestures toward Zaragoza were to no avail. Not much is known about this event, except that Morelos Zaragoza brought it to an end, more than likely with the use of force.[103]

Immediately after the metalworker-management agreement, 800 workers of the Compañía Minera, Fundidora y Afinadora de Monterrey, the Mexican-owned smelter, went on strike, demanding higher wages. *El*

Monterrey News reported seven years later that other workers from the steel mill, brewery, glass factory, and other industries also went out on strike. Except for *El Monterrey News,* neither the Reyista nor the independent press mentioned the other strikes in Monterrey. If the strikes did happen, one may conjecture that these workers either went out on strike in solidarity with the metalworkers or considered this the appropriate moment to present their own demands to their employers.[104] With so many workers on strike, this would have had the makings of a general strike. In any event, worker protest had been unknown in Monterrey until 1903, according to the *San Antonio Daily Express News;* as a result, "employers are becoming alarmed at the prospect of them [strikes] becoming as frequent as they are in the United States and some other countries."[105]

In the absence of more complete sources, one cannot help but conclude that the decision to go on strike was also influenced by the prevalent opinion in 1903 that Reyes had fallen from Díaz's grace—workers could have calculated that this was the right moment. David Montgomery, a U.S. labor historian, noted:

Workers in every industrializing country of the nineteenth century fought for civil and political rights within the national polity. In autocracies, where any popular mobilization could be regarded by the authorities as subversive, even strikes over economic issues frequently activated demands by workers for freedom of speech and association and for access to the decision-making powers of government.[106]

There is no reason to think that workers in Monterrey were an exception to this observation.

THE MIDDLE CLASS, BUSINESS, AND LABOR IN "MONTERREY'S SPRING"

The middle class mobilized to challenge Reyes immediately after the ending of Monterrey's labor unrest. Spurred to action by the presumption that Reyes no longer enjoyed the support of Díaz, a coalition emerged within a few weeks after Reyes's removal from the cabinet. The leadership of this emerging urban movement, headed by a trio of Monterrey lawyers, Francisco E. Reyes (no relation to Bernardo Reyes), Eusabio San Miguel, and Julio Galindo, perceived that the dismissal of Reyes from the cabinet presented the political opportunity to end Reyismo in Nuevo León. Lawyers, doctors, journalists, shopkeepers, and students actively participated in this movement to remove Reyes from office:

> For seventeen years the inhabitants of the state of Nuevo León have been patient and mute victims of a tyranny for which it is difficult to find a counterpart in another region of the Republic. A tyranny that becomes more oppressive, entrenched, and humiliating, and if it continues for much longer it will threaten to sweep away the most rudimentary features of personal dignity.[107]

As in the rest of Mexico, Reyes's hold over Nuevo León depended largely on his political machine, Club Unión y Progreso, which excluded everybody else from participating in government (including the judicial system). Monterrey's law school attracted students from throughout the northeast, whose professional future as lawyers was blocked by a handful of Reyistas who exercised control of the judicial system. Law students criticized Reyes for being "the lord of the three frontier states." [108] In one of the more critical public manifestos, the opposition denounced Reyes for being "everything: governor, legislator, judge, and even sheriff," and for appointing

> a Congress of tractable men, who are simply convenient fixtures and who omit [sic] such laws as he invents or draws up; who change the state constitution to suit his personal views and interests. . . . likewise for the courts of law he nominates judges and clerks equally irremovable while they bow before their patron.[109]

Convinced that the political conditions were ripe, the opposition gathered on February 5, 1903, marching in the streets of Monterrey to commemorate the anniversary of the 1857 Constitution and to present their demands to *regiomontano* society. The marchers carried banners that outlined their political demands, including an independent judicial system, an autonomous municipality (*municipio libre*), individual liberties, a representative political system, an end to dictatorial practices, freedom of the press, and public education for all, especially in the isolated municipalities.[110] The middle class was inspired to be the "bearers of public opinion" in the public sphere, to use a Jürgen Habermas phrase.

Both friends and foes and Reyes himself recognized that his political destiny rested in Porfirio Díaz's hands. The fact that Díaz had not made any public comment concerning the future of the ex-minister of war placed Reyes in a political straitjacket. Conscious that Díaz was closely monitoring the unfolding events in Nuevo León, Reyes could not move freely to deal with an opposition that kept growing numerically. In the first two months of 1903 the opposition fielded their own candidate, Francisco E. Reyes, to run for governor in the upcoming elections, held a large political rally in Monterrey, and articulated a political platform. Moreover, it had founded three Monterrey newspapers—*Redención, Constitución,* and *Justicia*—which along with *El Trueno* ended the Reyista monopoly of information in Monterrey.[111] During this time the opposition had grown numerically, gaining political momentum and greater confidence to challenge Reyismo.

While the opposition had its share of political opportunists (especially in the leadership, some of whom had been leading Reyistas), its agenda of civil liberties, political freedoms, honest government, and ending dictatorial practices was broad enough to attract Liberals, workers, students, teachers, and journalists, among others. The leadership was confident that Díaz "would allow the *pueblo* complete liberty to exercise its rights."[112] This movement grew because it involved activism and propaganda. Monterrey's law school, for instance, turned into a center of student activism. The "radical" intellectuals of the northeast—Martin Stecker, a Swiss émigré and the publisher of *El Trueno;* Benito Gónzalez, editor of *Rendición;* and Adolfo Duclos-Salinas, the son of a French émigré and the editor of *La Democracia Latina*—waged the propaganda war against Reyismo. All these groups, newspapers, and activists united under the Gran Convención Electoral Nuevoleonesa, an organization that had the blessing of Generals Francisco Naranjo and Lázaro Garza Ayala, two of Nuevo León's favorite sons. Naranjo wrote to the opposition leadership that he endorsed their cause "with all my heart and I will cooperate with all the legal means at my disposal so that your efforts can bring results and so that Don Bernardo will not govern the state for another four years."[113]

Regarding the growing opposition to his rule, Reyes wrote to Porfirio Díaz: "On my part, I am serene. I am in control of the situation."[114] Whether Reyes controlled the unfolding political developments is highly questionable. On one occasion he marred his own image when he lost his composure in public by beating a drunk who yelled "death to Reyes" as his carriage passed through a crowded street. Of course, the anti-Reyista press in Monterrey and in Mexico City had a field day with that incident. The fact that Reyes allowed his enemies to put together an electoral organization, run a candidate for the main office in the state, demonstrate in the streets, and publish their own newspapers did not mean that he passively sat and watched the opposition grow, however.

Reyes dealt with his mainly middle-class opponents by using methods he knew best, but without totally repressing the movement. Reyista goons and the secret police harassed opposition activists. They also arrested the publishers of the opposition press for brief periods.[115] None of these repressive measures silenced dissent. In fact, the opposition exploited these measures by publicizing them through the national press, a move aimed at embarrassing Reyes in public and in the eyes of Díaz. Desperation drove the Reyistas into more extortive measures. In early March Reyes ordered the director of the state-funded law school, a hotbed of student activism, to expel student leaders, including the core group of the Sociedad Estudiantil José Eleutario Gónzalez, which published *Renacimiento*. The expulsion of the student leaders backfired: in addition to being martyred as the victims of Reyista intimidation, the students belonged to a movement headed by lawyers. Thirteen lawyers affiliated with the leadership of the opposition volunteered to teach them the courses needed to complete their law requirements. The list included General Garza Ayala, Vicente Garza Cantú, a former State Supreme Court judge, and Francisco E. Reyes, the candidate for governor.[116] Student activism continued.

Three months passed without Díaz sending any clear message concerning Reyes's political fate. Moreover, the press coverage of the political divisions made Nuevo León a hot topic of national discussion. Thrust into the national spotlight, and with Díaz playing the role of a Greek god who watched the events unfold from the sidelines, the most Reyes could do was to arrest and intimidate dissenters. He was not worried about losing the election of 1903. He counted on his disciplined Unión y Progreso machine to bring out the vote on election day, especially on the caciques of the countryside. Moreover, Reyistas controlled the electoral commission that counted the votes. What apparently worried Reyes was winning the elections with some degree of credibility and gaining Díaz's unconditional support, the only "vote" that really counted.

With that in mind, Reyes recognized that he needed to give his campaign all the credibility he could manage. When he called on the Monterrey business community for aid, it responded by making a series of declarations supporting Reyes as the candidate of business.[117] Although business support helped Reyes's image, this alone was not enough, especially when the mobilization of people into the streets was becoming a barometer of how much popular support each candidate had. Club Unión y Progreso, for instance, countered opposition demonstrations and meetings with pro-Reyes rallies in Monterrey and the larger towns. The number of people mobilized had not yet reached the thousands, and the only way to attain these numbers, at least in Monterrey, was to mobilize the large working class.

Recognizing that he needed popular support to counter the growth of the middle-class opposition, Reyes (through intimidation or persuasion) integrated the workers and their organizations into his political machinery. Both the Gran Convención Electoral Nuevoleonesa and Club Unión y Progreso went into the factories and working-class communities and claimed that they had the support of workers. Courted by both factions, labor was considered a key political player for the first time ever, albeit not in a position of leadership.

In early March the big three sectors of "business"—banking, commerce, and industry—and "labor" jointly endorsed the candidacy of Bernardo Reyes because he "has been the main catalyst behind the prosperity of the state." [118] A few days earlier, on March 3, the leadership of the *gremios* had published a proclamation endorsing Reyes:

> Industry was born under his protective government, and it has developed into enterprises of all sizes. For other immense benefits [Reyes has provided], he deserves the gratitude of all inhabitants of Nuevo León.[119]

Over twenty labor organizations endorsed Reyes, including the Gran Círculo de Obreros de Monterrey, the largest working-class organization, of which Reyes was an honorary member.

On March 8, 1903, a few days after the joint business and labor endorsement of Reyes's candidacy, working-class organizations formed the Club Victoria, a Reyista workers' organization. It was specifically organized for all the "manifestations of endorsement" for Díaz's presidential and Reyes's gubernatorial campaigns. Club Victoria, according to Reyes, emerged from within Monterrey's labor organizations,

> which are quite numerous and have not been seduced by the agitators. I have arranged it so that, within due time, I can count on the *mayordomos* that oversee them . . . but I do not want to agitate these people [workers] and I will mobilize them at the time of the election.[120]

The Reyistas attempted to mobilize the working class with a top-down command approach. Industrialists allowed the Reyistas inside the factories, where they counted on the authority of the *mayordomos* to mobilize and organize workers. Workers could be used for mass meetings and as a large block of voters in the upcoming elections for governor. Reyes claimed that through Club Victoria he had "at my disposition around 4,000 industrial workers and they would be mobilized at the right opportunity."[121] With foremen and management overseeing the mobilization of the working class, workers had little choice but to participate under the Reyista banner.

The opposition also claimed that it had the vast support of the working class. According to Duclos-Salinas, an ardent anti-Reyista intellectual, workers were the most vocal supporters of the opposition movement. Metalworkers from Smelter Number Three actively participated in opposition politics, perhaps in retribution for the way Reyes intervened in ending the January strike. In a letter to the publisher of *El Trueno* a metalworker wrote: "Several liberal workers from Smelter Number Three in this city have collected from their *compañeros* [co-workers] a donation that could help you."[122] "Individuals who are the genuine representatives of the *pueblo*" collected 34.25 pesos for *El Trueno,* the only newspaper in Monterrey that had supported their strike.[123]

Closely monitored inside the factories by the *mayordomos,* workers participated in the opposition movement voluntarily and perhaps even clandestinely, given possible repercussions from the Reyista authorities. Some *mayordomos* from Smelter Number Three actively took part in opposition politics. For their courageous acts, Morelos Zaragoza sent them to the state penitentiary.[124] Of the approximately 200 people arrested after the "Massacre of April 2" only a dozen or so were workers, an indication that workers supported the opposition but that their participation was not as massive as Duclos-Salinas claimed.[125]

Was the business community forced to participate in the Reyista movement, just like the working class? In a "Manifesto to the Nation" the opposition accused Reyes of creating an atmosphere of "fright through [the] length and breadth of Nuevo León and in all the classes of society, the last to experience it being the mercantile and industrial people of Monterrey."[126] This manifesto indicated that capitalists were also victims of Reyista tyranny, suggesting that if they supported Reyes they did so because they had no choice, just like the workers of Club Victoria. An opposition newspaper presented a different view of business's participation. It asserted that capitalists supported Reyes because they were selfishly looking after their own class interests rather than the broader interests of society in ending authoritarian rule in Nuevo León. Accordingly, Reyes tamed big business by "favoring them with franchises and exemptions, but he wound up by laying his rod upon them and making them dance to the crack of his whip." [127]

This accusation was more accurate, because in essence Reyes "bribed" business leaders. As a class which had benefited from Reyista economic policies, capitalists had a vested interest in his political continuation. Adolfo Duclos-Salinas, a critic of Reyes, pointed out that Monterrey's capitalists did not join the opposition movement because they "form the conservative portion of society and, by general law, they are not strong supporters of changes that could affect their interests." [128]

These arguments suggest that Monterrey capitalists' support for Reyes was solely motivated by their economic concerns. It does not take into consideration that they could also act politically and independently of their most immediate economic interests. Prior to this political crisis, business leaders had never taken strong political stands. The only sign of their political involvement had been their frequent social events held with Reyes at the Casino Monterrey. Reyes wrote to Díaz that he did not want to "involve big business" in his political campaign and that he "told its main leaders that I would use the services that they have offered [me] at the opportune time." [129] Perhaps he wanted to give Díaz the impression that he had everything under control.

Regardless of whether Reyes requested their support or not, the bulk of the business community concluded that he was in deep political trouble. Capitalists came to oppose middle-class struggles for greater political liberties when they energetically endorsed Reyes and actively mobilized their resources for the cause of Reyismo. Not only did they allow the Reyistas into the factories, but they also had their *mayordomos* oversee the integration of the workers into the Club Victoria. Their support for Reyes also spilled outside of the factories. *Justicia* objected to their participation in political events: "Some foreign and degenerate Neoleonese businessmen are going from store to store soliciting signatures in favor of a 'vote of confidence' for the current governor." [130]

On April 1, 1903, the business sector made another announcement in *La Voz de Nuevo*, endorsing the presidential nomination of Díaz. They claimed that, although they were "removed from politics," the continual prosperity of "banking, commerce, and industry" in Monterrey depended on the rule of order.[131] Reading between the lines, it is clear that they associated the regional rule of order with Reyes because he had maintained political stability for many years. Essentially, they proposed that, in order for "capital and labor" to prosper in Nuevo León, strongmen such as Reyes and Díaz were needed for "the development of the industries that we represent."[132] Meanwhile, their older sons, the members of the Club Terpsicore and Club Atlético de Monterrey, manifested their class outlook. They denounced the challenger Francisco E. Reyes as "a man without much of a background and who has never been well-received by the *buena sociedad* [high society]" and said that he was supported by a "group of individuals without any prestige, and with little support other than from a few third-rate *letrados* [intellectuals] and a few agitated students."[133] These future business leaders endorsed the candidacy of Governor Reyes, signing the joint declaration as members of "the working classes of Nuevo León." The working class had suddenly been enlarged with individuals whose surnames included Sada, Ferrara, Zambrano, Sada Muguerza, and Cantú Treviño.

Both opposing groups recognized that regardless of the number of people who could be mobilized, the number of endorsers, and the newspapers published, the political outcome in Nuevo León would be determined by Díaz. Therefore, both pursued the strategy of linking their movements to Díaz's presidential campaign and endorsing the dictator's presidential candidacy before the rest of Mexico did so. Both political movements in Monterrey planned major street rallies on April 2 to commemorate Díaz's defeat of Maximilian's troops in Puebla in 1867.

On April 2 two separate rallies were held in different parts of the city. According to Pedro Martínez, the Reyista mayor of Monterrey, three to four hundred people participated in the opposition rally. They marched through the main streets of the city before holding a rally at Zaragoza Plaza, where they shouted "viva" to Díaz, Francisco Naranjo, Lázaro Garza Ayala, and Francisco Reyes, their candidate for governor. Bernardo Reyes raised the estimate to six to seven hundred people but still declared a victory in the battle of numbers, a barometer of popular support. He claimed that 2,500 Reyistas participated in his rally. The opposition, however, also declared a victory in the turnouts. In various letters to a Mexico City daily, *Diario del Hogar,* the opposition claimed to have mobilized from a low of 8,000 to a high of 18,000 people, while only 2,000 supporters marched in favor of Reyes.[134] With the existing evidence it is difficult to get reliable estimates, but it is not unusual for the governing parties to undercount the number of protesters and for the protesters to overcount their numbers; thus the opposition probably mobilized many more people than Reyes gave it credit for and fewer than it claimed. At any rate, it is highly possible that the opposition mobilized more people than the Reyistas did.

In the end, the number of people mobilized became insignificant, because Reyista repression put an end to Monterrey's "spring" on that day. According to Reyes, the opposition gathered at Zaragoza Plaza, many of them under the influence of alcohol, and insulted the police. After a squabble, two policemen and two civilians lay dead, with many others wounded. The police later dispersed the crowd and arrested the leadership.[135] Letters to *El Diario del Hogar* tell a different story. The participants wrote that thousands of people peacefully marched behind a procession headed by fifty *charros* (horsemen). Once they reached the municipal palace, snipers started shooting at them from the roofs of the Municipal Palace. Eight people were killed, dozens were wounded, and over two hundred were arrested.[136]

It is possible that Reyista agent provocateurs incited the violence. Two participants agree that there were drunks at the demonstration and that one of them initiated the disturbance. They also confirmed that some participants were armed; however, "take into account this fact: All the Nuevoleoneses have arms, guns, machetes, or a carbine at their homes." Yet they made it clear that "since the times of Catarino Garza, the first opponent of *continuismo* [reelection], Braulio Vargas, Parra, etc., the *fronterizos* have never attacked anybody from behind, always from the front, and they never slap around drunks."[137] This was a reference to the earlier occurrence when Reyes lost his composure and beat up a drunk who shouted "death to Reyes."

Regardless of the final verdict, the Reyistas had the most to gain from this incident. Reyes, still unsure of his political future, needed to take drastic measures in order to stop the opposition from growing into a larger movement that would have been more difficult to stop and that could seriously challenge him in the upcoming elections. He also needed to maintain the impression that he still controlled the region. Eventually, the results of the "massacre del 2 de abril" put an end to the opposition movement. Francisco E. Reyes fled to the safety of Mexico City, where he renounced his candidacy a few days later. The leadership was arrested or went into exile abroad or to Mexico City, the heartland of the Científicos. Although Reyismo emerged bruised from the 1903 events, no other opposition movement dared rise against Reyes in Nuevo León for the remainder of his tenure.

Reyes appreciated the support he received from business. A year later, after the dust had settled, the business community held one of its many dinners in his honor. Manuel Rivero began the party by saying that "the womb of *regiomontano* society"—the representatives of industry, commerce, and banking—had commissioned him to offer Reyes a toast. He also said that they were all personal friends of Reyes who were "removed from politics." [138] Reyes thanked them and then made a speech comparing Nuevo León to a "great concert" where one heard different sounds, from "the merry sounds of the workshops and factories" to the "rejoicing notes of the festivals," perhaps viewing himself as the conductor of these sounds of Nuevo León. He ended the speech with the following words: "Work, persevering work, harmony, and progress." [139] These were familiar words in Monterrey.

For the remainder of his tenure Reyes continued to build on the state government–business partnership initiated in 1890, when he passed the first pro-business laws in Nuevo León. This partnership was based on an agreed division of labor: Reyes dealt with politics and the business sector with the economy. Meanwhile, the discourse of big business in Monterrey—that clear distinctions existed between business and political activities—remained intact for the rest of the twentieth century. Concepts such as "political order" and "removed from politics" became the jargon of a class that viewed its main role as economic rather than political. But economics and politics had already become inseparable, as these groupings demonstrated by their voluntary participation in defense of Reyismo.

THE WORKING CLASS AND REYISTA SOCIAL POLICY

Beginning with the events of 1903, Bernardo Reyes worked at improving relations with workers and their organizations. He was one of the few Porfirian rulers who manifested genuine interest in the working class and their conditions. In 1903 he incorporated the mutual-aid organizations and *gremios* into the Club Victoria, which became a part of the overall Reyes machinery. Although he encouraged *mutualismo* and the formation of *gremios* and supported the railroad workers' strikes of 1906–1907, he made sure that these organizations remained free of radical impulses and that they operated within the boundaries of the Reyista political framework. The Reyista state legislature passed a minimum rural wage law in 1908 and a workers' accident compensation law in 1906, Reyes's two major labor landmarks. He also established a technical school aimed at training semiskilled workers for skilled positions. Well into the Mexican Revolution, Nuevo León had the most advanced workers' legislation in all of Mexico.

Reyes's "enlightened" outlook toward the working class had not evolved overnight. Monterrey's rapid industrial expansion and its eventual need for a permanent and more efficient labor force to operate many of the city's industries shaped his labor views. Given the shortage of workers within the emerging border labor market, Reyes regarded them as free laborers who could choose their own employers. He opposed the *enganche* system of advancing wages to recruit labor, a practice common throughout Mexico. Reyes refused to grant one of the outside requests for Nuevoleonese labor because advancing wages to recruit and retain labor affected the "liberties" of workers, who should have the "absolute independence" of laboring for anyone they chose.[140] Late in his tenure he came to oppose debt-peonage, the dominant form of labor retention in Nuevo León's hacienda. Reyes adhered to that opinion closely, and in 1908 the Reyista state government passed legislation targeted at ending debt-peonage (see Chapter 5).

Workers, in Reyes's view, were integral members of an orderly society that was organized with a division of labor. This outlook was clearly expressed in 1908, when the state legislature passed the accident insurance law: "The worker who works either materially or intellectually is an essential element in the creation and development of wealth, just like the other factors with which he cooperates to produce it [wealth]."[141] The Reyista state government had the role of ensuring the operations of that order—and if need be, pushing for reforms that guaranteed the functioning of that order. Governor Miguel Cárdenas of Coahuila asked Reyes for his advice concerning complaints from Sierra Mojada mineworkers who did not want to be paid bimonthly and in company tokens. Reyes suggested to Cárdenas that "if bimonthly pay produces so many complaints and for such a long time, it is, without a doubt, a bad system."[142] He advised Cárdenas to use his influence with the mine owners so that they could pay their workers weekly and in cash. Every so often the government made the needed reforms to ensure that the order worked. The *jornalero* and accident insurance laws were symptomatic of the reforms required for a more efficient capitalist system.

Monterrey's labor movement partly influenced the development of Reyes's social policy. In the last five years of the Porfiriato, the Mexican working class began to engage in more radical tactics to change its subordinate position in society. Labor unrest, exemplified by the workers' strikes in Cananea and Río Blanco and by the growing militancy of railroad workers, reached new heights. Monterrey was a center of the new "México para los mexicanos" nationalism that spread in the last years before the Revolution. This nationalism had various expressions. The business leaders' nationalism revolved around creating a nation of consumers who consumed Mexican rather than foreign goods. The middle class feared Mexico becoming an economic colony of the United States. Workers' nationalism concentrated on equality of pay and employment opportunities vis-à-vis U.S. workers. Monterrey gained the reputation as a center for this new nationalism. The U.S. press, such as *Harper's Weekly*, falsely reported that Reyes was the leader of an emerging antiforeigner movement that was gaining enough momentum to overthrow the Díaz government.[143]

Regiomontano working-class nationalism challenged the privileged position that U.S. workers enjoyed in Monterrey. U.S. machinists, for instance, earned 125 dollars a month, twice more than Mexicans with the same skills. Moreover, North American unions defended this privilege by not allowing Mexicans into their ranks.[144] José Morente, one of the leaders of Gran Liga Mexicana de Empleados de Ferrocarril, urged workers not to waste their "energies for a miserable wage when they have the right to equality."[145]

In July 1906 the Unión de Mecánicos Mexicanos (the railroad mechanics) went on strike throughout Mexico, including Monterrey, a leading railroad hub. The union demanded wage increases and an end to the discrimination against Mexican mechanics. When Reyes met with the leaders of the Unión de Mecánicos, they promised him that "they would not resort to any form of violence" and that they were aware that the "prestige and interests of the nation" came before "their improvement in wages."[146] The U.S. consul in Monterrey presented his view on the strike:

> It appears to me that the present labor agitation arises almost entirely from an incompetent and ignorant class who view the prosperity of Americans with envy. On the other hand, a substantial native element of Mexico welcomes American capital and competent American laborers as necessary guardians of such capital.[147]

Reyes neither repressed nor encouraged the mechanics' strike. He might even have been sympathetic to the workers' demands for wage increases and putting an end to discrimination. In fact, Reyes went as far as to suggest to Ramón Corral, the secretary of government, that the state should mediate in disputes between labor and capital as they related to the railroad strike. The object of that recommendation was to avoid more strikes that could disturb the social order.[148]

In an age of the radicalization of the Mexican working class, Reyes attempted to keep that wave from reaching *regiomontano* workers. While recognizing that workers had a role in society, he did not tolerate any labor movement not controlled by him. In 1906 the Gran Liga Mexicana de Empleados de Ferrocarril wanted to form a local chapter in Monterrey. This was the first railroad workers' group to organize all workers. Unlike the Unión de Mecánicos Mexicanos, which struggled only for the rights of mechanics, the Gran Liga Mexicana sought to end discrimination and improve wages for all railroad workers regardless of skill.[149]

Reyes considered this national organization to be tainted with socialist ideas and believed that if it was allowed into Monterrey the union could turn into a "center of anarchism." He met with the local promoters of the Gran Liga Mexicana and told them that they could establish a chapter in Monterrey just as long as they modified their program to exclude anything that could be construed as subversive.[150] Perhaps they heeded Reyes's recommendation, because he became an honorary member of the Gran Liga Mexicana. The Monterrey chapter later organized other locals in Saltillo and Tampico.

While he succeeded in controlling the labor organizations such as the railroad workers, Reyes was diligently on guard against the radical ideas that clandestinely began to permeate *regiomontano* working-class circles during the summer of railroad worker unrest. The radical *El Defensor del Pueblo,* a newspaper from Laredo, Texas, attempted to penetrate Monterrey's industrial workers' circles. Reyes, in coordination with the city's industrialists, prevented the newspapers from reaching the workers' hands by confiscating most of them in a few days.[151] Those were not the first attempts at socialist propaganda. In 1904 *La Voz de Nuevo León,* Reyes's mouthpiece, had denounced the presence of socialist literature, arguing that workers had a vested material interest in the capitalist system.[152]

This evidence suggests that Reyes tried to keep the working class uninformed about events outside of its immediate environment. The fact that Reyes, along with the industrialists, interfered in the distribution of radical propaganda further implies that both government and capitalists had a special interest in keeping the working class isolated from its counterparts in the rest of Mexico. Perhaps he even regarded radical ideas as alien to the formation of the *regiomontano* working class, believing that workers had prospered under his administration. There is a strong indication that he succeeded in isolating the *regiomontano* working class from radical ideas and from the rest of the labor movement in Mexico.

In 1909 José Limantour, Mexico's economic minister, urged E. N. Brown, the executive president of the "Mexicanized" Ferrocarriles Nacionales de México, to end policies that discriminated against native workers in the railroads and to equalize the pay between Mexican and U.S. workers. He also recommended that foreign workers learn Spanish and that the company open schools for the training of workers. Apparently the railroad workers' movement for equality influenced the upper echelons of Mexico's governing leaders.[153] Monterrey's labor movement of 1906 could also have influenced Reyista social policy in Nuevo León. Other governors from the most industrial states, such as Teodoro Dehesa of Veracruz and Pablo Escandón of the Federal District, shared similar concerns about the working class, but no one came close to matching Reyes's labor reforms. Reyes diffused probable workers' unrest by incorporating some of their key demands into legislation.

During the period 1900–1910, the working class had emerged as a large urban and industrial force of 10,000. A few thousand more labored as domestics, as sales clerks, and in building construction. A large sector of the industrial proletariat moved up from the ranks of the unskilled to the semiskilled in the last decade of the Porfiriato, as the result of native workers displacing foreign workers and industry's greater needs for skilled personnel. A newspaper reported on working-class upward mobility:

> our carpenters, blacksmiths, stonecutters, and bricklayers [albañiles], etc., receive wages that fluctuate between one and four pesos a day. Workers employed at the smelters and factories receive a minimum salary of seventy-five centavos a day that continues to increase proportionally according to the work that they do and the skills that are required.[154]

Although many workers moved to semiskilled occupations, they stagnated at that level because of their lack of technical knowledge. Those difficulties were compounded by a dearth of technical schools. Regarding the stagnation of semiskilled workers as a problem that could hamper Monterrey's industrial expansion in the near future, the Reyista state opened the Workers' School for Applied Sciences in the Arts (Cátedra de Ciencias Aplicadas a los Artes, para Obreros), a strange name for a technical school. This first attempt to sponsor a technical school failed because of the large number of workers and their diverse occupations. The school could not construct a common educational curriculum that met the needs of workers from varied occupations, ranging from tailors and shoemakers to plumbers and mechanics. Moreover, workers lacked the required basic education in mathematics (for example, in trigonometry).[155] In addition, workers toiled all day, leaving little time to study or to attend night classes.[156]

Reyes closed the first technical school, forcing workers to petition the governor to reopen it. They wrote that this school was important for their "material and intellectual improvement." They called the school the "Temple of Knowledge," a place where they learned skills and the consequent "endearment and respect of our *compañeros*."[157] Workers had a vested interest in the continuation of the school, arguing that this institution, besides satisfying the students' curiosity for learning, had created a sector of workers who had moved up in the skill ranks. This school had also produced public speakers, artists, and "mathematicians." In addition, it had served other purposes, such as settling "some strikes."[158]

It may have been working-class pressure that forced the state government to reopen the school in 1907, but with different educational goals that were aimed at servicing the specific needs of industry. The proposal for the school stated this aim very clearly: "it must be taken into consideration that a workers' night school does not have the mission of producing industrialists, but of producing people who are useful to industry based on the scientific notions that they have."[159] Expressing concern that Mexican mechanics were "very deficient [in skills] and in some cases they even lack primary education," the proposal stated that the mission of the school was to produce "modern mechanics" who could be master mechanics, supervisors, and *jefes de taller* (foremen of workshops).[160] The new technological school helped mostly industrial semiskilled workers, especially mechanics, rather than nonindustrial workers such as tailors, shoemakers, and bricklayers. Of the 239 students enrolled in 1907, the school had 129 mechanics, 20 carpenters, and 17 boilermakers. Only 3 *albañiles* were enrolled, even though they outnumbered mechanics in Monterrey. The school catered mainly to the members of the Unión de Mecánicos Mexicanos, the most combative of Monterrey working-class organizations prior to the Revolution.[161] This union established strong client ties with Reyes. Its members were among the most active supporters of his presidential bid in the succession crisis of 1909.

Given Monterrey's urban and industrial growth, and in view of the city's labor shortages, Reyes ordered a legislative commission to study and write a bill directed at industrial accidents. The result was Porfirian

Mexico's most important labor landmark, the "ley sobre accidentes de trabajo" (law on accident insurance). This bill was introduced into the state legislature in 1906 during a period of growing labor unrest throughout Mexico, including the railroad workers' strikes in Monterrey. "The modern industrial movement requires the existence of special ordinances," the proposed commission bill stated, "that provides compensation to the worker who has been injured by an unexpected event [suceso]." [162] The proposed legislation justified the need for this law because "the new forms of production and the great forces of energy that modern industry has appropriated, such as electricity and steam," caused industrial accidents. In this case, "neither the owner nor the worker is responsible. This is part of [the development] of industry." [163] Regardless of fault, the firm would be liable for paying the medical bill, for compensation time, or for providing payment in case of death.[164]

No study has yet been written on the impact of the law. It was a state policy to rationalize Monterrey's industrial environment, however. Unlike the rural workers' minimum wage legislation, which was heavily influenced by capitalists, it appears that the industrial accident legislation came as an initiative by the state government. There is no evidence suggesting that industrialists opposed this bill.

Nor is there any evidence that the workers approved of this law. Had it not been for the Revolution, the industrial accident bill would have meant the death of *mutualismo*. Workers formed mutual-aid societies to provide the members with money when faced with unemployment and work-related injuries. Industrialists were now responsible for compensating workers for injuries and death in the workplace. The law ended one of the most concrete and practical ways in which workers manifested their solidarity with each other, shifting a responsibility that had belonged to the working class to the industrialists and laying the first brick of the future edifice of capitalist paternalism.

CONCLUSION

In Monterrey all classes formed organizations, created cultures, and enjoyed distinctive forms of leisure. These collective identities were shaped inside and outside the workplace and also by the groups' relationships with each other and with the Reyista state. The local state applied specific political rules to each specific group. The primary aim of the Reyista state was to maintain political order and facilitate the expansion of industry. In this stratified society the Reyista press and, to a lesser extent, the middle-class press expressed an ideological outlook promoting progress, nationalism, and cooperative capital and labor relations. As far as we know, neither business leaders nor workers had newspapers through which they could express their ideology, concerns, and ambitions. Business leaders did not need to have their own means of communication, however, because the Reyista press and the middle-class press presented their views to society. According to Eric Hobsbawm:

> The world of the poor, however elaborate, self-contained, and separate, is a subaltern and therefore, in some senses, incomplete world, for it normally takes for granted the existence of those who have hegemony, or at any rate its inability for most of the time to do much about it. It accepts their hegemony, even when it challenges some of its implications because, largely, it has to.[165]

In the case of Monterrey, the ideological discourse emanating from above focused on the meaning of "progress," nationalism, and the supposed organic ties between capital and labor. Although the working class could not escape this dominant ideological framework, it did express its differences with business groups and the state through varying interpretations, for example, of education and natural catastrophes. Reyistas used workers' education to produce the first generation of Mexican skilled mechanics in Monterrey. Their goal was to create a specially trained group solely to meet the specific needs of industry. Workers, however, believed that education was essential, not just for skill acquisition, but for collective self-improvement, citizenship, and patriotism. A group of mechanics expressed these sentiments in a letter to Reyes:

> The true pueblo, the people who work and study, the people who struggle for life with dignity and heroism and who carry the hammer in the workshop to earn their bread just as they struggle with saber and rifle on the battlefield to defend the interests, honor, and dignity of the nation.[166]

Monterrey suffered two disasters that killed hundreds of people: the yellow fever epidemic of 1903 and the flooding of the Santa Catarina River in 1909. *La Voz de Nuevo León* viewed the yellow epidemic in terms of its effect on business: the quarantine cut the delivery of raw materials to the city; the lack of a mobile population induced labor shortages; and retail stores lacked consumers.[167] On August 26, 1909, the Santa Catarina River flooded, killing from 1,280 to 4,000 people in Monterrey and throughout Nuevo León. A popular song captures the attitude of the working people toward the flood of 1909:

Unos lloran por sus hijos,
y otros lloran por sus padres,
otros por sus hermanitos,
y varios señores
por sus capitales.

[Some cry for their children,
and others for their parents,
others for their little brothers and sisters,
and a few
for their money.] [168]

Monterrey was a city composed of different classes. It was also a city where each class had different conceptions of its reality and environment, as indicated by the examples of education and catastrophes. For the most part, the history of Monterrey has been written from the point of view of business, one that emphasizes class harmony and industrial progress. The other histories of Monterrey, especially from the perspective of its large working class, demonstrate that the city was not a conflict-free oasis.

CHAPTER SEVEN

A Tale of Two Porfirian Firms

THE CERVECERÍA CUAUHTÉMOC
AND THE FUNDIDORA DE MONTERREY

This chapter examines the Cuauhtémoc Brewery and the Compañía Fundidora de Fierro y Acero de Monterrey, the two firms that represented the pillars of Monterrey's industrial development. These firms were among the largest in Mexico, giving rise to industrial groups whose economic and political influence molded not only the city but the region during the late Porfiriato and most of the twentieth century. The Garzas and Sadas of the Brewery and Adolfo Prieto of the Fundidora were known not only as leading entrepreneurs but as important political actors. The Garzas and Sadas headed the Grupo Monterrey, the most combative postrevolutionary industrial grouping in Mexico in relation to the state. The Fundidora, in contrast, has been associated with pro-government policies.

The firms differed not only in their relation to the state but also in the types of working classes they produced, which established the organizational base of the *regiomontano* labor movement. Under the control and influence of management, brewery workers formed a *sindicato blanco,* the kind of company union which dominated the city's labor movement in the postrevolutionary era. Steelworkers, however, established a *sindicato rojo,* a union closely linked to the ruling party of Mexico.

This chapter explores the origins and early development of two of the most powerful industrial groupings in Monterrey and the makings of two different working-class organizations which would shape the structure of the city's labor movement in the aftermath of the Mexican Revolution. Both of these firms sought to attain a greater share of the market for their products, but in doing so they developed different strategies toward their competitors, their labor forces, and the state.

The Cuauhtémoc Brewery, the mother industry giving birth to a vast economic empire, produced the most politicized bloc of the present-day Mexican bourgeoisie. From its inception in 1890, the Cuauhtémoc Brewery competed with other large native breweries for the small but growing domestic market of beer consumers. In its attempt to gain a greater share of the beer market, it reduced its overall costs by vertically integrating bottling and packaging into its production network. Besides creating two new firms, for glass and packaging, this strategy allowed the company to become the largest brewery in Mexico. The firm also applied the strategy of reducing labor costs at all levels.

Reducing labor costs could only occur at the expense of semiskilled and skilled workers, who were largely foreigners who had originally been recruited at wages much higher than they could earn in their native lands. The predominantly unskilled labor force, earning much lower wages, would always be needed in a labor environment with great scarcities. In the last years of the Porfiriato, management used new technology, apprenticeships, schooling, and other labor cost-cutting measures to replace foreign workers, who earned "foreign wages," with Mexican workers, who earned "Mexican wages." This strategy, favoring the native workers, established a paternalistic relationship between management and its largely unskilled labor force.

Precisely because it was a competitive enterprise receiving the "protection" of the state against foreign competition, the Cuauhtémoc Brewery had weak ties to the Porfirian state and would remain independent of it. For the owners of the brewery, the Porfirian state was ideal, because it had aided in the integration of a domestic economy and had provided firms like the brewery with such benefits as long-term, tax-free concessions. During the first twenty years of its existence the brewery, a family-owned enterprise, produced an articulate economic group believing in an orderly society and a noninterventionist state in which capitalists and workers had a mutual interest in the so-called economic progress of Monterrey and Mexico.

Founded by Monterrey and Mexico City businessmen, the Fundidora de Monterrey began its steel operations in 1903 as a ten-million-peso investment. As the owners of the first integrated steel mill in Latin America, they enthusiastically set the goal of conquering the growing domestic market for steel and iron products. This goal was frustrated by the unexpected cutthroat competition from foreign importers of these goods, by high freight rates, and by expensive coal, the main source of energy for the Fundidora. Moreover, because of its inability to produce immediate profits for the stockholders, the company could not afford to recruit the large number of foreign semiskilled and skilled workers that it needed in order to operate the mill. It had to rely on unskilled Mexican workers, who learned their skills on the job and later through technical education, creating the highest-paid workforce in Monterrey. Confronted with a series of unexpected problems and with the Fundidora's survival at stake, the owners opted for closer ties to the Porfirian state, which then protected the steel mill with high tariffs and low-interest loans and, through the "Mexicanization" of the railroads, provided a secure market for the steel mill's products and reduced its transportation costs. The final result was a noncompetitive firm whose existence depended entirely on its close ties to the state.

THE CERVECERÍA CUAUHTÉMOC

In December 1890 Isaac Garza and Joseph Schnaider received a seven-year tax-free concession from the state government to establish the 125,000-peso Cuauhtémoc Brewery in Monterrey. In 1895 the state government extended the concession to twenty years after the cost of constructing the brewery exceeded 125,000 pesos. This was one of Monterrey's most notable ventures in a nonexport industry and a perilous one, especially since earlier attempts at brewing had ended in failure.[1] Twenty years later the Cuauhtémoc Brewery had become one of the "success" stories in Mexican entrepreneurship and a key symbol of Monterrey's industrial identity. By 1910 it was valued at between five and eight million pesos and employed 1,500 workers; by 1950 it was the third largest enterprise in Mexico, after the state-owned oil and railroad industries.[2]

The owners of the Cuauhtémoc Brewery represented a new generation of *regiomontano* entrepreneurs. The older and more established merchants, such as the Maderos, Riveras, Milmos, and others, had gained vast experience in legal and illegal frontier commerce extending as far back as the pre-1848 era and made their fortunes during the Vidaurri period (1854–1867). Francisco Sada, Isaac Garza, José Muguerza, and José Calderón Jr., the leading investors of the Cuauhtémoc Brewery, were all born after 1850 and initiated their business experience managing commercial houses during the economic crisis of 1867–1890. They administered northeastern commercial houses, which, in addition to selling goods, survived the long economic crisis by engaging in many activities such as investing in real estate and, in the absence of established banks, acted as financial institutions. Sada worked for seventeen years for the Armendáriz commercial house in Matamoros and later for the González Treviños' Monterrey outpost in Chihuahua. His commercial knowledge led him to invest in land and water speculations in the La Laguna area. Sada, the eldest of the Cuauhtémoc group, took over as general manager of the brewery at the age of thirty-eight, overseeing daily operations. Isaac Garza worked in a commercial house in San Luis Potosí before joining Casa Calderón in Monterrey as an associate of the firm. During his fifteen-year tenure, Casa Calderón emerged as one of the most prestigious commercial houses in Mexico. José Muguerza began his commercial apprenticeship at the age of fourteen, working under the supervision of Bernardo García, the owner of another large commercial establishment. With the merger of the García and Calderón commercial firms, both Muguerza and Garza became senior partners in the new commercial house, Casa Calderón. The commercial and financial experience that these young and talented businessmen gained at these different commercial establishments enabled them to invest merchant capital successfully in industrial ventures. Muguerza became the secretary of the brewery and Garza the president. José Calderón Jr., the son of the patriarch of Casa Calderón, became the treasurer of the Cervecería.[3]

Outside of the brewery, they all had investments in other industrial enterprises, commercial establishments, banking, and real estate ventures, making them prominent figures in Monterrey's elite circles. The brewery was their main economic concern, however, and the investment that glued them together. The relationships between the major figures of the Cuauhtémoc Brewery were not entirely business oriented. Besides their business ties to Casa Calderón and the brewery, they were all tied to one another by marriage.[4] This group of enterprising capitalists used the capital from Casa Calderón to maintain the Cuauhtémoc Brewery as a family enterprise and convert it into one of Mexico's most reputable and profitable native firms by the end of the Porfiriato. A second generation of family entrepreneurs headed by Eugenio and Roberto Garza Sada, engineering graduates of the Massachusetts Institute of Technology, were groomed to take over the firm after 1920; it has remained within the Garza Sada family to the present day.[5] The Cuauhtémoc Brewery follows the pattern of other Latin American family enterprises such as those of the Yarurs of Chile and Di Tellas of Argentina. Family enterprises, as Manuel Carlos and Louis Sellers argued, tended to produce internally a continuous flow of managerial talent and loyalty because family members identified the well-being of the company with the context of the family. Moreover, family enterprises created continuity and stability over a long period.[6]

The Cuauhtémoc Brewery emerged as Mexico's premier brewery in an era in which rising beer consumption, especially by the working classes, forced the restructuring of the entire industry at a worldwide level. Major technological innovations in fermentation, pasteurization, and biochemistry altered brewing from what had been for centuries a European cottage industry into a modern industry producing for mass consumption in the second half of the nineteenth century. In a highly competitive environment, mass-producing breweries facilitated the reduction of costs in all phases, especially in the bottling process. As brewing became more scientific, breweries that did not modernize could not compete with firms that were constantly lowering costs. The late nineteenth century witnessed the decline of hundreds of small breweries, especially in Europe and the United States, and the growth of a few large brewing firms.[7]

Before the rise of the modern brewing industry in 1890, Mexico contained thirty-one breweries.[8] These were small firms which employed a few workers who produced poor-quality beers. The growth of these breweries was thwarted by poor transportation services, the lack of refrigeration (ice), which caused beer to spoil after a few weeks, and the *alcabalas,* the infamous internal taxes.[9] The Cuauhtémoc Brewery opened its brewing operation in 1891 with seventy workers, who produced 1,500 bottles of beer daily and 10,000 barrels of beer annually. The brewery's low output indicates that its beer products were primarily consumed by *regiomontanos.* By 1903 the brewery had expanded its beer distribution throughout Mexico, producing 80,000 bottles of beer daily and 100,000 barrels of beer annually, while employing 500 to 600 workers.[10] By 1910 it employed 1,500 workers, who produced 300,000 bottles of beer daily and 300,000 barrels of beer annually.[11]

By 1910 the Cervecería Cuauhtémoc was one of three major breweries that dominated the Mexican beer market. Its success came from following patterns similar to those of other breweries in the industrial world which were in the process of becoming major firms. First, it competed with two large national companies, the Moctezuma Brewery and the Toluca-México Brewing Company, for the small but expanding domestic market, whose principal consumers were the working and middle classes. To enhance its competitiveness, it recruited Joseph Schnaider, a well-known brewer from St. Louis, Missouri, to oversee the brewing operations and brought other experienced brewers from Munich. Moreover, the plant had a first-class laboratory that experimented with various types of beer. Its best-known brands, Carta Blanca and Bohemia, continue to be popular today.

In spite of these achievements, success did not come easily for the Cuauhtémoc Brewery. The brewery encountered major barriers in its early efforts to penetrate the domestic market. Because the small Mexican elite preferred imported liquors and the peasants, the largest class in Mexico, were too poor to consume beer, the only possible consumers were the working and middle classes. Thus the firm's expansion hinged entirely on the growth of the domestic market, which meant the numerical growth of these two classes as consumers. Besides having to compete for a limited market, the brewery also faced the obstacle of convincing that market to consume beer, a product that was for all practical purposes unknown within these circles before 1890.[12] Nonetheless, the owners of the Cuauhtémoc Brewery understood that the beer business could be profitable. In 1889 Mexicans spent a million pesos on imported beers, mainly from Germany and the United States.[13] Imported beers had the market secured, as Mexico's elites preferred them over domestic products.[14] Consequently, one of the early challenges for the brewery was entering a domestic market dominated by foreign imports. Imported foreign beer in itself presented another problem:

> . . . because it was the belief [of storekeepers] that a national product could never compete with foreign beers. This error, which was deeply rooted in the storekeepers, reached such an extent that some of them were willing to sell the beers produced in Monterrey, and which were of equal quality to foreign beers, only on the condition that we labeled our products with names that gave the appearance of an imported beer.[15]

Notwithstanding the early preference consumers had expressed for foreign beers over domestic brands, and the limited size of the market, the Cuauhtémoc Brewery overcame these problems by pioneering advertising and organizing a network of distributors throughout Mexico. It launched an aggressive advertising campaign in newspapers that aimed to change the habits of the Mexican consumer. In 1900 it established *agencias distribudoras* (distributors) in Mexico's major urban and mining centers. These marketing strategies helped change consumer tastes, so that its various beer brands were well known throughout Mexico by 1910.[16]

The Cuauhtémoc Brewery's marketing strategy quickly paid off. The value of foreign beer imports had declined from a million pesos in 1889 to 300,000 pesos by 1910.[17] With the exception of small quantities of beer exports to Central and South America, the brewery depended almost en-

Table 7.1. CUAUHTÉMOC BREWERY SALES, 1892–1910

Sales Year	(ooo Liters)	Sales Year	(ooo Liters)
1892	498	1902	5,581
1893	986	1903	5,925
1894	1,123	1904	6,865
1895	1,980	1905	8,884
1896	2,151	1906	13,344
1897	2,474	1907	14,005
1898	3,743	1908	11,183
1899	4,504	1909	11,582
1900	4,866	1910	13,275
1901	4,685		

Source: Stephen H. Haber, *Industry and Underdevelopment: The Industrialization of Mexico, 1890–1945*, p. 53.

tirely on the expansion of the domestic market, as its products followed the railroad lines throughout Mexico. From Monterrey the Cuauhtémoc Brewery expanded its beer distributions to Mexico City, the largest urban market, and later to the northeastern border towns, followed by the urban centers of the Gulf of Mexico such as Tampico, Veracruz, and Mérida, and, finally, the mining districts of northern Mexico.[18] These areas contained high concentrations of workers.

If Mexico's economic growth was largely fueled by the export sectors of the economy, then the Cuauhtémoc Brewery's fate rested on the further expansion of that sector. This relationship was such that in boom periods the Cuauhtémoc Brewery prospered, while in periods of economic contraction it faltered. As Table 7.1 demonstrates, its sales increased considerably from 1892 to 1907, especially in the boom years of 1904 to 1907, when sales increased by over 100 percent. But the world economic crisis that began in 1907 and ended in 1909 thrust the Cuauhtémoc Brewery into a crisis, as the export-sectors of the economy dismissed thousands of workers, who became unemployed and therefore unable to purchase beer. Because of the economic crisis, Francisco Sada, the general manager of the Cervecería, presented a bleak picture of the brewery:

> . . . the suspension or considerable decrease in mining, upon which many businesses in Mexico depend, and the prolonged drought that the entire country has endured have deplorably paralyzed many busi-

nesses. . . . the operations of this enterprise cover the entire republic and are subjected to the success or decline of other businesses, and the result is that it has suffered considerable losses and will probably continue to do so for a long time.[19]

Beer sales dropped from 14,005,000 liters in 1907 to 11,183,000 the following year. Sales in La Laguna and Yucatán fell by half, and those in Guadalajara, Puebla, Veracruz, and Mexico City also fell, but not as severely.[20] Overall, the economic crisis hurt the brewery: beer sales in Mexico declined from 3,715,251 pesos (July 1907–June 1908) to 2,729,129 pesos (June 1908–July 1909), a drop of almost a million pesos.[21] The crisis ended in 1909; in the following years beer sales climbed to record highs until 1913, when the events of the Mexican Revolution forced the closure of the enterprise for three years.

For the Cuauhtémoc Brewery the greatest competition for the growing market of beer consumers came from the two other major breweries in Mexico, the French-owned Moctezuma Brewery of Orizaba, Veracruz, and the Spanish-owned Toluca-México Brewing Company. The Société Financière pour l'Industrie du Mexique, a large French consortium of banks and business groups that invested in Mexican industry, commerce, finance, and real estate, owned the Moctezuma Brewery, while the Toluca-México Brewing Company, formerly a family-owned firm, had emerged as a joint-stock company in 1898.[22] These breweries became large companies by early domination of the regional markets. The Moctezuma Brewery carved its niche in the humid Gulf region, the Toluca-México Brewing Company in the populous Mexico City area, and the Cuauhtémoc Brewery in the northeast. Monterrey was the beer-drinking capital of Mexico because of its hot climate and the absence of other alcoholic substitutes such as pulque, and the Cuauhtémoc Brewery had captured the *regiomontano* market at an early stage.[23] "If you stay in Monterrey don't forget to visit the Cuauhtémoc Brewery," a traveler wisely advised another traveler in 1904, and "don't ask for beer from another company because you will not find it; there is no consumer who will like it unless it comes from the Cuauhtémoc Brewery."[24]

Unlike other competitive native firms, the breweries did not seek to merge into a large company which could have monopolized the entire market or at least gain a greater share of it.[25] The three largest textile firms in the north, for example, merged into a 9,000,000-peso enterprise in 1908, while in Monterrey two large soft-drink companies merged in that same year.[26] Instead, the brewing industry was characterized by intense competition. In 1901 the Cuauhtémoc Brewery initiated a brewing war by moving aggressively into the large Mexico City market, the stronghold of the Toluca-México Brewing Company, with the founding of a subsidiary, the Cervecería Central, a large beer distribution company.[27] Likewise, the Cuauhtémoc Brewery's competitors entered Monterrey in 1905. Both the Toluca-México and Moctezuma breweries entered the large Monterrey market with much fanfare, mainly because this led to a price war which both reduced beer prices and ended the hope of escaping the *regiomontanos'* "ancient provincialism."[28] The Moctezuma Brewery spent 13,000 pesos, mainly in advertisements, simply to cover the first month of operations.[29] The domestic beer competition often reached hostile levels, especially during the 1907–1909 economic crisis, leading Francisco Garza Sada to write to Bernardo Reyes:

> Perhaps you have noted from our competitors' press that this enterprise has suffered, [but this is] due to causes that are entirely independent of our will and our correct conduct but are nevertheless well exploited by our enemies or competitors, of which there is no shortage in enterprises of this kind.[30]

In a competitive environment, the brewing firms sought to reduce costs in order to remain competitive. The Cuauhtémoc Brewery, just like all mass producers of beverages, confronted the problem of shortages of bottles, which for the most part had to be imported. Bottle imports had increased from 37,000 pesos in 1889 to 1.6 million in 1907.[31] "It is a well-known fact that there is a shortage of bottles for beer," a beer distributor in Monterrey complained, forcing the companies to pass the cost of the bottles on to the consumer.[32] The Mexican beverage industry, which depended on imported bottles, had grown because "of the climate in which consumers consume little strong alcohol and plenty of beer and soft drinks."[33] The value of the bottle represented one-third of the cost of the product sold to the consumer.[34] The common practice was for the consumer to purchase the product and then to receive a refund for the value of the bottle when it was returned to the store.

In its attempt to gain a greater share of the domestic beer market by following the patterns of other large competitive brewing firms in the industrial world, the Cuauhtémoc management's main goal was to reduce costs. To lower the cost of imported bottles, the business leaders of Monterrey, under the leadership of Isaac Garza, created the first large-scale glass

industry in 1899, the Fábrica de Vidrios y Cristales de Monterrey, an investment of 600,000 pesos. The Cuauhtémoc Brewery thus directly gave
birth to the modern Mexican glass industry. The glass company was vertically integrated with the brewery. For this enterprise Isaac Garza, the president of the brewery and the glass firm, recruited skilled glassblowers from
Germany, who, along with their Mexican apprentices, started producing
20,000 bottles a day. Garza's goal was to insure that the Cervecería had
plenty of bottles and to sell the surplus to its competitors. The glass company had secured contracts with the other breweries in Mexico to supply
them with 50,000 bottles a day.[35] The first attempt at glass manufacturing failed, however, because, among other factors, the German workers
went on strike in 1904.[36] While the bottling machine had been invented
in the 1880s, it was not employed until 1909, when Garza led another
attempt at glassmaking with the founding of the Vidriera de Monterrey.
This 1.2-million-peso enterprise used the latest technology, the Owens-
automated glass bottle machine, which produced forty thousand bottles a
day or twelve million in a working year. The Vidriera de Monterrey's impact was immediately felt: the value of imported bottles decreased from
1,649,000 pesos in 1907 to less than a million pesos by 1911.[37] More importantly, the Vidriera de Monterrey monopolized not only Mexican bottle
production but also other glass products, giving the Cuauhtémoc Brewery
the competitive advantage over the other breweries by reducing the cost
of bottles.[38] Consequently, the brewery's share of the domestic market increased from 29 percent in 1900 to 53 percent by 1910.[39]

THE STATE AND THE CUAUHTÉMOC BREWERY

From its start as a small enterprise in 1890, the Cuauhtémoc Brewery had
become one of Mexico's largest industrial enterprises by 1910. It was valued
between five to eight million pesos and had become the "mother" industry
to two new enterprises, La Vidriera de Monterrey and La Fábrica de Cartón
de Monterrey, a packaging firm. The emergence of this firm as "the leading
brewery of the republic," with an "international reputation," contributed
to Monterrey's identity as the industrial capital of Mexico.[40]

Before the brewery's emergence as a major firm, it is very likely that
its owners shared with the other frontier merchants of the northeast an anti-
statist view of government. This outlook had originally been shaped by the
subordinate economic relationship between the northeast and the center.
Since the late colonial era, northeastern economic interests had complained
that the central government's policies had prevented the region from devel-

oping economically. They opposed the Mexico City *consulado* (merchant guild), which monopolized trade between the center and northeast, and the internal taxes (*alcabalas*), which in their view kept the region subordinate to the center. After 1867 the northeastern merchants, especially those in Monterrey, opposed the federal government–sponsored border free zone, which had opened the door to large-scale contraband and directly contributed to the collapse of many commercial establishments.

In contrast to other major *regiomontano* firms, such as the Fundidora de Monterrey and Cementos Hidalgo, the Cuauhtémoc Brewery got little direct assistance from the state, other than the tax concessions from the state government which every new industrial enterprise received. It is doubtful that the Cuauhtémoc Brewery would have developed into a major firm, however, without "indirect" assistance from both the central and state governments. In 1896 the Porfirio Díaz regime legislated greater governmental regulation of the free-trade zone and abolished the *alcabala,* measures which facilitated greater domestic integration but also addressed the major commercial concerns of the northeast elites.[41] Of these two measures, the *alcabala* was of greater concern for mass-producing firms such as the Cuauhtémoc Brewery, which sold their products nationally. While a study on the impact of the abolishment of the *alcabala* on economic development has not been made, it at least appears to have benefited the alcohol industry, which depended on mass volume sales. For instance, Mexico City had previously collected 400,000 pesos a year from the *alcabala* on pulque alone, while wine from Parras, Coahuila, was taxed 5.70 pesos for each 100 kilograms in that same city, making sales very difficult.[42]

Although he was specifically discussing internal taxes, the U.S. consul at Nuevo Laredo succinctly captured the spirit of Porfirian economic legislation: "the alcabala belongs to the period of the ox-cart and pronunciamiento. It is out of place with steam, electricity and a virile national authority."[43] The gradual phasing out of the free-trade zone and its final elimination in 1905, the abolishment of *alcabalas,* and Díaz's protection of native industry with high tariffs on imports were key economic policies which contributed to greater domestic economic integration. These policies helped firms such as the Cuauhtémoc Brewery to survive and expand their operations.

Bernardo Reyes's tax-free concessions were another piece of probusiness legislation which favored *regiomontano* firms. The state government gave the Cuauhtémoc Brewery a seven-year tax-free concession in 1890, which was renewed for twelve years in 1892.[44] In addition to tax-free concessions, the Reyista government fostered a *laissez-faire* business climate in Monterrey in which the firms "enjoy the freedom of commerce."[45] Even José Limantour, the architect of Díaz's economic and fiscal policies, considered Reyes's economic policies, especially taxation, too lenient toward business. He counseled Reyes that "frequently it occurs that a reduction or exemption of taxes does not help those who need it most."[46] The idea behind the state government's 1889 legislation on tax-free concessions was to help new industries survive the first few years of operations. When their twelve-year tax-free concession was about to expire in 1904, Francisco Sada, the general manager of the Cuauhtémoc Brewery, petitioned Reyes for another concession, because

> the period of the concession, which was sufficient to start up an enterprise with relative ease, has not, however, provided the benefits [profits] to its owners which they could now only expect if these conditions [tax-free concessions] remain the same.[47]

By 1904 the Cuauhtémoc Brewery was considered the premier brewery in Mexico and was by no means a struggling firm.

In this "freedom of commerce" environment many industrial firms flourished in Monterrey. Nonetheless, abuses by the firms were, more often than not, the norm. As Bernardo Reyes noted, "the rich . . . do not reveal their wealth to the fiscal authorities so that it will not be used [as a base] in the payment of taxes. . . ."[48] The Cuauhtémoc Brewery was among those firms which did not reveal their wealth. To avoid a series of taxes on property and production output after their tax-free concession ended in 1910, the managers claimed that the value of the firm, whose real value was somewhere between five and eight million pesos, was three hundred thousand pesos. They continued to undervalue their firm as late as 1920, hence avoiding paying thousands of pesos in taxes.[49]

Monterrey's business community matured economically and politically under the Porfiriato. Business leaders shared a collective vision of the ideal role of the state and economic development, viewing the state as a promoter of domestic free trade and a protector of their interests from foreign competition. Both the Díaz and Reyes governments met their goals. In spite of government policies that favored industrial firms, the Cuauhtémoc Brewery was not entirely satisfied with the state government, primarily because of its taxation on beer distributors and sales. Because most industrial firms did not pay taxes, the state government, which had the lowest taxation policies in Mexico, received most of its revenue from property taxes, while the municipalities obtained it from sales taxes.[50] The Cuauhtémoc Brewery's managers griped about any type of taxation, from production taxes to sales taxes, associating it with "tribute" and "*alcabalas.*"[51] Thus, when the brewery's tax-free concession was about to expire and the managers faced an increase of taxes on the company, they argued that new taxes would cut into the brewery's "minimal profits" and would "endanger the life of the enterprise."[52] Moreover, additional taxes would weaken the company's ability to compete with other breweries.[53]

As minimal as the state sales tax was, taxation, at least until 1904, was based not on production output but rather on sales at the commercial outposts. Even though sales taxes in Nuevo León, including those on beer, were less than 1 percent, the Cuauhtémoc Brewery believed that such a tax was detrimental to the firm. The managers of the brewery, which sold thousands of pesos in goods a day, recognized that it was the consumer who carried the weight of taxation and not the company. Furthermore, they knew that beer consumers, primarily the working class, earned low wages; any tax on sales reduced the brewery's market considerably. Thus, in the economic crisis of 1907–1908, management petitioned once again for the reduction of taxes, arguing that the closure of mines and industries had led to a reduction of beer sales throughout Mexico.[54] The Reyista state must have agreed with the brewery management's view of economic development, because it renewed the concession for the third time.

MONTERREY'S BREWERY WORKERS

The Cuauhtémoc Brewery's labor force matured differently from the rest of the *regiomontano* industrial proletariat, not to mention that of Mexico as a whole. The development of the brewery's workforce has posed many problems for students of Monterrey's history and of Mexico's working class. Although other large firms in Monterrey produced militant working-class movements and forms of self-expression at certain stages of their history, workers at the brewery rarely showed such manifestations of class discontent. Why did the brewery's workforce, dominated mostly by unskilled laborers, became the highest paid workers in Monterrey by 1920? Why did they form the organizational core of the company unions (the *sindicatos blancos*) which dominated the labor movement in Monterrey after the Revolution?

One of the problems in examining the early history of the Cuauhtémoc Brewery's labor force is the dearth of both primary and secondary sources. It is difficult to study brewery workers from "below" because of the lack of concrete evidence on turnover rates, labor recruitment, age, sex, and other factors that might provide some clues as to why the brewery workers differed from the rest of the *regiomontano* working class. Therefore this analysis is based on a "history from above" approach by studying management's labor policies and practices. In examining the brewery workers' "uniqueness," I propose two hypotheses: first, that management's labor paternalism was based on a strong Catholic outlook and, second, that management attempted to court the unskilled by offering reduced work hours, upward mobility, and schooling. By 1920 these workers were the highest paid in Monterrey. A comparison of management's labor policies toward brewery workers and glass workers might clarify some patterns peculiar to the development of the brewery workers.

Other than sharing the same management, the two groups of workers had little in common. Glassworkers were an autonomous group of skilled and semiskilled workers with a long tradition of confronting management over many issues, while brewery workers were primarily unskilled workers without a history of combativeness. What explains the militancy of glassworkers (who waged major strikes in 1904, 1936, and in the early 1970s) and the relative passivity of brewery workers, especially when both were under the same management? Attempts to reduce costs often came at the expense of the higher-paid skilled and semiskilled glassworkers, who were most expendable, because the management sought to replace them with machinery. The unskilled brewery workers, however, were needed in the hundreds. Management was therefore anxious to curry their favor by offering incentives. Because brewing required uninterrupted production and distribution, a shutdown for even twenty-four hours would have paralyzed the company, especially given the expanding market and the highly competitive conditions. The unskilled workers were essential to maintaining constant production.

From its earliest years the Cuauhtémoc Brewery had been a family enterprise, noted for its promotion of Christian values among its workforce.[55] The Garzas and Sadas were known to be devout Catholics who had perhaps been influenced by Pope Leo XIII's influential encyclical *Rerum Novarum* of 1891, which emphasized that the institution of private property was part of the "natural order." In reference to the labor conflicts and the growth of the socialist movements in the advanced European capitalist countries during this period, however, it also recognized that the root of labor unrest could be located in the increasing income gap between rich and poor. It made an appeal to capitalists to provide workers with decent wages and better working conditions so that society could be governed by justice and peace. Moreover, it urged capitalists to participate in the welfare of workers by providing them with education and helping them to create Catholic labor organizations. Catholic entrepreneurs who followed the *Rerum Novarum* valued an orderly society, taking into consideration the welfare of their workers as long as workers did not question or challenge management and private property.[56]

It is probable that management exposed workers to Catholic forms of worker organizations which had had some influence in Europe, especially in Germany, France, and Italy. Ideologically, Catholic working-class organizations viewed workers and capitalists as sharing a mutually beneficial bond. While these organizations identified the source of worker discontent as poor working conditions, they rarely emerged as militant trade unions. Consequently, conservative worker organizations such as mutual-aid groups arose in many Monterrey enterprises, often sponsored by management, and dominated the early labor movement. For instance, Florentino Cantú, the owner of La Fama textile mill, organized his 110 workers into a mutual-aid organization. Cantú was elected president of the "Bernardo Reyes" mutual-aid society in 1900.[57] The brewery's workers' organization, the Sociedad Mutualista Cuauhtémoc, remained a self-help organization for the duration of the Porfiriato and the Revolution. By 1918, however, the organization, which would form the base of the company union, had clearly come under the control of management.

As a competitive enterprise whose goal was to dominate the growing domestic market for beer, the Cuauhtémoc Brewery constantly adopted the latest technology in brewing, employed German master brewers to develop its different brands of beer, and undertook advertising campaigns, among other innovative actions. Moreover, in order to gain the competitive advantage over its rivals, it vertically integrated new industries that revolved around brewing, specifically glassmaking and packaging. This modern enterprise created a division of labor in which foreign engineers oversaw new machines and supervised the different departments, semi-skilled workers were increasingly replaced by steam, and Mexican unskilled workers did the heavy work of rolling barrels, cleaning waste, and loading vehicles and other tasks that required, above all, physical strength.

Because of the shortage of sources, one can only hypothesize on the formation of the Cuauhtémoc Brewery's labor force. There is a strong probability that brewery workers shared many similarities with the great majority of the *regiomontano* working class. When the Cuauhtémoc Brewery opened its beer and ice works, it employed seventy workers, whose numbers increased in proportion to the growth of the firm as the most important brewery in Mexico. Like most of the first generation of *regiomontano* industrial workers, the great majority of the brewery's unskilled workers probably had rural roots with no tradition of factory life. For many brewery workers this was their first experience with industrial employment, in a labor market of scarcity and with the pressures characteristic of firms trying to mold a disciplined and permanent workforce.

To furnish the brewery with bottles, the Cuauhtémoc Brewery's management recruited fifty-one German skilled glassblowers, who were assigned Mexican apprentices. These glassblowers were paid six to seven pesos a day and produced twenty thousand bottles every day.[58] Before the mass production of glass, skilled glassworkers in Europe had gained considerable bargaining power with their employers over the centuries. Organized in guilds, glassworkers enjoyed control in the workplace by determining admissions to the guild, the hiring of apprentices, working conditions, production output, and wages. Moreover, because glassworkers enjoyed autonomy in production and in the workplace, management could not impose the rigid hierarchy then becoming common at mass-production firms such as the Cuauhtémoc Brewery.[59]

The Cuauhtémoc Brewery's managers had under their command workers with different skills: brewmasters, engineers, mechanics, glassblowers, ice workers, apprentices, and a majority of unskilled brewery workers. While Isaac Garza and Francisco Sada administered the firm, the brewery no doubt had to depend on highly skilled foreign personnel, at least during its first ten years of operations. In the absence of native skilled construction workers, U.S. workers were recruited to construct the brewery, just as all the other major enterprises had done in Monterrey. Once the brewery was constructed, U.S. mechanics installed the machinery and were retained to maintain it, while German brewers supervised the different departments and "oversaw the detailed responsibilities of producing beer."[60] Joseph Schnaider, one of the promoters of the brewery and its head brewmaster, played the key role in organizing the production process. He was followed throughout the brewery by a Spanish translator.[61]

Management's goal was to reduce costs at all levels, especially those for labor. To achieve this goal management developed two different sets of labor policies: one for skilled workers and another for the unskilled. Cutting labor costs came at the expense of the skilled and semiskilled workers, because the unskilled were already earning the lowest wages. In Monterrey's labor-starved environment, a reduction in the already low unskilled workers' wages would have led to massive desertions to other enterprises. Instead, management lowered the cost of labor by replacing the foreign workers with natives and by introducing new technologies.

After much fanfare, the first attempts at glass mass-production in Mexico faltered after just a year because of "the culpability of the German glassblowers."[62] German workers struck in 1904 over higher wages and better housing and working conditions. Management perhaps had not taken into account the fact that these highly paid workers had brought to Monterrey a powerful tradition of using their occupational skills to control the workplace and to confront management over many issues, including wages. In this dispute management preferred to fire them rather than negotiate and, with the help of the German consul in Monterrey, also paid for their one-way tickets back to Germany.[63] The glass works continued with Mexican apprentices, but management soon closed the plant because the "output of the native workmen was unsatisfactory and the industry did not prove a paying one."[64]

Following the imperative of constantly lowering costs at all levels of production, the Cuauhtémoc Brewery reorganized its glass works in 1909 into the Vidriera de Monterrey, a 1.2-million-peso enterprise using the latest technology in the mass production of glass, the Owens-automatic bottling machine. This enterprise had no use for glassblowers, a soon-to-be extinct occupation, because of the new technology in mass production. The new glass works depended on less costly semiskilled machine tenders, of unknown nationalities, who produced 40,000 bottles a day, twice the amount of the glassblowers.[65] The acquisition of new technology in 1923 reduced the workforce of 110 by half and tripled production to a 120,000 bottles a day. According to management, the new technology lowered the cost of labor, which was necessary "for the highest degree of perfection, the only way all enterprises could survive given the competition"—but the Vidriera de Monterrey had no competition in Mexico.[66]

In contrast to the glassworkers, management in the early years from 1890 to 1907 had not offered brewery workers many incentives. Considering that modern breweries only employed a handful of skilled workers and even fewer semiskilled workers, there was little room for upward mobility. The majority of the workforce earned 75 centavos to 1.25 pesos by 1910, the average wage for Monterrey's common laborers. Children, who in 1902 made up one-fifth of the labor force, earned the lowest wages.[67] In contrast to the larger *regiomontano* firms of the magnitude of the brewery, the Cuauhtémoc Brewery did not offer its predominantly unskilled labor force wage bonuses, housing, medical care, schools, or other types of incentives. Underneath the surface, however, management had initiated a series of paternalistic practices with its predominantly unskilled working class, beginning with gradual replacement of highly paid foreign skilled and semiskilled workers with native ones. These measures also, and more importantly, had a disciplining effect on the workforce and cut labor costs. While it is difficult to acquire data on labor turnover rates, one may reasonably speculate that the brewery shared the problem of other *regiomontano* firms: molding its workforce into a group of more efficient workers. A student of Mexican labor noted that the Cuauhtémoc ice workers could perform good work, "but as soon as they had finished what they were told to do they folded their arms and stood still until they received further instructions."[68] Knowing that its workforce performed better under Mexican supervision than under foreign supervision, the brewery's management gradually began to replace the highly valued foreign skilled workers with Mexicans who had gained experience as apprentices.[69] The German glassworkers had as apprentices

> young men from this country, who, by their talent, would soon be the only glassblowers. We had the opportunity to see the products that our compatriots produced and the company's technicians said that their work was of equal quality to the products that foreign workers made. These [foreign workers] are paid six to seven pesos a day, a salary that the Mexican workers could earn as soon as they could produce the same number of bottles as the German glassblowers.[70]

These apprentices, the so-called pride of the future of Mexico's glass industry, failed to produce quality goods and the same quantity of bottles after they displaced the German workers who had been deported for striking for higher wages and better working and living conditions.

Two early events suggest that employer paternalism evolved gradually with the expansion of the firm. In 1907 the Cuauhtémoc Brewery became the first enterprise in Mexico to lower the workday for workers from twelve hours to nine. According to *El Imparcial*, an influential Mexico City newspaper, attempts at labor reform, as in the case of the Cuauhtémoc Brewery, would not lead workers to socialism.[71] The other event was the establishment of a school for workers and their children in 1911. A few months after the Maderista triumph over Díaz, the brewery opened its own Escuela Politécnica Cuauhtémoc for its employees and their dependents. Following the state government's educational program, the Cuauhtémoc school offered a grammar and a high school for adults and their children. The overall objective of the school was to assist workers and their children in acquiring "the culture and skills that are required at work and in the occupation to which they are dedicated."[72] A few months after the school opened, it had enrolled 651 students: 240 children in the day classes and 411 adults in night classes. The brewery hired twelve employees to operate the school, including a director and eight teachers, at a monthly cost of 752.50 pesos. The school, including all school supplies, was free to all employees and their children.[73] True to management's strong antitax views, it requested a tax exemption for the school property. The state government exempted the brewery from the annual property tax of 81.36 pesos.[74]

Why did the brewery's management reduce the working hours from twelve to nine and invest large quantities of funds to educate a primarily unskilled working class and its children? Were these early reforms "enlightened" policies by a management that sought to improve the overall conditions of its workforce, as Nemesio García Naranjo, one of the Monterrey elite's leading ideologues and a former cabinet member in the Victoriano Huerta regime, emphasized?[75] These reforms were implemented in 1907 and 1911, two years of labor unrest not only in Monterrey but throughout Mexico. The managerial goal of these reforms probably was to foster a loyal and permanent workforce. The reduction of the workday came in the midst of two of the most publicized and violent strikes of the Porfiriato, the miners' rebellion of Cananea, Sonora, and the textile workers' strike at Río Blanco, Veracruz. These militant workers' strikes, along with agitation from railroad workers, sought higher wages and better working and living conditions, including a reduction of the workday. Monterrey was also hit by a major railroad workers' strike in 1906. Growing labor unrest could have contributed to the reduction of the workday—a strike of a few days or weeks at the brewery, in a highly competitive industry dependent on daily sales, would have jeopardized the firm's ability to retain its dominant share of the market.[76]

The brewery opened its school a few months after the success of the Madero rebellion that overthrew the Díaz regime. Immediately after the triumph of Madero's rebellion, the *regiomontano* working class began organizing not only for economic improvement but also for political participation in electoral movements independent of the bourgeoisie. Because labor unrest challenged the brewery owners' need for an orderly society, it perhaps forced them to invest in their workforce's "moral and cultural improvement" as a means of courting loyalty. With the exception of the 1903 glassworkers' strike, the Cuauhtémoc Brewery had not experienced any labor unrest in its first twenty years of operations.

There was also a very practical reason for establishing the school—to produce a native skilled and semiskilled labor force to satisfy what was perceived to be a limitless future of growth. The cost-minded managers continued their quest to cut labor costs, by replacing the foreign workers with native ones. "The export of talent harms nations that are developing, while importing it costs money," argued Rodrigo Mendirichaga, one of the ideologues of Monterrey's business class.[77] Management paid high wages to keep foreign skilled workers such as the German glassblowers, who earned six to seven pesos per day, probably equivalent to the salary earned by mechanics and brewmasters. The Escuela Politécnica Cuauhtémoc sought to produce native skilled and semiskilled workers so that the brewery would not have to depend on expensive foreign labor in the future. While the school followed the state curriculum of reading, writing, and arithmetic, it also placed a strong emphasis on classes in chemistry, physics, refrigeration, electricity, and fermentation, subjects needed in glassmaking, brewing, and machinery.[78]

The Cuauhtémoc Brewery's owners were committed to the children of the brewery workers. The directors of the school hoped that students would learn not only the basics, "but also the teachings of arts and crafts [artes y oficios] which could be used later to improve their social condition, and so that they could contribute to the greatness and prosperity of the country."[79] In educating the children, the company was investing in a future skilled and semiskilled native labor force, vital in a scarce labor environment. Management even offered scholarships to the brightest students so that they could study in Germany and the United States.

The Cuauhtémoc school also offered the children of workers extracurricular activities such as gymnastics, sports, music, theatre, and possibly even the Boy Scouts. Francisco Sada had the goal of creating a "new Mexican," based on the Boy Scout model recently founded by Lord Baden-Powell in 1907–1908, with the idea of creating a new generation of youth to serve the nation (and in the case of England to serve the empire).[80] According to Francisco Sada:

This system is in full harmony with the spirit of children, it awakens all of their faculties, and it is recognized to produce the best material for the soldier of the future, developing love for their neighbor, love for the country, honor, along with the best sentiments, and it accustoms children to the life of the countryside, and supplies them with and develops their full physical and intellectual skills.[81]

The brewery management's early paternalistic policies toward unskilled workers unmistakably laid the groundwork both for the future control of its labor force and for labor's loyalty to the firm.

THE FUNDIDORA DE MONTERREY

The Compañía Fundidora de Fierro y Acero de Monterrey, also known as the Fundidora de Monterrey, was founded in 1900 and began producing steel and iron products in 1903. Created as a venture of Monterrey and Mexico City capitalists, the Fundidora had a total investment of ten million pesos. It was the first integrated steel mill in Latin America and would remain so until the 1940s, with the creation of Altos Hornos in nearby Monclova, the Garza Sadas' Hojalata y Lámina SA (HyLSA) in Monterrey, and the Volta Redonda works in Brazil. Almost all of the leading Monterrey capitalists were involved in the founding of this Mexican venture as stockholders, holding over 28,000 shares, an amount almost equal to half of the 100,000 total shares if the Kelly interests of the Milmo family are included. Antonio Basagoiti and León Signoret, two Mexico City industrialists, held 40 percent of the total stocks.[82]

Vicente Ferrara, a Monterrey capitalist of Italian descent, became the leading promoter of the creation of a steel mill in Monterrey. Ferrara had had firsthand experience in the metal industry as general manager of the Compañía Minera, Fundidora y Afinadora de Monterrey, one of the most successful independent smelters in Mexico. Before promoting the Monterrey steel mill, Ferrara had visited the United States on a commission to study the steel industry and its organizational structure.[83] The United States was the ideal place to study the latest developments in the steel industry, mainly because of the constant technological innovations which had transformed the country from an insignificant iron and steel producer in the 1860s to the world's leading producer by the end of the century. Over those thirty years constant technological innovations and cutthroat competition propelled the steel industry's growth as it gave rise to Andrew Carnegie's "billion dollar steel trust" (U.S. Steel) and other large enterprises.

Equally important as Ferrara's inquiry into the United States steel industry was his preliminary examination of the future potential for a steel and iron industry in Mexico. Before inviting capitalists to this expensive project, Ferrara made a study of the major factors which could convince them to invest in the domestic steel industry. The secretary of economic development provided Ferrara with statistical data on foreign steel and iron imports.[84] This information showed that Mexico was progressively importing greater quantities of steel and iron products due to expansion in transportation, construction, and mining. In 1889 Mexico imported 2.3 million pesos in steel and iron products, increasing to 6.4 by 1897.[85] Ferrara, who was quite knowledgeable about the mining and smelting industry, noted that Mexico had all the key raw materials for this industry, especially iron and coal.[86] All that was needed was the necessary capital, because Mexico had the raw materials and the "mercantile conditions" to greatly reduce foreign imports.[87] Ferrara and the other promoters of the steel mill successfully convinced capitalists to invest in a ten-million-peso project.

Ferrara's firsthand examination of the U.S. steel industry and knowledge of the Mexican mineral ore industry convinced the Fundidora promoters that Monterrey was the natural site for building the steel plant. The city was located within an area that contained "the best mines and most important iron and coal deposits in this part of the country, and these resources could easily be transported to Monterrey by the three railroad lines and at a low cost."[88] According to a study on the Mexican economy, the location of the city made Monterrey a good place for the steel industry:

> The Coahuila coal fields are easily accessible and the ore from Durango meets their output here under conditions somewhat similar to the meeting of the ores of the Great Lakes and the coal from West Virginia and Pennsylvania in the Pittsburgh and Youngstown districts.[89]

The northeastern part of Coahuila was the only producer of coke and coal in Mexico, the two main sources of fuel for the industry.[90] The Fundidora promoters attempted to imitate the completely integrated U.S. steel industry: it operated its own mines for ores and coal and had the technological capacity to transform the raw material into finished goods.

In addition to the ownership of nearby raw materials, Monterrey, according to the Fundidora's seventy-fifth anniversary report, was the natural site for its steel works because it was a transportation center with six different outlets, including Nuevo Laredo, Rositas/Piedras Negras, and Reynosa/Matamoros on the U.S. border and Torreón/Durango, Tampico, and Mexico City in the interior. Moreover, ten years of industrialization in Monterrey had created the industrial infrastructure for a vast railroad network. The city also provided a settled population "accustomed" to the geography and climate and to a tradition of hard work in an industrial environment. Finally, the local state government favored industries of that magnitude.[91]

Imitating the U.S. steel industry, the Fundidora sought to reduce the costs of producing steel and iron by integrating its mines, shops, and stations into the steelworks. It owned its own iron mines in Cerralvo (Nuevo León), Monclova (Coahuila), and Concepción del Oro (Zacatecas) and its own coal deposits in Coahuila. These mines were connected to the Fundidora by three different railroad lines. The Fundidora also owned twenty-five kilometers of rail lines, with its own locomotive fleet.[92] The company's blast furnaces were capable of producing 300 tons of steel a day with three 35-ton open-hearth steel furnaces and a small Bessemer converter. The steelworks also contained rolling-mills for rails, structural shapes, and merchant bars.[93]

As in the case of the Cuauhtémoc Brewery, U.S. engineers designed the plant and skilled U.S. workers constructed the steel mill and installed the machinery. Once in operation, the Fundidora counted on a few foreign skilled workers to supervise the different departments and a large number of semiskilled Mexican laborers.[94] Vicente Ferrara supervised the construction of the mill and managed it until 1907, when he was replaced by Adolfo Prieto. Prieto would be the main figure behind the Fundidora for the next four decades while also playing an active part in the social and cultural life of Monterrey during his long tenure as manager and chairman of the board of the Fundidora. In contrast to the Cuauhtémoc Brewery, the Fundidora was not a family enterprise and instead operated under a Board of Directors under the leadership of Prieto.

Perhaps because steel output had become the new indicator of industrialization worldwide, the Fundidora became a symbol of Mexico's "modernization" drive. By the standards of the early 1900s, the Fundidora, which had acquired the latest technology, was a modern steel complex. The owners of the Fundidora expected that their expensive steel mill, with the capacity to produce 90,000 metric tons of steel a year, could take over the domestic steel and iron market. Those expectations were shared by the nationalist middle-class and Porfirian politicians, who viewed the Fundidora as a firm that represented Mexico's attempts to "liberate" itself from imports and foreign domination of the economy.[95]

The "patriotic" goal of "liberating" Mexico from steel imports seemed theoretically possible: the Fundidora had the latest technology and owned the raw materials and railroads that connected the mill to its resources and markets. Notwithstanding these hypothetical advantages, the reality of producing steel and iron in a developing country presented many difficulties for the Fundidora. From its inception it had encountered a series of costly problems threatening the survival of the firm, ranging from the lack of a large and much needed skilled and semiskilled labor force to finding consumers for its different products. First, the Fundidora had a difficult time lining up customers, despite the fact that the domestic market for steel and iron products was large and increasing because of the growing urban infrastructural improvements and the expansion of the railroad system. Although this was an early setback, management was optimistic about the future as it attempted to change the "habit of the customers who prefer imported products."[96] In trying to line up buyers, Ferrara met with José Limantour, the minister of economic development, and offered the government a 10 percent discount on all Fundidora products.[97] This was unnecessary—the concession to the steel mill called for a discount of 1 percent on all goods produced, a small price to pay for the considerable amount of assistance it would receive from the government.[98]

In addition to the problem of persuading buyers to switch to Fundidora products, management encountered the obstacle of surviving economically in a field entirely dominated by foreign imports. Even before the construction of the Fundidora began, Ferrara was convinced that this enterprise would have a difficult time surviving unless it received government protection so that it could "resist the competition."[99] Consequently, the Fundidora successfully lobbied for higher protective tariffs on steel and iron imports, which were already quite high.[100] With influential Fundidora Board members and investors, such as Signoret and Basagoiti, closely allied to José Limantour, the secretary of economic development, the Fundidora closely attached itself to the Porfirian state. On February 4, 1904, the secretary set a high tariff on steel and iron imports, beginning a state policy of protecting the native steel industry which continued to the mid-1980s.[101] La Voz de Nuevo León applauded the new tariff because it protected the Fundidora "against the unjustified competition that some importers could present to impede the nascent development of our industry. . . ."[102]

Notwithstanding the high tariffs on imports, iron and steel importers adamantly resisted the competition from a native industry whose principal goal was to dominate the profitable and expanding domestic market for those products. In 1904, the year that the secretary of economic development raised the tariffs on steel and iron imports, importing companies

Table 7.2. FUNDIDORA OUTPUT AND STEEL IMPORTS, 1903–1925

Year	Imports (tons)	Fundidora (tons)	Rails (tons)
1903	168,920	8,823	1,154
1904	139,392	29,552	1,565
1905	184,149	21,613	2,441
1906	210,726	33,463	—
1907	230,402	31,806	—
1908	184,996	28,900	—
1909	261,415	59,504	25,056
1910	208,242	67,944	23,546
1911	161,521	84,697	37,414
1912	171,417	66,820	25,056
1913	—	19,535	924
1914	—	—	—
1915	14,586	6,656	—
1916	33,109	19,247	506
1917	34,928	22,224	303
1918	31,305	25,995	4,087
1919	99,619	37,455	13,946
1920	105,869	32,291	8,806
1921	99,217	43,263	10,327
1922	99,681	52,726	14,342
1923	105,566	59,216	16,243
1924	118,162	37,612	8,901
1925	127,892	75,136	14,505

Source: Compañía Fundidora de Monterrey, *Informe de la Compañía Fundidora de Fierro y Acero de Monterrey, S.A, 1927*, pp. 14, 15, and 41.

lowered the prices on their products by as much as 30 percent, the lowest prices ever registered in Mexico for those commodities.[103] The price of imported goods continued to drop in the ensuing years. The price for a ton of billets fell from 140 to 150 pesos to 100 in 1905. Commercial steel, which used to sell for 220 pesos a ton, dropped to 160 that same year, while steel used in mining fell from 400 to 250 pesos.[104]

Prior to 1910, the Fundidora's impact was felt in the import market only in 1904 (see Table 7.2), the year in which the new tariffs were instituted. In fact, imports registered growth after 1905. The Fundidora's highest rate of output from 1903 to 1908 was in 1906, when it reached one-third of its productive capacity. In its early history the steel mill never even came close to competing with imports for the domestic market from 1903 to 1925 or even to reaching its total productive capacity. The closest it came was in 1911, when it reached output levels of 80 percent—it was not until the 1930s that the Fundidora produced at full capacity.

Management perhaps had not expected the strong resistance from steel importers, who, in order to keep the Fundidora out of the market, reduced the price of steel to its lowest ever in Mexico.[105] Competition perhaps also forced the Fundidora to abandon the production of rails, the most profitable steel product in Mexico. In fact, the expanding railroad system and its need for rails, bolts, and other goods provided the catalyst for Mexican entrepreneurs to invest in the steel mill.[106] During the Fundidora's first year of operation the managers had secured contracts from railroad companies to supply them with 8,000 tons of rails.[107] These types of contracts led to the *La Voz de Nuevo León*'s optimistic forecast in 1905 that the Fundidora's rails "will reduce the imports from Germany and the United States, and our railroad system could be supplied by the goods manufactured in Nuevo León's workshops." [108] After producing a dismal 5,160 tons of rails from 1903 to 1905, the Fundidora abandoned rails altogether for the next three years (see Table 7.2). With the Fundidora out of the rail market competition, foreign rail imports more than doubled from 23,871 tons in 1904 to 55,682 tons the following year, reaching a peak of 97,000 tons in 1908.[109]

After three years of operations the Fundidora's dream of controlling the steel and iron market quickly faded, and its new strategy centered on surviving in a hostile market. The early years of failure were in part of the company's own making. It closed a department for a year to repair machinery that had been poorly installed.[110] Other causes for the early troubles were not within the control of the Fundidora, such as the 1904 yellow fever quarantine on Monterrey, which closed off the city to raw materials for an extended period.[111]

These were small problems, however, compared to the high cost of coal and unexpectedly poor and expensive railroad services which prevailed throughout the 1900s. "Fuel is perhaps the greatest and most pressing need of Mexico," argued Matías Romero, Díaz's early minister of economic development.[112] According to his estimates, a ton of coal cost eighteen to twenty pesos in Mexico in 1892, but three pesos in Great Britain and five pesos in the United States.[113] Because wood was more expensive than coal (not to mention its limited supply) and oil was not yet used, coal became the costliest component of industry. In Monterrey both small and large enterprises spent more on coal and coke than on labor: for example, in 1902 the small La Leona textile mill and the Ladrillera Unión, a brick factory, spent over 40,000 pesos each for coal, while the Guggenheim's smelter consumed 825,000 pesos for coke.[114] Hence, the high cost of coal and coke hindered Mexican industrialization to the point that "it is impossible to manufacture cheaply when fuel commands a very high figure." [115] Domestic coal production, which was nonexistent before the arrival of the railroads, increased noticeably from 1900 to 1911, from 529,000 to 1,400,000 tons. This represented less than a third of what was required to fuel the railroads and industry, as Mexico had to import over three million tons of coal in 1911.[116] Preoccupation with coal forced many *regiomontano* firms to invest heavily in coal companies. Monterrey firms owned 77 percent of the Compañía Carbonífera de Monterrey, with the Fundidora owning 20 percent of the stock and the Cuauhtémoc Brewery 10 percent of this one-million-peso coal company.[117]

Well aware of the high cost of domestic and imported fuel, Ferrara and the other promoters of the Fundidora purchased coal mines in northeastern Coahuila, the only significant coal-producing region in Mexico. Ferrara understood that ownership of coal deposits and their proximity to Monterrey enhanced the Fundidora's ability to survive in the competitive market.[118] In the end, the location of the steel mill in Monterrey turned out to be an intelligent decision mainly because the city was the only industrial center in Mexico which could benefit from Coahuilan coal and coke. Coahuilan coal was more expensive than imported coal in central Mexico due to high freight costs, which raised the price by over 200 percent.[119]

Although the steel mill owned coal fields, they could not furnish it with enough coal, especially when the Fundidora consumed 10 percent of all the domestic and imported coal in Mexico.[120] Unable to satisfy its own coal needs, the Fundidora was forced to purchase much of the coal at a high cost. During the company's crucial first five years of operation (1900–1904) the price of coal increased at an annual rate of 40 percent.[121] In Monterrey it cost approximately eight pesos for a ton of Coahuilan coal in 1902. Given that the Fundidora consumed 270,000 tons of coal in Mexico in the early 1900s, it cost over two million pesos to fuel the steel mill every year.[122] The cost of coal was much higher than the cost of labor, which came to about a million pesos a year. According to Francisco Bulnes, a prominent Científico, the high cost of imported coal forced the Fundidora to abandon rail production from 1906 to 1908.[123]

The managers of the Fundidora had counted on Monterrey's excellent railroad connections to haul in raw materials and then to distribute the finished steel and iron products throughout Mexico. They had not expected that poor rail services and high freight rates would be the norm during the critical early years. Surprisingly, it cost the same to transport a ton of steel from Europe to Veracruz as from Monterrey to central Mexico.[124] High, perhaps even discriminatory, freight rates and poor rail services led *Renacimiento* to denounce the railroad companies, especially the Ferrocarril Central Mexico, which delivered most of the coal to the Fundidora:

> Given the great commercial importance of the steel mill, from the millions of pesos invested in it to the large number of workers it employs, it would seem impossible that it would suspend its works because of the lack of coal, but that was painfully true. For reasons that we should not mention, the foreigners who own the Ferrocarril Central used the pretext that they had no freight cars, and we justifiably say pretext, because once the Fundidora signed a new contract [with the railroad company] the coal problem ended. . . .[125]

The problems with "the deficiency of railroad service" continued for the Fundidora, often closing the steel works for a time.[126] Presumably, the problem of services ended when the Fundidora signed a new contract with the railroad company. After another "interruption" in 1908, the railroad company guaranteed the Fundidora at least "rail services for several months, regardless of any unforeseeable problem that could emerge. . . ."[127]

THE STATE AND THE FUNDIDORA

Poor rail services, high freight rates, and the company's inability to produce sufficient coal, coupled with cutthroat competition from iron and steel importers, seriously threatened the survival of the Fundidora. It had produced a total of 92,231 tons of steel between 1903 and 1906, less than 25 percent of its total productive capacity for those years. In spite of the many problems it had encountered during the first six years of operations, the Fundidora did register meager profits in three of those years.[128] Meanwhile, other Mexican-owned metal companies had performed much better. The Madero family's Compañía Metalúrgica de Torreón, a five-million-peso smelter, had returned up to 28 percent in dividends a year to its investors, while the Compañía Minera, Fundidora y Afinadora de Monterrey had returned to its investors dividends of 7, 8, 5, 3.5, and 3.5 percent for the years of 1905 to 1909, respectively.[129]

"Reviewing the adverse factors, it may be said that the Mexican capi-

Table 7.3. FUNDIDORA'S SALES AND PROFITS, 1905–1920 (IN PESOS)

Year	Total Sales	Monthly Average	Profits
1905	2,268,505	197,383	—
1906	3,700,691	308,390	637,619
1907	3,526,449	293,870	—
1908	2,351,109	195,925	—
1909	5,106,472	425,539	392,508
1910	6,206,691	517,224	670,133
1911	5,722,364	476,802	825,049
1912	2,269,128	189,094	784,746
1913	—	—	—
1914	786,946	65,831	—
1915	98,676	8,223	—
1916	1,588,930	132,410	—
1917	2,806,848	233,904	—
1918	5,255,369	437,947	—
1919	5,588,840	465,736	—
1920	8,096,402	674,700	—

Source: Compañía Fundidora de Monterrey, *Informe de la Compañía Fundidora de Fierro y Acero de Monterrey, 1927,* p. 18; Archivo General de la Nación, Caja de Préstamos, unclassified.

talists who have gone into the iron and steel and kindred industries are not easily discouraged," a trade study reported on the perseverance of the Fundidora's owners.[130] Forced out of the potentially profitable rail products because of the high cost of coal, the Fundidora concentrated its energies on steel goods destined for the construction and mining industries: "The failure of one experiment does not cause them to quit or to direct their capital into other currents. They have more patience than American capitalists and are willing to wait longer for returns on their investments."[131] Indeed, the shift in production strategy paid off: the Fundidora was able to secure over 2.5 million pesos in nonrail contracts for the first six months of 1906.[132] The total sales increased from 2.3 million pesos in 1905 to 3.7 in 1906 (see Table 7.3). The Fundidora registered profits of 637,619 pesos in 1906, raising the confidence of the shareholders.[133]

The possibility of profiting through concentration on nonrail products rapidly faded for the Fundidora with the world economic crisis of 1907–1908, which hurt the construction and mining industry in Mexico. These were the two other leading consumers of steel after railroads and the sectors on which the Fundidora had concentrated in 1906. The economic crisis directly brought the company to "the verge of a shipwreck, endangering its very existence."[134] Although the Fundidora had registered three years of profits prior to the economic crisis, these profits were meager and did not compensate for a net loss of 700,000 pesos during its short history.[135] In 1907 the board of the Fundidora could no longer endure further losses and replaced Vicente Ferrara with Adolfo Prieto as the main operative of the firm. Prieto, who represented the Basagoiti interests (which controlled 21.5 percent of the Fundidora's stocks), became chairman of the board in 1907 and would gain controlling interest of the firm in the 1920s.[136]

The change in management was a deliberate effort by the leading stockholders of the Fundidora to link the firm closely with the Porfirian government. Evidently the shareholders had concluded that the Fundidora could only survive by establishing strong ties to the central government. This was not an entirely new strategy. Even before the construction of the steel mill, Ferrara had clearly emphasized that the firm could only survive if it received the protection of the state.[137] In fact, Prieto continued the original strategy, outlined by Ferrara, of concentrating on rail production and enhancing the concept of an integrated steel mill by purchasing additional iron and coal mines. The difference between Prieto and Ferrara centered on the fact that Prieto was well connected to leading Porfirian political and business leaders.

New management was also accompanied by a major shift in the board of the Fundidora: influential Mexico City businessmen gained control of the new board.[138] Both of these changes reflected the new credo of ensuring the firm's ties to the central state. Prieto, a banker who had little experience in the metals industry, directed the Fundidora from his offices in Mexico City. He followed Ferrara's original outline of securing raw materials and concentrating on rail production. Under his leadership the Fundidora organized geological and technical expeditions to the different mining regions of Mexico with the objective of securing the needed coal and iron.[139] During this time the Fundidora purchased many mines, including the famed Iron Mountain of Durango, the most important iron mine in Mexico.[140] Prieto's political ties to Porfirian politicians also paid off: he secured rail contracts with the federal government in 1907, reviving the department which had been closed since 1905.[141]

The Fundidora's many troubles forced the Porfirian government to recognize that it could "not allow the disappearance of an enterprise of such high importance to the nation."[142] Indeed, Mexico's nascent steel industry was too important for the image-conscious Porfirian politicians to let it collapse. To begin with, steel production had become the new index of industrialization worldwide.[143] For the Porfirian elite the Fundidora represented "Mexican progress," while for the growing middle classes it was a symbol of Mexico's attempts to liberate itself from foreign domination of the economy. Moreover, supporting the Fundidora fitted perfectly with the government's desire to "Mexicanize" the railroads. In 1908 the government offered the Fundidora a major contract worth 2 million pesos.[144] Its closer ties to the government spawned a new era of hope for the struggling Fundidora. Contemplating this new relationship with the state, Prieto emphasized that the company still had an "ample field yet to conquer."[145] Protected by tariffs and wholeheartedly supported by the "Supreme Government," all the Fundidora needed, according to Prieto, was leadership that could "take advantage of the favorable circumstances that surround it."[146] The leadership that would take the Fundidora into a new era included Prieto, the firm's main operative in Mexico City, and a new Board of Directors which included such prominent Porfirian businessmen as Fernando Pimentel, Pablo Macedo, Hugo Scherer, and León Signoret.

The "favorable circumstances" that favored the Fundidora pertain to the "Mexicanization" of the railroad industry. Between 1903 and 1910 Díaz's government aggressively began to purchase controlling shares of railroad companies' stock. In 1907 the National Railways of Mexico was formed to administer the railroad operations of the government, which owned two-thirds of all lines.[147] The post-1907 Fundidora success could largely be attributed to the "Mexicanization" of the railway system and the fact that Pablo Macedo, Hugo Scherer, and José Signoret sat on the Board of Directors of both the Fundidora and the National Railways of Mexico.[148] The National Railways of Mexico–Fundidora ties led to the firm's concentration on rail production, which had been abandoned earlier due to the high cost of coal. In 1908 the Fundidora received a government contract worth two million pesos to supply the National Railways of Mexico with 20,000 tons, a production figure it never met.[149] Two years later the contract called for 32,000 tons of rails.[150] By 1911 rails constituted more than half of all the Fundidora's steel output.[151]

The Fundidora profited from its new relationship with the government-owned National Railways of Mexico not just because of the purchase of rails but in other ways. Perhaps the fact that Macedo, Scherer, and Signoret were board members of both companies helped shape Mexico's Porfirian energy policies to the benefit of domestic industries, which, in the end, favored the Fundidora. In 1909 the directors of the National Railways of Mexico decided to lower the freight cost of Coahuilan coal. The government also imposed a tariff of one peso per ton of imported coal, thus protecting Mexican coal producers such as the Fundidora. These policies led immediately to a decrease of imported coal and an increase in the domestic production of those indispensable sources of fuel, not to mention lower fuel costs for Mexican industries.[152] The Fundidora, which consumed about 10 percent of all the domestic and imported coal in Mexico, felt the impact of these protectionist energy policies: 70 percent of the coke it used in 1909 came from abroad—a year later it was reduced to 37 percent.[153] Likewise, the Fundidora no longer had to confront unfriendly railroad companies, which had provided poor services to the firm and perhaps even charged discriminatory freight rates.

Conceivably, no other native enterprise in Mexico had closer ties to the Porfirian state than the Fundidora de Monterrey. The state had ensured the survival of the firm by posting high tariffs on steel and iron imports in 1904. In 1909 the National Railways of Mexico lowered the transportation fares for Coahuilan coal and coke, while the federal government imposed a tariff on those imported goods. By 1908 the federal government had become one of the Fundidora's principal customers. Foreigners criticized those government policies on grounds that they gave native enterprises preferential treatment.[154]

Finally, the ties between the Fundidora and the Porfirian state were further cemented with a major loan from the Caja de Préstamos, a financial institution promoted by both private banks and the government to help mainly hacendados with long-term, low-interest loans. In 1908 the Fundidora received a 3.9-million-peso loan from the Caja de Préstamos, payable in fifteen years at an annual interest rate of 7 percent.[155] This was the largest loan from the Caja de Préstamos to an enterprise, either industrial or agrarian, during the Porfiriato.[156] With the new loan the Fundidora had become one of the largest enterprises in Mexico, valued at over sixteen million pesos by 1911. The future had never looked so bright for the Fundidora as in the waning years of the Porfiriato.

MONTERREY'S STEELWORKERS

Monterrey's first ten years of industrialization had attracted thousands of workers to the city. The city's large working-class population, who had been "socialized" as industrial workers, and its excellent railroad connections and access to nearby raw materials were key factors in locating the steel mill in Monterrey. Securing a large labor force, usually a problem for most enterprises, was not the issue for the Fundidora's managers. Rather, management faced the problem of creating a large semiskilled labor force from predominantly unskilled workers. Management needed semiskilled labor which could operate all the departments of a modern and expensive integrated steel complex.

Unlike the Cuauhtémoc Brewery, which began as a small 125,000-peso firm that required a handful of skilled brewmasters and large numbers of unskilled laborers, the Fundidora was from its inception prepared to mass-produce steel using the latest technology. The Cuauhtémoc Brewery had expanded by acquiring the latest technological innovations, but without radically changing the occupational structure of its labor force. The turn-of-the-century steel industry, however, having undergone revolutionary technological innovations, had replaced its large number of skilled and unskilled workers with semiskilled workers.[157] While it had been possible to build a steel mill like the Fundidora for ten million pesos in 1900, a new mill with the latest technology cost twenty million dollars in 1911.[158] Because of the high cost of the constantly changing steel technology, the Fundidora kept its original machinery for the first thirty years. In effect, the first generation of steelworkers learned their skills with technology that was considered archaic by 1910 standards.

Although the Fundidora opened its doors in mid-June of 1903, it did not actually begin production until late July because it needed to experiment with the organization of production and to adjust the machinery. This dress rehearsal also had the objective of teaching "our workers the skills that they experienced [to which they were exposed] for the first time." [159] The Fundidora needed a large labor force with diverse skills, but especially a few highly skilled workers and numerous semiskilled laborers. It solved the problem of obtaining a skilled labor force by recruiting most of them in Austria.[160] These twenty-five highly skilled steelworkers supervised the various departments of the mill. The company also hired 500 workers who were classified in semiskilled occupations and 1,250 workers of diverse occupations, such as common laborers (*peones*), coal and iron miners, and apprentices. The number of semiskilled workers was actually higher because of the many apprentices and miners the firm employed.[161] To maintain these workers, especially the skilled group, it also constructed a company store, a hospital, and a three-story hotel with fifty-five rooms and offered housing for some of its employees.[162]

In a country dominated by an unskilled working class, semiskilled workers were in great demand. "The severe lack of workers who understand the operations of different machines that are being employed with the growth of our businesses is becoming more and more notable every day," as a local newspaper reported on the problems that firms like the Fundidora encountered because of the lack of semiskilled laborers in Monterrey. It also noted that "some businesses have never gotten off the ground because of this." [163] Barely surviving financially, the Fundidora could not afford to recruit from abroad the many semiskilled workers it needed. Foreign workers demanded higher wages than they could receive in their home country. Therefore, Mexico's steelmakers had no choice except to produce their own semiskilled steelworkers. The Fundidora's original goal of dominating the home market for steel, especially rails, rested on its ability to train a semiskilled labor force rapidly. Without a large and experienced semiskilled labor force, a trade study on Mexico noted,

> it does not appear likely that for many years the Mexican demand for rails will be supplied by domestic production. The chief trouble is said to be securing the class of skilled labor that is essential. Iron and steel works from the United States demand higher wages than they obtain at home, and no plant can expect to manufacture and profitably market steel rails on such a wage basis. The future of the industry therefore lies in developing in Mexico workman [sic] of the same type that are found in the mills of the United States. . . . The process is a slow one. The lack of available skilled native labor must be taken into consideration in determining the time in the future when Mexican iron and steel industries will render the country measurably independent of foreign importation, allowing that the raw materials of the right quantity can be assembled on an even plane economically with those of foreign countries.[164]

Forced to rely on native workers, the Fundidora underwent a slow process of trial and error in the workplace, shaping a large semiskilled labor force. Indeed, incapable of attracting or competing for foreign workers, the Fundidora, also known as the *maestranza* (the teacher), became "a school . . . for the first generation of national technicians [*técnicos nacionales*]." [165] In an age when the Porfirian state did not provide technical schools to train and produce future skilled and semiskilled workers, it was up to the firms to train their own workforce. The Reyes-sponsored technical school mostly served railroad workers rather than workers from other occupations, who needed to learn skills different from those in the state school. Under the leadership of Adolfo Prieto the Fundidora founded its own technical schools in 1912, the Escuelas Acero (Steel Schools). Prieto, a strong proponent of technical schools, stressed that "[f]rom these schools and these workshops we must produce the true aristocracy of the national proletariat."[166]

On-the-job training by trial and error and the establishment of the Escuelas Acero succeeded in producing the first generation of "national technicians" (*técnicos nacionales*). There was much room for upward mobility at the plant level: through apprenticeships and on-the-job experience, unskilled workers could move up to the ranks of the semiskilled, and perhaps a few could even move to the ranks of the skilled. The acquisition of steelmaking skills made the company's labor force the best-paid workers in Monterrey. The Fundidora paid an average daily wage of 3.73 pesos, while the Compañía Fundidora y Afinadora de Monterrey paid 1.92 pesos; ASARCO, 1.61 pesos; and the Cuauhtémoc Brewery, 1 peso.[167] By 1908 the Fundidora had a weekly payroll of 20,000 pesos for its 1,000 steelworkers (excluding its mining operations) or over a million pesos a year.[168] It paid an average of 20 pesos a week to each worker, perhaps the highest wages in the country for Mexican workers.

In its first seven years of operations the Fundidora succeeded in producing a well-paid, upwardly mobile semiskilled labor force. Privileged by Mexican standards and aware of the power of their skills, steelworkers would use their technical knowledge as a bargaining chip in future disputes with the Fundidora's management during the Revolution and afterward. Those skills were so specialized and limited to steelmaking, however, that they could only be used in the Fundidora, the only enterprise of this kind in Mexico and in Latin America. Simply stated, management and steelworkers needed each other.

CONCLUSION

Both of the firms examined developed into powerful economic groups during the Porfiriato. The Cuauhtémoc Brewery began as a small enterprise and by 1910 had become Mexico's premier brewery. The Fundidora de Monterrey started out as a large enterprise that sought to corner Mexico's domestic steel market. In the process of emerging as powerful industrial groups the two firms developed different strategies toward the state and working class. By the end of the Porfiriato these strategies had produced different working-class formations, with various kinds of ties to the Porfirian state.

The firms developed different strategies for seeking to gain control of their respective markets. The Cuauhtémoc Brewery had to compete with other large and small native breweries for the small domestic market of beer consumers. Competition forced the brewery to adopt innovative strategies like pioneering advertisement in Mexico and expanding into other areas such as packaging and bottling. Each new division of the brewery evolved into a new firm which in turn strengthened the economic power of the Cuauhtémoc group. The brewery's future economic interests depended on the growth of the domestic market and on social peace. Because it did not depend on the government for protective tariffs and credits, the Cuauhtémoc Brewery became an independent grouping with little ties to the Porfirian state.

As in other brewing firms in the world, the management maintained a stable labor force through paternalistic methods. While it paid the average wage in Monterrey and did not offer any incentives to its workforce, the brewery's management—unlike other firms which depended largely on unskilled laborers—introduced reforms with the intention of creating a permanent labor force. It reduced the workday from twelve hours to nine and opened a school for its workers and their children. While these types of reforms were limited and perhaps even contributed little to the formation of a permanent labor force, they did establish paternalistic patterns of interaction with the labor force which would increasingly be relied upon as management sought to exert even more influence over its workers during the Mexican Revolution and beyond.

With higher hopes than the Cervecería, the Fundidora de Monterrey began production in 1903, having already anticipated gaining control of the profitable steel and iron domestic market. But the intense competition from foreign imports, expensive raw materials, poor rail services, and discriminatory freight rates quickly shattered those expectations. Not only did the Fundidora never even come close to gaining control of the domestic market, but it in fact appeared to have been a costly and poor investment. The future indeed looked bleak for the steel mill when it changed management in 1907. The new managers, however, who were mainly Mexico City businessmen, used their contacts with the Porfirian government to ensure the survival of the Fundidora through the use of tariff protection, credits, and, most importantly, the purchase of rails for the "Mexicanized" railway system, markedly improving the firm's fortunes.

Among the many obstacles the Fundidora faced at an early stage were recruiting, maintaining, and training a large labor force needed for the different departments of the mill. Management solved the problem of the lack of skilled workers by simply recruiting them from Austria. Due to the Fundidora's financial problems, it could not afford to recruit the large numbers of semiskilled laborers needed from abroad and thus depended on native laborers to fulfill those tasks. These workers acquired their occupational skills through trial and error and later by attending the firm's technical school. Because the Fundidora had to create a large semiskilled workforce, it offered native workers high wages and opportunities for advancement within the firm. By 1910 Monterrey's steelworkers were the best-paid workers in the city and perhaps in all of Mexico.

Epilogue

Across the plains,
Between two hills, two villages, two trees, two friends,
The barbed wire runs which neither argues nor explains
But where it likes a place, a path, a railroad ends,
The humor, the cuisine, the rites, the taste,
The pattern of the City, are erased.
             W. H. AUDEN, "MEMORIAL FOR THE CITY"

El otro México que aquí hemos construido
en este suelo que ha sido territorio nacional,
es el esfuerzo de todos nuestros hermanos
y latinoamericanos que han sabido progresar.
Mientras los ricos se van por el extranjero
para esconder su dinero y por Europa pasear
los campesinos que venimos de mojados
casi todo se lo enviamos a los que quedan allá.
[The other Mexico that we have built here
in this land that had been national territory
is the effort of all our brothers and sisters
and Latin Americans who have known how to progress.
Meanwhile the rich go to foreign lands
to hide their money and to tour Europe,
the peasants who have come as wetbacks
send almost everything to those who are left behind.]
             "EL OTRO MÉXICO" (NORTEÑO SONG)

In this age of the globalization of economies, labor, information, and cultures, Mexico and the United States provide numerous examples relevant to the current debates about the future role of the nation-state. Many of these debates center on the issues of mass migration of labor from the "periphery" of capitalism (Mexico) to its "core" (the United States) as well as the unrestricted movement of capital between the two. In particular, the contradictions created by the intense push for greater economic integration between the two nations in the midst of efforts to control the massive emigration (both legal and unauthorized) of Mexicans to the United States stand out in these debates, as one of today's most pressing scholarly and policy-making issues.

The 1994 North American Free Trade Agreement (NAFTA) allows for the relatively free movement of investments, goods, and services across borders and thus serves as an example of capital eroding national sovereignty when it comes to the state's abilities to formulate domestic economic policies. The increasing militarization of the border, which is aimed at preventing drugs and unauthorized immigrants from entering the United States, is an example of the state exercising greater sovereignty over its boundaries. Mexico's recent granting of dual citizenship to the millions of Mexicans residing abroad, especially in the United States, and of their right to vote in future Mexican presidential elections is an example of the state extending citizenship rights across borders.

The urgency with which the media present these issues and the heated polemics that they provoke within academic, diplomatic, and policy-making circles give the impression that these concerns have only recently developed. For the most part, these discussions have been devoid of a historical content. The integration of economies, the policing of boundaries, and the mass movement of millions of people from south to north along with the reverse transfer of billions of dollars in capital, as well as other issues dominating U.S.-Mexican relations, are not recent developments. These issues did not exist prior to 1848; the imposition of the 1848 boundary gave birth to them. The starting point for elaborating on the complexities of these modern phenomena is 1848.

After 1848 the "problems" of migration, policing, and economic integration became permanent fixtures of the U.S.-Mexican borderlands. Law enforcement along the international line (contraband, Indian raids, etc.), the Mexican Free Trade Zone, and the unauthorized movements of people (such as Mexican indentured servants escaping into Texas) emerged in 1848 as fundamentally new and tension-driven issues dominating *fronterizo* and U.S.-Mexican diplomatic affairs. These issues have not disappeared—they have just assumed more complex forms today: the present mass immigration of poor Mexicans to all corners of the United States has a direct connection to the post-1848 exodus of hundreds of indentured servants who escaped to Texas. Contraband, just as in the post-1848 era, continues to be a well-organized enterprise: today it is a billion-dollar industry controlled by groups such as the Tijuana and Ciudad Juárez cartels.

The borderlands are unique and volatile because this is one of the few regions in the world, if not the only one, where two large nations that are so different come into permanent contact. Why does the United States have a strikingly greater police presence (military, customs, immigration, and other policing agencies) on its southern boundary than on the border with Canada, a nation with a boundary line that is twice as large as the Mexican border? The way nations police their boundaries tells us much about how they perceive their neighbors.

More than any other catalyst, the economic power of U.S. capitalism has been the driving force shaping the development of the borderlands ever since the two countries became neighbors. From the start, the process of economic integration occurred between nations that were on two completely different tracks of historical development. A report from a Mexican congressional committee emphasized this important distinction in 1878, noting that on the southern side of the boundary one could not be indifferent to "the poverty and decadence in which they [Mexicans] live, when they are only separated from prosperity and abundance by an imaginary line, which some view as a wall which shuts off material prosperity and intellectual progress." [1]

I took on the task of mapping the distinct shapes that these phenomena took in Nuevo León from 1848 to 1910. The north emerged as a geographical area distinct from the rest of Mexico during this era, as the location of permanent contact between the United States and Mexico. The "frontier to border" process produced profound changes in the economy and in rural-urban and periphery-center relationships. At the same time, it shaped group identities, class formations, and conflicts. Three of the main developments emerging from the frontier to border transition included the dominance of capitalism in the north, where it expanded more rapidly and thoroughly than in the rest of Mexico; the rise of powerful native business groups; and the creation of a labor market based on competitive wage labor and largely dependent on thousands of migrants from central Mexico.

Today the Mexican borderlands continue to play the role of a magnet that attracts millions of people and promotes economic integration. For example, the *maquiladora* industry generates about ten billion dollars a year in foreign exchange for Mexico and employs close to a million workers in border cities. Monterrey, Ciudad Juárez, and Tijuana are among the six largest cities in Mexico.

Business leaders, academics, and politicians from both countries have praised the new era of NAFTA, even though economic integration has never been between equals. They expect greater integration to generate employment in both countries and reduce Mexican immigration and income inequalities. U.S. labor unions, however, oppose NAFTA because of the prospects of greater deindustrialization of the U.S. economy as corporations move their manufacturing operations to the low-wage paradise of Mexico. The boundary and the borderlands have existed for over a century and a half, long enough to be better understood. The heated discussions on the new economic integration and other border- and boundary-related themes have ignored the historical foundations that have shaped these modern developments. I hope that this book will contribute to discussions of these themes; they are, for better or worse, permanent fixtures of the borderlands and will certainly not disappear in the near future.

Notes

INTRODUCTION

1. Alan Knight boldly states that these business groupings would have emerged as Mexico's "national bourgeoisie." See Alan Knight, *The Mexican Revolution*, 1:11.

2. David J. Weber, *The Spanish Frontier in North America*, p. 11.

3. Quoted in Peter Sahlins, *Boundaries: The Making of France and Spain in the Pyrenees*, p. xv.

4. Malcolm Anderson, *Frontiers: Territory and State Formation in the Modern World*, p. 1.

5. John H. Coatsworth, "Obstacles to Economic Growth in Nineteenth-Century Mexico," *American Historical Review* 83 (1978): 82.

6. Matías Romero to T. F. Bayard, Washington, D.C., February 10, 1888, *Papers Related to the Foreign Relations of the United States 1888*, p. 1270.

7. See John H. Coatsworth, *Growth against Development: The Economic Impact of Railroads in Porfirian Mexico*, pp. 28–29.

CHAPTER 1. THE SIGNIFICANCE OF 1848

1. Edward Moseley, "The Public Career of Santiago Vidaurri, 1855–1858," p. 82; Ronnie C. Tyler, *Santiago Vidaurri and the Southern Confederacy*, pp. 15–40.

2. Quoted in Moseley, "The Public Career," p. 74.

3. República Mexicana, *Nuevo León: Reseña geográfica y estadística*, p. 47.

4. See the second footnote in Santiago Roel, *Nuevo León, apuntes históricos*, p. 169.

5. Quoted in Tomás Mendirichaga, "Después de la derrota," in *Nuevo León: Textos de su historia*, ed. Celso Garza Guajardo, 1:435.

6. Santiago Vidaurri to Benito Juárez, Monterrey, January 31, 1858, in *Correspondencia particular de Don Santiago Vidaurri, gobernador de Nuevo León, 1855–1864*, ed. Santiago Roel, p. 9.

7. Ibid.

8. Eugenio del Hoyo, "La economía del Nuevo Reino de León," in *Nuevo León*, ed. Garza Guajardo, 1:53.

9. Alberdi was one of Argentina's foremost intellectuals of the mid-nineteenth century. See David Rock, *Argentina, 1516-1987: From Spanish Colonialism to Alfonsín*, p. 114.

10. José E. González, *Datos estadísticos que pueden servir de base para formar una estadística del estado de Nuevo León*, p. 16.

11. François Chevalier, *Land and Society in Colonial Mexico*, p. 181.

12. Daniel Nugent, *Spent Cartridges of the Revolution: An Anthropological History of Namiquipa, Chihuahua*, p. 39; Ramón A. Gutiérrez, *When Jesus Came, the Corn Mother Went Away: Marriage, Sexuality and Power in New Mexico, 1500-1846*.

13. J. H. Elliott, "Spain and America before 1700," in *Colonial Spanish America*, ed. Leslie Bethell, p. 65.

14. González, *Datos estadísticos*, p. 17.

15. In Nuevo León the *encomienda* was better known as a *congrega*, short for *congregación*. Legally the *encomienda* gave the *encomendero* the right to receive tribute from Indians, while the *congregación* was defined as a settlement of Indians for the purpose of conversion and protection. In Nuevo León, as a scholar pointed out, the difference between the two was only a difference in words—they were polite terms for Indian slavery. See Israel Cavazos Garza, *Breve historia de Nuevo León*, p. 56.

16. Quoted in Cavazos Garza, *Breve historia*, p. 48; Eugenio Del Hoyo, *Historia del Nuevo Reino de León, 1577-1723*, 1:316-317.

17. Chevalier, *Land and Society*, p. 157.

18. Andrés Montemayor Hernández, "La congrega o encomienda en el Nuevo Reino de León desde finales del siglo XVI hasta el siglo XVIII," in *Nuevo León*, ed. Garza Guajardo, 1:95.

19. Ibid., 1:340-399.

20. Ibid., 2:435-436.

21. Quoted in Garza Guajardo, *Nuevo León*, 1:325. For a general survey of Indian-settler conflicts, see María Teresa Huerta Presiado, *Rebeliones indígenas en el noreste de México en la época colonial*.

22. Quoted in Garza Guajardo, *Nuevo León*, p. 116.

23. Cited in Cavazos Garza, *Breve historia*, p. 78.

24. González, *Datos estadísticos*, pp. 16-17.

25. For an excellent collection of letters that *vecinos* wrote to the governors, see Israel Cavazos Garza, *Cedulario autobiográfico de pobladores y conquistadores de Nuevo León*.

26. Ibid.; Cavazos Garza, *Breve historia*, pp. 78-79.

27. The arrival of new settlers and the expansion of Indian enslavement into other areas expanded settlements into Nuevo Santander (Tamaulipas) and Texas. See José E. González, *Lecciones orales de la historia de Nuevo León*, pp. 254-255; Montemayor Hernández, "La congrega," p. 100.

28. Cavazos Garza, *Breve historia*, pp. 77-78.

29. For the case of Coahuila, see Charles H. Harris III, *The Sánchez Navarros: A Socio-economic Study of a Coahuilan Latifundio, 1846-1856*.

30. Cavazos Garza, *Breve historia*, p. 77.

31. For a chronology of the municipalities, see Gustavo Garza Guajardo, *Las cabeceras municipales de Nuevo León*.

32. Although the historiography of colonial Nuevo León strongly emphasizes the Spanish and Tlaxcalan roots of the colonization period, other ethnic groups also played a major role, especially African slaves. In all likelihood, the slaves and *castas* played a far greater role than has been attributed to them. For example, Sabinas Hidalgo had 1,529 residents in 1821. The *castas* and Africans made up 84 percent of the population. Meanwhile, over 80 percent of the children baptized in Linares from 1771 to 1795 were non-Spaniard. See Roel, *Nuevo León*, pp. 83–87; Cavazos Garza, *Breve historia*, p. 78; Guajardo Garza, *Nuevo León*, 1:287; Raúl García Flores, "Formación de la sociedad mestiza y la estructura de castas en el noreste: El caso de Linares."

33. David J. Weber, *The Spanish Frontier in North America*, pp. 327–328.

34. D. W. Meinig, *The Shaping of America: A Geographical Perspective of 500 Years of History*, 2:128.

35. Roel, *Nuevo León*, p. 163; Comisión Pesquisidora, in Oscar Martínez, ed., *U.S.-Mexico Borderlands: Historical and Contemporary Perspectives*, pp. 58–65; David Vigness, "El intento de la separación," in *Nuevo León*, ed. Guajardo Garza, 1:438–448.

36. Quoted in Rodrigo Mendirichaga, "Los nuevos vecinos," in *Nuevo León*, ed. Garza Guajardo, 1:381–382; John S. D. Eisenhower, *So Far from God: The U.S. War with Mexico, 1846–1848*, p. 148.

37. Mendirichaga, "Los nuevos vecinos," p. 382.

38. Chevalier, *Land and Society*, pp. 178–184. For studies on the Mexican *mesta*, see del Hoyo, "La economía"; Richard Salvucci, *Textiles and Capitalism in Mexico: An Economic History of the Obrajes, 1539–1840*; William H. Dusemberry, *The Mexican Mesta: The Administration of Ranching in Colonial Mexico*.

39. D. A. Brading, "Bourbon Spain and Its American Empire," in *Colonial Spanish America*, ed. Leslie Bethell, pp. 151–154.

40. Del Hoyo, "La economía," pp. 57–59, 71; Cavazos Garza, *Breve historia*, pp. 59–60.

41. Chevalier, *Land and Society*, p. 183.

42. Del Hoyo, "La economía," p. 56. For an excellent study on the profound impact that the introduction of sheep had in the Mezquital Valley (Hidalgo), see Elinor G. K. Melville, *A Plague of Sheep: Environmental Consequences of the Conquest of Mexico*.

43. José E. Gónzalez, *Colección de noticias, documentos para la historia del estado de Nuevo León*, pp. 92–96; Jaime Del Toro Reyna, "Aramberrí, Nuevo León, 1626–1950," pp. 23–32; "Galeana," *Boletín del Archivo General del Estado de Nuevo León* 1 (January–April 1984).

44. Doris M. Ladd, *The Mexican Nobility at Independence, 1780–1826*, pp. 41, 45, 63, 77, 184, 185, 206, 210.

45. Ibid., p. 63.

46. John Tutino, *From Insurrection to Revolution in Mexico: The Social Bases of Agrarian Violence, 1750–1940*, pp. 228–240.

47. Isidro Viscaya Canales, "Composición étnica de la población de Nuevo León a la consumación de la independencia," in *Nuevo León*, ed. Garza Guajardo, 1:287.

48. "Galeana," p. 25.

49. Ibid.

50. Ibid.

51. Ibid.

52. Quoted in Paul S. Taylor, *An American-Mexican Frontier: Nueces County, Texas*, p. 36.

53. Meanwhile, Mexicans welcomed U.S. slaves who had escaped to Mexico. A Mexican "underground railroad" helped slaves, as a Texas Ranger reported: "The possession of slaves in Western Texas was rendered insecure owing to the contiguity of Mexico, and to the efforts of Mexicans to induce them to run away. They assisted them in every way they could. When once on Mexican soil they were free from pursuit—free, and very popular. The Mexicans expressed horror at the idea of slavery as it existed in the United States, and seemed to forget that they made their own countrymen slaves . . . for inability to pay a debt" (quoted in ibid.).

54. Ibid.; Moisés González Navarro, *Los extranjeros en México y los mexicanos en el extranjero, 1821–1970*, 2:45–46.

55. Ibid.

56. "Extract from a letter of Hon. Antonio Moreno, senator in the Mexican Congress from Sonora, n.d., n.p.," in *Foreign Relations of the United States 1878* (Washington, D.C.: Government Printing Office, 1878), p. 832.

57. Mrs. William L. Casneau (Cora Montgomery), *Eagle Pass or Life at the Border*, p. 103.

58. Quoted in Isidro Viscaya Canales, "Razones que retardaron el desarrollo de las provincias internas," in *Nuevo León*, ed. Garza Guajardo, 1:149.

59. Isidro Viscaya Canales, "Factores adversos para el desarrollo de las provincias internas en los últimos años de la dominación española," in *Estudios de historia del noreste*, ed. Sociedad Nuevoleonesa de Historia, Geografía y Estadística, p. 175.

60. Quoted in Eric Wolf, "The Mexican Bajío in the Eighteenth Century," in *Synoptic Studies of Mexican Culture*, p. 185.

61. Ibid.

62. Ibid.

63. Viscaya Canales, "Razones," 1:150.

64. See John M. Hart, *Revolutionary Mexico: The Coming Process of the Mexican Revolution*, pp. 105–128; David Montejano, *Anglos and Mexicans in the Making of Texas, 1836–1986*; Mario Cerutti, *Economía de guerra y poder regional en el siglo XIX, gastos militares, aduanas y comerciantes en los años de Vidaurri (1855–1864)*.

65. Matías Romero to Bayard, Washington, D.C., February 10, 1888, *Papers Related to the Foreign Relations of the United States, 1888*, 2:1266.

66. Ibid., 2:1266–1267.

67. Milo Kearney and Anthony Knopp, *Border Cuates: A History of U.S.-Mexican Twin Cities* (Austin, Tex.: Eakin Press, 1995), pp. 38–37, 82–83.

68. Matías Romero to Bayard, Washington, D.C., February 10, 1888, 2:1266–1267.

69. J. Fred Rippy, *The United States and Mexico*, p. 88.

70. See John K. Winkler, *The First Billion: The Stillmans and the National City Bank.*

71. William Emory, *Report on the United States and Mexican Survey*, 1:63-64.

72. Ibid., 1:60-62.

73. Helen Chapman to father, Fort Brown, Texas, January 4, 1849, in *The News from Brownsville: Helen Chapman's Letters from the Texas Military Frontier, 1848-1852*, ed. Caleb Coker, p. 101.

74. Mario Cerutti, *Burguesía y capitalismo en Monterrey (1850-1910)*, pp. 20-21.

75. Helen Chapman to her father, Fort Brown, Texas, January 4, 1849, p. 107.

76. Quoted in Taylor, *An American-Mexican Frontier*, p. 69.

77. See José Vasconcelos, *Don Evaristo Madero, biografía de un patricio*, pp. 77-104; Cerutti, *Burguesía y capitalismo*, pp. 70-76.

78. For his business skills and perseverance in frontier trade, González Treviño was known in the northeast as "judíos grandes todos hermanos" after the first initial of the firm's name—Jesús Gónzalez Treviño Hermanos. See Sara Aguilar Belden de Garza, *Una ciudad y dos familias*, pp. 265-267.

79. For the northwest trade, see John Mayo, "Consuls and Contraband on Mexico's West Coast in the Era of Santa Ana," *Journal of Latin American Studies* 19, no. 2 (November 1987): 389-411.

80. Luis G. Zorilla, *Historia de las relaciones entre México y los Estados Unidos de América, 1800-1958*, 1:246-247.

81. Américo Paredes, *A Texas-Mexican Cancionero: Folksongs of the Lower Border*, p. 41.

82. Ibid., pp. 96-107.

83. See Vasconcelos, *Don Evaristo Madero*; Bill Karras, ed., "First Impressions of Mexico, 1828, by Reuben Potter," *Southwestern Historical Quarterly* 79, no. 1 (July 1975): 55-68.

84. Emory, *Report on the United States*, 1:61.

85. Ibid., 1:64.

86. Quoted in Rodrigo Mendirichaga, "Los tribus salvajes," in *Nuevo León*, ed. Garza Guajardo, 1:344.

87. See Weber, *The Spanish Frontier*, pp. 204-235.

88. See Isidro Viscaya Canales, "El fin de los indios lipaneses," in *Monterrey, Nuevo León, el noreste: Siete estudios históricos*, ed. Mario Cerutti; "Historical Sketch of the Indians," in *Papers Related to the Foreign Relations of the United States 1878*, pp. 538-539.

89. Robert M. Utley, *The Indian Frontier in the American West, 1846-1890*, p. 4; Meinig, *The Shaping of America*, 2:141.

90. Meinig, *The Shaping of America*, 2:138.

91. Israel Cavazos Garza, "Las incursiones de los bárbaros en el noreste de México durante el siglo XIX," in *Nuevo León*, ed. Garza Guajardo, 1:352-353.

92. Viscaya Canales, "El fin de los indios lipaneses," pp. 62-67. See Isidro Viscaya Canales, *La invasión de los indios bárbaros al noreste de México en los años de 1840-1841*. On conflicts between Chihuahua and Sonora over Indian policies, see Joseph F. Park, "The Apaches in Mexican-American Relations, 1848-1861," in *U.S.-Mexico Borderlands*, ed. Martínez, pp. 50-51.

93. Viscaya Canales, "El fin de los indios lipaneses," p. 67.

94. Mendirichaga, "Los tribus salvajes," 1:343.

95. Mexican officials estimated that between 1848 and 1870 over 10,000 Nuevoleoneses participated (some more than once) in actions against Indians. Indian raids left 388 *vecinos* dead. See *Informe de la Comisión Pesquisidora de la frontera norte sobre descripción de los indios y otros males que sufre la frontera norte* (Mexico City: Imprenta de Díaz de León y White, 1874), p. 37; J. Fred Rippy, "The Indians of the Southwest in the Diplomacy of the United States and Mexico, 1848-1853," *Hispanic American Historical Review* 2, no. 3 (August 1919): 386; Park, "The Apaches," p. 50.

96. Viscaya Canales, "El fin de los indios lipaneses," pp. 61-62.

97. Quoted in Rippy, "The Indians of the Southwest," p. 390.

98. Nuevo León had had three civilian governors since 1848 before the military came to govern it in 1853. Meanwhile, the state budget averaged a meager 50,000 pesos per year. See Roel, *Nuevo León*, pp. 158-162; República Mexicana, *Nuevo León*, pp. 46-47.

99. Quoted in Mendirichaga, "Los tribus salvajes," 1:344.

100. Quoted in ibid., p. 346.

101. See Mendirichaga, "Los nuevos vecinos," p. 374; Vigness, "El intento de la separación," pp. 438-448; Martínez, *U.S.-Mexico Borderlands*, pp. 58-60; Rippy, *The United States and Mexico*, pp. 89-91; Zorilla, *Historia*, 1:299-304.

102. Quoted in Utley, *The Indian Frontier*, p. 31.

103. Her name was María de Jesús Dosamantes. See Eisenhower, *So Far from God*, p. 155; Roel, *Nuevo León*, p. 157.

104. Junta de Representantes, "Plan para la defensa de los estados (México, 1849)," Archivo General de la Nación (henceforth AGN), Gobernación, Indios bárbaros, e. 3; Cavazos Garza, *Breve historia*, pp. 136-137; Cavazos Garza, "Las incursiones de los bárbaros," pp. 358-360.

105. Cormac McCarthy, *Blue Meridian: Or the Evening Redness in the West*, p. 65.

106. Viscaya Canales, *La invasión de los indios bárbaros*, p. 219.

107. Barrington Moore Jr., *Injustice: The Social Bases of Obedience and Revolt*, p. 22.

108. Quoted in *La Voz de Nuevo León*, March 9, 1889.

109. Moore, *Injustice*, p. 22.

110. Quoted in Martínez, *U.S.-Mexico Borderlands*, pp. 61-62. This filibuster army attempted to cross the boundary to recover stolen horses and runaway African-American slaves.

111. Santiago Vidaurri to Benito Juárez, Monterrey, September 29, 1861, in Roel, *Correspondencia particular de don Santiago Vidaurri*, 1:81.

112. Ibid.

113. Quoted in Roel, *Nuevo León*, pp. 146-147.

114. Evaristo Madero to Santiago Vidaurri, Río Grande, Coahuila, December 15, 1862, in Vasconcelos, *Don Evaristo Madero*, p. 125.

115. Karl Marx, *Grundrisse: Foundations of the Critique of Political Economy*, translated with a foreword by Martin Nicholas, p. 471.

116. Quoted in Mendirichaga, "Después de la derrota," p. 435.

117. Justo Sierra, *Juárez: Su obra, su tiempo*, p. 106; Cavazos Garza, "Las incursiones de los bárbaros," p. 358.

118. Hermenegildo Dávila, *Biografía del Señor General Don Juan Zuazua*, p. 12; Guillermo Colín Sánchez, *Ignacio Zaragoza: Evolucíon de un héroe*, p. 22.

119. Marx, *Grundrisse*, p. 475.

120. Sierra, *Juárez*, p. 106.

121. José Vasconcelos, *Memorias*, 1:553–554.

122. See Edward H. Moseley, "El benefactor de la causa liberal," in *Nuevo León*, ed. Garza Guajardo, 1:484–496.

123. Quoted in Mendirichaga, "Después de la derrota," p. 435.

124. For a history of the split between Juárez and Vidaurri, see Cerutti, *Economía de guerra y poder regional*; Garza Guajardo, *Nuevo León*, 1:429–580; Moseley, "The Public Career"; Roel, *Correspondencia particular de don Santiago Vidaurri*; Tyler, *Santiago Vidaurri*.

125. Quoted in Mario Cerutti, "Economía de guerra, frontera norte y formación de capitales a mediados del siglo XIX," in *De los Borbones a la Revolución Mexicana: Ocho estudios regionales*, ed. Mario Cerutti, p. 72.

126. Fernando Iglesias Calderón, *Rectificaciones históricas: Un libro del ex-Ministro de Guerra*, pp. 150–151.

127. Quoted in Cerutti, "Economía de guerra," p. 72.

128. See Cerutti, *Economía de guerra y poder regional*.

129. James W. Daddyman, *The Matamoros Trade: Confederate Commerce, Diplomacy and Intrigue*, p. 34.

130. Cerutti, "Economía de guerra," pp. 82–89.

131. Daddyman, *The Matamoros Trade*, pp. 31–32.

132. Matías Romero, *Mexico and the United States*, 1:442.

133. Ibid.

134. Quoted in Daddyman, *The Matamoros Trade*, p. 35.

135. Rippy, *The United States and Mexico*, p. 238; R. Curtis Tyler, "Santiago Vidaurri and the Confederacy," *Americas* 26 (1969): 66–79.

136. Quoted in Marilyn McAdams Sibley, "Charles Stillman: A Case Study of Entrepreneurship on the Rio Grande, 1861–1865," *Southwestern Historical Quarterly* 77 (October 1973): 237.

137. José E. González, *Algunos apuntes y datos estadísticos que pueden servir de base para formar una estadística del estado de Nuevo León*, p. 64.

138. Vasconcelos, *Don Evaristo Madero*, p. 130.

139. Ibid., p. 125.

140. Romero, *Mexico and the United States*, 1:442.

141. Daddyman, *The Matamoros Trade*, pp. 34–35, 137–140; Hart, *Revolutionary Mexico*, p. 113.

142. Daddyman, *The Matamoros Trade*, pp. 134–140.

143. Dominico Sindico, *Ensayo sobre problemas agrícolas en Nuevo León (1820–1906)*, p. 16.

144. Quoted in Daddyman, *The Matamoros Trade*, p. 34.

145. Vasconcelos, *Don Evaristo Madero*, p. 135.

146. Quoted in ibid., p. 130.

147. Charles Harris III, *The Mexican Family Empire: The Latifundio of the Sánchez Navarros, 1765–1867*, pp. 305–306.

148. Aguilar Belden de Garza, *Una ciudad y dos familias*, p. 111.

CHAPTER 2. THE TAMING OF THE PERIPHERY, 1867-1890

1. Cited in Justo Sierra, *La evolución de un pueblo*, p. 420.

2. For the best study on the politics of the Restored Republic era, see Laurens Ballard Perry, *Juárez and Díaz: Machine Politics in Mexico*.

3. See Roel, *Nuevo León*, pp. 208-241; José Luis García Valero, *Nuevo León, una historia compartida*, pp. 111-138.

4. Quoted in Roel, *Nuevo León*, p. 223.

5. Quoted in Perry, *Juárez and Díaz*, p. 167.

6. John W. Foster to Eleutario Avila, Mexico City, November 26, 1878, in *Papers Related to the Foreign Relations of the United States 1879*, p. 761.

7. Ibid.

8. Ibid., p. 764.

9. Gaspar Sánchez Ochoa Report on an interoceanic railway across the States of Sonora and Chihuahua, in *Papers Related to the Foreign Relations of the United States 1879*, p. 830.

10. See Lorenzo Meyer and Josefina Zoraida Vásquez, *México frente a Estados Unidos: Un ensayo histórico, 1776-1980*, pp. 85-86; Mario Cerutti, "Militares, terratenientes y empresarios en el noreste: Los generales Treviño y Naranjo (1880-1910)," in *Monterrey, Nuevo León, el noreste*, ed. Cerutti; García Valero, *Nuevo León*, pp. 127-128.

11. Wilbert H. Timmons, ed., *John F. Finerty Reports Porfirian Mexico, 1879*, p. 96.

12. Quoted in Cerutti, "Militares, terratenientes y empresarios," pp. 144-145, n. 38.

13. Rudolf Dresel to William Hunter, Monterrey, June 15, 1878, in Consular Despatches from the Consul in Monterrey, 1849-1908, U.S. Department of State.

14. González, *Datos estadísticos*, p. 47.

15. González, *Algunos apuntes*, pp. 63-64; Romero, *Mexico and the United States*, p. 442; Nuevo León, *Memorias de gobierno del estado de Nuevo León 1880*, p. 21 (hereafter cited as *Memorias de gobierno*); *Memorias de gobierno 1885*, supplement no. 27 (not paginated).

16. Population estimates for Matamoros differ. Matías Romero claimed Matamoros had 4,000 inhabitants, while a more recent estimate has 18,444 in 1900. See Romero, *Mexico and the United States*, p. 451; Antonio N. Zavaleta, "The Socioeconomic Interdependence of the Brownsville-Matamoros Border Community," in *Studies in Brownsville History*, ed. Milo Kearney, p. 147; José Fuentes Mares, "Monterrey, una ciudad creadora y sus capitanes," in *Nuevo León*, ed. Garza Guajardo, 2:6.

17. The population of the northeastern border towns increased from 12,000 in 1848, including Ciudad Juárez (El Paso del Norte), to over 50,000 by 1862. See Romero, *Mexico and the United States*, p. 442; Angela Mayano Pahissa, *Frontera: Así se hizo la frontera norte*.

18. Captured in Mexico, Erresuris was killed while "attempting to escape." See *Papers Related to the Foreign Relations of the United States 1886*, p. 721.

19. Zavaleta, "The Socio-economic Interdependence of the Brownsville-Mata-

moros Border Community," p. 148; Informe del general Francisco Naranjo, Monterrey, July 5, 1878, AGENL, Ramo Militar 1878–1885.

20. César Sepúlveda, *La frontera norte: Historia y conflictos 1762–1975*, p. 81.

21. Quoted in Timmons, *John F. Finerty Reports*, p. 14.

22. *Informe de la Comisión Pesquisidora*, pp. 13, 16, 70.

23. Informe del General Francisco Naranjo, Monterrey, July 5, 1878, AGENL, Ramo Militar 1878–1885.

24. Bernardo Reyes to Porfirio Díaz, Monterrey, July 23, 1886, Archivo de Bernardo Reyes (henceforth ABR), no. 781; Adolfo Duclos-Salinas, *Méjico pacificado: El progreso de Méjico y los hombres que lo gobiernan, Porfirio Díaz–Bernardo Reyes*, p. 187.

25. Isidro Viscaya Canales, *Los orígenes de la industrialización de Monterrey*, pp. 21–22.

26. *Memorias de gobierno 1880*, p. 21.

27. Informe del general Francisco Naranjo, Monterrey, July 5, 1878, AGENL, Ramo Militar 1878–1885; *Informe de la Comisión Pesquisidora de la frontera norte al Ejecutivo de la Unión* (Mexico City: Imprenta de Díaz de León White, 1874), p. 99; Romero, *Mexico and the United States*, p. 434.

28. Matías Romero to Bayard, Washington, D.C., February 10, 1888, in *Papers Related to the Foreign Relations of the United States 1888*, 2:1270.

29. See Samuel Bell and James B. Smallwood, *The Zona Libre, 1858–1905: A Problem in American Diplomacy*.

30. Quoted in Emiliano Bustos, *Estadísticas de la República Mexicana* (Mexico City: Imprenta de Ignacio Cumplido, 1880), p. 150.

31. *Informe de la Comisión Pesquisidora*, p. 52; González, *Datos estadísticos*, pp. 24–25.

32. The value of cattle in Nueces County increased from 2,145 dollars in 1848 to 942,040 dollars in 1871. See Taylor, *An American-Mexican Frontier*, p. 71.

33. *Informe de la Comisión Pesquisidora*, p. 52.

34. *La Revista*, February 2, 1886, found in AGENL, Concluidos 1886.

35. *Memorias de gobierno 1876*, pp. 18–19.

36. *Memorias de gobierno 1883*, pp. 10–11.

37. Eduardo Zambrano to Genaro Garza García, Monterrey, July 24, 1883, in *Memorias de gobierno 1884*, document 23.

38. *Memorias de gobierno 1885*, p. 20.

39. Ibid., p. 14; *Memorias de gobierno 1883*, pp. 10–11; *La Revista*, February 2, 1886.

40. *Memorias de gobierno 1885*, supplement no. 27.

41. Ibid., p. 14.

42. *El Pueblo*, March 13, 1887.

43. *Memorias de gobierno 1885*, p. 14.

44. Alfonso Luis Velasco, *Geografía y estadística de la República Mexicana, 1895*, p. 29; *Memorias de gobierno 1887*, p. 288.

45. Duclos-Salinas, *Méjico pacificado*, p. 188.

46. *Memorias de gobierno 1885*, supplement no. 27.

47. Antonio González Sepúlveda to Bernardo Reyes, Monterrey, July 30, 1886, AGENL, Concluidos 1886.

48. Quoted in Anita Edgar Jones, "Conditions Surrounding Mexicans in Chicago," p. 79.

49. *La Voz de Nuevo León*, February 20, 1889.

50. Quoted in Viscaya Canales, *Los orígenes*, pp. 23-24.

51. Ibid., p. 24; Fuentes Mares, "Monterrey, una ciudad creadora y sus capitanes," 2:6.

52. *Memorias de gobierno 1885*, no. 27.

53. Matías Romero to Bayard, Washington, D.C., February 10, 1888, in *Papers Related to the Foreign Relations of the United States 1888*, 2:1268.

54. *Progreso*, January 4, 1872, in *Papers Related to the Foreign Relations of the United States 1872*, p. 404.

55. *Memorias de gobierno 1889*, p. 320.

56. Reau Campbell, *Travels in Mexico*, p. 41.

57. Cerutti, *Burguesía y capitalismo*, pp. 21-25.

58. Ildefonso Villarello Vélez, *Historia de la Revolución Mexicana en Coahuila*, pp. 33-34.

59. Don Evaristo Madero also pioneered the modern agro-industrial organization that combined "cultivation, transportation, fabrication, and marketing of the cotton products" (William K. Meyers, *Forge of Progress, Crucible of Revolt: The Origins of the Mexican Revolution in La Comarca Lagunera, 1880-1911*, p. 28); Cerutti, *Burguesía y capitalismo*, pp. 57-106; Vasconcelos, *Don Evaristo Madero*.

60. Vasconcelos, *Don Evaristo Madero*, p. 139.

61. For the early years of cotton cultivation, see Meyers, *Forge of Progress*, pp. 37-43; Cerutti, *Burguesía y capitalismo*, pp. 47-49.

62. Cerutti, *Burguesía y capitalismo*, p. 47-49.

63. Quoted in María Eugenia Ramírez España, "La importancia de La Laguna como zona de producción de algodón: La participación de capitales regiomontanos en su desarrollo," *Boletín del Archivo General del Estado de Nuevo León* 3, no. 2 (May-August 1982): 23-24.

64. John Weber to State Department, Monterrey, April 1, 1879, Consular Despatches from the Consul in Monterrey.

65. Tyler, *Santiago Vidaurri*, p. 152. Today Milmo's descendants, the Azcarraga Milmos, play a leading part in TELEVISA, the large Mexican communications conglomerate.

66. See Ferrocarriles Nacionales de México, *Album mercantil, industrial, pintoresco, ciudad de Monterrey*, pp. 43-45.

67. This represented the largest acquisition of public lands granted to a surveying company in Mexico after Jesús Valenzuela in Chihuahua (6.9 million hectares) and Luis Huller in Baja California (5.3 million). See Cerutti, "Militares, terratenientes y empresarios," pp. 102-106.

68. Cerutti, "Militares, terratenientes y empresarios," pp. 113-124; *Boletín del Archivo General del Estado de Nuevo León* 3, no. 1 (January-April 1982): 3-9.

69. Cerutti, "Militares, terratenientes y empresarios," pp. 122-123.

70. See El Colegio de México, *Estadísticas sociales del porfiriato, 1877-1910*, p. 42.

71. Gónzalez, *Algunos apuntes*, pp. 32-33.

72. *La Voz de Nuevo León*, March 23, 1889.

73. Francisco Salazar to Secretario de Estado, Galeana, July 12, 1893, AGENL, Comisión Agraria 1892–1927.

74. For an excellent study on Namiquipa, Chihuahua, see Nugent, *Spent Cartridges of the Revolution*.

75. Benito Juárez to Mariano Escobedo, Chihuahua, March 27, 1865 in *Mariano Escobedo*, ed. Masea Sugarawa, p. 136.

76. Ibid.

77. Harris, *The Mexican Family Empire*, pp. 301–309; Meyers, *Forge of Progress*, pp. 24–27.

78. Lázaro Gutiérrez de Lara and Edgcomb Pinchon, *The Mexican People: The Struggle for Freedom* (Garden City: Doubleday, Page and Co., 1914), p. 318; *Memorias de gobierno 1883*, p. 7.

79. *Memorias de gobierno 1883*, p. 7.

80. At most, Díaz urged Governor Garza Ayala to break up the municipal *ejidos* because "the pueblos do not have legal power to possess land [*bienes y raices*]." He suggested that the *ejidos* be divided into private plots of fifteen to twenty hectares and that community members have the first choice in purchasing the land. Most municipalities had *ejidos*, but communally owned lands did not constitute the majority. Land was owned in *comunidad*, the collective management of private property. Each community member owned a portion of specified farming land and water rights, but most of the community lands were grazing lands; each individual had an unspecified portion. Porfirio Díaz to Lázaro Gutiérrez de Lara, Mexico City, April 8, 1889, and April 22, 1889, AGENL, Tierras y Fomento.

81. Mariano Escobedo to Benito Juárez, Monterrey, August 26, 1866, in *Mariano Escobedo*, ed. Masea Sugarawa, p. 191.

82. Juan de Dios Frias, *Reseña histórica de la formación y operaciones del cuerpo del ejército del norte durante la intervención francesa, sitio en Querétaro y noticias sobre la captura de Maximiliano, su proceso íntegro y su muerte*, pp. 12–15.

83. Ibid., pp. 146–147. Francisco Villa shared similar views. In an interview with John Reed, Villa declared: "We will put the army to work. In all parts of the Republic we will establish military colonies composed of veterans of the Revolution. The state will give them grants of agricultural lands and establish big industrial enterprises to give them work. Three days a week they will work and work hard, because honest work is more important than fighting, and honest work makes good citizens. . . . My intention is to live my life in one of those military colonies among my compañeros whom I love, who have suffered so long and so deeply with me" (John Reed, *Insurgent Mexico*, pp. 145–146).

84. Meyers, *Forge of Progress*, pp. 24–27.

85. Romero to Mariano Escobedo, Mexico City, n.d., AGENL, Tierras y Fomento; Fernando Ibarra to Secretary of State of Nuevo León, Aramberrí, December 15, 1886, AGENL, Tierras y Fomento; Francisco Mier's land distribution plan, Monterrey, August 30, 1876, AGENL, Tierras y Fomento.

86. Francisco I. Mier, author of the land distribution plan, Monterrey, August 30, 1876, AGENL, Tierras y Fomento.

87. George M. McBride, *The Land System of Mexico*, p. 95. Apparently, the three grants came from the nationalization of La Soledad hacienda.

88. Ibid.

89. González, *Algunos apuntes*, pp. 32-33.

90. See Governor Garza Ayala's description of the changing countryside in *Memorias de gobierno 1887-1889*, pp. 21-22.

91. Informe del General Francisco Naranjo, Monterrey, July 5, 1878, AGENL, Ramo Militar, 1878-1885.

92. Margarita Garza to Bernardo Reyes, Monterrey, December 18, 1889, AGENL, Concluidos 1889.

93. Ibid.

94. Luis Terrazas, the governor of Chihuahua, was also considered an ally of González and Treviño, thus giving the northern frontier caudillos considerable power at the regional and national level.

95. *Mexican Financial Review*, March 28, 1890.

96. Victor E. Niemeyer Jr., *El general Bernardo Reyes*, p. 34.

97. *Memorias de gobierno 1885*, pp. 35-38; Andrés Montemayor Hernández, "Monterrey," in *Nuevo León*, ed. Garza Guajardo, 2:63-65; *El Pueblo*, July 16, 1885.

98. Ibid.

99. On the divisions between the Liberals in the region, see *El Pueblo*, July 16, 1885.

100. *El Pueblo*, July 16, 1885.

101. Quoted in Viscaya Canales, *Los orígenes*, p. 3.

102. Montemayor Hernández, "Monterrey," 2:68-69.

103. Bernardo Reyes's 1885 "Proclamation to the *Sirvientes*" in *El Trueno*, October 31, 1909.

104. Viscaya Canales, *Los orígenes*, p. 4.

105. Montemayor Hernández, "Monterrey," 2:69.

106. *El Pueblo*, November 15, 1885.

107. Ibid., December 17, 1885.

108. Montemayor Hernández, "Monterrey," 2:68-69; García Valero, *Nuevo León*, pp. 136-138; Duclos-Salinas, *Méjico pacificado*, pp. 65-93.

109. *El Pueblo*, December 17, 1885.

110. García Valero, *Nuevo León*, p. 137; Montemayor Hernández, "Monterrey," pp. 68-69; Duclos-Salinas, *Méjico pacificado*, p. 93.

111. Ibid.; Niemeyer, *El general Bernardo Reyes*, pp. 37-39; *El Pueblo*, December 17, 1885.

112. Robert Campbell to James Porter, Monterrey, December 13, 1885, Consular Despatches from the Consul in Monterrey; Bernardo Reyes to Manuel Romero Rubio, Monterrey, October 29, 1886, ABR, no. 954.

113. On the northeast caudillo-Díaz conflict, see Daniel Cosío Villegas, "Porfirio v.s. Jerónimo," *Humanitas* 11 (1970): 577-584.

114. In 1893 Bernardo Reyes supported the Carranza brothers' rebellion against Governor Garza Galán. Díaz advised Reyes that, in spite of his removal as governor, Garza Galán should be treated with "all due respect and consideration—it dignifies more the one who gives this tribute than the one who receives it" (Porfirio Díaz to Bernardo Reyes, Mexico City, August 29, 1893, ABR, no. 3640).

115. For studies on Reyes, see Niemeyer, *El general Bernardo Reyes*; Anthony Bryan, "Mexican Politics in Transition, 1900-1913: The Role of General Bernardo

Reyes"; Josefina G. de Arellano, *El general Bernardo Reyes y el movimiento Reyista* (Mexico City: Instituto de Antropología y Historia, Colección Científica, 1982).

116. Bernardo Reyes to Rosendo Piñeda, Monterrey, August 10, 1886, ABR, no. 805; Reyes to R. Chausal, Monterrey, May 23, 1888, ABR, no. 1451.

117. Bernardo Reyes to Manuel Romero Rubio, Monterrey, October 29, 1886, ABR, no. 954; Bernardo Reyes to Porfirio Díaz, Monterrey, July 23, 1886, ABR, no. 780.

118. *El Pueblo*, January 4, 1888.

119. See letter to the editor, *La Revista*, February 2, 1886, found in AGENL, Concluidos 1886.

120. Bernardo Reyes to Porfirio Díaz, Monterrey, July 23, 1886, ABR, no. 908.

121. *Alcance,* no date, no location, found in AGENL, Concluidos 1886.

122. Bernardo Reyes to Porfirio Díaz, Monterrey, September 29, 1886, ABR, no. 908.

123. Porfirio Díaz to Bernardo Reyes, Mexico City, February 14, 1890, ABR, no. 2101.

124. Porfirio Díaz to Bernardo Reyes, Mexico City, May 18, 1890, ABR, no. 2177.

125. Porfirio Díaz to Bernardo Reyes, Mexico City, November 17, 1887, ABR, no. 1317.

126. Manuel Romero Rubio to Bernardo Reyes, Mexico City, April 5, 1887, ABR, no. 1144; Bernardo Reyes to Manuel Romero Rubio, Monterrey, May 24, 1887, ABR, no. 1136.

127. Bernardo Reyes to Manuel Romero Rubio, Monterrey, May 24, 1887, ABR, no. 1136.

128. Bernardo Reyes to Porfirio Díaz, Monterrey, March 11, 1903, ABR, no number.

129. Meanwhile, the United States had close to 2,000 soldiers on the Texas side of the border in 1893. See *Papers Related to the Foreign Relations of the United States 1893,* pp. 435–442; Matías Romero, *Geographical and Statistical Notes on Mexico,* p. 100.

130. *El Pueblo*, January 4, 1888; Niemeyer, *El general Bernardo Reyes,* p. 85.

131. *El Pueblo*, March 13, 1887.

132. General Pedro Martínez's report to the State of Nuevo León, Monterrey, June, 1888, ABR, no. 1464.

133. Ibid.

134. R. Chousal to Bernardo Reyes, Mexico City, May 24, 1888, ABR, no. 1452.

135. Report of Pedro Martínez to the State Government of Nuevo León, June 1888, Monterrey, ABR, no. 1464.

136. *El Pueblo*, March 8, 1888.

CHAPTER 3. CITY AND COUNTRYSIDE, 1890–1910

1. On the origins of industrialization, see Cerutti, *Burguesía y capitalismo;* Viscaya Canales, *Los orígenes;* Andrés Montemayor Hernández, *Historia de Monterrey;* Frédéric Mauro, "Le développement économique de Monterrey," *Caravelle* 2 (1964): 35–129. On the formation of the Monterrey bourgeoisie, see Alex M. Saragoza, *The Monterrey Elite and the Mexican State, 1880–1940.* On modern class rela-

tions, see Jorge Balán, Harley L. Browning, and Elizabeth Jelin, *Men in a Developing Society: Geographic and Social Mobility in Monterrey, Mexico;* Abraham Nuncio, *El Grupo Monterrey;* Menno Velinga, *Industrialización, burguesía y clase obrera en Monterrey.*

2. Campbell, *Travels in Mexico,* p. 41.

3. J. A. Robertson to Bernardo Reyes, Monterrey, April 1, 1890, AGENL, Ferrocarriles Nacionales de México, 1873-1913.

4. Of the estimated 1.04 billion dollars invested by Americans, 61.7 percent went into railroads and 23.9 percent into mining, for a total of 85.6 percent of total investments. See David Pletcher, *Rails, Mines and Progress,* p. 313.

5. Andrew Barlow, "United States Enterprises in Mexico," *Daily Consular Reports,* Bureau of Foreign and Domestic Commerce (Department of Commerce and Labor) 168 (October 29, 1902): 500-504.

6. Enrique Creel to Juan Creel, Mexico City, April 21, 1927, AGN, Caja de Préstamos, unclassified.

7. U.S. Department of Commerce and Labor, Bureau of Manufacturers, *Monthly Consular and Trade Results* 352 (January 1910): 63-65.

8. Archivo General del Estado de Nuevo León, *Permisos y concesiones 1890-1912,* pp. 30-31; Montemayor Hernández, *Historia de Monterrey,* p. 277; García Valero, *Nuevo León,* p. 160.

9. Edwin P. Hoyt, *The Guggenheims and the American Dream,* p. 76.

10. Eric Hobsbawm, *The Age of Empire, 1875-1914,* p. 39.

11. Hoyt, *The Guggenheims,* p. 77.

12. Harvey O'Conner, *The Guggenheims,* pp. 88-89.

13. Juan Weber to Philip Hannah, Monterrey, February 20, 1904, Consular Despatches from the Consul in Monterrey.

14. Antonio Peñafiel, *Anuario estadístico de la República Mexicana, 1900,* p. 315. Nuevo León produced only 1.5 million pesos in mineral ores during the 1897-1900 period.

15. *Modern Mexico,* February 1896; Marvin S. Bernstein, *The Mexican Mining Industry, 1890-1950,* p. 37.

16. *Modern Mexico,* February 1896.

17. *El Espectador,* January 17, 1897.

18. García Valero, *Nuevo León,* p. 160.

19. The smelters employed over 1,400 workers in 1900, while hundreds toiled in the railroad yards of Monterrey. By 1907 the smelting industry employed 1,700 workers, who produced over nineteen million pesos in ores and earned from eighty-seven centavos a day to a maximum of ten pesos. Three mines near Monterrey employed close to 1,000 mine workers in 1897. See AGENL, Minutas de Gobierno 1901; AGN, Sección Fomento y Obras Públicas, Minas y Petróleo, c. 37, l. 92, e. 12; *El Espectador,* January 17, 1897.

20. *La Voz de Nuevo León* provided lists of the new enterprises that received tax-free concessions. It described the nature of the enterprises, the number of workers employed, wages, capital invested, and their markets. See, for example, *La Voz de Nuevo León,* December 26, 1891, and January 2, 1892.

21. Agustín Basave, "Monterrey pre-industrial," *Historia Mexicana* 10 (January-March 1961): 419-424.

22. Ferrocarriles Nacionales de México, *Album mercantil*, pp. 43–45.

23. One of the exceptions involved the partners of Casa Calderón, who were the sole investors in the Cuauhtémoc Brewery.

24. For instance, Ramón E. Treviño took on the task of organizing other capitalists for an insurance company in 1908. See Ramón E. Treviño to Bernardo Reyes, Monterrey, February 18, 1908, AGENL, Concesiones 1908, c. 2, n. 95.

25. Dominico Sindico and Guillermo Beata, "The Beginnings of Industrialization in Northeastern Mexico," unpublished manuscript, p. 20, AGENL.

26. In 1918 the Compañía Minera, Fundidora y Afinadora de Monterrey was sold to the American Metal Company. It was renamed Compañía Metalúrgica de Peñoles.

27. Timmons, *John F. Finerty Reports*, p. 96.

28. Colin M. MacLachlan and William Beezley, *El Gran Pueblo: A History of Greater Mexico*, p. 96; Bell and Smallwood, *The Zona Libre*, pp. 49–56.

29. Even before investing in industrial firms Monterrey capitalists recognized that imports were subjected to high tariffs. See, for instance, the import duties for the 1889–1890 fiscal year on two key goods that Monterrey would later produce: food imports had an invoice value of 5,954,813 pesos and paid a duty of 4,627,227 pesos; cotton had an invoice value of 7,667,131 pesos and paid a duty of 8,109,445 pesos. For a list of import duties, see Romero, *Mexico and the United States*, p. 157.

30. See Mauro, "Le développement," pp. 90–97; *La Voz de Nuevo León*, March 28, 1903, and April 22, 1905.

31. U.S. Department of Commerce and Labor, Bureau of Manufacturers, *Monthly Consular and Trade Reports* (January–April 1899): 313–314.

32. Ibid.; Philip Hannah to Francis Loomis, Monterrey, January 21, 1904, Consular Despatches from the Consul in Monterrey.

33. Concesiones a la Compañía Fundidora de Fierro y Acero de Monterrey, AGENL, Concesiones 1900.

34. Concesión a Cementos Hidalgo, Anexo 23/217; AGENL, Concesiones 1901, c. 3, e. 217. For a similar argument, see Francisco G. Sada to Bernardo Reyes, Monterrey, April 20, 1904, AGENL, Concesiones a la industria 1884–1890, c. 125, e. 136, f. 291.

35. José I. Limantour to Bernardo Reyes, Mexico City, July 4, 1908, ABR, no. 7545.

36. Knight, *The Mexican Revolution*, 1:23, 92; Stephen H. Haber, *Industry and Underdevelopment: The Industrialization of Mexico, 1890–1945*, pp. 23, 40.

37. *El Espectador*, October 22, 1897.

38. Sindico and Beata, "The Beginnings of Industrialization," p. 20.

39. See Mario Cerutti, "El caso de los Maderos," in *Nuevo León*, ed. Garza Guajardo, 3:4–55.

40. For the best discussion of the relationship of marriage, family, and joint investments in the "making" of the Monterrey elite, see Saragoza, *The Monterrey Elite*, pp. 41–51; Cerutti, *Burguesía y capitalismo*, pp. 57–106.

41. Nuevo León was followed by the Federal District with 11.7 percent. Monterrey and Mexico City produced one-fourth of Mexico's total industrial output. See Daniel Cosío Villegas, ed., *Historia moderna de México*, 1:392.

42. Mauro, "Le développement," p. 70. For the most recent study on Mexico's industrialization, see Haber, *Industry and Underdevelopment.*

43. *Modern Mexico,* June 1896, reprinted from *Voz de Nuevo León,* n.d.

44. *Memorias de gobierno 1903–1907,* p. xlviii.

45. U.S. Department of Commerce, *Monthly Consular and Trade Reports* (August 1907): 89–90; *Modern Mexico,* February 1896; Niemeyer, *El general Bernardo Reyes,* p. 133.

46. Only new houses built within three *manzanas* (blocks) from Unión and Progreso streets and one *manzana* within the Alameda Porfirio Díaz. See Archivo General del Estado de Nuevo León, *Permisos y concesiones,* p. 32.

47. Bernardo Reyes to H. Congreso del Estado, Monterrey, December 1, 1890, AGENL, Minutas de Gobierno 1888–1893; Decreto del Congreso del Estado, Monterrey, December 19, 1890, in *Memorias de gobierno 1891,* pp. 173–174.

48. Eleutario Martínez to Alcalde Constitucional, Monterrey, August 25, 1903, Monterrey municipal archives (microfilm located in Trinity University, San Antonio, Texas).

49. Esteban Horcasista to Presidente Municipal, Monterrey, September 17, 1903, November 11, 1904, and March 22, 1904, Monterrey Municipal Archive (microfilm held at Trinity University).

50. Quoted in Viscaya Canales, *Los orígenes,* p. 98.

51. *Modern Mexico,* June 1896, reprinted from *Voz de Nuevo León,* n.d.; see also the January 1896 issue.

52. Humberto Buentello Chapa, *La inundación de 1909: Sus aspectos trágicos y políticos,* pp. 31–32.

53. The Monterrey Real Estate and Mining Company, owned by Patricio Milmo and General Gerónimo Treviño, even advertised its real estate business in the U.S. press. Public notary records are an excellent source on the elite's involvement in real estate transactions. See *Modern Mexico,* March 1896. For a partial list of real estate transactions between 1889 and 1904, see Garza Guajardo, *Nuevo León,* 3:88–90.

54. Garza Guajardo, *Nuevo León,* 3:76–77.

55. Comisión Nacional Agraria, *Resoluciones presidenciales, 1926,* 35:200–204.

56. Percy F. Martin, *Mexico of the Twentieth Century,* 2:83.

57. *El Trueno,* November 17, 1903.

58. *La Voz de Nuevo León,* January 19, 1907.

59. Manuel Cortés to Municipal President, Monterrey, January 1, 1903, Archivo Municipal de Monterrey (microfilm held at Trinity University).

60. In 1880 Monterrey contained 350 commercial establishments; thirty years later, they had grown to 1,100. Pablo Livas, *El estado de Nuevo León: Su situación económica al aproximarse el Centenario de la Independencia de México,* p. 28.

61. C. Holck y Compañía had sales of 1,797,963 pesos; Suc. de Hernández, 1,181,388; Manuel Cantú Treviño, 872,417; Valentín Rivera Suc., 735,651; José Calderón, 521,877; for a total of 5,109,296 pesos. Presidencia municipal, April 25, 1904, AGENL, Concesiones a la industria, 1884–1890.

62. Livas, *El estado de Nuevo León,* p. 28.

63. *El Trueno,* May 14, 1905.

64. *Modern Mexico,* June 1896, reprinted from *La Voz de Nuevo León,* n.d.

65. Francisco G. Sada to Bernardo Reyes, Monterrey, April 20, 1904, AGENL, Concesiones a la Industria 1884–1890, c. 125, e. 136, f. 291.

66. *La Voz de Nuevo León,* February 6, 1904.

67. In 1887 the value of agriculture was 1,308,823 pesos, while industry for 1889 had a value of 326,360 pesos. *Memorias de gobierno 1887,* p. 288; *Memorias de gobierno 1889,* p. 320.

68. See Cerutti, *Burguesía y capitalismo,* p. 108.

69. El Colegio de México, *Estadísticas sociales del porfiriato,* pp. 68–69.

70. Ibid., pp. 16–17, 34–35.

71. Duclos-Salinas, *Méjico pacificado,* p. 184. Duclos-Salinas wrote this book from exile. He participated in the anti-Reyes opposition movement of 1903.

72. Bernardo Reyes echoed those same words twenty years later. González, *Algunos apuntes,* p. 32; Bernardo Reyes to Manuel Fernández Leal, Monterrey, July 21, 1893, ABR, no. 130.

73. *La Voz de Nuevo León,* December 28, 1908; Livas, *El estado de Nuevo León,* p. 18.

74. *Estadísticas sociales del porfiriato,* p. 41; *México Industrial,* December 15, 1905; Livas, *El estado de Nuevo León,* pp. 18–19; "Boleta relativa a estadística agrícola de los estados de la República," AGN, Fomento, c. 8, e. 5, l. 2.

75. AGENL, Correspondencia con la Secretaría de Fomento, 1912.

76. Petition from the *vecinos* of Hualahuises to Bernardo Reyes, Hualahuises, September 1, 1907, AGENL, Concluidos 1907.

77. "Projecto de ley sobre comunidades en el estado de Nuevo León, 1894," AGENL, Minutas de Gobierno 1894, no. 31.

78. González, *Algunos apuntes,* pp. 32–33.

79. These calculations were made from the information provided in AGENL, Correspondencia con Fomento 1913, c. 2, and the Secretaría de Fomento's "Boleta relativa a estadística agrícola de los estados de la República," AGN, Fomento, c. 8, e. 5, l. 2.

80. Ibid.; Livas, *El estado de Nuevo León,* pp. 18–19.

81. Livas, *El estado de Nuevo León,* p. 5.

82. González, *Datos estadísticos,* p. 26.

83. Bernardo Reyes to Manuel Fernández Leal, Monterrey, July 21, 1893, ABR, no. 130.

84. Narciso Dávila's report to the Secretaría de Fomento, Mexico City, October 25, 1889, AGENL, Correspondencia con Fomento, 1890–1892; Comisión Nacional Agraria, *Resoluciones presidenciales, 1926,* 40:167–171; Petition from *vecinos* of Lampazos, Lampazos, June 1921, AGENL, Correspondencia con Fomento, 1912–1923.

85. The founding of the "pueblo" of Cadereyta Jímenez provides an excellent description of colonial policy toward new settlers. See Tribunal Especial para Arreglo de Aguas en Cadereyta Jímenez, Monterrey, July 10, 1852, AGENL, Correspondencia con Alcaldes Primeros (Cadereyta Jímenez) 1878–1884, c. 136.

86. Comisión Nacional Agraria, *Resoluciones presidenciales, 1925,* 22:318–319.

87. See Narciso Dávila's report to the Secretaría de Fomento, Mexico City, October 25, 1889, AGENL, Correspondencia con Fomento 1890–1892.

88. Comisión Nacional Agraria, *Resoluciones presidenciales, 1926,* 40:167–171; Bernardo Reyes to Pedro Benítez Leal, Mexico City, April 6, 1900, ABR, nos. 429–430.

89. Petition from Cerralvo *vecinos* to Nicéforo Zambrano, 1918, AGENL, Correspondencia con Fomento 1918–1922. Felipe Martínez to Leobardo Chapa, Cerralvo, July 19, 1911, AGENL, Concluidos 1910.

90. Petition from *vecinos* of Cerralvo and Dr. González to Leobardo Chapa, Dr. González, June 24, 1911, AGENL, Concluidos 1910.

91. Comisión Nacional Agraria, *Resoluciones presidenciales, 1927,* 44:284–290.

92. Ibid., 44:278–283.

93. Luis Leal to José María Mier, Cadereyta Jiménez, March 29, 1910, AGENL, Concluidos 1910–1913.

94. Inocente González to José María Mier, Agueleguas, April 17, 1910, AGENL, Concluidos 1910–1913.

95. González, *Algunos apuntes,* p. 33.

96. Comunidad de Denunciantes to José María Mier, Los Herreras, January 23, 1911, AGENL, Concluidos 1911; Petition from the community of Garza García to José María Mier, November 13, 1909, AGENL, Concluidos 1910.

97. Matilde de la Garza to Bernardo Reyes, Monterrey, November 27, 1899, AGENL, Concluidos 1900–1904.

98. Benigno R. Davis to Secretaría de Fomento, Los Ramones, June 8, 1905, AGENL, Correspondencia con Fomento 1905. For the impact of the 1878 drought in this municipality, see Antonio García to the Governor, Cadereyta Jímenez, n.d., AGENL, Correspondencia con Alcaldes Primeros 1878–1884.

99. Alvino Guerra to Ramón G. Chavarrí, Doctor Coss, February 18, 1892, AGENL, Correspondencia de Bernardo Reyes 1886–1906.

100. Chapa, *La inundación de 1909,* p. 16. For a similar case in the same municipality, see Luis Ramos to Bernardo Reyes, Saltillo, April 6, 1896, AGENL, Correspondencia del General Bernardo Reyes 1886–1909.

101. Chapa, *La inundación de 1909,* p. 16.

102. González, *Datos estadísticos,* p. 26.

103. Ibid.

104. Petition from the *vecinos* of Huilahuises to Bernardo Reyes, Huilahuises, September 1, 1907; AGENL, Concluidos 1907, c. 1, e. 475.

105. Bernardo Reyes to Porfirio Díaz, Monterrey, August 12, 1896, ABR, nos. 43–44.

106. Jesús M. Guzmán to Porfirio Díaz, found in Bernardo Reyes to Pedro Benítez Leal, Mexico City, September 6, 1900, ABR, nos. 429–430.

107. Comisión Nacional Agraria, *Resoluciones presidenciales, 1926,* 40:167–171.

108. A member of the Comisión Nacional Agraria reported that "each of the contending sides in this litigation represents more than fifty heads of families, and if it can not be proven that the actual inhabitants of the land that is in dispute are legitimate heirs of José Cantú, then the opposing side cannot demonstrate being the legal heirs either" (Comisión Nacional Agraria, *Resoluciones presidenciales, 1926,* 40:167–171; quotation on 168–169).

109. For other intracommunity conflicts, see Narciso Dávila's report to the Secretaría de Fomento, Mexico City, October 25, 1889, AGENL, Correspondencia con

Fomento 1890–1892; Comisión Nacional Agraria, *Resoluciones presidenciales, 1927*, 44:278–290; *Periódico Oficial*, September 29, 1905.

110. On the problematic legal meaning of *comunidad* and *heredero*, see *La Voz de Nuevo León*, August 13, 1892, and December 26, 1908; Livas, *El estado de Nuevo León*, p. 18.

111. Comisión Nacional Agraria, *Resoluciones presidenciales 1927*, 44:278–290.

112. *Periódico Oficial*, September 29, 1905.

113. F. Villareal's Project to Break Up the Communities, Monterrey, April 24, 1917, AGENL, Ramo Comisión Local Agraria, 1914, 1917, and 1919.

114. Comunidad de Denunciantes to José María Mier, Los Herrera, June 23, 1911, AGENL, Concluidos 1911.

115. F. Villareal's Project to Break Up the Communities, Monterrey, April 24, 1917, AGENL, Ramo Comisión Local Agraria, 1914, 1917, and 1919.

116. Comunidad de Denunciantes to José María Mier, Los Herreras, June 23, 1911, AGENL, Concluidos 1911.

117. Juan Zuazua to Bernardo Reyes, Lampazos, August 10, 1905, AGENL, Concluidos 1905.

118. Germán Carrillo to Bernardo Reyes, Los Aldamas, March 3, 1909, AGENL, Concluidos 1910–1911.

119. Luciano Peña to Bernardo Reyes, Los Aldamas, March 17, 1909, AGENL, Concluidos 1910–1911.

120. Inocente González and *representación común* to José María Mier, Agueleguas, April 17, 1910, AGENL, Concluidos 1910–1913.

121. Ibid.; Inocencio González and others to Constitutional Governor, Agueleguas, August 24, 1915, AGENL, Concluidos 1910–1913.

122. In Huilahuises cattle were worth 15 pesos each and a goat had a value of 1.25 pesos. *Vecinos* of Los Herrera to José María Mier, Los Herreras, January 23, 1911, AGENL, Concluidos 1911; Petition from *vecinos* of Huilahuises to Bernardo Reyes, September 1, 1907, AGENL, Concluidos 1907, c. 1, e. 475.

123. Bernardo Reyes to José F. Godoy, Monterrey, August 23, 1897, AGENL, Correspondencia del General Bernardo Reyes 1896–1906.

124. David Silva to Secretaría de Fomento, Cadereyta Jiménez, n.d., AGENL, Correspondencia con Fomento 1905.

125. Petition from the *vecinos* of Huilahuises to Bernardo Reyes, Huilahuises, September 1, 1907, AGENL, Concluidos 1907, c. 1, e. 475.

126. *Vecinos* from Cerralvo and Doctor González to Leobardo Chapa, Doctor González, June 24, 1911, AGENL, Concluidos 1910.

127. Felipe Martínez to Leobardo Chapa, Doctor González, July 3, 1911, AGENL, Concluidos 1910.

128. For another case dealing with the creation of ranchos from community lands, see Jesus González Treviño to José María Mier, Minas, March 15, 1910, AGENL, Concluidos 1910–1913.

129. *Vecinos* from General Terán to José María Mier, General Terán, April 11, 1910, AGENL, Concluidos 1910.

130. *Vecinos* of Garza García to José María Mier, Garza García, November 13, 1909, AGENL, Concluido 1910.

131. Ibid.

132. Mark Wasserman, *Capitalists, Caciques and Revolution: The Native Elite and Foreign Enterprise in Chihuahua, Mexico, 1854–1911,* pp. 44–46, 152.

133. On the eve of the Revolution, the Richardson Irrigation and Land Company reported on the future prospects of the Yaqui Valley: "Various products of the Yaqui have a high demand in faraway markets. For example, almost all the chickpeas are exported and the buyers come to purchase them where they are produced. Fruits, especially cantaloupes, mature three to four weeks earlier than in the United States, where there is a high demand" (Informe Relativo de los Terrenos de la Compañía Richardson, 1911, AGN, Caja de Préstamos).

134. For a brief description of the Banco Minero de Chihuahua in the Chihuahua economy, see Enrique Creel to Juan Creel, Mexico City, April 21, 1927, AGN, Caja de Préstamos, unclassified.

135. Vasconcelos, *Don Evaristo Madero,* p. 212.

136. An agricultural experimentation station increased oats, maize, barley, beans, chickpeas, and other products by 168 percent in one year (1910–1911) by the use of irrigation. See Informe de la Compañía Constructora Richardson, Esperanza, September 1, 1911, AGN, Caja de Préstamos.

137. Bernardo Reyes to Porfirio Díaz, Monterrey, May 16, 1892, ABR, no. 235; *Memorias de gobierno 1889,* p. 19.

138. Livas, *El estado de Nuevo León,* p. 17.

139. Montemayor Hernández, *Historia de Monterrey,* pp. 278–279.

140. José Antonio Olvera Sandoval, "La citricultura en Montemorelos: Sus inicios (1890–1910)," in *Monterrey, Nuevo León, el noreste,* ed. Cerutti, pp. 164–165.

141. Bernardo Reyes to Porfirio Díaz, Monterrey, May 16, 1892, ABR, no. 235.

142. Bernardo Reyes to Porfirio Díaz, Monterrey, May 16, 1892, ABR, no. 235.

143. AGN, Caja de Préstamos.

144. González Treviño also received a 2.4-million-peso loan from the Caja de Préstamos for establishing a land company near Piedras Negras. See Informe de Hacienda de la Caja de Préstamos para Obras de Irrigación y Fomento de la Agricultura 1912, S.A., AGN, unclassified; Apuntes de la Compañía Agrícola y Ganadera del Río San Diego, S.A., Caja de Préstamos, AGN, unclassified.

145. Francisco de la Fuente to State Secretary, Linares, July 9, 1888, AGENL, Correspondencia con Alcaldes Primeros 1887–1895, c. 24, no. 29.

146. *El Hacendado Mexicano,* reprinted in *La Voz de Nuevo León,* August 20, 1904.

147. Ibid.

148. Bernardo Reyes to José F. Godoy, Monterrey, August 23, 1897, AGENL, Correspondencia de Bernardo Reyes 1896–1906.

149. For a list of sugar producers, see copy of sugar planter census sent to *El Hacendado Mexicano,* Monterrey, August 26, 1901, AGENL, Concluidos 1900, c. 9; Francisco de la Fuente to State Secretary, Linares, July 9, 1888, AGENL, Correspondencia con Alcaldes Primeros 1887–1895, c. 24, no. 29.

150. John Womack, *Zapata and the Mexican Revolution,* pp. 42–50.

151. Olvera Sandoval, "La citricultura en Montemorelos," pp. 151–175.

152. Livas, *El estado de Nuevo León,* pp. 20–21.

153. Bernardo Reyes to Porfirio Díaz, Monterrey, August 12, 1896, ABR, nos. 43–44.

154. Comisión Nacional Agraria, *Resoluciones presidenciales, 1925–1926*, 30:151–155.

155. Ibid., *1925*, 22:180–181; Informe de Hacienda to Caja de Préstamos para Obras de Irrigación y Fomento de la Agricultura, 1912, AGN, unclassified.

156. Estatutos y Informes de la Compañía Agrícola y Ganadera del Río San Diego, S.A., AGN, Caja de Préstamos, unclassified.

157. Mark Wasserman, "Oligarchy and Foreign Enterprise in Porfirian Chihuahua, Mexico, 1876–1911," p. 334.

158. Ballesteros had 23,168 pesos in assets, with water rights constituting 11,759. Echeverría had 9,406 pesos in assets, with water representing 3,829. Good profits could still be made from *piloncillos* even if they simply invested in irrigation and not in technology. A well-irrigated hectare of sugarcane could produce anywhere from eighty to one hundred *cargas* of *piloncillos* that sold for between 12 and 18 pesos each. The cost to produce a *carga* was 5 pesos, mainly for water and labor. See Olvera Sandoval, "La citricultura en Montemorelos," pp. 163–165; Livas, *El estado de Nuevo León*, pp. 22–23.

159. *La Voz de Nuevo León*, August 20, 1904.

160. *Modern Mexico*, January 1896.

161. Bernardo Reyes to Gregorio Zambrano and Vicente Ferrara, Mexico City, June 3, 1900, ABR, no. 328; Bernardo Reyes to José I. Limantour, Monterrey, June 29, 1908, ABR, no. 7555; José Limantour to Bernardo Reyes, Mexico City, June 4, 1908, ABR, no. 7545.

162. Reyes's renewal of the Concession to the Compañía de Tranvías, Luz y Fuerza Motriz de Monterrey, S.A., Monterrey, May, 1909, AGENL, Correspondencia con Fomento 1912–1923; Bernardo Reyes to Ramón Chavarrí, Mexico City, March 3, 1900, ABR, no. 182.

163. Manuel Cantú Treviño to Bernardo Reyes, Monterrey, May 8, 1908, AGENL, Concesiones 1908.

164. José I. Limantour to Bernardo Reyes, Mexico City, June 4, 1908, ABR, no. 7545.

165. Bernardo Reyes to José I. Limantour, Monterrey, June 29, 1908, ABR, no. 7555; *El Economista Mexicano*, January 18, 1908.

166. Francisco de la Fuente to Secretary of State, Linares, July 9, 1888, AGENL, Correspondencia con Alcaldes Primeros 1887–1895, c. 24, d. 29.

167. Aurelio Torres to Ramón Chavarrí, Galeana, July 17, 1908, AGENL, Correspondencia con Alcaldes Primeros (Galeana) 1908–1909, c. 15, d. 542; Presidencia Municipal, Monterrey, April 25, 1904, AGENL, Concesiones a la Industria 1884–1890, e. 136.

168. Livas, *El estado de Nuevo León*, p. 76.

169. *La Voz de Nuevo León*, May 2, 1903.

170. Enrique Creel to Juan Creel, Mexico City, April 21, 1927, AGN, Caja de Préstamos, unclassified.

171. República Mexicana, *Nuevo León*, p. 47; Boleta del Estado, Monterrey, March 17, 1907, AGENL, Correspondencia con la Secretaría de Hacienda; Mauro, "Le développement," p. 126.

172. José Delgado to Bernardo Reyes, Cadereyta Jiménez, March 13, 1893, AGENL, Correspondencia con Bernardo Reyes 1891–1903.

173. Bernardo Reyes to Francisco Lozano, Monterrey, February 9, 1897, ABR, no. 478.

174. *Memorias de gobierno 1903-1907*, p. xlix; Presidencia Municipal, Monterrey, April 25, 1904, AGENL, Concesiones a la Industria 1884-1890.

175. *Modern Mexico*, January 1896.

176. Livas, *El estado de Nuevo León*, p. 71.

177. República Mexicana, *Nuevo León*, p. 47; Boleta del Estado, Monterrey, March 17, 1907, AGENL, Correspondencia con la Secretaría de Hacienda; Mauro, "Le développement," p. 126.

178. Quoted in José Luis Martínez, ed., *Alfonso Reyes/Pedro Henríquez Ureña: Correspondencia 1907-1914*, p. 89.

179. José I. Limantour, *Apuntes sobre mi vida pública*, p. 114.

180. Colonel Adolfo Iberrí, Colonel Felipe Angeles, and Colonel Gilberto Luna to Vicente Ferrara, Mexico City, November 24, 1905, cited in Manuel González Caballero, *La fundidora en el tiempo, 1900-1986*, p. 55.

181. Ibid.

182. *El Contemporáneo* (San Luis Potosí), May 11, 1897.

183. *La Voz de Nuevo León*, August 13, 1892. For other examples, see ibid., December 26, 1908, and August 20, 1904; *El Trueno*, November 10, 1901; Livas, *El estado de Nuevo León*, p. 18.

184. Cited in Garza Guajardo, *Nuevo León*, 3:249.

CHAPTER 4. NUEVO LEÓN AND THE MAKING OF
THE BORDER LABOR MARKET, 1890-1910

1. Garza Guajardo, *Nuevo León*, 2:233.

2. Only two studies have examined urban labor during the Porfiriato. No study on labor in the countryside has been published. See Cerutti, *Burguesía y capitalismo*, pp. 137-167; Javier Rojas, *Antecedentes del movimiento obrero de Monterrey: El mutualismo* (Monterrey: OIDMO, 1980).

3. *La Voz de Nuevo León*, February 23, 1889.

4. See *Memorias de gobierno 1887*, p. 288; *Memorias de gobierno 1889*, p. 320.

5. E. P. Thompson, "Time, Work-Discipline, and Industrial Capitalism," *Past and Present* 39 (December 1967): 90.

6. David C. Montgomery, *The Fall of the House of Labor: The Workplace, the State, and American Labor Activism, 1865-1925*, p. 71.

7. Victor S. Clark, "Mexican Labor in the United States," *Bulletin of the Bureau of Labor*, 17, no. 78 (September 1908): 472.

8. *El Nuevo Mundo* (Torreón), October 10, 1907.

9. Ibid.

10. *El Estado de Coahuila* (Saltillo), March 15, 1907.

11. *Estadísticas sociales del porfiriato*, pp. 68, 73-74, 107.

12. *Boletín de la Sociedad Agrícola Mexicana*, December 9, 1909.

13. Clark, "Mexican Labor in the United States," p. 470.

14. Ibid., p. 493; Hoyt, *The Guggenheims*, p. 91.

15. Ibid.

16. *El Nuevo Mundo,* October 10, 1907. Two and a half silver pesos were worth a dollar (gold).

17. The common call of Texan farm owners from 1890 to 1929 was "we have to have Mexicans as cheap labor" (Paul S. Taylor, *Mexican Labor in the United States: Dimmit County, Winter Garden District, South Texas,* p. 338).

18. *La Zona Libre,* reprinted in *El Trueno,* October 23, 1904.

19. *El Monterrey News,* April 10, 1909.

20. *Boletín Commercial,* Secretaría de Relaciones Exteriores, Dirección General Consular, 1, no. 1 (January 1911): 78–80.

21. United States Bureau of the Census, *Thirteenth Census of the United States, 1910: Abstracts of the Census,* p. 190.

22. Ibid., pp. 208–209.

23. Ibid., p. 190.

24. *La Voz de Nuevo León,* January 31, 1903.

25. *El Trueno,* May 5, 1901.

26. AGENL, Minutas de Gobierno 1896.

27. Viscaya Canales, *Los orígenes,* p. 93.

28. García Valero, *Nuevo León,* p. 183.

29. Buentello Chapa, *La inundación de 1909,* p. 40.

30. George D. Barron to Bernardo Reyes, Monterrey, October 5, 1897, AGENL, Correspondencia con Bernardo Reyes 1896–1898.

31. J. S. Williams to Bernardo Reyes, Nacozari, June 5, 1907, AGENL, Concluidos 1907. For other examples of out-of-state employers seeking to recruit in Monterrey and Nuevo León, see George D. Barron to Bernardo Reyes, Monterrey, October 5, 1897, AGENL, Correspondencia de Bernardo Reyes 1896–1898; Guillermo Leaske to Bernardo Reyes, Mexico City, August 4, 1893, AGENL, Correspondencia de Bernardo Reyes 1886–1894.

32. *El Monterrey News,* November 5, 1907. The results of this study were published in Clark, "Mexican Labor in the United States."

33. George D. Barron to Bernardo Reyes, Monterrey, October 5, 1897, AGENL, Correspondencia con Bernardo Reyes 1896–1898.

34. Martin, *Mexico,* 2:86.

35. Hoyt, *The Guggenheims,* p. 91.

36. In a year the payroll at their Pueblo plant reached a million dollars, while Monterrey's 200,000-dollar payroll represented a huge savings for the Guggenheims. See ibid.

37. Hoyt, *The Guggenheims,* p. 91.

38. *La Voz de Nuevo León,* April 18, 1891; Viscaya Canales, *Los orígenes,* p. 93.

39. *La Voz de Nuevo León,* April 18, 1891.

40. *El Espectador,* January 23, 1897.

41. Ibid.

42. Serafín Cantú González and others to Bernardo Reyes, Colombia, January 23, 1908, AGENL, Concluidos 1908; Adolfo Zambrano to Ramón Chavarrí, Monterrey, February 13, 1908, AGENL, Concluidos 1908.

43. Serafín Cantú González to Bernardo Reyes, Colombia, AGENL, Concluidos 1908.

44. J. Treviño to Ramón Chavarrí, Colombia, April 16, 1901; AGENL, Concluidos 1908.

45. Quoted in Basave, "Monterrey pre-industrial," p. 423.

46. *Memorias del gobierno 1903-1907*, pp. 66-67. The government officials might have lost their memory. On the first day of 1903 workers from this firm and almost all the major enterprises in the city waged what appeared to be a general strike that lasted almost two weeks.

47. Nuevo León's labor force in 1906 can be broken down as follows: 32,472 were employed in agriculture; 9,940 in mining; and 19,940 in industry. See *La Voz de Nuevo León*, August 1, 1891; *Memorias de gobierno 1903-1907*, p. 50.

48. *La Defensa del Pueblo*, September 14, 1890.

49. *El Trueno*, January 11, 1903.

50. Ibid. Apparently the companies which practiced the bonus wage had two policies. Some required workers to work for twenty-five consecutive days, and others the entire month.

51. Hoyt, *The Guggenheims*, p. 226.

52. George D. Barron to Bernardo Reyes, Monterrey, October 5, 1897, AGENL, Correspondencia con Bernardo Reyes 1896-1898.

53. *El Monterrey News*, July 12, 1907.

54. Ibid.

55. Memoria Mensual de la Compañía Aurífera del Pánuco, S.A., April 30, 1900, AGENL, Correspondencia con el Ministerio de Fomento 1900.

56. Daniel Nelson, *Managers and Workers: Origins of the New Factory System in the United States, 1880-1920*, p. 43.

57. *El Trueno*, November 24, 1901.

58. Ibid.

59. See *La Voz de Nuevo León*, March 30, 1907; George K. G. Conway, "The Water-Works and Sewage of Monterrey," *Transactions* 72 (1911): 552.

60. *La Voz de Nuevo León*, December 26, 1891, and January 2, 1892.

61. See the occupation section of Monterrey, *Censo de la municipalidad de Monterrey 1900*.

62. Elizabeth Viscre McGary, *An American Girl in Mexico*, pp. 21-22.

63. Clark, "Mexican Labor in the United States," p. 493.

64. Bernstein, *The Mexican Mining Industry*, p. 41; Isaac F. Marcosson, *Metal Magic: The Story of the American Smelting and Refining Company*, p. 203; U.S. Department of Commerce, *Monthly Consular and Trade Reports* (August 1907): 90.

65. Conway, "The Water-Works and Sewage of Monterrey," p. 552.

66. Clark, "Mexican Labor in the United States," p. 493.

67. Quoted in Haber, *Industry and Underdevelopment*, p. 36.

68. Jonathan C. Brown, "Foreign and Native-Born Workers in Porfirian Mexico," *American Historical Review* 98, no. 3 (June 1993): 790.

69. *La Voz de Nuevo León*, August 15, 1903.

70. Hoyt, *The Guggenheims*, p. 91.

71. González Caballero, *La fundidora en el tiempo, 1900-1986*, pp. 120-121; *La Voz de Nuevo León*, April 12, 1903; Montemayor Hernández, *Historia de Monterrey*, p. 278.

72. On the railroad craft unions, see Lorena M. Parlee, "The Impact of United States Railroad Unions on Organized Labor and Government Policy in Mexico, 1880–1911," *Hispanic American Historical Review* 64, no. 3 (August 1984): 443–475; Brown, "Foreign and Native-Born Workers in Porfirian Mexico," 786–818.

73. *La Voz de Nuevo León*, August 15, 1903.

74. Ibid.

75. James Feeney to Bernardo Reyes, Monterrey, February 29, 1904, AGENL, Minutas de Gobierno 1904.

76. Clark, "Mexican Labor in the United States," p. 495.

77. Bernardo Reyes to George Conway, Monterrey, August 10, 1907, AGENL, Minutas de Gobierno 1907.

78. Quoted in Jones, "Conditions Surrounding Mexicans," p. 79. It is possible that Jones made a mistake in equating dollars to pesos. It is doubtful any worker, foreign or native, earned ten dollars a day in that period.

79. Ibid.

80. Clark, "Mexican Labor in the United States," p. 481.

81. *La Voz de Nuevo León*, March 26, 1898.

82. Javier Rojas, "El mutualismo en Monterrey," in *Nuevo León*, ed. Garza Guajardo, 2:191.

83. James Feeney to Bernardo Reyes, Monterrey, February 29, 1904, AGENL, Minutas de Gobierno 1904.

84. *La Voz de Nuevo León*, December 17, 1903.

85. AGENL, Minutas de Gobierno 1896, d. 136.

86. Data compiled from Quarterly Demographic Reports sent by the State Government of Nuevo León State to Secretaría de Gobernación, January 1, 1903, to December 31, 1910, AGN, Gobernación, c. 769, e. 7.

87. See *Estadísticas sociales*, pp. 68, 73–74, 107.

88. Excluding Monterrey, children who died before their first birthday made up 25 percent of all deaths in Nuevo León. Data compiled from Nuevo León's Quarterly Population Reports, January 1, 1903, to December 31, 1910, AGN, Gobernación, c. 769, e. 7.

89. Petition from residents of barrio Estación del Golfo to Viviano Villareal, Monterrey, November 27, 1912, AGENL, Concluidos 1912; American Consul General to Francis Loomis, Monterrey, March 17, 1905, Consular Despatches from the Consul in Monterrey; AGENL, Minutas de Gobierno 1896, d. 136.

90. In spite of the doubling in the city's population from 1890 to 1910, the number of children attending school did not increase by the same proportions. In 1891 the city contained 29 public schools that served 4,640 students. By 1909 the number of public schools had increased to 57, serving close to 7,000 students. See Viscaya Canales, *Los orígenes;* Monterrey, *Censo de la municipalidad de Monterrey 1900;* Miguel F. Martínez's report, Monterrey, March 10, 1900, AGENL, Minutas de Gobierno 1900; Livas, *El estado de Nuevo León,* p. 63.

91. Data collected from the communities of Fábrica de Ladrillos, El Golfo, San Pedro, San Pablo, and Zaragoza. See Monterrey, *Censo de la municipalidad de Monterrey 1900.*

92. *La Voz de Nuevo León*, August 15, 1903.

93. Quoted in Sandra Arenal, *En Monterrey no sólo hay ricos*, p. 26. My father, Magdaleno Mora Rojas, started working at the age of ten in the mines of Tlalpujahua, Michoacán. He shared the opinion of the young man in Arenal's book. So did other children who worked with him.

94. Dámaso O. Martínez to José María Mier, Monterrey, January 4, 1910, AGENL, Concluidos 1910-1911.

95. Arenal, *En Monterrey no sólo hay ricos*, pp. 54-57.

96. Ibid., pp. 57-60.

97. Ibid., 54-57.

98. [Illegible name] to Antonio I. Villareal, Monterrey, November 24, 1914, AGENL, Correspondencia con Alcaldes Primeros (Monterrey) 1913-1914, d. 583.

99. Guillermo Leaske to Bernardo Reyes, Mexico, August 4, 1893, AGENL, Correspondencia con Bernardo Reyes 1886-1894.

100. Ibid.

101. Romero, *Mexico and the United States*, p. 513.

102. *El Trueno*, November 10, 1901.

103. *Informe de la Comisión Pesquisidora*, p. 24.

104. Ibid., pp. 116-125; Juan M. Salazar to [illegible name], Villa de Allende, November 29, 1905, AGENL, Concluidos 1905.

105. Taylor, *Mexican Labor in the United States*, pp. 300-301.

106. For the transformation of the south Texas economy and the role of Mexican workers, see Montejano, *Anglos and Mexicans*, pp. 103-128; Emilio Zamora, *The World of the Mexican Worker in Texas*, pp. 10-85; Taylor, *An American-Mexican Frontier;* Frank Pierce, *A Brief History of the Lower Rio Grande Valley* (Menasha, Wis.: George Banta Publishing, 1917).

107. Quoted in Taylor, *An American-Mexican Frontier*, pp. 317-318.

108. Taylor, *Mexican Labor in the United States*, p. 307.

109. Zamora, *The World of the Mexican Worker in Texas*, p. 59. The following passage describes the migration of poor northeastern Mexicans to neighboring Texas during the 1930s: "[the family head] takes his family and his dog. Many of those going into the cotton fields of Texas are accompanied by their entire families. . . . Those who have come from Mexico have, in addition to the family and the dog, their donkey. It is not an uncommon sight to see long trains of Mexicans in small wagons en route to the cotton fields."

110. Ibid.

111. Taylor, *Mexican Labor in the United States*, pp. 300-301.

112. Juan M. Salazar to [illegible name], Villa de Allende, November 29, 1905, AGENL, Concluidos 1905. After three years in Mexico he only had seven thousand pesos left.

113. Juan Delgado to Viviano Villareal, Cadereyta Jiménez, October 25, 1911, AGENL, Concluidos 1911-1912.

114. Francisco Salazar to Ramón Chavarrí, Galeana, October 21, 1898, AGENL, Correspondencia con Alcaldes Primeros 1895-1902.

115. For an excellent examination of labor conditions on the Mexican haciendas and plantations, see Friedrich Katz, "Labor Conditions on Haciendas in Porfirian Mexico: Some Trends and Tendencies," *Hispanic American Historical Review* 54, no. 1 (February 1974): 1-47.

116. Even Luis Terrazas, who created a family empire in Chihuahua at the expense of peasants, practiced paternalism. In visits to his haciendas, Terrazas offered each of his peons gifts. See Katz, *The Secret War*, p. 10.

117. Francisco I. Madero to Evaristo Madero, San Pedro, Coahuila, September 19, 1908, INAH, Archivo de Francisco I. Madero, 2 vols., 2:232.

118. Report of the Yaqui Valley Experimental Station, 1911, AGN, Caja de Préstamos.

119. In turn, the Yaqui Indians loyally followed him during the Mexican Revolution. That was not the case with other hacendados, however, as R. G. Kennedy, the former director of British irrigation projects in India, reported on Yaqui laborers: "... in general they do not bother the foreigners, although they do not have the same considerations with the Mexicans. The few who have been civilized are often prosperous and resourceful. The Yaqui tribe are some of the most industrious people as well as excellent warriors." Informe del Ingeniero R. G. Kennedy, "Projecto de Irrigación del Yaquí," December 20, 1911, AGN, Caja de Préstamos; and Katz, *The Secret War*, p. 10.

120. *El Azote*, April 4, 1903, found in AGENL, Correspondencia de Bernardo Reyes, 1886-1908; Andrés Martínez to Leobardo Chapa, Galeana, July 12, 1911, AGENL, Concluidos 1910; Juana Vargas to Viviano Villareal, Mier y Noriega, November 20, 1911, AGENL, Concluidos 1911.

121. Ynes Morales to José María Mier, Bustamante, n.d., AGENL, Concluidos 1910-1911.

122. José Lozano to Leobardo Chapa, Bustamante, July 10, 1911; AGENL, Concluidos 1910-1911; Benito Sánchez to José María Mier, Topo Chico, February 12, 1910, AGENL, Concluidos 1910.

123. Albina Guevara to José María Mier, Colombia, February 20, 1910, AGENL, Concluidos 1910-1911.

124. Manuel Aguilar to Bernardo Reyes, Apodaca, December 13, 1889, AGENL, Correspondencia con Bernardo Reyes 1897-1902.

125. Pedro Salas to José María Mier, Monterrey, March 10, 1910, AGENL, Correspondencia con Bernardo Reyes 1897-1902.

126. Luis Elizondo to Viviano Villarreal, Los Aldamas, October 14, 1911, AGENL, Minutas de Gobierno 1911.

127. Francisco Salazar to Ramón Chavarrí, Galeana, October 21, 1898, AGENL, Correspondencia con Alcaldes Primeros 1895-1902.

128. Ibid.

129. Famosa López to Bernardo Reyes, Mina, April 1893, AGENL, Correspondencia con Bernardo Reyes 1897-1902.

130. Reyes disapproved of Dávila's abusive conduct because he was a family member and it "affected his reputation." Bernardo Reyes to Rodolfo Reyes, Monterrey, July 16, 1897, ABR, nos. 36-37. For other cases of conscripting people into the army, see Captain Juan Ibarra to José María Mier, Monterrey, April 7, 1911, AGENL, Ramo Militar 1911-1917; Santos Cavazos to Leobardo Chapa, Monterrey, July 18, 1911, AGENL, Concluidos 1911; Plutarco Gónzalez to Leobardo Chapa, China, July 27, 1911, AGENL, Concluidos 1911.

131. Juan Charles Luna's oral history in Colección Divulgación, *Mi pueblo durante la Revolución Mexicana*, 3:173.

132. Informe del Evaluador de la Hacienda San Antonio y Anexas to Caja de Préstamos, n.p., n.d., AGN, Caja de Préstamos.

133. Ruiz y García to Bernardo Reyes, Montemorelos, August 31, 1908, AGENL, Minutas de Gobierno 1908.

134. José Delgado to Viviano Villareal, Cadereyta Jiménez, October 25, 1911, AGENL, Concluidos 1911–1912.

135. Emilio Hinojosa to Ramón Chavarrí, Doctor Arroyo, February 4, 1907, AGENL, Correspondencia con Alcaldes Primeros 1903–1907.

136. Ibid.

137. Desperate for the well-being of his daughter, the father complained to Bernardo Reyes that she had been kidnapped by the landlord. Teodoro Cepeda to Bernardo Reyes, Mina, April 1893, AGENL, Correspondencia con Bernardo Reyes 1897–1902.

138. Encarnación Pérez to José María Mier, Linares, April 16, 1910, AGENL, Concluidos 1910–1913.

139. Ibid.

140. Miguel Mireles to José María Mier, Linares, April 25, 1910, AGENL, Concluido 1910–1913.

141. Nacario Román to Bernardo Reyes, Villa de Santiago, February 22, 1907; Encarnación Pérez to José María Mier, Linares, April 16, 1910, AGENL, Concluidos 1910–1913.

142. Sebastián Rodríguez to Bernardo Reyes, Monterrey, May 1902, AGENL, Correspondencia con Bernardo Reyes 1897–1902.

143. Pedro Salas to José María Mier, n.p., March 10, 1910, AGENL, Correspondencia con Bernardo Reyes 1897–1902; Emilio Hinojosa to Ramón Chavarrí, Doctor Arroyo, February 4, 1907, AGENL, Correspondencia con Alcaldes Primeros; Cerutti, Burguesía y capitalismo, p. 144.

144. Manuel Aguilar to Bernardo Reyes, Apodaca, December 13, 1889, AGENL, Correspondencia con Bernardo Reyes 1897–1902.

145. Ibid.

146. Nacario Román to Bernardo Reyes, Villa de Santiago, February 22, 1907, AGENL, Correspondencia con Bernardo Reyes 1897–1902.

CHAPTER 5. THE CRISIS OF THE COUNTRYSIDE
AND PUBLIC POLICY IN THE LATE PORFIRIATO

1. Memorias de gobierno 1903–1907, p. xlix.

2. Data collected from the Secretaría de Fomento.

3. Vecinos of Hualahuises to Bernardo Reyes, Hualahuises, September 1, 1907, AGENL, Concluidos 1907.

4. Berger, Pig Earth, p. xv.

5. Luis Leal to José María Mier, Cadereyta Jiménez, March 28, 1910, AGENL, Concluidos 1910–1913.

6. E. Flores to Bernardo Reyes, Bustamantes, May 7, 1909, AGENL, Minutas de Gobierno 1909.

7. Felipe Yslas and Lorenzo Cazárez to Bernardo Reyes, Bustamante, April 16, 1909, AGENL, Minutas de Gobierno 1909.

8. E. Flores to Bernardo Reyes, Bustamantes, May 7, 1909, AGENL, Minutas de Gobierno 1909.

9. Eutemio Calzado to Bernardo Reyes, Bustamantes, May 15, 1909, AGENL, Minutas de Gobierno 1909. The mayor claimed that only 500 people had left Bustamantes.

10. Ibid.

11. Secretaría de Agricultura y Fomento, *Tercer censo de población: Censo de 1910 de los Estados Unidos Mexicanos* (Mexico City: Oficina Impresora de la Secretaría de Hacienda, 1918), pp. 218–220.

12. Ibid., pp. 19–20.

13. See Narciso Dávila's report to the Secretaría de Fomento, Mexico City, October 25, 1889, AGENL, Correspondencia con la Secretaría de Fomento 1890–1892.

14. República Mexicana, *Nuevo León*, p. 55.

15. See, for instance, *La Voz de Nuevo León*, October 11, 1907.

16. Resolution of Bernardo Reyes on the community dispute in China, Monterrey, July 30, 1892, AGENL, Concluidos 1892.

17. Andrés Cantú to Bernardo Reyes, China, August 23, 1892, AGENL, Correspondencia con Fomento 1890–1892.

18. F. Villareal's Project to Break Up the Communities, Monterrey, April 24, 1917, AGENL, Ramo Comisión Local Agraria, 1914, 1917, and 1919.

19. *La Voz de Nuevo León*, December 26, 1908.

20. Ibid., August 13, 1892.

21. Quoted in Jerónimo Garza Hernández, "Las comunidades rurales en el Estado de Nuevo León, vistas a través de la historia, la sociología y el derecho," p. 61.

22. República Mexicana, *Nuevo León*, p. 55.

23. Livas, *El estado de Nuevo León*, p. 18.

24. Gobierno del Estado de Nuevo León, "Projecto de ley sobre comunidades en el estado de Nuevo León, 1894," AGENL, Minutas de Gobierno 1894.

25. Juan Zuazua to Bernardo Reyes, Lampazos, August 10, 1905, AGENL, Concluidos 1905.

26. For a full text of the article, see *La Voz de Nuevo León*, December 26, 1908; República Mexicana, *Nuevo León*, p. 56.

27. Jesús González Treviño to José María Mier, Mina, March 15, 1910, AGENL, Concluidos 1910–1913.

28. *Periódico Oficial*, December 12, 1911.

29. Quoted in Garza Hernández, "Las comunidades rurales," p. 61.

30. Colección Divulgación, *Mi pueblo*, 3:171–173; quotation on 173.

31. Del Toro Reyna, *Aramberri*, p. 33.

32. Emilio Hinojosa to Ramón Chavarrí, Doctor Arroyo, February 4, 1907, AGENL, Correspondencia con Alcaldes Primeros (Galeana) 1903–1907.

33. Comisión Pesquisidora de la Frontera del Norte, *Reports of the Commission of Investigation Sent in 1873 by the Mexican Government to the Frontier of Texas*, p. 403.

34. *Arrendatarios* (tenants) constituted 30 percent and *propietarios* (landowners) the remaining 10 percent of the "farming class" in Mexico. See Caja de Préstamos, "Apuntes para discutir sobre la manera de ayudar a los terratenientes y agricultores en pequeño," AGN, Caja de Préstamos, unclassified (1909?).

35. Ibid.

36. Luis Cortés to Ramón Chavarrí, Galeana, September 29, 1906, AGENL, Correspondencia con Alcaldes Primeros 1903–1909.

37. Ibid., January 29, 1907.

38. República Mexicana, *Nuevo León*, pp. 42, 56.

39. Emilio Hinojosa to Ramón Chavarrí, Doctor Arroyo, February 4, 1907, AGENL, Correspondencia con Alcaldes Primeros 1903–1907.

40. Of the twenty-four producers of ixtle in Galeana, four had ceased to produce it and three were on the verge of doing so in the summer of 1908. See *Extracto* (Monterrey), July 24, 1908, AGENL, Correspondencia con Alcaldes Primeros 1903–1909; Aurelio Torres to Ramón Chavarrí, Galeana, July 17, 1908, AGENL, Correspondencia con Alcaldes Primeros 1903–1909.

41. *Extracto* (Monterrey), July 24, 1908, AGENL, Correspondencia con Alcaldes Primeros 1903–1909.

42. Ibid.

43. Luis Cortés to Ramón Chavarrí, Galeana, June 16 and June 21, 1908, AGENL, Correspondencia con Alcaldes Primeros 1903–1909.

44. Ibid., June 21, 1908.

45. Emilio Hinojosa to Ramón Chavarrí, Doctor Arroyo, February 4, 1907, AGENL, Correspondencia con Alcaldes Primeros 1903–1907.

46. Ibid.

47. Emilio Hinojosa to Ramón Chavarrí, Doctor Arroyo, February 18, 1907, AGENL, Correspondencia con Alcaldes Primeros 1903–1909.

48. Ramón Chavarrí to Emilio Hinojosa, Monterrey, February 11, 1907, AGENL, Correspondencia con Alcaldes Primeros 1903–1907; Israel Cavazos Garza, *Diccionario bibliográfico de Nuevo León*, 1:240.

49. Ibid.

50. Ibid.

51. Ibid.

52. Bernardo Reyes to Miguel Cárdenas, Monterrey, November 10, 1894, ABR, nos. 216–217.

53. *La Voz de Nuevo León*, February 2, 1907.

54. Ibid.

55. *Informe del ciudadano gobernador de Nuevo León, General Bernardo Reyes, al XXXIV congreso del estado* (Monterrey: Tipografía del Gobierno en Palacio, 1908), pp. 12–13.

56. Proyecto de Ley, Monterrey, July 11, 1908, AGENL, Minutas de Gobierno 1908; *Periódico Oficial*, July 17, 1908; *La Voz de Nuevo León*, July 18, 1908.

57. Ibid.

58. *El Economista Mexicano*, April 24, 1909.

59. Ibid.

60. José Delgado and Antonio Leal Cantú to Viviano Villareal, October 25, 1911, AGENL, Asuntos Concluidos 1911–1912.

61. Eutemio Flores to Bernardo Reyes, Bustamantes, May 15, 1909, AGENL, Minutas de Gobierno 1909.

62. Fuentes Hermanos to Bernardo Reyes, Galeana, July 19, 1909, ABR, no. 7690.

63. José Delgado to Antonio Leal Cantú to Viviano Villareal, Cadereyta Jiménez, October 25, 1911, AGENL, Concluidos 1911-1912.

64. B. Traven, *The Carreta*, p. 46.

65. Ruiz y García to Bernardo Reyes, August 31 and October 21 and 31, 1908; Ruiz y García to Ramón Chavarrí, November 25, 1908, Montemorelos, AGENL, Minutas de Gobierno 1908.

66. Comisión Pesquisidora, *Reports of the Commission of Investigation*, pp. 401-402.

67. Caja de Préstamos, "Apuntes para discutir."

68. Ruiz y García to Bernardo Reyes, August 31, October 21 and 31, 1908; Ruiz y García to Ramón Chavarrí, November 25, 1908, Montemorelos, AGENL, Minutas de Gobierno 1908.

69. Andrés Martínez to Secretary of State, Galeana, February 11, 1910, AGENL, 1910-1919; Luis Cortés to Bernardo Reyes, Galeana, October 24, 1908, AGENL, Minutas de Gobierno 1908.

70. Luis Cortés to Bernardo Reyes, Galeana, October 24, 1908, AGENL, Minutas de Gobierno 1908.

71. Andrés Martínez to Secretary of Government, Galeana, February 11, 1910, AGENL, Correspondencia con Alcaldes Primeros 1910-1919.

72. Fuentes Hermanos to Bernardo Reyes, Galeana, July 19, 1909, ABR, no. 7690.

73. Andrés Martínez to Secretary of State, Galeana, February 11, 1910, AGENL, 1910-1919; Luis Cortés to Bernardo Reyes, Galeana, October 24, 1908, AGENL, Minutas de Gobierno 1908.

74. Bernardo Reyes to Luis Cortés, Monterrey, October 31, 1908, AGENL, Minutas de Gobierno 1908.

75. Miguel Mireles to José María Mier, Linares, April 25, 1910; Encarnación Pérez to José María Mier, Linares, AGENL, Asuntos Concluidos 1910-1913.

76. Fuentes Hermanos to Caja de Préstamos para Obras y Fomento de la Agricultura, S.A., Mexico City, October 18, 1912, AGN, Caja de Préstamos 1908-1912.

77. Informe de Fuentes Hermanos to Caja de Préstamos, n.p., n.d., AGN, Caja de Préstamos; Fuentes Hermanos to Caja de Préstamos, Mexico City, October 18, 1912, AGN, Caja de Préstamos.

78. *Tercieros* received two-thirds of what they harvested because the hacienda only provided the land. *Tercieros* had to provide the seeds, animals, tools, and other equipment for the harvest. Enterprising *tercieros* who owned these resources often worked large tracts of land and recruited their own labor force. *Tercieros* lacking these resources received a loan of thirty-seven centavos a day from the hacienda which was to be repaid with the goods from the harvest. The hacienda provided *medieros* with land, animals, and tools, in exchange for half of the harvest of whatever crop was under cultivation. See Fuentes Hermanos to Caja de Préstamos, n.p., October 18, 1912, AGN, Caja de Préstamos; Informe de Manuel R. Vara to the Gerente de la Caja de Préstamos, Mexico City, June 1, 1909, AGN, Caja de Préstamos.

79. Fuentes Hermanos to Caja de Préstamos, n.p., October 18, 1912, AGN, Caja de Préstamos.

80. For a *tercero* and *mediero* contract between Ciénega de Toros and the share-

croppers, see Fuentes Hermanos to Bernardo Reyes, Galeana, July 19, 1909, ABR, no. 7690.

81. Informe de Manuel R. Vera to Gerente de la Caja de Préstamos, Mexico City, June 1, 1909, AGN, Caja de Préstamos.

82. Ibid.

83. Luis Cortés to Bernardo Reyes, Galeana, October 24, 1908, Minutas de Gobierno 1908.

84. *El Economista Mexicano*, January 6, 1912.

CHAPTER 6. CLASS, CULTURE, AND POLITICS
IN MONTERREY, 1890–1910

1. *La Voz de Nuevo León*, July 2, 1904.

2. Studies that stress class harmony include Rodrigo Mendirichaga, *Monterrey en el desarrollo;* Fuentes Mares, "Monterrey"; and Montemayor Hernández, *Historia de Monterrey.*

3. *La Voz de Nuevo León*, January 31, 1903.

4. See the advertisement section of *La Unión*, April 14, 1907.

5. Viscaya Canales, *Los orígenes*, p. 24; *La Voz de Nuevo León*, March 28, 1903.

6. *La Voz de Nuevo León*, December 19, 1891.

7. McGary, *An American Girl*, p. 118.

8. *La Unión*, March 10, 1907.

9. *La Voz de Nuevo León*, November 1, 1902.

10. Quoted in Viscaya Canales, *Los orígenes*, p. 113.

11. Nuevo León had 67 Catholic priests to attend a population of 327,937 or one priest for 4,894 people. Data compiled from Antonio Peñafiel, *Censo y división territorial 1904*, pp. 50–73; Monterrey, *Censo de la municipalidad de Monterrey 1900.*

12. Viscaya Canales, *Los orígenes*, p. 113.

13. *Renacimiento*, July 22, 1906.

14. Ibid., July 29, 1906.

15. Ibid., February 26, 1905.

16. A. N. Lovett to Bernardo Reyes, September, 1909, ABR, no. 1,7807.

17. Francisco G. Sada to Bernardo Reyes, Monterrey, April 20, 1904, AGENL, Concesiones a la Industria 1884–1890.

18. *El Trueno*, November 17, 1903.

19. Ibid., January 11, 1903.

20. Buentello Chapa, *La inundación de 1909*, pp. 31–32.

21. Ibid., p. 40.

22. Viscaya Canales, *Los orígenes*, p. 93.

23. *La Voz de Nuevo León*, March 28, 1903: *Modern Mexico*, June 1896; Viscaya Canales, *Los orígenes*, p. 24.

24. *El Trueno*, November 17, 1903. Nevertheless, it is possible that a portion of the working class did own their homes. The most likely group were workers who with time entered the ranks of the semiskilled and skilled, many of whom earned over five pesos a day. It is also likely that some city-born workers inherited a home or a plot of land to build a dwelling from their parents. In public auctions the municipal

government sold city-owned property that was exclusively reserved for the "vecinos pobres." Manuel Cortés, a blacksmith, outbid other *vecinos* for a plot of land. He built his "jacalito" in San Luisito. Manuel Cortés to Municipal President, Monterrey, January 1, 1903, Monterrey Municipal Archives (microfilm held at Trinity University, San Antonio, Texas).

25. Data compiled from Monterrey, *Censo de la municipalidad de Monterrey 1900*.

26. *Memorias de gobierno 1903-1907*, p. 17.

27. *El Monterrey News*, September 16, 1910. Bernardo Reyes served as the president of the casino from 1894 to 1909. The 1910 board of directors included Ernesto Madero, Antonio V. Hernández, and Gustavo Madero. A year later they joined Francisco I. Madero's cabinet.

28. See Carlos Pérez-Maldonado, *El Casino de Monterrey, bosquejo histórico de la sociedad regiomontana*, pp. 87–90, 145–147.

29. Saragoza, *The Monterrey Elite*, pp. 74–84.

30. See the advertisement section of *La Unión*, April 14, 1907.

31. See photographs of the event in Pérez-Maldonado, *El Casino*, p. 168.

32. Quoted in Viscaya Canales, *Los orígenes*, p. 115.

33. Monterrey also had one of the largest concentrations of Masonic lodges in Mexico. Their most distinguished member was Bernardo Reyes, holding one of the highest degrees of one of orders. Viscaya Canales, *Los orígenes*, p. 113.

34. *El Monterrey News*, September 16, 1910; Saragoza, *The Monterrey Elite*, pp. 74–84; Pérez-Maldonado, *El Casino*, pp. 87–89, 145–147.

35. *La Unión*, April 14, 1907. The third generation would later form new organizations such as Nine Cats and Alpha-Phi-Sigma, which was made up of young men and women who had studied in U.S. colleges. Sara Aguilar Belden de Garza, herself the product of one of the elite marriages that included the Madero family, recalled the "stuck-up" attitude of this new generation: "The 'American boys' always spoke to us in English and always repeated a slogan that was in mode in the United States: 'Every day and in every way, I am getting better and better.' Besides a new vocabulary, they introduced the latest artistic novelties such as jazz, also the fox trot and art nouveau" (Sara Aguilar Belden de Garza, *Una ciudad y dos familias*, pp. 91–92); Viscaya Canales, *Los orígenes*, p. 117.

36. Pérez-Maldonado, *El Casino*, pp. 70–71. See also the photograph of the event on p. 188.

37. Quoted in ibid., p. 62.

38. Eugenio Sada on the finance committee; Antonio V. Hernández on the public works committee; Patricio Milmo on the ornaments and public parks committee; and Domingo Treviño on the municipal jail committee. *Memorias de gobierno 1903-1907*, p. 387.

39. On Díaz's two visits to Monterrey and the receptions he received, see Pérez-Maldonado, *El Casino*.

40. Florentino Cantú Treviño to Bernardo Reyes, Santa Catarina, March 28, 1900, AGENL, Minutas de Gobierno 1908.

41. The Círculo Mercantil Mutualista de Monterrey had 6,123 members in 1946. See Carlos Pérez Maldonado, *Nuestra Señora de Monterrey*, pp. 194–197.

42. *La Unión*, March 10, 1907.

43. Reyes drew salaries from the secretary of war and as governor of Nuevo León. In addition to his salary, the secretary of war gave him 2,000 pesos a year for "extraordinary" expenses. Reyes also controlled the budget for the Tamaulipas and Nuevo León *rurales*. When Reyes died, he left only 70,000 pesos to his wife. While his salary was sufficient to support his family, he could not afford to send his son Alfonso to college in the United States (Alfonso Reyes wanted to pursue his literary leanings at Columbia University). See Rodolfo Reyes, *De mi vida: Memorias políticas*, 2:254–255.

44. Francisco I. Madero, *La sucesión presidencial en 1910*, p. 269.

45. Henry Baerlin, *Mexico: The Land of Unrest*, pp. 223–224; Ernest Gruening, *Mexico and its Heritage*.

46. Bernardo Reyes to Hernández Hermanos, Monterrey, August 26, 1896, ABR, no. 1–394.

47. Reyes, *De mi vida*, 2:254–255.

48. Duclos-Salinas, *Méjico pacificado*, p. 253.

49. The U.S. consul in Monterrey reported the deaths of seventeen North Americans, and North Americans probably represented less than 3 percent of the city's total population. The number of deaths will never be known exactly, but if the number of U.S. casualties is an index, then the Mexicans who died probably numbered in the hundreds. See *La Voz de Nuevo León*, February 6, 1904; *San Antonio Daily Express News*, October 29, 1903; U.S. Consul, Monterrey, January 24, 1904, Consular Despatches from the Consul in Monterrey.

50. Prospero Villareal to Bernardo Reyes, Lampazos, February 5, 1885, AGENL, Concluidos 1885.

51. *El Pueblo*, November 14, 1886.

52. Concepción Uno de Gracia's letter in *El Pueblo*, October 17, 1886.

53. *La Voz de Nuevo León*, November 4, 1905.

54. Florentino Cantú Treviño to Bernardo Reyes, Santa Catarina, March 28, 1900, AGENL, Minutas de Gobierno 1908.

55. Vicente Cavazos to Pedro Benítez Leal, Monterrey, October 26, 1900, AGENL, Concluidos 1900.

56. Cosío Villegas, *Historia moderna de México, El Porfiriato: La vida social*, 1:355.

57. *La Voz de Nuevo León*, March 4, 1903.

58. Rojas, "El mutualismo en Monterrey," 2:187.

59. Código Penal: Delito contra el orden público, Monterrey, March 5, 1885, AGENL, Circulares 1883–1887.

60. Quoted in Viscaya Canales, *Los orígenes*, p. 147.

61. Ibid., *Los orígenes*, p. 118.

62. See the advertisement section of *La Unión*, April 14, 1907.

63. Gustavo López Castro, *El Río Bravo es un charco*, p. 12.

64. *Norteño* is as popular today as in the past. It has given birth to new musical styles such as Tex-Mex and *cumbias norteñas*. Meanwhile, Nuevo León has produced dozens of the most famous *conjuntos* in Mexico and the United States, including Los Alegres de Terán, Los Gorriones del Topo Chico, Los Cadetes de Linares, Los Invasores de Nuevo León, and Los Cardenales de Nuevo León.

65. Alfonso Reyes to Pedro Henríquez Ureña, Monterrey, January 14, 1908, in *Alfonso Reyes/Pedro Henríquez Ureña: Correspondencia 1907-1914,* ed. Martínez, 1:50.

66. Monterrey, *Censo de la municipalidad de Monterrey 1900,* p. 5.

67. McGary, *An American Girl,* pp. 22-23.

68. Ibid., pp. 21-23.

69. J. Cram to Salomé Botello, Monterrey, February 3, 1914, AGENL, Correspondencia con Alcaldes Primeros (Monterrey) 1913-1914.

70. Ibid.

71. Ibid.

72. Martin, *Mexico,* 2:87.

73. McGary, *An American Girl,* p. 8.

74. *La Unión,* February 17, 1907.

75. Martin, *Mexico,* 2:87. I have not found newspaper or government reports concerning this riot.

76. *Renacimiento,* July 12, 1904, quoted in Viscaya Canales, *Los orígenes,* p. 118.

77. *La Defensa del Pueblo,* September 14, 1890.

78. *El Trueno,* November 3, 1901.

79. Ibid.

80. Ibid.

81. Petition from the *vecinos* of El Porvenir to Viviano Villareal, General Terán, October 5, 1912, AGENL, Concluidos 1912.

82. Quoted in Jones, "Conditions Surrounding Mexicans," p. 79.

83. *La Unión,* February 10, 1907.

84. Quoted in Israel Cavazo Garza, *Diccionario bibliográfico de Nuevo León,* 2:399.

85. Bernardo Reyes's letter of resignation in *La Voz de Nuevo León,* December 28, 1902.

86. Ibid., January 3, 1903; *San Antonio Daily Express News,* January 1, 1903.

87. Duclos-Salinas, *Méjico pacificado,* pp. 238-239.

88. Ibid.

89. *Justicia,* March 30, 1903, found in AGENL, Minutas de Gobierno 1903.

90. *El Trueno,* January 11, 1903. What little is known about the metalworkers' strike comes from *El Trueno,* an anti-Reyista newspaper, and from the *San Antonio Daily Express News.* As expected, the local Reyista press did not report on Monterrey's labor unrest of 1903.

91. *El Trueno,* January 11, 1903.

92. *San Antonio Daily Express,* January 4, 1903.

93. República Mexicana, *Nuevo León,* p. 55; *Memorias de gobierno 1903-1907,* p. xlix.

94. *La Voz de Nuevo León,* January 31, 1903.

95. Ibid.

96. The increasing cost of living also shaped the working class as consumers. The price of basic goods increased considerably throughout this formative period of the working class. Maize, the main staple of the lower classes and a good indicator for examining the rise in the cost of living, doubled in price from 1893 to 1910, from

four centavos a kilo to eight centavos. The average "tortilla basket" increased considerably, especially in the last years before the Revolution. The wholesale price for a kilogram of sugar, coffee, chile peppers, rice, maize, flour, beans, and lard increased from 2.63 pesos in 1909 to 3.10 pesos in 1911, an increase of 47 centavos. Beans, flour, and maize were sold by *cargas* (140 kilograms). The price of maize was calculated from the price list of 1910. For the price of these and other goods, see AGENL, Correspondencia con el Ministro de Hacienda 1891–1893, c. 2; *El Monterrey News,* January 19, 1909, July 11, 1910, and January 5, 1911.

97. *San Antonio Daily Express News,* January 1, 1903.

98. *El Trueno,* January 11, 1903.

99. *San Antonio Daily Express News,* January 7, 1903, and January 5, 1903.

100. Ibid., January 10, 1903.

101. *El Trueno,* January 11, 1903.

102. Ibid.

103. *El Monterrey News,* September 16, 1910.

104. Ibid.

105. Ibid., January 8, 1910, and January 10, 1910.

106. David Montgomery, *Citizen Worker: The Experience of Workers in the United States with Democracy and the Free Market during the Nineteenth Century,* p. 1.

107. *Justicia,* March 30, 1903. Of the approximately two hundred people arrested in the April 2, 1903, "massacre," most were journalists, shopkeepers, teachers, lawyers, law students, and urban landlords (*propietarios*). Less than twenty workers were arrested. For a list of the people arrested and their occupations, see Duclos-Salinas, *Méjico pacificado,* pp. 387–389.

108. Quoted in Villarello Vélez, *Historia de la Revolución Mexicana en Coahuila,* p. 47.

109. Manifesto to the Nation, Mexico City, April 13, 1903, found in Consular Despatches from the Consul in Monterrey.

110. Carlos Cantú Cantú, "Los sucesos del 2 de abril de 1903 en Monterrey," *Humanitas* 12 (1971): 339; *Diario del Hogar,* February 25, 1903.

111. *El Trueno,* March 1, 1903.

112. *Justicia,* March 30, 1903.

113. Quoted in Duclos-Salinas, *Méjico pacificado,* pp. 384–385; *Diario del Hogar,* April 15, 1903, and May 12, 1903.

114. Bernardo Reyes to Porfirio Díaz, Monterrey, March 18, 1903, ABR, no. 89.

115. *El Trueno,* March 1, 1903; *El Diario del Hogar,* January 16, 1903.

116. *El Diario del Hogar,* March 11 and March 14, 1903.

117. Ibid., March 8, 1903.

118. *La Voz de Nuevo León,* March 4 and March 8, 1903.

119. Ibid. (quotation on March 4).

120. Bernardo Reyes to Porfirio Díaz, Monterrey, March 11, 1903, ABR, no. 72.

121. Ibid., March 10, 1903, ABR, no. 85.

122. *El Trueno,* February 24, 1903.

123. Ibid.

124. Duclos-Salinas, *Méjico pacificado,* pp. 269, 387–389.

125. Duclos-Salinas provided a list of all those arrested after the events of April 2, 1903. See ibid., pp. 387–389.

126. Manifesto to the Nation, Mexico City, April 13, 1903, Consular Despatches from the Consul in Monterrey.

127. *Justicia,* March 30, 1903.

128. Duclos-Salinas, *Méjico pacificado,* pp. 267–268.

129. Bernardo Reyes to Porfirio Díaz, Monterrey, March 18, 1903, ABR, no. 89.

130. *Justicia,* March 30, 1903.

131. *La Voz de Nuevo León,* April 1, 1903.

132. Ibid.

133. *El Espectador,* March 31, 1903.

134. Pedro Martínez to Bernardo Reyes, Monterrey, April 2, 1903, AGENL, Minutas de Gobierno 1903, no. 111; Bernardo Reyes to Secretario de Gobernación, April 2, 1903, AGENL, Minutas de Gobierno, no. 111; *Diario del Hogar,* April 7, 8, and 15, 1903; Villarello Vélez, *Historia de la Revolución,* p. 51.

135. Bernardo Reyes to Secretario de Gobernación, Monterrey, April 2, 1903, AGENL, Minutas de Gobierno, no. 111.

136. See *El Diario del Hogar,* April 7, 8, and 15, 1903; Duclos-Salinas, *Méjico pacificado.* Duclos-Salinas was arrested during the Reyista crackdown on the opposition. Later he went into exile in the United States, where he wrote *Méjico pacificado.*

137. *El Diario del Hogar,* April 15, 1903.

138. Quoted in *La Voz de Nuevo León,* February 13, 1904.

139. Ibid.

140. J. S. William to Bernardo Reyes, Nacozari, Sonora, January 5, 1907, AGENL, Concluidos 1907.

141. Introduction to Ley del Trabajo, Sala de Diputados, Monterrey, October 26, 1906, AGENL, Minutas de Gobierno 1906.

142. Bernardo Reyes to Manuel Cárdenas, Monterrey, November 8, 1894, ABR, nos. 216–217.

143. See *Harper's Weekly,* August 25, 1906; Villarello Vélez, *Historia de la Revolución,* p. 78.

144. Clark, "Mexican Labor in the United States," pp. 481, 492.

145. Quoted in Villarello Vélez, *Historia de la Revolución,* p. 78.

146. Bernardo Reyes to Porfirio Díaz, Monterrey, July 29, 1906, ABR, no. 7231.

147. Consul Hannah to Robert Bacon, Monterrey, July 25, 1906, Consular Despatches from the Consul in Monterrey.

148. Rodney Anderson, *Outcasts in Their Own Land,* p. 211.

149. Villarello Vélez, *Historia de la Revolución,* pp. 77–78.

150. Bernardo Reyes to Porfirio Díaz, Monterrey, March 28, 1906, ABR, no. 7184.

151. Bernardo Reyes to Porfirio Díaz, Monterrey, July 24, 1906, ABR, no. 7227; July 27, 1906, ABR, no. 7230.

152. *La Voz de Nuevo León,* July 2, 1904.

153. Jaime Gurza, *La política ferrocarrilera del gobierno,* p. 130.

154. *La Voz de Nuevo León,* July 2, 1904.

155. M. Moreno to Serafín Peña, Monterrey, November 1, 1905, AGENL, Minutas de Gobierno 1907.

156. Ibid.

157. Workers' petition to Bernardo Reyes, Monterrey, March 11, 1907, AGENL, Minutas de Gobierno 1907.

158. Ibid.

159. Education Program proposal, Monterrey, January 1, 1908, AGENL, Minutas de Gobierno 1908.

160. See Juan Ayala's Educational Proposal to Bernardo Reyes, Monterrey, December 25, 1907, AGENL, Minutas de Gobierno 1908, d. 119.

161. For the occupation list of workers enrolled in school, see AGENL, Minutas de Gobierno 1907; Unión de Mecánicos Mexicanos, sucursal no. 9 to Ramón Chavarrí, Monterrey, February 8, 1908, AGENL, Minutas de Gobierno 1907.

162. C. Madrigal and Virgilio Garza's exposition on the Ley del Trabajo, Monterrey, August 15, 1906, AGENL, Minutas de Gobierno 1906.

163. Ibid.

164. Introduction to the Ley del Trabajo, Sala de Diputados, Monterrey, October 26, 1906, AGENL, Minutas de Gobierno 1906.

165. Eric Hobsbawm, *Workers: The World of Labor*, p. 39.

166. Unión de Mecánicos Mexicanos, sucursal no. 9 to Ramón Chavarrí, Monterrey, February 8, 1908, AGENL, Minutas de Gobierno.

167. *La Voz de Nuevo León*, February 6, 1904, and May 21, 1904.

168. Quoted in Buentello Chapa, *La inundación de 1909*, p. 73.

CHAPTER 7. A TALE OF TWO PORFIRIAN FIRMS:
THE CERVECERÍA CUAUHTÉMOC AND THE
FUNDIDORA DE MONTERREY

1. José Calderón, the first patriarch of what later became the Cuauhtémoc economic group, had attempted a similar enterprise years before, but it had failed. See Saragoza, *The Monterrey Elite*, pp. 62-63.

2. Barbara Hibino, "Cervecería Cuauhtémoc: A Case Study of Technological and Industrial Development in Mexico," *Mexican Studies/Estudios Mexicanos* 8, no. 1 (Winter 1992): 23-24.

3. For brief biographies of the leading functionaries of the Cuauhtémoc Brewery, see Cavazos Garza, *Diccionario bibliográfico de Nuevo León*; Saragoza, *The Monterrey Elite*, pp. 27-28. For a Cuauhtémoc Brewery account, see Cervecería Cuauhtémoc, *Cuarenta años, 1890-1930*; Fuentes Mares, "Monterrey"; Hibino, "Cervecería Cuauhtémoc"; Nemesio García Naranjo, *Una industria en marcha*; Nora Hamilton, *The Limits of State Autonomy: Post-revolutionary Mexico*, pp. 306-317. For a more critical examination of "Grupo Monterrey," see Nuncio, *El Grupo Monterrey*.

4. For a genealogy of the Garza-Sada family, see Hamilton, *The Limits of State Autonomy*, pp. 308-310; and Saragoza, *The Monterrey Elite*, pp. 27-28, 77.

5. Other key second-generation family figures included Luis G. Sada, who studied brewing in Germany and the United States. See Fuentes Mares, "Monterrey," p. 122; Hibino, "Cervecería Cuauhtémoc," pp. 31-33.

6. Manuel Carlos and Louis Sellers, "Family, Kinship, Structures, and Modernization," *Latin American Research Review* 7, no. 2 (1972): 95-124; Peter Wynn, *Weavers of the Revolution: The Yarur Workers and Chile's Road to Socialism* (Oxford: Oxford University Press, 1986).

7. On the major technological changes underway at the turn of the century, see John Vaizly, *The Brewing Industry, 1886-1950,* pp. 4-6. For the U.S. brewing industry, see Stanley Baron, *Brewed in America: A History of Beer and Ale in the United States.*

8. Romero, *Mexico and the United States,* p. 236.

9. See Daniel Cosío Villegas, ed., *Historia moderna de México, El Porfiriato: La vida económica,* 1:361; and *La Voz de Nuevo León,* August 1, 1891.

10. See *La Voz de Nuevo León,* August 15, 1903, March 28, 1903, April 22, 1905.

11. Viscaya Canales, *Los orígenes,* pp. 81-82. The Cuauhtémoc Brewery, a family enterprise, does not provide the public with annual reports. Thus it is difficult to acquire exact data on the development of the firm.

12. Cervecería Cuauhtémoc, *Cuarenta años,* p. 6.

13. Cosío Villegas, *La vida económica,* 1:361.

14. Imported beer was considered an "aristocratic drink" because only the small national and foreign elite consumed it. See Hibino, "Cervecería Cuauhtémoc," p. 26.

15. Cervecería Cuauhtémoc, *Cuarenta años,* p. 6.

16. Ferrocarriles Nacionales de México, *Album mercantil,* p. 45.

17. Cosío Villegas, *La vida económica,* 1:361.

18. Cervecería Cuauhtémoc, *Cuarenta años,* p. 6.

19. Francisco Garza Sada to Bernardo Reyes, Monterrey, August 30, 1909, AGENL, Concesiones a la Industria 1884-1890.

20. Francisco Garza Sada to Bernardo Reyes, Monterrey, August 17, 1909, ABR, no. 7752.

21. Francisco Garza Sada to Bernardo Reyes, Monterrey, August 30, 1909, AGENL, Concesiones a la Industria 1884-1890.

22. Haber, *Industry and Underdevelopment,* pp. 52-53; Hamilton, *The Limits of State Autonomy,* pp. 46-47. The French consortium owned the large Compañía Industrial de Orizaba, Sociedad Anónima (CIDOSA) textile complex at Orizaba, Veracruz, and the San Rafael Paper Company.

23. Beer sales declined considerably in most of Mexico during the winter. In Monterrey beer sales were prolonged for longer periods.

24. *La Voz de Nuevo León,* February 7, 1903. Even today it is difficult to find beer brands in Monterrey other than those from the Cuauhtémoc Brewery.

25. The brewing wars became a permanent feature of this industry. The three big breweries enjoyed over 80 percent of the market in the 1930s. In their attempts to gain a greater share of the market, the breweries lowered the price of their products. During this time the Cuauhtémoc Brewery unsuccessfully sought to buy the Moctezuma Brewery. If it had succeeded it would have gained control of 70 percent of the market. See Hamilton, *The Limits of State Autonomy,* pp. 310-312, 331-333.

26. *El Economista Mexicano,* January 18, 1908; Manuel Cantú Treviño to Bernardo Reyes, Monterrey, AGENL, Concesiones a la Industria, c. 24, e. 232.

27. Hamilton, *The Limits of State Autonomy,* pp. 310-311.

28. *Renacimiento,* April 30, 1905, and May 14, 1905. Besides competing with other breweries for the local market, the Cuauhtémoc Brewery had to compete with the local soft-drink enterprises for the ice market in Monterrey. Apparently the

brewery won the ice war, because by 1913 the soft-drink industry did not produce ice for the market. General Manager of the Compañía Embotelladora del Topo Chico to Secretary of Government, Monterrey, January 25, 1913, AGENL, Correspondencia con Fomento 1913, c. 1, f. 14.

29. Luis de Oliva to Bernardo Reyes, Monterrey, October 4, 1905, AGENL, Concluidos 1905, c. 6, e. 483.

30. Francisco Garza Sada to Bernardo Reyes, Monterrey, August 30, 1909, AGENL, Concesiones a la Industria 1884-1890. On the effects of the economic crisis on Nuevo León's mining industry, see *El Economista Mexicano*, August 29, 1908.

31. Cosío Villegas, *Vida económica*, 1:374.

32. Luis de la Oliva to Bernardo Reyes, Monterrey, October 4, 1905, AGENL, Concluidos 1905.

33. Cosío Villegas, *La vida económica*, 1:361.

34. Ibid.

35. Ibid., 1:374.

36. Charles M. Pepper, *Trade Conditions in Mexico*, p. 15.

37. Cosío Villegas, *La vida económica*, 1:374.

38. Haber, *Industry and Underdevelopment*, pp. 90-91.

39. In 1900 Mexico produced 17,000,000 liters of beer, while the Cuauhtémoc Brewery produced 4,866,000. In 1910 the domestic production had increased to 25,000,000 liters, while the Cuauhtémoc Brewery produced 13,275,000. These data come from Cosío Villegas, *La vida económica*, 1:361; and Haber, *Industry and Underdevelopment*, p. 53.

40. *Renacimiento*, April 30, 1905; Luis de la Oliva to Bernardo Reyes, Monterrey, October 4, 1905, AGENL, Concluidos 1905, c. 6, e. 483.

41. In 1896 an 18.5 percent tax was imposed on all goods leaving the free-trade zone to the interior. The free-trade zone was abolished in 1905. MacLachlan and Beezley, *El Gran Pueblo*, pp. 95-97.

42. Cosío Villegas, *La vida económica*, 1:473; Joseph Donnally to Edwin F. Uhl, Nuevo Laredo, June 17, 1895, Consular Despatches from the Consul in Monterrey.

43. Joseph Donnally to Edwin F. Uhl, Nuevo Laredo, June 17, 1895, Consular Despatches from the Consul in Monterrey.

44. AGENL, Permisos y Concesiones 1890-1912, p. 28.

45. José López Portillo, a federal deputy from Nuevo León and one of the leading Reyistas in Mexico, requested information on Monterrey's industrial production, domestic and foreign investments, and exports. Ramón Chavarrí, Reyes's secretary, wrote that this type of information was unavailable because enterprises enjoy "all kinds of freedoms." Thus the state government was unable to collect such data. See Ramón Chavarrí to José López Portillo, Monterrey, June 16, 1903, AGENL, Minutas de Gobierno 1903, d. 215.

46. José I. Limantour to Bernardo Reyes, Mexico City, May 22, 1908, ABR, no. 7535.

47. Francisco G. Sada to Bernardo Reyes, Monterrey, April 20, 1904, AGENL, Concesiones a la Industria 1884-1890, c. 125-136, e. 136, f. 291.

48. Bernardo Reyes to Manuel Z. Doria, Monterrey, December 3, 1891, ABR,

no. 336–338. Pablo Livas noted that in 1886 the state collected 35,871 pesos in taxes from industrial firms. In spite of the millions of pesos in industrial investments, the state collected only 87,366 pesos in 1908. Livas observed that it was the larger enterprises which undervalued their firms most for purposes of avoiding higher taxes. See Livas, *El estado de Nuevo León,* p. 76.

49. See Oscar Flores Torres, "De la edad de acero a los tiempos revolucionarios: Dos empresas industriales regiomontanas (1909–1923)," in *Monterrey, Nuevo León, el noreste,* ed. Cerutti.

50. Livas, *El estado de Nuevo León,* pp. 70–71.

51. Francisco G. Sada to Bernardo Reyes, Monterrey, April 21, 1904, AGENL, Concesiones a la Industria 1884–1890, c. 125–136, e. 136, f. 209; Francisco G. Sada to José Santos, Monterrey, February 25, 1920, AGENL, Permisos y Concesiones 1920–1922, c. 26, e. 274.

52. Francisco G. Sada to Bernardo Reyes, Monterrey, April 21, 1904, AGENL, Concesiones a la Industria 1884–1890, c. 125–136, e. 136, f. 209.

53. Francisco G. Sada to Bernardo Reyes, Monterrey, April 20, 1904, AGENL, Concesiones a la Industria 1884–1890, c. 125–136, e. 136, f. 291.

54. Francisco G. Sada to Bernardo Reyes, Monterrey, August 17, 1909, ABR, no. 7752; Francisco G. Sada to Bernardo Reyes, Monterrey, August 30, 1909, AGENL, Concesiones a la Industria 1886–1890, e. 136, f. 497.

55. Other studies on the Cuauhtémoc economic group have suggested that Christian values were the foundation of management's paternalism. See Fuentes Mares, *Monterrey;* and Nuncio, *El grupo Monterrey.*

56. For an examination of the Catholic church's role in Latin American politics during this period, see John Lynch, "The Catholic Church," in *Latin America: Economy and Society, 1870–1930,* ed. Leslie Bethell (Cambridge: Cambridge University Press, 1989), pp. 360–364.

57. Florentino Cantú Treviño to Bernardo Reyes, Santa Catarina, March 28, 1900, AGENL, Minutas de Gobierno 1908. See also Vicente Cavazo to Pedro Benítez Leal, Monterrey, October 26, 1900, AGENL, Concluidos 1900.

58. *La Voz de Nuevo León,* August 15, 1903; Viscaya Canales, *Los orígenes,* p. 79.

59. For an excellent study on glassworkers in France, see Joan Wallach Scott, *The Glassworkers of Carmaux: French Craftsmen and Political Action in a Nineteenth-Century City.*

60. Cervecería Cuauhtémoc, *Cuarenta años,* pp. 4–5; *La Voz de Nuevo León,* August 15, 1903.

61. Hibino, "Cervecería Cuauhtémoc," pp. 30–31.

62. Flores Torres, "De la edad de acero," p. 246.

63. Ibid.

64. Clark, "Mexican Labor in the United States," pp. 14–15.

65. Haber, *Industry and Underdevelopment,* p. 90.

66. Flores Torres, "De la edad de acero," p. 247.

67. Censo Industrial, 1902, AGENL, Censos.

68. Clark, "Mexican Labor in the United States," p. 495.

69. Ibid.

70. *La Voz de Nuevo León,* August 15, 1903.

71. Cosío Villegas, *Historia Moderna de México, El Porfiriato: La vida social,* 1:289.

72. Francisco Sada to Leobardo Chapa, Monterrey, September 1, 1911, AGENL, Concluidos 1911.

73. School Report, n.d., AGENL, Concluidos 1912.

74. Ibid.

75. See Nuncio, *El grupo Monterrey,* p. 123.

76. Unlike most industries, the brewing industry depends on daily sales. For instance, Chicago was the brewing capital in the United States until the fire of 1871. Within weeks of the fire, brewing firms of the city fled to Milwaukee, which quickly became the brewing capital.

77. Mendirichaga, *Monterrey en el desarrollo,* p. 153.

78. Ibid., pp. 153-154; Hibino, "Cervecería Cuauhtémoc," p. 121.

79. Manuel González Garza to Viviano Villareal, Monterrey, March 4, 1912, AGENL, Concluidos 1912.

80. Edward W. Said, *Culture and Imperialism,* pp. 109-110, 135-136.

81. Quoted in Oscar Flores Torres, *Burguesía, militares y movimiento obrero en Monterrey: Revolución y comuna empresarial,* pp. 63-64.

82. While the stocks were almost equally divided between Mexico City and Monterrey interests, the first Board of Directors of the Fundidora was controlled by Monterrey capitalists. Its first directors were Antonio Basagoiti, León Signoret, Isaac Garza, Vicente Ferrara, Adolfo Zambrano, Valentín Rivero, and Ernesto Madero. Ferrara was the first manager of the Fundidora. Saragoza, *The Monterrey Elite,* p. 59.

83. Ferrocarriles Nacionales de México, *Album mercantil,* p. 45.

84. Compañía Fundidora de Fierro y Acero de Monterrey S.A., *Informe anual de 1901 de la Compañía Fundidora de Fierro y Acero de Monterrey S.A.,* in *Informes anuales 1900 a 1927.*

85. Romero, *Mexico and the United States,* 183.

86. "Ruta panorámica, descriptiva," in Ferrocarriles Nacionales de México, *Album mercantil,* pp. 45-49.

87. Concesiones a la Compañía Fundidora de Fierro y Acero de Monterrey, AGENL, Concesiones 1900.

88. Ferrocarriles Nacionales de México, *Album mercantil,* p. 49.

89. Pepper, *Trade Conditions in Mexico,* p. 14.

90. Ferrocarriles Nacionales de México, *Album mercantil,* pp. 45-49.

91. Fundidora de Monterrey, *Memorias, 1900-1975* (Monterrey: n.p., n.d.), p. 14.

92. *La Voz de Nuevo León,* August 12, 1903.

93. *Mining Magazine,* October 1910.

94. Ibid.

95. For examples of the nationalist sentiment, see *La Voz de Nuevo León,* June 17, 1905; *Renacimiento,* February 26, 1905.

96. *Renacimiento,* February 26, 1905.

97. Bernardo Reyes to Adolfo Zambrano and Vicente Ferrara, Mexico City, June 3, 1900, ABR, no. 328.

98. See articles three and four of the concession, in Concesión a la Compañía Fundidora de Fierro y Acero de Monterrey, AGENL, Concesiones 1900.

99. Concesiones a la Compañía Fundidora de Fierro y Acero de Monterrey, AGENL, Concesiones 1900.

100. The Mexican government received a large part of its revenue from import taxes. For instance, for the business year of 1888–1889 the government received 1.25 million pesos from taxes on steel and iron imports which were valued at 1.50 million pesos, a tax of 83 percent on the value of the product. The following year it collected 1.50 million pesos in taxes from imports of these two products valued at 2.03 million pesos. See Romero, *Mexico and the United States*, p. 157.

101. Fundidora de Monterrey, *Informe anual 1903*, p. 87; Pepper, *Trade Conditions in Mexico*, pp. 20–21.

102. *La Voz de Nuevo León*, May 21, 1904.

103. Fundidora de Monterrey, *Informe anual 1904*, pp. 111–112.

104. *La Voz de Nuevo León*, June 17, 1905.

105. Fundidora de Monterrey, *Informe anual 1904*, pp. 111–112.

106. William E. Cole, *Steel and Economic Growth in Mexico*, pp. 8–9.

107. *La Voz de Nuevo León*, August 1, 1903.

108. Ibid., June 17, 1905.

109. Pepper, *Trade Conditions in Mexico*, pp. 20–21; Cosío Villegas, *Vida económica*, 1:382.

110. Cosío Villegas, *Vida económica*, 1:381.

111. *La Voz de Nuevo León*, February 6, 1904.

112. Romero, *Mexico and the United States*, p. 23.

113. Cosío Villegas, *Vida económica*, 1:424.

114. See statistical data of the 1902 industrial census, AGENL, Censos 1902.

115. Romero, *Mexico and the United States*, p. 23.

116. Cosío Villegas, *Vida económica*, 1:200; Bernstein, *The Mexican Mining Industry*, p. 36; Diego G. López Rosado, *Curso de historia económica de México*, p. 295.

117. Sindico and Beato, "The Beginnings of Industrialization," p. 20; The Madero family was very active in coal mining. It owned the Compañía Carbonífera de Sabinas, capitalized at 5.5 million pesos, and two other companies worth over a million pesos each. See Bernstein, *The Mexican Mining Industry*, p. 36.

118. Bernstein, *The Mexican Mining Industry*, p. 36; Cosío Villegas, *Vida económica*, 1:424.

119. Bernstein, *The Mexican Mining Industry*, p. 36; Cosío Villegas, *Vida económica*, 1:424.

120. Railroads and vessels consumed 67 percent of the coal. See López Rosado, *Curso de historia económica*, p. 296; Cosío Villegas, *Vida económica*, 1:234.

121. Cosío Villegas, *Vida económica*, 1:210.

122. The price for coal is from the 1902 industrial census of Nuevo León. See AGENL, Censos de 1902.

123. Quoted in Miguel Othón de Mendizabal, *La minería y metalurgia en México, 1520–1943*, p. 111.

124. Fundidora de Monterrey, *Informe anual 1904*, pp. 111–112.

125. *Renacimiento*, July 22, 1906.

126. *El Economista Mexicano*, November 21, 1908.

127. Ibid.

128. Haber, *Industry and Underdevelopment*, p. 71.

129. Carlos Díaz Dufoo, *México y los capitales extranjeros*, p. 321.
130. Pepper, *Trade Conditions in Mexico*, p. 15.
131. Ibid.
132. For a list of contracts for the first six months of 1906, see *La Voz de Nuevo León*, February 3, 1906.
133. Caja de Préstamos, Fundidora file, AGN (unclassified).
134. Fundidora de Monterrey, *Informes anuales 1900–1975*, p. 14.
135. Haber, *Industry and Underdevelopment*, p. 71.
136. On Adolfo Prieto, see ibid., pp. 69–72.
137. Concesiones a la Compañía Fundidora de Fierro y Acero de Monterrey, AGENL, Concesiones 1900.
138. Monterrey capitalists dominated the 1900 board. The 1910 board of the Fundidora was expanded to twelve, with Mexico City capitalists in the majority. For a list of the original board members, see Montemayor Hernández, *Monterrey*, p. 278. For a list of the new board members, see Livas, *El estado de Nuevo León*, p. 46.
139. Cosío Villegas, *Vida económica*, 1:235–236.
140. Ibid.; *Mining Magazine*, October 1910.
141. Fundidora de Monterrey, *Informe anual 1907*, pp. viii–ix.
142. Fundidora de Monterrey, *Informes anuales 1900–1975*, p. 15.
143. Hobsbawm, *The Age of Empire*, p. 35.
144. Fundidora de Monterrey, *Informe anual 1907*, pp. viii–ix.
145. Ibid., p. ix.
146. Ibid.
147. Coatsworth, *Growth against Development*, pp. 45–46.
148. Ferrocarriles Nacionales de México, *Second Annual Report, 1910*.
149. *El Economista Mexicano*, November 21, 1908.
150. *Mining Magazine*, October 1910.
151. Fundidora de Monterrey, *Informe anual 1927*, p. 16.
152. Bernstein, *The Mexican Mining Industry*, p. 36; *Mining Magazine*, December 1910.
153. Of the 59,000 tons of coke it consumed in 1910, 22,000 tons were imported. See Cosío Villegas, *Vida económica*, 1:380.
154. Baerlin, *Mexico*, pp. 301–302.
155. Caja de Préstamos loan contract with the Fundidora, AGN, unclassified.
156. Nuevo León was the leading recipient of Caja de Préstamos loans for the years 1908–1910, receiving 3.9 million pesos out of a total of 26.8 million pesos. Obviously, the Fundidora de Monterrey received all the money destined for Nuevo León. See AGN, Caja de Préstamos 1910–1914, c. 47, e. 1 (unclassified).
157. For an excellent examination of the transformation of labor in the U.S. steel industry, see Chapter 2 of David Brody, *Steelworkers in America: The Nonunion Era*.
158. Ibid., p. 16.
159. *La Voz de Nuevo León*, May 21, 1904.
160. Montemayor Hernández, *Historia de Monterrey*, p. 278.
161. *La Voz de Nuevo León*, April 12, 1903; Montemayor Hernández, *Historia de Monterrey*, p. 278.
162. *La Voz de Nuevo León*, April 12, 1903.

163. Quoted in Haber, *Industry and Underdevelopment*, p. 36.

164. Pepper, *Trade Conditions in Mexico*, p. 14.

165. Fundidora de Monterrey, *Informes anuales 1900–1975*, p. 14.

166. Manuel González Caballero, *La maestranza de ayer . . . la fundidora de hoy*, p. 129. Prior to the Escuelas Acero, steelworkers had sought the help of city officials to establish a night school at the steel plant. To meet the demands of the 110 workers enrolled in the night school, the city government paid for two teachers and an assistant. Alfredo Peña to state secretary, Monterrey, May 10, 1912, AGENL, Correspondencia con Alcaldes Primeros 1912.

167. AGENL, Correspondencia del Gobierno de Nuevo León con la Secretaría de Fomento 1896–1910, 1902–1906, and 1902–1907; *Memorias de gobierno, 1903–1907*, 2:806–814.

168. *El Economista Mexicano*, November 21, 1908.

EPILOGUE

1. Congressional Committee's "Report on General Gaspar Sánchez Ochoa's Proposal," in *Papers Related to the Foreign Relations of the United States 1879*, p. 831.

Selected Bibliography

MANUSCRIPT SOURCES

Archivo General de la Nación. Mexico City.
    Caja de Préstamos, unclassified.
    Fomento y Obras Públicas, Minas y Petróleo.
    Gobernación.
Archivo General del Estado de Nuevo León (AGENL). Monterrey.
    Asuntos Concluidos, 1886–1910.
    Comisión Agraria, 1892–1927.
    Concesiones, 1890–1910.
    Correspondencia con Alcaldes Primeros.
    Correspondencia con Bernardo Reyes.
    Correspondencia con la Secretaría de Fomento.
    Ferrocarriles Nacionales de México, 1873–1913.
    Militares, 1878–1885.
    Minutas de Gobierno.
    Tierras y Fomento.
Archivo de Francisco I. Madero. Instituto de Antropología y Historia. 2 vols. Mexico City.
Archivo Municipal de Monterrey. Monterrey.
Archivo de Bernardo Reyes (microfilm held at Universidad Autónoma de Nuevo León, Capilla Alfonsina). Monterrey.

NEWSPAPERS

Boletín de la Sociedad Agrícola Mexicana. Mexico City. 1906–1910.
El Contemporáneo. San Luis Potosí. 1897.
El Diario del Hogar. Mexico City. 1902–1904.

El Economista Mexicano. Mexico City. 1900–1910.
El Espectador. Monterrey. 1900–1907.
El Estado de Coahuila. Saltillo. 1906–1910.
El Nuevo Mundo. Torreón. 1906–1909.
El Pueblo. Monterrey. 1885–1887.
El Trueno. Monterrey and Linares. 1902–1909.
Harper's Weekly. New York. 1906.
La Defensa del Pueblo. Monterrey. 1886–1890.
La Revista. Monterrey. 1886.
La Unión. Monterrey. 1907.
La Voz de Nuevo León. Monterrey. 1890–1909.
Mexican Financial Review. 1890.
Mexico Industrial. Mexico City. 1905.
Mining Magazine. 1907–1910.
Modern Mexico. Topeka. 1896.
Monterrey News. Monterrey. 1900–1910.
Periódico Oficial. Monterrey. 1903–1909.
Renacimiento. Monterrey. 1904–1907.
San Antonio Daily Express News. 1902–1905.

PRIMARY AND SECONDARY SOURCES

Aguilar Belden de Garza, Sara. *Una ciudad y dos familias.* Mexico City: Editorial Jus, 1970.

Anderson, Malcolm. *Frontiers: Territory and State Formation in the Modern World.* Cambridge: Polity Press, 1996.

Anderson, Rodney. *Outcasts in Their Own Land.* De Kalb: Northern Illinois University Press, 1976.

Archivo General del Estado de Nuevo León. *Permisos y concesiones, 1890–1912.* Monterrey: Archivo General del Estado de Nuevo León, n.d.

Arenal, Sandra. *En Monterrey no sólo hay ricos.* Mexico City: Editoriales Nuestro Tiempo, 1988.

Auden, W. H. *City and Other Poems.* New York: Random House, 1965.

Baerlin, Henry. *Mexico: The Land of Unrest.* Philadelphia: J.B. Lippicott, n.d.

Balán, Jorge, Harley L. Browning, and Elizabeth Jelin. *Men in a Developing Society: Geographic and Social Mobility in Monterrey, Mexico.* Austin: Institute of Latin American Studies, University of Texas Press, 1973.

Ballard Perry, Laurens. *Juárez and Díaz: Machine Politics in Mexico.* De Kalb: Northern Illinois University Press, 1978.

Barlow, Andrew. "United States Enterprises in Mexico." *Consular Reports,* Bureau of Foreign and Domestic Commerce (Department of Commerce and Labor) 168 (October 29, 1902): 500–504.

Baron, Stanley. *Brewed in America: A History of Beer and Ale in the United States.* Boston: Little, Brown, and Company, 1962.

Bartra, Armando, ed. *Regeneración, 1900–1918.* Mexico City: Era, 1977.

Basave, Agustín. "Monterrey pre-industrial." *Historia Mexicana* 10 (January–March 1961): 413–424.

Bell, Samuel, and James B. Smallwood. *The Zona Libre, 1858-1905: A Problem in American Diplomacy.* El Paso: Texas Western Press, 1982.

Benjamin, Walter. *Illuminations.* New York: Schocken Books, 1968.

Berger, John. *Pig Earth.* New York: Vintage International, 1992.

Bernstein, Marvin S. *The Mexican Mining Industry, 1890-1950.* Albany: State University of New York, 1964.

Bethell, Leslie, ed. *Colonial Spanish America.* Cambridge: Cambridge University Press, 1987.

Boletín del Archivo General del Estado de Nuevo León. Monterrey. 1982-1986.

Brody, David. *Steelworkers in America: The Nonunion Era.* New York: Harper Torchbooks, 1969.

Brown, Jonathan C. "Foreign and Native-Born Workers in Porfirian Mexico." *American Historical Review* 98, no. 3 (June 1993): 786-818.

Bryant, Anthony. "Mexican Politics in Transition, 1900-1913: The Role of General Bernardo Reyes." Ph.D. diss., University of Nebraska, 1970.

Buentello Chapa, Humberto. *La inundación de 1909: Sus aspectos trágicos y políticos.* Monterrey: Universidad Regiomontana, 1970.

Campbell, Reau. *Travels in Mexico.* New York: C. G. Crawford, 1890.

Cantú Cantú, Carlos. "Los sucesos del 2 de abril de 1903 en Monterrey." *Humanitas* 12 (1971): 331-360.

Carlos, Manuel, and Louis Sellers. "Family, Kinship, Structures and Modernization." *Latin American Research Review* 7, no. 2 (1972): 95-124.

Casneau, Mrs. William L. (Cora Montgomery). *Eagle Pass or Life at the Border.* Austin, Tex.: Pemberton Press, 1966.

Cavazos Garza, Israel. *Breve historia de Nuevo León.* Mexico City: El Colegio de México, 1994.

———. *Cedulario autobiográfico de pobladores y conquistadores de Nuevo León.* 2 vols. Monterrey: Biblioteca de Nuevo León, 1964.

———. *Diccionario bibliográfico de Nuevo León.* 2 vols. Monterrey: Universidad Autónoma de Nuevo León, 1985.

Cerutti, Mario. *Burguesía y capitalismo en Monterrey (1850-1910).* Mexico City: Claves Latinoamericanas, 1983.

———. *Economía de guerra y poder regional en el siglo XIX: Gastos militares, aduanas, y comerciantes en los años de Vidaurri (1855-1864).* Monterrey: Archivo General del Estado de Nuevo León, 1983.

———, ed. *De los Borbones a la Revolución Mexicana: Ocho estudios regionales.* Mexico City: G.V. Editores, S.A. de C.V., 1986.

———. *Monterrey, Nuevo León, el noreste: Siete estudios históricos.* Monterrey: Universidad Autónoma de Nuevo León, 1987.

Cervecería Cuauhtémoc. *Cuarenta años, 1890-1930.* Monterrey: Tipografía Lozano, n.d.

Chevalier, François. *Land and Society in Colonial Mexico.* Berkeley: University of California Press, 1966.

Clark, Victor S. "Mexican Labor in the United States." *Bulletin of the Bureau of Labor* 17, no. 78 (September 1908): 466-522.

Coatworth, John H. *Growth against Development: The Economic Impact of Railroads in Porfirian Mexico.* De Kalb: Northern Illinois University Press, 1981.

————. "Obstacles to Economic Growth in Nineteenth-Century Mexico." *American Historical Review* 83 (1978): 80–100.

Coker, Caleb, ed. *The News from Brownsville: Helen Champan's Letters from the Texas Military Frontier, 1848–1852.* Austin: Texas State Historical Association, 1992.

Cole, William E. *Steel and Economic Growth in Mexico.* Austin: University of Texas Press, 1967.

Colección Divulgación. *Mi pueblo durante la Revolución mexicana.* 3 vols. Mexico City: INAH, 1985.

Colín Sánchez, Guillermo. *Ignacio Zaragoza: Evolución de un héroe.* Mexico City: Editorial Porrúa, S.A., 1963.

Comisión Pesquisidora de la Frontera del Norte. *Reports of the Commission of Investigation Sent in 1873 by the Mexican Government to the Frontier of Texas.* New York: Baker and Goodwin, 1875.

Compañía Fundidora de Fierro y Acero de Monterrey, S.A. *Informes anuales, 1900 a 1927.* Monterrey: n.d., n.p.

————. *Memorias, 1900–1975.* Monterrey: n.d., n.p.

Conway, George K. G. "The Water-Works and Sewage of Monterrey." *Transactions* 72 (1911): 531–563.

Cosío Villegas, Daniel. "Porfirio v.s. Jerónimo." *Humanitas* 11 (1970): 577–584.

————, ed. *Historia moderna de México.* 9 vols. Mexico City: Editorial Hermes, 1955–72.

Daddyman, James W. *The Matamoros Trade: Confederate Commerce, Diplomacy and Intrigue.* Newark: University of Delaware Press, 1984.

Dávila, Hermenegildo. *Biografía del Señor General Don Juan Zuazua.* Monterrey: Edición del Archivo General del Estado de Nuevo León, 1983.

De Arrellano, Josefina G. *El general Bernardo Reyes y el movimiento reyista.* Colección Científica. Mexico City: Instituto de Antropología y Historía, 1982.

Del Hoyos, Eugenio. *Historia del Nuevo Reino de Nuevo León, 1577–1723.* 2 vols. Monterrey: Instituto Tecnológico de Estudios Superiores de Monterrey, 1972.

Del Toro Reyna, Jaime. "Aramberrí, Nuevo León, 1626–1950." Monterrey: Archivo General del Estado de Nuevo León, 1988.

Díaz Dufoo, Carlos. *México y los capitales extranjeros.* Mexico City: Librería de la Vda. de Ch. Bouret, 1918.

Duclos-Salinas, Adolfo. *Méjico pacificado: El progreso de Méjico y los hombres que lo gobiernan, Porfirio Díaz–Bernardo Reyes.* St. Louis: Imprenta de J. Hughes y Company, 1904.

Dusemberry, William H. *The Mexican Mesta: The Administration of Ranching in Colonial Mexico.* Urbana: University of Illinois Press, 1963.

Eisenhower, John S. D. *So Far from God: The U.S. War with Mexico, 1846–1848.* New York: Doubleday, 1989.

El Colegio de México. *Estadísticas sociales del porfiriato, 1877–1910.* Mexico City: El Colegio de México, 1956.

Emory, William, *Report on the United States and Mexican Survey.* 2 vols. Washington, D.C.: Cornelius Wendell, Printers, 1857.

Ferrocarriles Nacionales de México. *Album mercantil, industrial, pintoresco, ciudad de Monterrey.* Mexico City: Tipografía "la Luz," 1904.

———. *Second Annual Report, 1910.* English ed. Mexico City: Ferrocarriles Nacionales de México, 1910.

Flores Torres, Oscar. *Burguesía, militares y movimiento obrero en Monterrey: Revolución y comuna empresarial.* Monterrey: Universidad Autónoma de Nuevo León.

Frias, Juan de Dios. *Reseña histórica de la formación y operaciones del cuerpo del ejército del norte durante la intervención francesa, sitio en Querétaro y noticias sobre la captura de Maximiliano, su proceso íntegro y su muerte.* Mexico City: Imprenta de Narón Chávez, 1867.

Fuentes Mares, José. *Monterrey, una ciudad creadora y sus capitanes.* Mexico City: Editorial Jus, 1976.

Fyfe, Henry H. *The Real Mexico: A Study on the Spot.* London: William Heinemann, 1914.

García Flores, Raúl. "Formación de la sociedad mestiza y la estructura de castas en el noreste: El caso de Linares." Serie Orgullosamente Bárbaros, no. 12. Monterrey: Archivo General del Estado de Nuevo León, 1996.

García Naranjo, Nemesio. *Una industria en marcha.* Mexico City: n.p., n.d.

García Valero, José Luis. *Nuevo León, una historia compartida.* Mexico City: Instituto de Investigaciones Dr. José María Luis Mora, 1989.

Garza Guajardo, Celso, ed. *Nuevo León: Textos de su historia.* 3 vols. Mexico City: Instituto de Investigaciones Dr. José María Mora, 1989.

Garza Guajardo, Gustavo. *Las cabeceras municipales de Nuevo León.* Monterrey: Universidad Autónoma de Nuevo León, 1986.

Garza Hernández, Jerónimo. "Las comunidades rurales en el Estado de Nuevo León, vistas a través de la historia, sociología y el derecho." Tesis de Licenciatura de Derecho, Universidad Autónoma Nacional de México, 1956.

Gómez Serrano, Jesús. *Aguascalientes, imperio de los Guggenheims.* Mexico City: SEP, 1982.

González, José E. *Algunos apuntes y datos estadísticos que pueden servir de base para formar una estadística del estado de Nuevo León.* Monterrey: Imprenta de Gobierno, 1873.

———. *Colección de noticias y documentos para la historia del estado de Nuevo León.* Monterrey: Tipografía de Antonio Mier, 1867.

———. *Lecciones orales de la historia de Nuevo León.* Monterrey: Imprenta de Gobierno, 1887.

Gónzalez Caballero, Manuel. *La Fundidora en el tiempo, 1900-1986.* Monterrey: Gobierno del Estado de Nuevo León, 1989.

———. *La Maestranza de ayer . . . La Fundidora de hoy.* Monterrey: Fundidora de Monterrey, S.A., 1980.

González Navarro, Moisés. *Los extranjeros en México y los mexicanos en el extranjero, 1821-1970.* Mexico City: El Colegio de México, 1994.

Gruening, Ernest. *Mexico and Its Heritage.* London: Stanley Paul and Co., Ltd., 1928.

Gurza, Jaime. *La política ferrocarrilera del gobierno.* Mexico City: Tipografía de la Oficina Impresora de Estampillas, Palacio Nacional, 1911.

Gutiérrez, Ramón A. *When Jesus Came, the Corn Mother Went Away: Marriage, Sexuality and Power in New Mexico, 1500–1846*. Stanford: Stanford University Press, 1991.

Gutiérrez de Lara, Lázaro, and Edgcomb Pinchon. *The Mexican People: The Struggle for Freedom*. Garden City: Doubleday, Page and Co., 1914.

Haber, Stephen H. *Industry and Underdevelopment: The Industrialization of Mexico, 1890–1945*. Stanford: Stanford University Press, 1989.

Hamilton, Nora. *The Limits of State Autonomy: Post-Revolutionary Mexico*. Princeton: Princeton University Press, 1982.

Harris, Charles H., III. *The Mexican Family Empire: The Latifundio of the Sánchez Navarros, 1765–1867*. Austin: University of Texas Press, 1975.

———. *The Sánchez Navarros: A Socio-economic Study of a Coahuilian Latifundio, 1846–1856*. Chicago: Loyola University Press, 1964.

Hart, John M. *Anarchism and the Mexican Working Class, 1860–1931*. Austin: University of Texas Press, 1978.

———. *Revolutionary Mexico: The Coming Process of the Mexican Revolution*. Berkeley: University of California Press, 1987.

Hernández Molina, Moisés. *Los partidos políticos en México, 1891–1913*. Puebla: Editorial de José M. Cajica Jr., S.A., 1972.

Hibino, Barbara. "Cervecería Cuauhtémoc: A Case Study of Technological and Industrial Development in Mexico." *Mexican Studies/Estudios Mexicanos* 8, no. 1 (Winter 1992): 23–43.

Hobsbawm, Eric. *The Age of Empire, 1875–1914*. New York: Pantheon, 1987.

———. *Workers: The World of Labor*. New York: Pantheon, 1984.

Hoyt, Edwin P. *The Guggenheims and the American Dream*. New York: Funk and Wagnalls, 1967.

Huerta Presiado, María Teresa. *Rebeliones indígenas en el noreste de México en la época colonial*. Mexico City: Instituto Nacional de Antropología y Historia, 1966.

Iglesias Calderón, Fernando. *Rectificaciones históricas: Un libro del ex-Ministro de Guerra*. Mexico City: Imprenta de A. Carranza e Hijos, 1910.

Jones, Anita Edgar. "Conditions Surrounding Mexicans in Chicago." Ph.D. diss., University of Chicago, 1928.

Katz, Friedrich. "Labor Conditions on Haciendas in Porfirian Mexico: Some Trends and Tendencies." *Hispanic American Historical Review* 54, no. 1 (February 1974): 1–47.

———. *The Life and Times of Pancho Villa*. Stanford: Stanford University Press, 1998.

———. *The Secret War in Mexico: Europe, the United States and the Mexican Revolution*. Chicago: University of Chicago Press, 1981.

Kearney, Milo, ed. *Studies in Brownsville History*. Brownsville: Pan American University, 1986.

Knight, Alan. *The Mexican Revolution*. 2 vols. Cambridge: Cambridge University Press, 1986.

Ladd, Doris M. *The Mexican Nobility at Independence, 1780–1826*. Austin: University of Texas Press, 1976.

Laslett, John. *Labor and the Left: A Study of Socialist and Radical Influences in the American Labor Movement, 1881-1924*. New York: Basic Books, Inc., 1970.

Limantour, José I. *Apuntes sobre mi vida pública*. Mexico City: Editorial Porrúa S.A., 1965.

Livas, Pablo. *El estado de Nuevo León: Su situación económica al aproximarse el Centenario de la Independencia de México*. Monterrey: Imprenta de J. Cantú, 1910.

López Castro, Gustavo. *El Río Bravo es un charco*. Zamora: El Colegio de Michoacán, 1995.

López Rosado, Diego G. *Curso de historia económica de México*. Mexico City: UNAM, 1973.

Maceda, Pablo. *La evolución mercantil*. Mexico City: J. Ballesca y Compañía, Sucesores, 1905.

MacLachlan, Colin M., and William Beezley. *El Gran Pueblo: A History of Greater Mexico*. Englewood Cliffs: Prentice-Hall, 1994.

Madero, Francisco I. *La sucesión presidencial en 1910*. Mexico City: Editorial Nacional, 1960.

Marcosson, Isaac F. *Metal Magic: The Story of the American Smelting and Refining Company*. New York: Farrar, Strauss and Co., 1949.

Martin, Percy F. *Mexico of the Twentieth Century*. 2 vols. London: Edward Arnold, 1907.

Martínez, José Luis, ed. *Alfonso Reyes/Pedro Henríquez Ureña: Correspondencia 1907-1914*. Mexico City: Fondo de Cultura Económica, 1986.

Martínez, Oscar, ed. *U.S.-Mexico Borderlands: Historical and Contemporary Perspectives*. Wilmington, Del.: Scholarly Resources, Inc., 1996.

Marx, Karl. *Grundrisse: Foundations of the Critique of Political Economy*. Translated with a foreword by Martin Nicholas. New York: Vantage Books, 1973.

Mauro, Frédéric. "Le développement économique de Monterrey." *Caravelle* 2 (1964): 35-129.

Mayano Pahissa, Angela. *Frontera: Así se hizo la frontera norte*. Mexico City: Ariel México, 1996.

Mayo, John. "Consuls and Contraband on Mexico's West Coast in the Era of Santa Ana." *Journal of Latin American Studies* 19, no. 2 (November 1987): 389-411.

McAdams Sibley, Marilyn. "Charles Stillman: A Case Study of Entrepeneurship on the Rio Grande, 1861-1865." *Southwestern Historical Quarterly* 77 (October 1973): 227-240.

McBride, George M. *The Land System of Mexico*. New York: American Geographical Society, 1923.

McCarthy, Cormac. *Blue Meridian: Or the Evening Redness in the West*. New York: Vintage Edition, 1992.

McGary, Elizabeth Viscre. *An American Girl in Mexico*. New York: Dodd, Mead and Company, 1904.

Meinig, D. W. *The Shaping of America: A Geographical Perspective of 500 Years of History*. 3 vols. New Haven: Yale University Press, 1993.

Melville, Elinor G. K. *A Plague of Sheep: Environmental Consequences of the Conquest of Mexico*. Cambridge: Cambridge University Press, 1994.

Mendirichaga, Rodrigo. *Monterrey en el desarrollo.* Monterrey: Impresora del Norte, 1975.

México. Comisión Nacional Agraria. *Resoluciones presidentiales.* 57 vols. N.p.

México. Secretaría de Fomento. *Censo de la République mexicana, Estado de Nuevo León.* Mexico City: Oficina de Tipografía de la Secretaría de Fomento, 1904.

Meyer, Lorenzo, and Josefina Zoraida Vásquez. *México frente a los Estados Unidos: Un ensayo histórico, 1776-1980.* Mexico City: El Colegio de México, 1982.

Meyers, William K. *Forge of Progress, Crucible of Revolt: The Origins of the Mexican Revolution in La Comarca Lagunera, 1880-1911.* Albuquerque: University of New Mexico Press, 1994.

Montejano, David. *Anglos and Mexicans in the Making of Texas, 1836-1986.* Austin: University of Texas Press, 1987.

Montemayor Hernández, Andrés. *Historia de Monterrey.* Monterrey: Asociación de Editores de Libros de Monterrey, A.C., 1971.

Monterrey. *Censo de la municipalidad de Monterrey 1900.* Monterrey: Tipográfico del Gobierno del Estado, 1902.

Montgomery, David C. *Citizen Worker: The Experience of Workers in the United States with Democracy and the Free Market during the Nineteenth Century.* Cambridge: Cambridge University Press, 1993.

———. *The Fall of the House of Labor: The Workplace, the State, and American Labor Activism, 1865-1925.* Cambridge: Cambridge University Press, 1987.

Moore, Barrington, Jr. *Injustice: The Social Bases of Obedience and Revolt.* White Plains, N.Y.: M. E. Sharpe, Inc., 1978.

Moseley, Edward. "The Public Career of Santiago Vidaurri, 1855-1858." Ph.D. diss., University of Alabama, 1963.

Nelson, Daniel. *Managers and Workers: Origins of the New Factory System in the United States, 1880-1920.* Madison: University of Wisconsin Press, 1975.

Niemeyer, Victor E., Jr. *El general Bernardo Reyes.* Monterrey: Centro de Estudios Humanísticos, Universidad Autónoma de Nuevo León, 1966.

Nuevo León. *Memorias de gobierno del Estado de Nuevo Léon, 1874-1920.* Monterrey: Imprenta de Gobierno, 1874-1921.

Nugent, Daniel. *Spent Cartridges of the Revolution: An Anthropological History of Namiquipa, Chihuahua.* Chicago: University of Chicago Press, 1993.

Nuncio, Abraham. *El Grupo Monterrey.* Monterrey: Editorial Nueva Imagen, 1982.

O'Conner, Harvey. *The Guggenheims.* New York: Covici Friede, 1937.

Othón de Mendizabal, Miguel. *La minería y metalurgia en México, 1520-1943.* Mexico City: CEHMO, 1980.

Papers Related to the Foreign Relations of the United States 1872-1900. Washington, D.C.: Government Printing Office, 1873-1901.

Paredes, Américo. *A Texas-Mexican Cancionero: Folksongs of the Lower Border.* Urbana: University of Illinois Press, 1976.

Parlee, Lorena M. "The Impact of United States Railroad Unions on Organized Labor and Government Policy in Mexico, 1880-1911." *Hispanic American Historical Review* 64, no. 3 (August 1984): 443-475.

Peñafiel, Antonio. *Anuario estadístico de la República Mexicana, 1900.* Mexico City: Oficina de Tipografía de la Secretaría de Fomento, 1901.

————. *Censo y división territorial 1904*. Mexico City: Secretaría de Fomento, 1905.

Pepper, Charles M. *Trade Conditions in Mexico*. United States Department of Commerce and Labor. Washington, D.C.: Government Printing Office.

Pérez-Maldonado, Carlos. *El Casino de Monterrey, bosquejo histórico de la sociedad regiomontana*. Monterrey: Impresora Monterrey, 1950.

————. *Nuestra Señora de Monterrey*. Monterrey: Impresa Monterrey, 1946.

Pletcher, David. *Rails, Mines and Progress*. New York: Kennikat Press, 1972.

Reed, John. *Insurgent Mexico*. New York: International Publishers, 1969.

República Mexicana. *Nuevo León: Reseña geográfica y estadística*. Mexico City: Librería de la Vda. de Ch. Bouret, 1910.

Reyes, Rodolfo. *De mi vida: Memorias políticas*. 2 vols. Barcelona: Biblioteca Nueva, 1929.

Rippy, J. Fred. "The Indians of the Southwest in the Diplomacy of the United States and Mexico, 1848–1853." *Hispanic American Historical Review* 2, no. 3 (August 1919): 363–396.

————. *The United States and Mexico*. New York: F. S. Crofts and Company, 1931.

Rock, David. *Argentina, 1516–1987: From Spanish Colonialism to Alfonsín*. Berkeley: University of California Press, 1985.

Roel, Santiago. *Nuevo León: Apuntes históricos*. Monterrey: Ediciones Castillo, S.A., 1980.

————, ed. *Correspondencia particular de Don Santiago Vidaurri, gobernador de Nuevo León, 1855–1864*. Monterrey: Universidad de Nuevo León, 1946.

Rojas, Javier. *Movimiento obrero y partidos políticos en Nuevo León*. Monterrey: Oficina de Información y Difusión del Movimiento Obrero, 1982.

Romero, Matías. *Geographical and Statistical Notes on Mexico*. New York: G. P. Putnam's Sons, 1898.

————. *Mexico and the United States*. 2 vols. New York: G. P. Putnam's Sons, 1898.

Sahlins, Peter. *Boundaries: The Making of France and Spain in the Pyrenees*. Berkeley: University of California Press, 1989.

Said, Edward W. *Culture and Imperialism*. New York: Vintage Books, 1994.

Salvucci, Richard. *Textiles and Capitalism in Mexico: An Economic History of the Obrajes, 1539–1840*. Princeton: Princeton University Press, 1987.

Saragoza, Alex M. *The Monterrey Elite and the Mexican State, 1880–1940*. Austin: University of Texas Press, 1988.

Scott, Joan Wallach. *The Glassworkers of Carmaux: French Craftsmen and Political Action in a Nineteenth-Century City*. Cambridge, Mass.: Harvard University Press, 1974.

Sepúlveda, César. *La frontera norte: Historia y conflictos 1762–1975*. Mexico City: Editorial Porrúa, 1976.

Sierra, Justo. *Juárez: Su obra, su tiempo*. Mexico City: Editorial Porrúa, S.A., 1980.

————. *La evolución de un pueblo*. Mexico City: La Casa de España en México, 1940.

Sindico, Dominico. *Ensayo sobre problemas agrícolas en Nuevo León (1820–1906)*. Mexico City: Departamento de Investigaciones Históricas, INAH, 1975.

Sociedad Nuevoleonesa de Historia, Geografía y Estadística, ed. *Estudios de historia del noreste*. Monterrey: Editorial Alfonso Reyes, 1972.

Sugarawa, Masea, ed. *Mariano Escobedo.* Mexico City: Cámara de los Senadores de la Républica Mexicana, 1987.

Taylor, Paul S. *An American-Mexican Frontier: Nueces County, Texas.* Chapel Hill: University of North Carolina Press, 1934.

———. *Mexican Labor in the United States: Dimmit County, Winter Garden District, South Texas.* Berkeley: University of California, 1930.

Thompson, E. P. "Time, Work-Discipline, and Industrial Capitalism." *Past and Present* 38 (December 1967): 56–97.

Timmons, Wilbert H., ed. *John F. Finerty Reports Porfirian Mexico, 1879.* El Paso: Texas Western Press, 1974.

Traven, B. *The Carreta.* London: Allison and Busby, 1981.

Tutino, John. *From Insurrection to Revolution in Mexico: The Social Bases of Agrarian Violence, 1750–1940.* Princeton: Princeton University Press, 1986.

Tyler, R. Curtis. "Santiago Vidaurri and the Confederacy." *Americas* 26 (1969): 66–79.

Tyler, Ronnie C. *Santiago Vidaurri and the Southern Confederacy.* Austin: Texas State Historical Association, 1973.

United States Bureau of the Census. *Thirteenth Census of the United States, 1910: Abstracts of the Census.* Washington, D.C.: Government Printing Office, 1913.

United States Department of Commerce and Labor. Bureau of Manufacturers. *Monthly Consular and Trade Reports* (January–April 1899): 313–314.

———. *Monthly Consular and Trade Reports* (August 1907): 88–90.

———. *Monthly Consular and Trade Reports* (January 1910): 63–65.

United States State Department. Consular Despatches from the Consul in Monterrey, 1849–1908. Microfilm.

Utley, Robert M. *The Indian Frontier in the American West, 1846–1890.* Albuquerque: University of New Mexico Press, 1984.

Vaizly, John. *The Brewing Industry, 1886–1950.* London: Sir Isaac Pitman and Sons, Ltd., 1960.

Vasconcelos, José. *Don Evaristo Madero, biografía de un patricio.* Mexico City: Talleres Gráficos de Impresiones Modernas, S.A., 1958.

———. *Memorias.* 2 vols. Mexico City: Fondo de Cultura Económica, 1983.

Velasco, Alfonso Luis. *Geografía y estadística de la República Mexicana, 1895.* Mexico City: Oficina de la Secretaría de Fomento, 1898.

Velinga, Menno. *Industrialización, burguesía y clase obrera en Monterrey.* Mexico City: Siglo Veintiuno Editores, 1979.

Villarello Vélez, Ildefonso. *Historia de la Revolución Mexicana en Coahuila.* Mexico City: Instituto Nacional de Estudios de la Revolución Mexicana, 1970.

Viscaya Canales, Isidro. *Los orígenes de la industrialización de Monterrey.* Monterrey: Instituto Tecnológico de Estudios Superiores de Monterrey, 1968.

———, ed. *La invasión de los indios bárbaros al noreste de México en los años de 1840–1841.* Monterrey: Instituto Tecnológico de Estudios Superiores de Monterrey, 1968.

Wasserman, Mark. *Capitalists, Caciques and Revolution: The Native Elite and Foreign Enterprise in Chihuahua, Mexico, 1854–1911.* Chapel Hill: University of North Carolina Press, 1984.

————. "Oligarchy and Foreign Enterprise in Porfirian Chihuahua, Mexico, 1876-1911." Ph.D. diss., University of Chicago, 1975.

Weber, David J. *The Spanish Frontier in North America*. New Haven: Yale University Press, 1992.

Winkler, John K. *The First Billion: The Stillmans and the National City Bank*. New York: Vanguard Press, 1934.

Wolf, Eric. "The Mexican Bajío in the Eighteenth Century." In *Synoptic Studies of Mexican Culture*, 181-198. New Orleans: Tulane University, Middle America Research Institute, 1957.

Womack, John. *Zapata and the Mexican Revolution*. New York: Vintage, 1968.

Zamora, Emilio. *The World of the Mexican Worker in Texas*. College Station: Texas A & M University Press, 1993.

Zorilla, Luis G. *Historia de las relaciones entre México y los Estados Unidos de América, 1800-1958*. 2 vols. Mexico City: Editorial Porrúa, S.A., 1965.

Index